THE JEWEL HUNTER

For my parents who started the whole thing off.
And for my wife who saw it through to the end.

Chris Gooddie

The
Jewel Hunter

First published in Great Britain in 2010 by WILD*Guides* Ltd

WILD*Guides* Ltd, Parr House, 63 Hatch Lane, Old Basing,
Hampshire, RG24 7EB

Website: www.wildguides.co.uk
Tel: +44 (0)1628 529297 Fax: +44 (0)1628 525314
info@wildguides.co.uk

ISBN: 978-1-903657-16-4

Cover Design: Andy Swash & Rob Still (**WILD***Guides* Ltd)
Edited by: Bernardine Freud, Chris Gooddie,
Sheila Gooddie, Andy Swash
Author Photo: Cliff Smith

Production and design by WILD*Guides* Ltd., Old Basing,
Hampshire, UK.

WILD*Guides* Ltd. is a publishing organisation committed
to supporting nature conservation. All our titles are printed
on Greenpeace approved FSC certified paper and carry the
FSC logo. WILD*Guides'* policy is to use paper that is natural,
renewable and recyclable, and which is made from wood
grown in sustainable forests.

Thanks to Tricor plc for their generous sponsorship in
covering the costs of offsetting the carbon footprint involved
in creating this work.

Contents

Glossary: 8

Chapter 1: Quitting the Day Job. High Wycombe, UK 13

Chapter 2: The Storm Before the Calm. Southern Thailand 20

Chapter 3: Dry Country Blues. Central, Northern Thailand 39

Chapter 4: Missing in Action. Luzon, The Philippines 57

Chapter 5: Jeepneys and Jeopardy. Mindanao, The Philippines 71

Chapter 6: The Swimming Pool Trail. Southern Vietnam 88

Chapter 7: One Cup of Tea? Northeast India 103

Chapter 8: Rusty's Return. Peninsular Malaysia 123

Chapter 9: The *Toktor* Will See You Now.
    Southwest Sumatra 147

Chapter 10: The Eight Colour Bird. Taiwan 169

Chapter 11: Who's the Daddy? Sabah, Borneo 189

Chapter 12: The Famous Five. Sabah, Borneo 208

Chapter 13: The Heart of Darkness. Southwest Uganda 228

Chapter 14: Mad Dogs and Englishman. Halmahera,
    Sulawesi, Peleng 249

Chapter 15: The Mysterious Mr. Klau. Bali, Sumba,
    West Timor, Flores 278

Chapter 16: Billabongs and Bowers. Northern Australia 293

Chapter 17: Strange Days. Manus 304

Chapter 18: Adrift in Time. The Solomon Islands 313

Chapter 19: A Rare Bird Indeed. Sri Lanka 324

Chapter 20: And the First Shall Be Last. Zambia 330

Acknowledgements 341

The Treasure Chest 345

Glossary

Birders' Tapas: The infinitely varied range of junk-food on which birders choose to survive in preference to nutritious, healthy fare.

Birding: Looking for birds in a fairly serious way. Like bird-watching but cooler, with go-faster stripes. As my other half would put it, 'it's not a hobby, it's a bloody obsession.'

Bird-race: An attempt to see and/or hear as many different species of bird as possible in a twenty-four hour period. It does not involve people riding chickens from one end of a farmyard to the other. That would be cruel.

Blade Runner: Ridley Scott's sci-fi magnum opus. A working knowledge of the movie is required to understand what the hell I'm on about when describing a Golden Bush-robin in Chapter 7.

Chum: A disgusting mix of fish offal, cooking oil and popcorn (or in an emergency, cheesy puffs) used to attract seabirds.

Dipping: Failing to see a target bird. e.g. *'I dipped the Rail-babbler.'* Not to be confused with 'skinny-dipping', which is altogether more fun.

Endemic: A species that lives solely in one particular locale. Hence *regional endemic, country endemic* etc. The sought-after rock stars of the bird world.

Gripping/ *Gripping off:*	Seeing a type of bird that another birder hasn't seen. e.g. *'He was really gripped off by my Long-billed Partridge.'* As good as it gets in the insane world of competitive birding.
Heterodactyl:	Trogon-toed. See Chapter 9.
Jizz:	Essentially, 'avian character.' The combined effect of a bird's shape, stance, and other traits that distinguish it from other species. You know how you can recognize a good friend a hundred metres away because of that slight shuffle in his walk, the permanently connected iPod in only one ear and the way he tips his head fractionally to the left with every second step? Apply that to a bird and you've got the gist. (Note: not literally. Attempting to apply an iPod to either of a bird's ears will quite correctly earn you a spell at her majesty's pleasure.)
Lek/ *Exploded Lek:*	A *lek* is a communal display ground. An *exploded lek* is a display ground on which the participating males are spread out over a greater distance and so compete solely by means of vocalizations. (The latter thus has nothing to do with the TNT mentioned in Chapter 2.)
Lists:	Essential for any birder's mental wellbeing. Lists can be 'Birds I have seen during my life', 'Birds I have seen in my garden,' 'Birds I have seen since waking up this morning' and so on. I have even known birders keep lists of birds they have seen on TV. No really.

Man City:	Manchester City Football Club. God's own team. Unlike Manchester United, actually supported by people who come from Manchester. Last won a trophy in 1976.
Pittas: aka *Jewel- thrushes:*	A family of thirty-two species (Pittidae) of bird which live primarily in tropical Asia, and which have cost the author everything. The most beautiful creatures on the face of the earth. See Chapters 1 through 20. Not to be confused with the Greek bread of the same name, jokes about which, I can confirm from bitter experience, tend to wear thin after the first couple of thousand outings. Also not to be confused with the new world antpittas, another wonderful family of ground-dwelling birds (though sadly bereft for the most part of the pittas' glorious colours. They may still get a book of their own one of these days though.)
Species:	Ah, well the definition of course depends on whether one adheres to the Biological Species Concept (BSC) or the Phylogenetic Species Concept (PSC). An explanation of either of these will take far more time and a considerably deeper knowledge of molecular biology than I possess. In the interests of brevity, and of you not putting this book straight back on the shelf, let's just say that for the purposes of this volume, a species is a kind of bird or animal which can be visually and/ or audibly distinguished from another type, and which will generally interbreed only with others of its own type.

Splitting: The act of separating a single species or set of sub-species into two entities with their own specific status. In birding circles this is a fabulous thing if valid, since it means that if you have seen both races you now get to add more species to your world list. In the vernacular this is known as an 'armchair tick.' See below. The opposite process is known as 'lumping', and is tragic in equal measure.

Tick: i.) The twitcher's *raison d'être*. Literally, a tick next to a bird's name on a checklist indicating that the list-owner has seen that particular species. Hence by extension, any bird that is new for the observer.

ii.) Small, round-bodied bugs found in tropical grasslands and forest, which attach themselves to you to suck your blood. A pain in the arse. Or leg, arm etc.

Twitching: the obsessive art of chasing rare birds that one has not seen before, yea, unto death. Hence 'twitchers' are those who indulge in this ludicrous activity, and a 'twitch' is a gathering of said maniacs at a place where a rare bird has been sighted.

Vismig: Visible migration. The spectacle of actually observing birds in the act of migration. The most exciting aspect of bird-watching after pittas/rainforest.

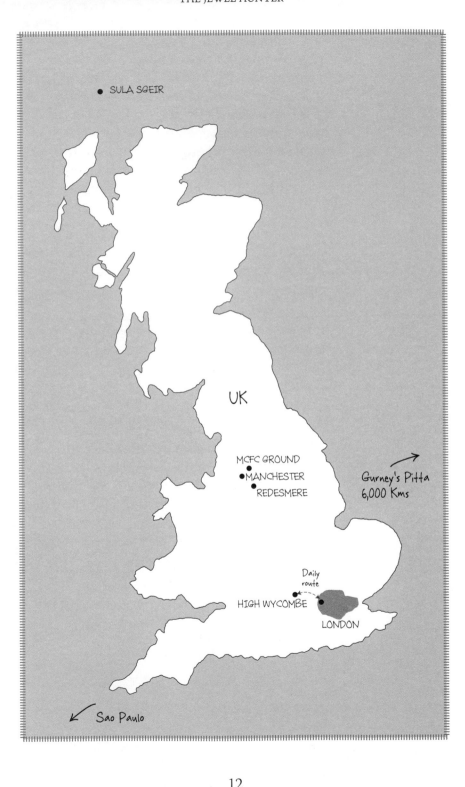

Chapter 1

Quitting the Day Job. High Wycombe, UK

Blood pounded in my ears. My heart rate was up in the stratosphere. I crouched on a disused hunting trail in a remote forest in southwest Sumatra. There was no mistaking the hulking black figure in front of me; it was, beyond question, a Malayan Sun Bear. Big, brutish, and armed with a set of raking, razor-sharp claws ideal for cracking open trees and the skulls of wayward ornithologists. I analysed the known data: it was definitely a bear. Quite a big one. It was making uncomfortably rapid progress down the narrow trail towards me. Six metres away and closing. What one was supposed to do came to me in a flash. Run away. Now.

Six months earlier, slumped over a desk in the Home Counties, the best method of flight from large, hairy and quite possibly hungry wild animals was not my primary concern. I was trying to figure out which formulae did what, and where. Which spreadsheets linked to which others. And beyond that, exactly why it was that we had decided to link the damn things in the first place.

I was pretty sure that it had something to do with gross profit margin. Or turnover by product sector. Or possibly the square on the hypotenuse. Whichever of these was the case it was certainly important, which is why I, as Sales Director of an English professional audio manufacturing company, had been charged with the task of building the whole byzantine, interlocking, mathematical structure by nine o'clock the following morning: get all the company's financial ducks in a row, make them add up, and ensure they spelled out the right answer in commercial terms. I had put together a thousand spreadsheets like this before, but this time something was bothering me, and it was not something numerical, but something existential; when all the numbers did finally line up, what would they actually *mean*?

By some curious quirk of fate, the faceless little office in Buckinghamshire in which I now found myself was where I spent an indecent proportion of my waking hours. (When I wasn't suffering the slow, traffic-clogged commute west out of London along the

13

A40 in my ageing Audi that is.) This desk-bound existence was one I had fashioned for myself. This is what I had won in adversity, and it had come to define who I was. I was in charge of stuff, quite big stuff involving a lot of zeros, and this meant that I was, by definition of a host of capitalists far more learned than myself, quite important in the general scheme of things. The company was doing well. Our competitors were perhaps not quite quaking in their boots, but they were at least sitting up and taking notice. I was winning. The problem was it just didn't feel that way.

This state of affairs was largely the result of my own making, but the exact mechanism escaped me. I had started out in UK sales, quickly graduating to international sales management, developing a network of third party distributors to sell the company's products all over the world. It was challenging and fun, the commercial equivalent of those circus plate-spinners who keep fifty different dinner plates aloft simultaneously, wobbling precariously atop bamboo poles. However, as I took on more responsibility, the job entailed more office-based overseeing and less field-work; someone else would now spin the plates, while I would mostly build spreadsheets to calculate whether we could add more plates, or whether each one could ten percent spin faster. Gazing out of my first-floor window over the urban sprawl below, I tried to remember exactly when my success had started to separate me from doing what I enjoyed. When had I moved from a life visiting new markets in a slew of fascinating countries in Asia and South America, to gently banging my head against a computer screen in an industrial park in High Wycombe? Somewhere along the line, it seemed, I had swapped the thrilling life of an explorer for the humdrum existence of an office drone.

In the nineties I travelled widely and revelled in the eclecticism: dropped into cantinas in São Paulo to drink Caipirinhas before any London barman had ever heard of Cachaça; bought delicate snuff bottles in Shanghai, each with an exquisite scene from the Karma Sutra painted on the inside, pieces of art which made our own humdrum, ship-in-a-bottle British culture look distinctly provincial. In Peru, over monumental tumblers of whisky, a mysterious man whose name translated as 'Mr. Luxurious' had showed me a collection of Nazi memorabilia. I had even managed to have a good time in Belgium.

Throwing off the shackles of traditional British linguistic shyness, I had learned to say *'hello'*, *'beer'*, and *'thank-you'* in seventeen different languages. What's more, I knew that in Mandarin it was important to get the intonation *just so*, in order to avoid inadvertently ordering a banjo-playing mule in a manner that might offend one's hosts. I had broadened my horizons, mind and waistline. And then, as if time was up on this Faustian pact, I had apparently agreed to swap all of this in order to oversee a collection of spreadsheets, some of which had quite big numbers in them. Nice trade.

It was seven thirty in the evening, and my colleagues had all packed up for the day leaving me alone in the office. Inspiration. I toggled through my MacBook Pro's open applications, fired up Safari, and prepared to indulge my secret passion.

The fact is I have been a bird-watcher almost since I can remember. My father had bought me my first bird book when I was eleven years old. This was probably driven by the parental fear that if he didn't get me interested in healthy outdoor pursuits, I would be set on the inner city urchin road to heroin, glue sniffing or, worse, a life-long obsession with Manchester United. (Whatever the motivation, it worked on all levels; I became fascinated by birds, I have yet to try heroin, and I still support Manchester City.)

We lived in northwest England, on the southern edge of God's own city, Manchester, and I vividly recall my first ever bird-watching trip. My father had driven me to a local lake, Redesmere, which nestled amidst the rolling Cheshire hills, surrounded by mature woodland. The first bird we saw on getting out of the car was blue on top, pink underneath and had what I described in my notebook at the time as 'a powerful, pointy beak.' It was upside-down, clinging tenaciously to a vertical tree trunk, with the business end pointing downwards. I remember thinking, 'if it falls off now it'll be a hell of a job to get it out of the ground.'

I knew it was a Nuthatch, and smugly identified it as such. My father to this day claims that I was only able to identify it because it was in exactly the same upside-down pose as the one in the book. I was incensed when he suggested this at the time, not least because there was a large element of truth in the observation. Nonetheless, I had identified it correctly, and it was duly written down in my notebook. A very small, single-entry, amoebic list maybe, but events had been set in motion; I was well and truly hooked.

As my bird-watching interests matured, I started to travel further afield, firstly cycling to the next lake a little further from home in pursuit of wintering ducks, then hitching to the neighbouring county to look for wading birds on the Wirral peninsula. As soon as I had passed my test, I started driving to the farthest-flung corners of the country in pursuit of storm-driven waifs that had pitched up on a desolate promontory that still somehow qualified as part of England. This allowed me to add crucial ticks to the list of birds I had seen within the British Isles; the all important 'British List'. By the time I was twenty-five, I was developing an enviable tan on the shores of the Red Sea in Israel while searching for maroon and azure-blue White-throated Kingfishers and tiny, long-tailed Namaqua Doves. My hobby was responsible for me nearly freezing to death at the top of a black run in the French Pyrenees in pursuit of a White-winged Snowfinch while dressed, for reasons I prefer to forget, as a pantomime cat. My widening circle of travel required me to start a 'Western Palaearctic' List to record all the species of bird I had seen in Europe and immediately beyond, and once I discovered Asia and South America, their forests teeming with unparalleled biodiversity, there was no way back, and my world list was born.

With bird-watchers there is always a list. Preferably more than one. They are the Wagnerian *leitmotif* that recurs through every birder's life. You will find a number of lists dotted throughout this volume, and I make no apologies for their presence. Lists to me, and to bird-watchers in general, are like vodka-tonics; you make one and it seems like such a good idea you end up making a few. Before long you can't remember why you embarked on the first one, but you're having such a good time you no longer care. Saying that birders like making lists is like saying Homer Simpson likes Duff Beer, that politicians are fond of lying, or that Catholics are well disposed towards the Pope. The truth is, we bird-watchers have a burning need to catalogue, record and sort; a trait my long-suffering other half refers to as 'drawers within drawers'.

Having visited Asia for the first time (a riotous trip to Beidaihe in eastern China with a group of hard-drinking, culturally insensitive fellow bird-watchers) I started a passionate affair with rainforests and their many inhabitants. While getting to grips with the huge number of birds that can be found in Asian forests, I discovered the pittas; love at first sight. Richly colourful and yet highly elusive, they are the ultimate forest prize, and they quickly became my favourites.

Awaking from my reverie, I glanced at my watch again. Seven thirty-five, time for a quick clandestine diversion. I knew there were certain websites I really should not be perusing on company premises, but I couldn't help myself. I googled 'Pittas', clicked a likely link, and the screen glowed as a male Banded Pitta appeared. A gorgeous creature, emblazoned with a broad golden arc that sweeps over the eye, deepening to a burnished orange at the nape. Below the neck the bird is all deep, dipped-in-ink blue. I smiled as I recalled seeing my first Banded Pitta on a narrow forest path known as the Jenet Muda trail, situated in a quiet corner of the Taman Negara rainforest in Peninsular Malaysia, May 2000. My mind wandered further back, to my first ever pitta sighting, a Noisy Pitta bouncing across the lower slopes of Mount Whitfield in northeast Australia in 1995; I googled 'Noisy Pitta' and found a full-frame shot of a bird perched on a log, its mouth stuffed with worms. A wave of nostalgia washed over me. I had spent a couple of days searching for the species, hearing its cheerful, far-carrying *walk-to-work* whistle echoing through the forest, but as always, it had been much easier to hear than to see. After a lot of careful stalking I had got close to a bird, and I sat down on the trail, flicking leeches away and whistling my best impression of a Noisy Pitta to entice the bird closer.

And to my astonishment it had worked; as I scanned the forest floor for a glimpse of colour I heard a tell-tale rustle in the leaf-litter behind me, and I slowly swivelled around while trying to remain inconspicuous. There, not ten metres from me, was a Noisy Pitta, a jumble of green, blue, buff and red. It hopped through a dense patch of cover on the forest floor, and eventually, unbelievably, stood out on the trail with its head cocked on one side, trying to figure out whether this crouching, sweaty creature in a pile of crumpled, camouflaged clothing was a threat or not.

It had taken my breath away, this bird, all vital energy and astonishing, unfathomable beauty, like those unattainable girls on TV adverts who somehow make you buy toothpaste, but whom you secretly know will never come home with you to do the brushing. Yet now I found myself some nine thousand miles away from the nearest Noisy Pitta, reduced to gazing at the bird's image on my computer screen in the English Home Counties. I became horribly aware of the unpalatable, jarring truth; my life was out of whack. I was spending fifty weeks of the year wishing I was in the rainforests of Asia and Australasia hunting for pittas, and at best a scant two weeks actually in those forests. Those two snatched weeks a year would see me frenetically rushing around, trying to grab as many avian experiences as I possibly could, so that I could squirrel away enough material to get me through the long winter of work until the next trip. I scarcely had time to list the birds I saw, let alone glory in the poetry of their existence.

50:2, the ratio sucked. Something had to change. At this rate I'd be over the hill before all of the world's thirty-two pittas were under the belt.

I had banished such thoughts and immersed myself in work. I ran the London Marathon twice (raising money to save the rainforest home of the Gurney's Pitta in Thailand) and the endless training filled every available second, preventing any more dark thoughts of throwing away everything I had worked for. But those questioning voices in my head had grown ever louder, and I was now forced to consider my position. The truth was that I no longer loved my job. I no longer sprang out of bed of a morning, desperate to get to the office. I resented all those working weekends as lost birding opportunities that I would never get back. And I was tired; stress and long hours were wearing me down, and I wasn't getting any younger. The next step was obvious. Being a bird-watcher, I did what countless generations of bird-watchers had done. I made a list.

Stay in the job	Leave the job to watch pittas
Good salary	*Get by on savings*
Stay on career ladder	*Set fire to career ladder, warm hands over flames*
Buy new Audi	*Rent rickshaws and motorbike-taxis*
New Armani suit	*New leech socks*
Steak and kidney pie, office canteen	*Roti Canai, riverside food stall*
Safe, secure, dull life	*Risky, unstable, exciting life*
No pittas	*Lots of pittas*
Continue to be frustrated	*Start to be fulfilled*

I stared at the list. Not too many things going for staying in the job. OK, financial security was a positive, but the correlative cost to health, sanity and missed birds was high.

A friend of mine summed it up succinctly: 'you don't see great birds in your living room'. This stick of philosophical dynamite had been offered up on the deck of an ice-breaker, a long way off the northwest tip of Scotland, heading out to Sula Sgeir, one of the British Isles' most remote rocky outposts. We had spent a restless night getting tossed around our bunks in rough seas, on our way we hoped to a rendezvous with a wayward Black-browed Albatross that had taken up residence on the rock for the previous two summers.

We left empty-handed, but I knew what he meant. *Faint heart ne'er won fair bird.* Or something like that. *Carpe diem.* Those rosebuds needed to be gathered, and they did not grow in my front room, nor in my office. I wanted to see all the world's pittas, but I was already forty-five years old and thus no spring chicken, and lengthy sojourns in the world's rainforests would be physically demanding. If I didn't do it soon, it would be impossible for me to scale peaks in order to find the montane species, and to ford rivers and hack my way through choked ravines to access the remote home ranges of some of the more difficult lowland ones.

Deforestation was depriving a number of pittas of their habitat. If I left it too late, it was possible that some species would be extinct, or so scarce that they would be impossible to find. Gurney's Pitta, the species that I had run two fund-raising London marathons to help save was already on the edge, with less than twenty pairs left in the whole of Thailand.

In the final analysis, the hierarchy was reassuringly simple:

> *Animals are the best things in the world*
> *Birds are the best animals*
> *Pittas are the best birds*
> *Gurney's Pitta is the best pitta*

Gurney's Pitta was top of the pile, cock of the walk, king of the hill. And almost extinct. The clock was ticking.

I closed the spreadsheet, typed out a resignation letter, and quietly cleared my desk.

Chapter 2

The Storm Before the Calm. Southern Thailand

Snow. Thick, thick snow. Tons of the stuff. The heaviest UK snowfall, the radio announcer intoned, in the last fifty years. As omens go, not exactly what the meteorologist ordered for my first day as a free man.

My taxi did not arrive. Not a single bus was running across the entire country. My quest began, rather inauspiciously, on foot. I swung my rucksack onto my back and slithered my way across north London, with the vague idea of heading for King's Cross Station. A few hardy commuters were battling against the elements in a bid to reach the office, and we exchanged sympathetic glances as we passed, the maximum communication London locals can tolerate without alarm bells ringing. As I reached the station a few alarm bells of my own were ringing; the gates were firmly shut. Somehow, it seemed, the snow had penetrated underground too (points frozen solid at Lancaster Gate no doubt) and no trains would be running from King's Cross in the foreseeable future.

I trudged further west, mentally tracing a route along the Circle Line. Euston Square station was also closed, and my attempts to flag down the few taxis on the snow-clogged streets were as successful as Man City's away record. The next station was closed too, and with snow still falling, I walked onward, the weight of my rucksack bearing down on my aching shoulders, my footfall uncertain on the icy pavements. I'd rashly decided to try and set a record by seeing all of the world's thirty-two species of pitta in a year, but at this rate it looked like I might stand a better chance of seeing all of London's underground stations. I backtracked to Euston station, which by some merciful oversight on London Transport's part had been allowed to remain open.

Four hours after leaving home I finally completed the twenty-mile journey and made it to the British Airways counter with five minutes to spare before check-in closed. Some shameless sweet-talking meant that my old friend (and companion for this first leg of the journey) Graham Hogan was also able to make the flight. We had met in the late 1970s when mere fledgling bird-watchers,

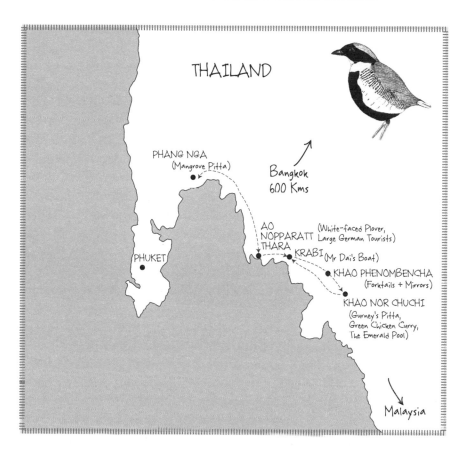

sleeping rough on the North Norfolk coast and birding all the hours God sends. Graham had saved my life by offering me a space to sleep in the back of his van during a storm. Now, having survived another storm, we were hoping for more clement Thai weather and some rather more exotic birds. My co-traveller had abandoned Manchester Airport at five a.m. and schlepped down on one of the few trains still running, before hitching a ride in a friendly Saudi family's minibus. His timely arrival was largely due to the Herculean efforts of the driver, who had glanced over his shoulder to assure his charges that he 'daren't risk driving at more than a hundred miles per hour in this weather and with so many passengers.'

Having cheated the weather gods, we breezed through the deserted immigration area, downed the traditional pre-flight pint of Guinness, bought the prerequisite bottle of rum at duty free and ran to the gate, crashing out in our seats and giggling at our good fortune. Against all the odds, despite the country being

21

at a standstill and with London's premier airport reduced by the ongoing arctic mayhem to a single runway, the flight was allegedly on time. After a two-hour wait for de-icing we did indeed take off, and thirteen hours later arrived at Bangkok's brand new, unfeasibly shiny Suvarnabhumi airport. We raced through endless fake marble corridors and made our onward connection with barely five minutes to spare. An hour later we finally ground to a halt at the tidy but reassuringly provincial 'Krabi International Airport.' This new structure was billed as being Thailand's next big thing, yet today it was as quiet as a Monday afternoon in a country church.

We drove east. *En route* we passed dusty towns whose names sounded decidedly saucy, but which doubtless in the original Thai meant something tranquil like *green trees by blue water* or *the white house by the one-horned water buffalo*. Most were desperately poor and neglected, sagging in the heat like the listless dogs that mooched around the margins.

Bang Thieo is an unassuming locale, squatting in the shadow of the Khao Nor Chuchi mountain. The peak itself is but an insignificant dot on most maps, but is nonetheless hallowed ground to bird-watchers the world over for one simple reason; for many years it was thought to be the last known refuge of Gurney's Pitta, a bird almost too beautiful to exist. Indeed, prior to the pitta's rediscovery in southern Thailand, it had been thought extinct for many years, until a tiny relict population was found hiding deep in the forest. I had decided that the jewel hunt needed to start with a bang, and so had chosen this same, tiger-striped avian gem to kick things off. The tiny creature, barely seven inches tall on tiptoe, had almost single-handedly caused me to quit my job, jeopardise my long-term relationship, and willingly embrace my mid-life crisis. And there was a real risk that it wouldn't even show up to explain itself.

The problem is that pittas in general, and Gurney's in particular, are really difficult to see. Despite its bright colours, Gurney's Pitta is both a master of disguise and extraordinarily shy and retiring. Its song, so often a critical element in finding pittas, is an unassuming and apologetic *'whilip'*, over almost before it's begun. It's frighteningly easy to miss in the cacophony of the forest, competing as it does for aural space with legions of other birds, monkeys and mosquitoes. And that's before one takes into account the cicadas, whose incessant, buzz saw whining drowns out everything else in the vicinity – like children in a restaurant whose overindulgent parents have allowed them too many litres of Tizer before lunch. Despite such concerns, I needed to start the campaign with a grand gesture, a statement of intent, so Gurney's it was. Graham and I planned to lose little time in dumping our baggage, breaking out our jungle fatigues, and hitting the trails.

Firstly however, after fourteen hours of exposure to the oxymoronic concept of 'airline food', there was the important matter of lunch to consider. With Thailand unquestionably the home of the world's finest cuisine, we needed to ingratiate ourselves with our hosts and sample the local fare. A glance at the menu had us salivating, and we plumped for *Gaeng Keowan Gai* (green chicken curry) with fragrant slices of galangal, juicy, refreshingly bitter pea aubergines, and twists of crispy Thai basil. A bowl of Jasmine rice apiece rounded things off, washed down with an iced glass of fresh lime juice. The reckless abandonment of my career was already starting to seem like a good idea.

As we mopped up the last of the curry, I was horrified to see a coach-load of tourists pull up in a shiny double-decker with a Gurney's Pitta painted on the door. Our fellow guests descended on the buffet like the proverbial plague of locusts. It transpired that they were on a day trip out of Krabi, a coastal resort a couple of hours to the west, and were intent on bathing in the Emerald Pool, the latest attraction to be pitched by the ever growing throng of tourist operators that had sprung up on the outskirts of Krabi town. Things had changed since my last visit in the late nineties, when I had been the only swimmer in this oasis, whose waters spilled over into the rainforest like an organic infinity pool. (At least, I was the only swimmer once I'd persuaded a four-foot monitor lizard to vacate the pool.) Clearly Khao Nor Chuchi was no longer the unknown backwater it had once been, and I shuddered at the thought that at dawn the next day we might spend an hour manoeuvring ourselves into position to catch a glimpse of a pitta, only to have our carefully laid plans wrecked by a portly German squeezed into a tiny thong, clutching a towel and bellowing '*Ja! Hello! Wo ist das Schwimmbad bitte?*'

I need not have worried. The tour rep. swung into view and effortlessly swept everyone back onto the bus in a flurry of flip-flops, and they departed to the bathing pavilion as quickly as they had arrived.

In our quest to find the Gurney's, we had an ace up our sleeve. A local man, Yothin Meekao, had for years been helping to keep the Gurney's Pitta population intact, helping to promote the site, warden the birds, and prevent the worst of the deforestation. Almost single-handedly he had fought a rearguard action to protect this last fragment of lowland forest in southern Thailand. Having met him in the past I knew him to be a skilled jungle operator, and we had contacted him ahead of time to help us track down our quarry. Unfortunately he was only free on the day of our arrival, which meant looking for Gurney's in the heat of the afternoon. Pittas, like many forest birds, are most active during the first few hours of daylight, and I did not fancy our chances of tracking down one of the world's most elusive species after midday. If we missed Gurney's on our first afternoon however, we would have our work cut out trying to locate a calling bird over the coming days. The season was also less than perfect, since the birds do not settle down to breed until the rains arrive. Thus the best time to look for them is March/April; on the face of it we were at least a month too early. The odds were against us.

Yothin duly appeared around two o'clock. After catching up on the latest news in Thaiglish and being reacquainted with Yothin's endearing laugh that suggested a shared lineage with Dick Dastardly's pooch Muttley, we drove down a succession of deeply rutted tracks to a secret location. Hanging our sweat-towels around our necks, we crept silently along a narrow muddy trail through secondary forest to a small, camouflaged hide. We hunkered down inside on the forest floor, confident of our invisibility thanks to the protection afforded by the hide. In seconds the tropical heat had soaked our clothes in perspiration, as we prepared for what I was sure would be a long and fruitless wait. Sweat ran into our eyes, temporarily blinding us, before dripping from our noses onto our binoculars. Mosquitoes whined irritably around our heads, denied a feeding frenzy only by the thin layer of chemicals we had laboured to apply to every inch of exposed flesh. We ignored them all, and I smiled, delighted to be back in the fray with all its discomforts.

We had waited only twenty minutes when I glimpsed a movement to the right of the hide. I motioned to the others, and a moment later we were rubbing our eyes in disbelief as a stunning male Gurney's Pitta bounced past the hide, not three metres from us! Fifteen minutes later, a female followed suit. A few moments more, and the male returned, and the pair posed for photographs as if born to the role. They fed unconcernedly in front of us, so close I felt I could almost reach out and touch them, though their nervous twitching each time my camera's motor drive whirred was evidence of their true shy and elusive nature. Even the mosquitoes' continuous assault failed to divert our attention from the theatre unfolding in front of us. I had glimpsed Gurney's Pitta on previous visits, but it had taken days to manage even the briefest of views. We had beaten the worst the English weather could throw at us, and yet were now watching one of the most difficult pitta species in the world at point blank range within a few short hours of the start of the quest. As curtain raisers go, it was tough to beat. Day one, species one, and we had barely set foot on a trail.

The next couple of days ran a little more true to form. Birds that had suffered years of hunting pressure gave us the run-around as they hid behind every conceivable bough and twig, and our forays into the forest after dark to spotlight night birds were similarly unsuccessful. However, we heard a Blue-winged Pitta at dawn on the third day, and spent two mornings and an evening in wet, trashy forest locked in a tense struggle with a pair of birds that stubbornly refused to show themselves. An occasional sharp, whipcrack 'skeaoow' of alarm would betray the birds' presence, but they lurked in the densest cover and kept themselves to themselves. During our third attempt we got smart, and figured that the male might respond if we played a tape of his call from up in the canopy. Blue winged Pittas, like most of their cousins, spend the vast majority of their lives on the forest floor, but when they sing to declare their territory they fly up and call from a hidden perch a few metres off the ground. Logically then, if we simulated a bird in the position from which it would normally call, we ought to get a response.

It seemed to be a flawed plan however. We were three months too early for the breeding season, and these Blue-wings were wintering birds, far more interested in feeding than breeding. The other problem was that there really was no canopy to speak of in this tiny plot of marshy wasteland, just a ragtag collection of scraggy bushes barely fit to uproot and burn as firewood. There was, however, a single sapling of slightly more significant stature in one corner of the plot, and it was growing out of a small muddy mound, raising it a few yards above the rest. That would have to do. We clawed our way up the sticky slope, clambered into the tree as quietly as possible, and played my pre-recorded Blue-winged Pitta call. 'Tae-raew, tae-raew... tae-raew, tae-raew...' the familiar, almost mechanical sound of the pitta rang out through the morning air, and within seconds a medium-sized blue, green and red bird with large white wing-patches flew out of the trash-swamp, arced in towards us, and landed in the very tree in which we were so ineptly hiding.

To say we were astonished would be putting it mildly. Our plan of attack was born of desperation not genius, and we had really not expected anything other than the same result we'd been experiencing for the last two days. The pitta too seemed amazed to see us, and after pausing for a few seconds, looking quizzically at us with its head cocked slightly to one side (one eyebrow raised expressing disbelief and disapprobation in equal measure) it quickly flew back into the plot. We played one more snippet of tape, and the bird returned. It was rather more circumspect this time, defiantly calling at us from a nearby bush.

Three days in, and the second pitta species secured. A bonus species too, for I had not expected to see Blue-winged (a scarce wintering bird here in southern Thailand) until late May, by which time birds are vocalizing on their Malaysian breeding grounds. We had been put to the sword by the local mosquitoes, the spiny rattan bushes had torn into our arms and legs and tested our patience and we were liberally plastered with marsh juice, but we had our prize.

The days at Khao Nor Chuchi were relentlessly hot; it had not rained for six weeks, and although the reserve held many rare species, I knew many were at very low population densities. As a result, the next couple of days were hard work. We saw little, and were forced to sit out the stultifying heat of the day when avian activity slowed almost to a standstill. Happily this meant we could indulge in a succession of delicious slow lunches, featuring a varied assortment of rural Thai cuisine. These inevitably involved *Som Tam*, a northeastern salad comprising firm papaya, crunchy peanuts, and tiny dried freshwater prawns, all marinaded in pungent fish sauce, garlic and bird's eye chillies. With our mouths on fire, we eased back a little on the heat, plumping for something sensible like steamed fish in tamarind, but my Mancunian palate, educated by years of post-libation curries in Rusholme, would always mean I'd finish by re-entering the fray with a fiery *Gaeng Tang Moo Gap Nor Mai*. This red curry of pork and bamboo shoots was chock-full of torn kaffir lime leaves, fragrant lemongrass and chopped coriander root, all simmered in cooling, fresh coconut milk, but cunningly laced with searingly hot, long red chillies. Our endorphins well and truly set in motion by the spice assault we were raring to go again by three o'clock, our senses alive and finely tuned.

While we waited for the temperature to drop, we staked out a fruiting tree on the main trail close to the Emerald Pool. Fruiting trees act like magnets to forest birds, and sitting quietly beneath the canopy we were treated to a cavalcade of bright green and red barbets (including the scarce Red-crowned and Brown Barbets along with their commoner congeners) subtle-shade green-pigeons, and a host of tiny flowerpeckers and sunbirds, daintily feeding on the blooms that decorated the end of each spindly branch.

At dawn on our fourth day, I sat sipping coffee while I waited for Graham, listening to the eerie, ringing *'pee-WHEEAH'* calls of the Great Eared-nightjars, perennial wardens of the night shift, in the darkness above me. As the village started to stir, I heard the world's most surreal sound; a speeding motorbike-and-sidecar ice cream vendor blaring Thai pop music, which shifted in pitch with his passage as the Doppler effect kicked in. Who wants to buy ice cream at five-thirty in the morning? Was there a major turf war under way, this vendor making an early start to ensure he snaffled the best pitch for the day's trading? It would remain a mystery.

We worked our way up Trail B, the heat a physical presence already by six a.m. Eventually we reached primary forest, the well-formed canopy high above our heads blocking much of the light, the temperature distinctly and thankfully cooler as a result. We tiptoed respectfully through the rainforest cathedral soaking up its quiet majesty, dwarfed by the huge dipterocarps soaring up towards the heavens, cloistering us within. Huge flocks of butterflies disturbed by our passage flickered in the sun-gaps, blizzards of colour around our knees. The ghostly chimes of an Indian Cuckoo rippled down to us from a high perch deep in the forest, but all too soon the chorus of birdsong died, replaced by the tortured-metal screaming of the cicadas. As we returned to the main track, we passed a small rickety bridge with missing struts and a hand-rail long since rotted into oblivion; the famous 'Pole Bridge', around which the Gurney's Pittas used to play. I had waited for four days on my first visit to KNC in 1997, hoping against hope to hear the pitta's sharp *'whilip'* call. I neither heard nor saw the bird back then, and it was another three years before I finally got my first glimpse.

On 21st January 1999, a date forever etched in my memory, I'd sat for five hours on a small muddy trail, at a spot universally known as 'U22'. A pair of Gurney's Pittas had taken up residence in the gully that crossed the trail, and I was determined to see them. My patience was ultimately rewarded, when in a tiny gap in the vegetation, I caught a flash of something blue. A crisp bag? A discarded drink carton? The patch of blue rippled, a delicate shiver, but undeniably a movement. It was the tail of a female pitta, and a few moments later the bird bounced into view. A stripy yellow-and-black vision appeared for a few brief seconds, before it bounced further into cover and was gone. I stared at the same gap for ten more minutes, and eventually a yet more gorgeous vision appeared; blocks of yellow, black and brown, even more outrageous tiger-striping down the flanks, and an iridescent blue cap set at a rakish angle on the back of the head. A male Gurney's! Again, a few seconds of paradise before, *boink, boink*, the vision had evaporated back into the forest.

In the late afternoon we birded the very same trails that had provided my first views of Gurney's Pitta ten years earlier. We saw very little, KNC living up to its reputation as a tough place to work. It's one of the inconveniences of tropical bird-watching that one can walk for hours seeing and hearing almost nothing. Suddenly from nowhere a flock appears, and a mass of birds, all feeding actively, move at speed through the forest. The only option is to scan frantically, trying to make sense of the jumble of colours, wing-bars, spots and stripes, and hope to identify the less common members of the assembly before they move on and are lost forever. No such problems beset us on this airless afternoon, and we saw only a pair of Ferruginous Babblers next to the road at the end of our long and dusty walk. We could have sat in the blissful cool of the car and seen just as much, but that's the way the forest is some days.

That evening we drove to a nearby spa to join the ranks of the alternative tourist crowd. Our intention was not to take the waters, despite their impeccable mineral content credentials proudly displayed on numerous municipal signs, but rather to look for a particular night bird, the Blyth's Frogmouth. Frogmouths are cute, in a gawky, ill-proportioned, adolescent kind of way. They look roughly like an owl that has been stretched out a little and has had a capacious comedy beak stuck on by some mean-spirited prankster. (The name 'frogmouth' is more than merely coincidental.) Facially they are blessed with wispy, frond-like appendages that resemble massively overgrown eyebrows, giving them the air of an eccentric but kindly agèd professor. Plumage-wise they are decked out in a range of sombre but subtly beautiful greys and browns. A rufous gorget adorns the upper breast, as if they had just dined and spilled a particularly rich gravy all down their best dress shirt.

They are as strange vocally as they are aesthetically. The repertoire includes an endearing, fruity, gurgling laugh, *'Waa hurgh hurghh hurghl'*, that descends down the scale; definitely in weird uncle territory. This particular Blyth's Frogmouth was most accommodating. In response to our audio playback, the bird graciously flew out of the forest and perched just above our heads, posing for photographs as we illuminated his finer features in our torch beams. As we exited the spa we showed the lady at the gate our photograph to reassure her that although we looked a bit odd (sporting binoculars and recording equipment unlike her other patrons) we had not been up to any mischief. In typical Thai style she broke into a broad smile, nodded sagely, and said *'Noc Hoo'*, which presumably means either *'Blyth's Frogmouth'* or *'crazy foreigners'* in Thai.

The following dawn found us back at the Pole Bridge, and after a prolonged bout of lurking, our stealth was rewarded with another pitta. I know I'm biased and tend to think that all pittas are mouth wateringly beautiful, but a male Banded Pitta is genuinely a sight to behold. Broad stripes, crisply delineated above and below in black sweep back above the eyes. Primrose yellow at first, they deepen to a burnished orange that lights up the forest. A series of concentric vermilion waves washes across the shining royal blue breast, rippling out towards each of the racing-striped wings. An electric blue tail adds a final breathtaking flash of colour, jutting out from beneath the chocolate mantle.

You can keep your Sistine Chapel ceiling and your Mona Lisa; this is the most astonishing work of art on the planet. Despite being aware of our presence, the bird seemed loath to leave its favoured feeding area, and by keeping still and silent we were able to enjoy unparalleled views of this stunning creature. Less than a week of

February gone, and I had already found my third pitta. I had worried that my inability to leave work until the end of January (thus leaving me just eleven short months in which to find all thirty-two pittas rather than the twelve I had planned) would cost me dear. Suddenly it seemed less of a problem. At this rate it would all be wrapped up before summer was out.

Buoyed by our success, we returned to a trail on the Khao Nor Chuchi reserve after dark to try again for Gould's Frogmouth, a close relative of the Blyth's Frogmouth that had frolicked above our heads the previous evening. We had visited the trail earlier in the day to familiarise ourselves with the layout, having had prior experience of becoming lost in rainforest at night. We had cunningly marked the trail into (and hopefully out of) the forest with bright orange ice cream wrappers, tied to trees at strategic intervals. This, in the absence of any over-zealous litter-gatherers, ought to ensure our successful passage back to the sanctity of the road even on the darkest night.

Bird-watchers are divided regarding the subject of the joys of night-birding. Personally I enter dark forest in a state of barely suspended terror, convinced that every rustle in the inky blackness is an enormous deadly snake, coiling itself in readiness for the perfect angle of attack. In truth the problem is purely one of overactive imagination, and in all my nocturnal woodland wanderings in Asia, I must admit I have yet to actually experience an attack by a mammoth killer snake. It's just the thought of what *could* lie unseen in the black void of the night, the razor-sharp fangs dripping venom mere inches away from my vulnerable body that chills the blood.

The fact is that the only things that tripped us up on this night, as on all such nights, were unseen tree roots and thorn-laden rattans. We failed to encounter a single snake, or indeed, a voracious Tiger bent on our destruction. Sad to relate, it is almost certain that all the big cats in southern Thailand have long since been despatched by an animal far more dangerous than themselves. They have been systematically slaughtered, rendered down and packaged to satisfy the insecurities of urban Chinese customers, convinced despite all the evidence to the contrary that powdered Tiger penis will somehow enhance their own faltering virility.

We did, however, finally persuade a Gould's Frogmouth to show itself. Not quite as beautiful as the Blyth's, nor as much of a show-off, but after a last stab at invisibility, relatively helpful in perching above us for a minute or two as our headlamp beams wove patterns around his head, illuminating his fleeting moment of stardom. As we left, we conscientiously picked up our ice cream wrappers behind us, like Theseus re-ravelling his string back to the labyrinth entrance having slain the Minotaur. *Leave only footprints* as the mantra runs. And definitely no Orange Maid wrappers.

Celebrating back at the ranch with a couple of unfeasibly cold beers, we met Dean, a solo birder newly arrived. In time-honoured style we shared our bird information from the last few days, drawing detailed maps that would have been incomprehensible to the laymen, but which to the initiated represented a golden key unlocking the door to avian treasure. Dean had moved to India from Liverpool in the 1980s, and I innocently asked what had prompted the move. The answer was unexpected and uncompromising: 'Heroin.'

I did not like to ask whether the move to Asia had been to pursue a career involving the drug or to escape its clutches, but as the conversation progressed it became clear that our new friend had fled northern England's urban wastelands to escape the tenacious grip of narcotics, and with great success. Fifteen years on he was engaged in various volunteer projects and thriving in his new home. His week in Thailand was a rekindling of a childhood interest in bird-watching. I thought of my abandoned in-tray in the UK, all the seventeen-hour days and endless trade shows, the weekends worked and lost forever. Sometimes a clean break is the only way. As we sank another couple of beers, Dean demonstrated an unnerving familiarity with India's larger and more venomous snakes, and we traded scare stories. Dean won hands down with his tale of being bitten by a keelback while trying to free it from a fishing net. So much for karma. Keen though I am on looking after the planet, I must admit, I'd have let the bugger drown.

Well before dawn we said our goodbyes to the kindly ladies at the Morakot who had hosted us so splendidly for the last few days. An hour's starlit drive brought us to Khao Phenombencha, a site we had visited in previous years in search of the Chestnut-naped Forktail. Forktails are small, long-tailed riverine birds, decked out in a range of black and white patterns. In flight they resemble a tiny upset chess board, all contrasting spots and stripes, a chiaroscuro in motion. The Chestnut-napes trump other forktails in the fashion stakes however, boasting as they do a foxy red crown and upper back. Like most forktails, they are also very shy. All too often a high-pitched call is the only evidence of their presence, as the bird dodges around a river-bend moments before you round the previous one. My theory is that they construct complex sets of mirrors at each twist in the river to remain one step ahead. This particular pair of forktails at Phenombencha were only ever seen at first light, thereafter (doubtless alerted to potential disturbance by their bespoke mirror set-up) moving up-river to quieter, inaccessible reaches beyond the waterfalls.

However, by arriving before dawn we had stolen a march, and before the first glimmers of daylight had turned the sky blue at the edges we were in position. We crouched inconspicuously on the bridge over the river, like a pair of marines poised to blow up an enemy position with one of those antiquated box-with-plunger TNT trigger boxes. (I should point out in the interests of ensuring future readmission into Thailand, that we had not brought any *actual* dynamite with us, and happily it proved superfluous to mission success.) Only five minutes after dawn however, despite our caution the forktail departed, and we trooped back to the rental car, heads held high. We were greeted by the sight of a tame Peacock standing on the roof of our vehicle, and it took a not inconsiderable amount of shooing to persuade the bird to abandon its newly-claimed perch.

Delightful though the forktail was, it was undeniably a distraction from the pitta mission. The nearby tourist town of Krabi was our next destination, specifically the mangrove boardwalk on the edge of town, home to the Mangrove Pitta. The species shares a large number of genes with the superficially similar Blue-winged Pitta, but at some point back in the mists of time a few Blue-winged Pittas developed a taste for marine crustacea, and decamped to the mangroves to pursue a crab-centric lifestyle.* As a result, their descendents are armed with a fearsome outsize bill, ideal for breaking into crab shells (or for removing the caps from bottles of beer when no-one can remember where the opener is).

To enter a mangrove swamp is to wander into a strange alternative universe, largely silent except for random 'smacks' as gas bursts through the slimy mud-skin. These tiny explosions reverberate

---

* The town is thus Krabi by name, and crabby by nature.

around the gnarled, convoluted knots of the Tolkeinesque root systems that draw succour from the glutinous tidal nutrients below. The pittas are fond of feeding beneath these tangled roots, and the secret is to try to catch a glimpse of blue, red and green as they scurry around the darker recesses in search of their crabby prey. I have always thought that it should be pretty easy to snatch the latter, given that they can only move sideways. Certainly the pittas seem for the most part to manage it without ever having to make themselves overtly visible, and we spent a fruitless morning pacing up and down the boardwalk getting no closer than hearing pittas call in the distance, scant reward for our efforts.

Eventually the heat drove us back on to *terra firma*, and we abandoned the chase in favour of food, reconnecting with Yothin and a group of American birders. All were enjoying a bird-watching tour organized by US company WINGS. We had bumped into their group almost every day since arriving in Thailand. Lunch was an incendiary affair at a local restaurant a few blocks back from the main drag. We eschewed the menu's suggestion of fried wasps and red ant eggs, plumping instead for fresh prawns marinaded in local herbs and laced with the ubiquitous chillies that as ever set off thrilling spot-fires in the mouth.

Since the afternoon remained as searingly hot as the local cuisine, we suspended pitta operations and sought out the famous Mr. Dai, Krabi's most redoubtable longtail boat captain, and persuaded him to pilot us out to the fish traps in the estuary mouth. In his late fifties, our coxswain's weather-beaten, sun-cracked features are a living document of the passage of time. His awkward gait is exaggerated by the bunched grey trousers strung uncertainly about his waist, which swing as he walks like a badly hung pair of curtains in a gale.

He had sprung to fame amongst the birding fraternity in the early 1990s, having located a rare and sought-after bird, a Masked Finfoot, in the myriad mangrove channels adjacent to Krabi town. The finfoot – aesthetically a curious cross between a duck and some strange prehistoric fish – had lured countless bird-watchers to Krabi, and Mr. Dai had become the pilot of choice. He had subsequently learned to whistle the songs of the other hard-to-find birds of the mangroves, Mangrove Blue-flycatcher, Mangrove Whistler and even in season, Mangrove Pitta. (On a previous trip, while being paddled slowly along the minor tributaries and in danger of slumbering in the heat, we had been disturbed by Mr. Dai mooring up and swiftly climbing one of the taller trees with a nimbleness belying his advancing years to persuade a Mangrove Pitta to show itself on an exposed perch up in the canopy.) Today we asked after the finfoot, but Mr. Dai looked mournful, saying only *'bad people Thailand'* before mimicking the sound of a shotgun. The finfoot, it seems, had ended its days by joining the wasps and the ants' eggs on a local menu.

The tide was so low that we had to walk the last mile, squelching barefoot across vast expanses of mudflats, assuring ourselves that benefits would accrue. (Was this not the very same treatment for which rich European ladies paid a small fortune in pursuit of perfect toe and heel skin?) We remained convinced right up to the moment when we sank through the gloop up to our knees and lacerated our feet on the solid layer of razor-clams concealed beneath the surface. Choosing areas that looked rather more solid and deftly weaving our way between the stranded corpses of huge purple jellyfish, we picked our way out to distant groups of birds, finding a Chinese Egret, a Great Knot, and a mixed flock of Terek Sandpipers and Greater Sand Plovers, though not the Spotted Greenshank we were looking for. Eventually we admitted defeat and gingerly picked our way back to the creaking longtail to inspect our shellfish-inflicted wounds and wash a billion microscopic creatures from between our toes. I toyed with the idea of bringing a couple of glamorous spiral shells back home as a gift for my girlfriend, but decided against it upon discovering the shells' occupants alive and all too active within.

Opting for an easier life, we sped over to Ao Nopparatt Thara, one of Krabi's immaculate, white-sand, straight-out-of-the-brochure beaches. Our strategy in heading to the beach was less to do with lounging on multi-striped towels, and more to do with searching through the flocks of small sandpipers scurrying about like clockwork toys at the water's edge in pursuit of a recently rediscovered species, the White-faced Plover. Our gaze was irresistibly drawn to the sight of two clinically obese septuagenarian tourists waddling towards the sea, threatening to set off a chain reaction that would surely result in a sizeable tsunami. Never would the protective powers of the mangroves face a sterner test...

We returned to the job in hand and started to hunt for the White-faced Plover in earnest. This diminutive wading bird, no taller than a jam jar, was first noticed in Singapore in 1993, and has yet to be formally described to science. Birds had since occasionally been seen around the Malaysian and Thai coast, and luckily for us, one had been found on this very beach twenty-four hours earlier by an English birder we'd bumped into in the mangroves. He had shown us jaw-dropping, frame-filling photographs, and had drawn us a map of the location. We were dismayed not to find a huge flock of Kentish Plovers (the commoner species with which the bird had been seen) but only a small group of ten birds. Miraculously, nine of these birds were Kentish Plovers, and the tenth was the White-faced. It was strikingly pale in the face as one might expect, with a short white stripe above the eye. Plain above with tiny, delicate brown bands at the side of the breast, the bird was slightly smaller than most examples of the new species so far recorded, but there was no doubting its identity – a major result.

A bonus for sure, but still indisputably not a pitta, and with only one morning left in the south I was running out of time to find a Mangrove Pitta. If I missed it here, the only other site I knew where the bird could reliably be seen was Pulau Ubin, a small island off Singapore, which would require a separate trip in May. I already had plans for May, a key month in the world of pittas since many species are getting ready to breed as the wet season kicks in and hence are at their most vocal. Thus I could ill afford the time to bunk off on an extra-limital mission to Singapore's outlying islands. There was no doubt in my mind; I needed to find the bird tomorrow.

The problem was that the Krabi mangroves did not look at all promising. We had heard the rough 'tae-RAEW, tae-RAEW' call shortly after dawn near Krabi, but the bird was depressingly distant and the songster's location wholly inaccessible. What we needed was a small site that could be accessed on foot and where multiple birds would be hanging out.

Yothin had mentioned a remnant scrap of mangroves just south of Phang Nga. The latter town was only a couple of hours' drive north from Krabi, and although he had not seen the birds recently, Yothin recommended the site as our best option. Thus after a comfortable but woefully short night in a smart hotel in Krabi (Pool! Buffet! Carafe of local wine!) we found ourselves at Phang Nga before dawn. This charming location sat at the junction of two busy main roads, squeezed in between a petrol station and a stinking toilet block.

I have never understood why, given that birds can fly wherever they want, so many of them choose to spend their time at the most degraded sites in the least auspicious locales. Nevertheless they do, and what's more, as we clambered wearily from our rental car fifteen minutes before dawn, I could hear the unmistakable song of a Mangrove Pitta not thirty metres from where we stood, with a second bird calling beyond. Graham was all for drinking our coffee and unpacking breakfast, but I was convinced that this early in the season the birds would sing only until the first hint of daylight. Thereafter they would drop into the mangroves where they would doubtless elude us for the rest of the day, sniggering to themselves as we stomped past while they continued their crab banquets, secreted beneath the forest of roots. I grabbed a flashlight, and, berated by Graham for being an impatient so and so, advanced stealthily down the boardwalk, here bizarrely paved with ceramic tiles, perhaps left over from the construction of the aforementioned public conveniences. The bird was further away than it seemed, ventriloquial as ever, but within ten minutes we had located the bird high in a mangrove tree, lustily singing its heart out. Illuminating the bird in the throw of our spotlight, I managed a quick photograph in the darkness. As the first rays of light pierced the gloom the bird stopped calling, dropped into the darkness and disappeared.

We spent the next two and a half hours trudging around the tiny boardwalk, incredulous that at least two Mangrove Pittas could execute a vanishing trick with such aplomb. Even the odd brief burst of Mangrove Pitta song from my iPod failed to stimulate them to show themselves again, or to respond. At around eight o'clock however, the respective feeding circuits of the two male birds must have coincided, and they flew back up into the canopy and started calling. We crept towards the closer bird, firing off photographs as we went, but our caution was unwarranted. Over the next forty minutes the bird perched in full view, allowing us to wander around choosing the best light, background and *mise-en-scène* for our photographs. As we left the swamp the bird was still on the same bough, singing away in defence of its territory.

Such is the way with pittas. You spend a week flogging yourself to death working twelve hours a day in good habitat walking right by them a hundred times without so much as a glimpse, and then inexplicably you get lucky and watch one for an age, the bird seemingly unconcerned by your presence. The former situation is far commoner than the latter, but that's what makes the few precious moments in the presence of a pitta so special. It is not a privilege afforded to all. One must work hard, plan ahead, and start before it gets light, out-thinking the birds so that you see them before they see you. Developing the stealthy field-skills of a forest ninja and the reflexes of a hunter won't go amiss either.

A list of things to remember when hunting for pittas

- *Dress in sober colours. Look as much like a tree as possible. Forgo the fashion statement for once.*

- *Move silently on the trail. Never take your transistor radio with you. Whispering may sound quiet to you, but to a pitta it sounds like Motorhead at 120 dB.*

- *When you see that critical movement on the forest floor, move your hands/binoculars/camera v-e-r-y s-l-o-w-l-y.*

- *Keep still. For a long time. Still people see stuff.*

- *When you think you've missed a pitta, you haven't. It's extremely close, and probably just behind you.**

- *If you are lucky enough to see a pitta, never point. Ever. You see a helpful soul indicating the direction of the bird for the benefit of others. The pitta sees a large and lethal animal pointing one of those sticks that spits fire and which killed his mama.*

- *Use cover. If you are going to search an open area, hide behind something: a tree, some other miscellaneous foliage, a mound. (But note, not a passing dog. I have tried this and it doesn't work.)*

---

* For example, ALL the Blue-rumped Pittas I have ever seen (in Vietnam) have approached to within two metres without me seeing a single feather on their sneaky behinds. They will be watching from a hidden vantage point closer than you think humanly possible. That's because whilst it's impossible for a human, it's eminently possible for a pitta, which is able to take the subway, or glide through the forest without touching the floor. Despite their typically rather chubby frames, they are able to flatten themselves behind single blades of grass. They can travel through space-time without leaving a ripple in the continuum in a way that even Stephen Hawking could not begin to explain.

- *Sit. The f*ck. Down. (Imagine Al Pacino saying this for the full impact.) Honestly it works. Never mind the leeches and the mozzies, you are suffering for your cause. You are way less visible as a short creature than as a tall one.*

- *Get up-to-date, accurate information from anyone who knows exactly where the birds are. Shock news, pittas move around over time.*

- *Go where the birds are high density. It's theoretically possible that I'll see the one and only Giant Pitta that lives at Khao Nor Chuchi, but then it's theoretically possible that Kylie Minogue will call me and ask me round to her place for a candlelit dinner à deux. A man can dream, but neither is likely to happen in my lifetime.*

Relieved to have cornered pitta number four, we drove back to Krabi, dodging the decrepit *songthaews* that sagged beneath their cargoes. Unserviceable motorbikes spluttered past, bearing everything from three generations of the same family to gleaming, just-built-and-off-to-market bamboo furniture. On arrival we adjourned to Ao Nang's beautiful beach for a final meal, enjoying the fake watch salesmen's cheesy patter. *'OK, you have one watch, but what about the other arm?'* The sartorial contrast between dusty backpackers and the beachfront waiters, immaculate in their light blue, shot silk uniforms was hard to miss, and I pondered the problems of sustainable tourism. Ten years before Krabi had been truly idyllic. I'd dined on a deserted beach overlooking the monumental limestone pillars, which rose like leviathans from the azure depths. Now the view was backed by a bustling high street, populated with Burger Kings, MacDonalds and Starbucks, providing at a stroke all the things one comes to Thailand to forget.

We made the best of it, ordering Seafood *Som Tam*, my favourite unripe papaya salad dotted with denizens of the deep, carried all of five yards from the net to the table. Chillies, as bitter and wicked as a wife cut from her husband's will, provided the kick; definitely a shade ahead of a quarter pounder with cheese. As we ate I wondered how long the Thailand I loved would survive the onslaught of globalisation. It was time to find a quieter corner of The Land of Smiles.

Chapter 3

Dry Country Blues. Central, Northern Thailand

Our time in the south was up. After waving Graham off on a flight back to snowy London, I flew to Bangkok before driving northeast on quiet roads, my passage slowed only by the occasional grubby trucks, and a fruitless quest for alcohol. My next destination, Khao Yai, one of Thailand's premier National Parks, was infamous for its government-enforced beer drought, and the thought of arriving without the odd snifter for a six-day stay was less than appealing.

After checking the shelves of the fourth garage in a row without success, it dawned on me that Thai laws must have changed; presumably tying driving and alcohol together quite so tightly had claimed one too many victims. Out in the sticks I found an all night stall that sold not only beer but also *Hong Thong*. The latter tipple claims to be whisky, but tastes just like dark rum when poured into an empty mineral water bottle and smothered in flat coke. Into the small hours I pulled up at Khao Yai's entrance gate, and wriggled into the back of the car for a couple of hours sleep. The local dogs had noted my arrival however, and I was driven away up a quieter road by a volley of community barks that woke the entire neighbourhood.

The park gates opened at six, and I made for the visitor's centre to sort out the inescapable paperwork. The park HQ was stocked with pickled snake specimens (including a deadly Banded Krait, which had been wedged extra tightly into a jar in case it made a last lunge at the *'I've been to Khao Yai!'* baseball cap salesperson).

Administrative duties completed, I grabbed a bottle of water, sprayed myself liberally with toxic DEET to dissuade mosquitoes and leeches, and sashayed across the swaying, wooden suspension bridge that leads to the Huay Suwat trail. I'd been tipped off by a Singaporean friend that Eared Pittas had recently been seen feeding in the dry leaf-litter here. Since my record at Khao Yai over the years had been pretty woeful with regard to Eared Pitta – one sighting in seven visits – I had allowed six full days to cover as much ground as possible to maximise my chances of finding this cryptically coloured and deeply anti-social pitta.

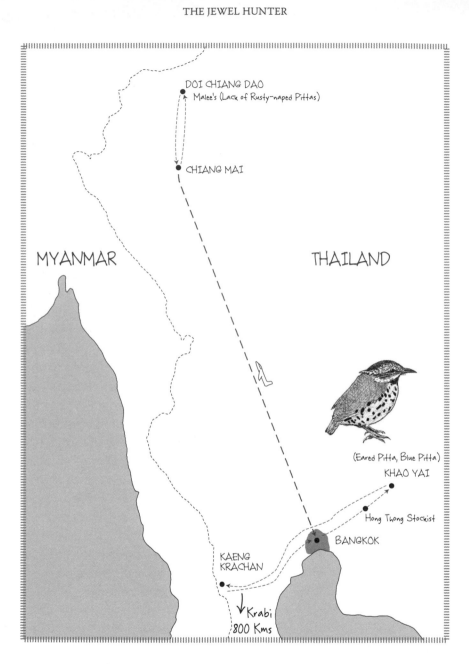

Eared Pittas are immaculately camouflaged creatures. Both male and female sport an array of rich chestnuts, subdued oranges and sombre browns, dappled with fawn and silver about the head and flecked with black and white crescents below. The male has black and silver crescents above each eye that stretch backwards to the nape, and which can be erected when excited; a neat party trick. These scattered, subtle markings break up the birds' outline, and allow them to blend effortlessly into the leaves that cover their forest floor home. Added to this is the fact that, being way too smart to fall for old birders' tricks, they steadfastly ignore recordings of their own vocalizations. Even when setting up territories before breeding, they only call at first light for a few minutes, and for an equally short period at dusk. If they sense danger, rather than bounce off into the forest, they freeze for a minute or two, rendering them invisible. All in all, worthy adversaries, more than capable of hiding away in their chosen habitat for as long as they please.

There are, however, a couple of positives. They tend to live in relatively dry forest, which means if you proceed slowly and silently along a suitable trail, you may hear their furtive rustling in the leaf-litter as they ferret out juicy bugs. Ninety-nine times out of a hundred, when you hear such rustling it's a squirrel/tree rat/lost child/killer cobra, but just occasionally it's an Eared Pitta. When you do finally manage to track one down, a cautious approach will often allow amazing views at extremely close range for minutes on end. The birds assume their camouflage is so good you couldn't possibly have seen them, even if you are virtually standing on their tail.

And that, your honour, is why I was loitering on a Thai trail in a suspicious fashion, creeping along oh-so-slowly, lifting my feet to avoid any rustling of my own, and stopping every twenty metres to cup my hands behind my ears while swivelling from side to side. Most serious birders do this to enhance the efficiency of the human ear. The posture looks truly ludicrous, like some long-abandoned, pseudo-robotic New Romantic dance-floor move from the 1980s, but unfortunately it does actually work. One hears more and the ability to pinpoint direction improves, which means that sadly I will continue to look like a complete retro-retard.

After an hour of slow-motion eighties choreography I was amazed to hear an unmistakably Pitta-ish rustling further along the trail. I tiptoed forward, approaching the sound's source. Whatever was foraging in the undergrowth was no more than five metres away. My progress slowed even further as I painstakingly checked each clump of vegetation for movement. As I passed a frondy patch, I caught sight of just what I had hoped to see: dead leaves apparently flipping themselves into the air, as if caught in a miniature whirlwind.

Another few seconds and I located the source of the disturbance, a male Eared Pitta! A second rustle beneath an adjacent bush indicated the presence of another bird, not a complete surprise since Eared Pittas often feed in pairs, and sure enough I quickly unearthed an adult female. I trailed the birds for half an hour, trying to anticipate their wanderings so that I could catch them in a photogenic pose as they whipped across gaps in the vegetation. I managed to capture a couple of worthwhile images, satisfyingly sharp close-ups that captured the birds' shuffling, hunched profiles as they searched for prey.

The whole episode encapsulated for me why pittas are so maddening, and, for exactly the same reasons, so alluring. They provide the ultimate hunt; they are variously wily, elusive, cryptic, sneaky, crepuscular, shy and unpredictable. Their habits are mercurial, mysterious and contrary. If you say 'pot-ay-to,' you can guarantee that they will say 'pot-ah-to.'*

They will frustrate your best-laid plans, and just when you think you have your pitta-finding technique honed to perfection, they will change tack and fail to make an appearance. Just occasionally however, the really tricky species will grant you an audience, often when you least expect it, and blow your socks off. I expected Eared Pitta to be a real challenge, and had already allowed time in my schedule to return to Khao Yai, assuming I would miss them in just six short days. So what do they do? They show up on my first morning in the park, and all but wave a cheery wing in my direction while signing autographs.

Keen to share my good fortune, I drew maps for all the other birders I met showing the exact location of the Eared ones, maps which included a few distinctive forest features to guide the massing crowds straight to the birds. It was a guaranteed stakeout, the birds could not have been more certain if I had tied their compliant, silvery ear tufts to the nearest tree.

At least fifteen birders were in place at dawn the next day to catch up with these beauties, the park's star birds. Nobody saw them.

Thanks to the Eared Pittas' newly discovered appeasement policy, I had five and three-quarter days left at Khao Yai to find my other target here, Blue Pitta. A collision of incendiary orange and frosty

---

* Actually this is unlikely. The only thing eared Pittas say on a regular basis is 'Wheoooooooowh-WIT.' And they don't even say that very often.

blue, they are marked below with a riot of spots and bars that help to break up their outline as they skulk in wet forest. Despite this, compared to finding Eared Pitta, locating a Blue Pitta ought to be a walk in the park. I had never missed them in all my visits to Khao Yai. I knew where they liked to feed, and the best way to approach them. (Which, incidentally, is not to.) The technique is as follows: scan the forest floor from a long way off with your binoculars and find them before they see you coming. Then hide in a bush, play a smidge of tape and watch them sneak in all self-satisfied, convinced of their cloak of invisibility, while all the time you have already nailed them. One can even smugly observe how they use cover in an attempt to avoid being discovered, *but it's too late my friend because I have already got...your...number.* Finally they realize and hide, peeking out at you with a worried glance, their little brows furrowed as they realise what has gone on, and then they melt back into the forest, just to prove that they can. But by then it's way too late and the game is won.

I had one good stakeout for them that had proved itself time and again over the years. This was a small muddy pond fed by waste water from a restaurant shack at the edge of the park's campsite where Blue Pittas would come to drink, bathe, read the papers and catch up on the gossip. I, however, would not be relying on the stakeout, because I was a real birder who would not sully himself by lying in wait for the Blue Pitta that everyone else ticked off. That would be far too easy. Instead, I would use all my skill and experience to win my own Blue Pitta in the wilds of the forest. I would venture into virgin territory, refusing to rest until it was mapped and conquered. I grinned to myself, thinking how I would order a slap-up Thai dinner that evening with both the central Thailand pitta targets in the bag. Big mistake.

I walked Trail Six, where Blue Pittas have lived for generations. I glimpsed a nice White-crowned Forktail, that most flirtatious tease of the Asian streams, and met some lovely high volume Thai school kids out on a rainforest experience course. (Their experience: shout a lot with bouts of occasional squealing. See nothing. Go home again.) I beamed at them, and exercised one half of my immense Thai vocabulary, *'Sawatdee krup.'* Because despite their cacophonous merriment, I simply knew that as soon as they had disappeared up the trail I would be watching a Blue Pitta in the streambed.

I wasn't.

Undeterred, I was out in the field before dawn the next day, investigating a quiet side-trail on the other side of the park. I heard a pitta. It was about a mile away, deep in the forest, and unresponsive to the male Blue Pitta territorial calls I had pre-recorded onto my iPod. I channelled my energy, ignoring any activity more than a metre above the forest floor. Nothing. By evening on day two I had already spent eighteen hours looking for Blue Pitta, and had not come close to seeing one. Hot, exhausted and shocked into despondency, I consoled myself with a curry from the new 'improved' park facilities. The bad old days, where the staff cooked fresh food to order had long since been banished, and a 'new and improved' streamlined service allowed customers to point at dishes and receive them immediately. True, they had been cooked ten hours earlier, were now barely lukewarm, and had functioned in the meantime as a skating rink for all manner of flies and other creepy-crawlies, but that's the price of progress. To cap it all, the universal Thai friendliness has largely been abandoned at Khao Yai, where one feels the park authorities must place adverts that run *'Are you an atypically surly caterer? One of the seven people in The Land of Smiles who would struggle to raise a grin if you won the lottery? Then come and join us at one of Thailand's premier tourist attractions and make visitors feel like they are back home in Britain experiencing sloppy service and sub-standard cuisine!'*

I sipped a can of bitter orange fizz which, as it slid over my parched lips, felt like those little polystyrene balls designed to stop mail order purchases from getting trashed in transit, but which fail to prevent your purchase from arriving with a large piece chipped off the corner. (It serves you right for ordering a scale model of a Dickensian village with real interior lighting in the first place.) I reflected sourly on the fact that in the bad old days the park canteen had also sold beer. Thank goodness that particular avenue of consumer pleasure had been firmly closed off.

My visit to the park shop in search of insect repellent had not been a success, since the shelves had been ransacked by hordes of ill-prepared local Thai visitors visiting the park during the previous day, a National holiday. My own two cans of mosquito death juice had been liberated by a light-fingered baggage handler. This combination of minor annoyances had built into a groundswell of barely suppressed, embittered rage. My mood worsened as I conceded that I had smugly underestimated the Blue Pittas' level of resistance.

At that moment, a cheery greeting rescued me from my tantrum, as my secret weapon appeared in the form of Andy Pierce. A UK expat, Andy has been running the research project at Khao Yai for the last seven years. He knows the forest extremely well, and works his research plots almost every day. He has the jungle mapped, divided into a complex series of tetrads, identified by coloured ribbons discreetly pinned to various trees which, to the tutored eye, mark the boundaries of each section. This is a man with his finger on the throbbing pulse of the forest. This, in short, is the man who would know where the Blue Pittas were hiding.

Having been advised of my pitta mission, Andy had kindly asked his fellow research workers to look out for Blue and Eared Pittas during the previous week, and both had been seen in and around the plots. At least one Blue Pitta, I learned, had been seen only the day before on the main approach trail. Andy indicated how best to access the area in the inimitable language used by birders since time immemorial. *Right at the fruiting tree, past the Sambar feeding spot by the river, skirt around the edge of the slum housing and then take the trail up the steep clay bank. Keep left at the second fork and look for a jagged stump that has a black mark in the middle of it that in a certain light looks like a map of Australia. Cross the stream there, double back on yourself for ten metres and if you reach the small cave you've gone too far...* After a couple of purchased-in-advance beers I pleaded exhaustion, left Andy to the perils of pre-cooked, air-cooled chicken curry and crashed out in my forest chalet.

Next morning I followed Andy's instructions and was in the pitta zone well before first light. I heard a Blue Pitta call just after dawn and decided that guerrilla tactics were in order. Creeping off-trail, I concealed myself inside a bush before firing up the iPod and pretending to be a rival male Blue Pitta. A rapid-fire *'Wheeoow-WIP'* cracked out of my portable speaker. (Blue Pitta sounds like an Eared Pitta that's late for work.) I waited for the bird to come in, confident of success. The bird would surely be fooled into a show of bravado to protect his home patch and his young lady-pitta. I soon heard a rustle in the leaves behind me, and carefully swivelled round so I could peer over my shoulder without moving too radically and thus flushing the Blue Pitta that was about to show at any moment. A few seconds more, and a shape appeared no more than a metre away. A black head, too far off the forest floor for any pitta, a patch of bare red skin around the eye and a gleaming red bill were perfectly framed in a sunlit gap. It was a Coral-billed Ground-cuckoo!

Ground-cuckoos are even harder to see than some pittas, and spend their lives following the packs of wild pigs that inhabit the park. To bump into one by chance was incredible good fortune, and to have such amazing views at close range unprecedented. After a few seconds the ground-cuckoo continued on its way, having never even noticed me lurking in the shadows. I congratulated myself, and waited in silence for another half an hour. No pitta. A second bird called further up the trail, but despite supreme field skills and a further five hours' sleuthing, I could not find anything remotely resembling a pitta, blue or otherwise. The fact was that it had been exceptionally dry in Thailand, with not a drop of rain in the last six weeks. Blue Pittas are wet season breeders, so they become active, responsive and vocal when the rains start in earnest. In short, they were not yet territorial nor the tiniest bit frisky, and not remotely interested in my tape. I swallowed my pride and drove over to the stakeout I had sworn to shun. It was time for route one tactics.

At the stakeout however, things were afoot. Two idiot photographers had erected a hide right on top of the Blue Pitta's favoured drinking pool, and were trying to photograph Long-tailed Macaques, the local monkey species. To help the process along they had laid out a fine selection of fruit in front of the hide, which the monkeys were steadily munching their way through. In fact they were making such inroads into the fruit-fest that the photographers had to emerge once an hour to replenish supplies, an action guaranteed to persuade any neighbourhood pittas to keep their distance. The stakeout's efficacy was thus in shambles, and the Blue Pitta revue cancelled until further notice.

I returned to my pitta-pioneering, walking a few more trails, scanning endless acres of forest floor, and comparing notes with the few birders I bumped into. It was the same story everywhere; no-one had seen any Blue Pittas. After another thirteen-hour day I admitted defeat and gladly accepted Andy's invitation to dinner. The conversation included the usual snake horror stories, a gory comparison of the world's forest parasites and what they can do within the human frame, and the finer points of porcupine deterrence. (Porcupines I learned are notorious scavengers, and can do an immense amount of damage to a well-appointed kitchen.)

One of the dinner guests was a lady called Jen, a researcher from Chicago who had spent the day setting up insect traps. She explained that she was moonlighting for a few days and that she was really a monkey follower. This role was new to me, and did not, as I first thought, involve the machinations of some arcane religious cult. In fact it was a serious academic pursuit in which simian researchers track apes in order to chart their movements and behaviour. I had observed some unsavoury onanistic monkey behaviour earlier in the day, but my report was greeted with little enthusiasm; clearly this was not an unusual sighting. We soon descended into typical birders' tales, an intoxicating blend of fact, folklore and fantasy. After a delicious home-cooked vegetarian stir-fry I made my excuses, keen to get a good night's sleep. I left Andy and his team dealing with a termite invasion, only to find an ant invasion in my own poorly appointed bathroom. A quick sluice down washed most of the interlopers back to whence they came, and peace was restored.

At an unfeasibly early hour, I returned to Andy's recommended spot to try once more to track down my uncooperative target, but the results were worryingly similar to the previous morning. Occasionally a pitta would call from deep within the forest, but would not respond to tape, going about its business at a range unlikely to yield any views. I scoured the understorey for a hint of a plump groundbird, and minutely examining anything that moved. Very little did, and there was no hint of that glorious, characteristic bounce that heralds the imminent arrival of a pitta.

As I worked the forest it occurred to me that I had fondly imagined my year in pursuit of pittas being the perfect antidote to my usual tropical forest birding; a snatched couple of weeks during which myself and my fellow avian addicts frantically tried to compile a huge list of species in our escape from the rat-race. I would, I'd decided, finally be able to truly learn the birds of Asia, become intimately acquainted with their habits, be able to identify every squeak and warble emanating from the darkest corners of the densest habitats. In short, I would become a truly proficient birder rather than a charlatan who sneaks into the forest on occasion to sample its gaudiest delights in a highly superficial manner.

The reality, I now had cause to reflect, was rather different. Pitta hunting involves spending an inordinate amount of time staring at the forest floor, and is antithetical to seeing the vast majority of forest birds, which, as birds will, habitually live in the air or at the top of tall trees. Not to put too fine a point on it, I was looking down, when the smart money was looking up. Up is where a panoply of gorgeous kingfishers, resplendent trogons, imperious hornbills, streamlined swifts, mischievous monkeys, and improbably cute flying squirrels live. Down is where dowdy, brown birds and a few beetles do their thing. This was not how I had envisaged things panning out.

After three hopeless hours I resolved to try another spot, and abandoning my usual stealthy gait I trudged noisily out of the forest barely glancing around me, keen to check another trail before the last of the morning cool burned off. Given the contrary nature of pittas, I should have known this would be the very moment at which I'd stumble across a Blue Pitta. It bounced into view, a vision in blue and orange, with a scatter of black and white polka dots thrown in for good measure. It was a fine male, and doubtless one of the birds that had been tormenting me at long range for the past couple of days. My victory was all the sweeter for having been postponed, and once the pitta had departed I punched the air gleefully, desperate to meet someone who would care about my success, or at least feign interest for a short while. A glorious euphoria swept through me, the cumulative frustration of the previous days instantly forgotten. I mentally checked the tally; nine days, six pittas, no snakes. Life doesn't get any better.

I had a decision to make. Having seen Eared Pitta so easily, and having caught up at last with the only other likely central Thailand pitta species, I had three days free to do as I pleased. After a brief debate with myself (my favourite kind, you always win) I threw the chaotic contents of the bungalow into my bag and drove west, skirting Bangkok on the elevated expressways, following a route I had driven before to the Myanmar border. My destination was a much quieter forest named Kaeng Krachan, an unbroken tract of wilderness that stretches all the way to the border and beyond. Its single lonely access road cuts directly through primary forest, where wardens warn of unplanned meetings with wild Asian Elephants by day and Leopards by night. (Of course birders routinely ignore such sensible instruction. How are you supposed to find White-fronted Scops-owls if you don't wander around after dark?)

Kaeng Krachan is also allegedly home to the daddy of them all, the Giant Pitta, and I figured I may as well spend time in the GP's neck of the woods as anywhere else. I knew I wouldn't see one. Giant Pittas, after all, do not really exist, other people's photographs notwithstanding, but it wouldn't hurt to hang around and perhaps whistle like a Giant Pitta now and then on the off-chance. Was Kaeng Krachan not the very place where I had come so close to seeing Giant Pitta three years earlier?

I had been approached by two other birders, Rob Hutchinson and James Eaton. Rob, knowing my burning desire to see Giant Pitta, had sidled up to me holding a digital camera in the palm of his left hand.

'James has a photo of a mystery bird,' Rob innocently announced, 'and he thinks you'll know what it is.'

I stared at the proffered camera screen and recognized the shape; a sharp-focus, frame-filling image of a female Giant Pitta. I grinned at Rob.

'Wow, amazing shot, where was it taken?'

'Oh...over there.'

Rob waved his hand vaguely, gesturing at some scrappy forest not five yards from where we stood. The grin faded from my face.

'*When* did you take it?'

Rob's cheery insouciance continued.

'Hmm, lets see, I suppose, ooh, four, maybe five minutes ago.'

My jaw dropped as I let the news sink in. The facts were plain. 1. Apparently Giant Pittas do exist after all. 2. In all probability, if we could vapourize all the trees in our immediate vicinity, a Giant Pitta would be exposed within fifty metres of our current location. 3. It had already shown itself, which meant that it was extremely unlikely that it would show itself again. That is the way with Giant Pittas. It is the law. It is immutable. 4. We had not been there when it showed. We were screwed.

Nonetheless, we had gone through the motions. We walked the trail on which Rob and James had seen the bird. We kept silent. We played the mournful, falling whistle of a Giant Pitta. We saw nothing. Next morning before dawn we were back at the same spot. We saw more nothing. For quite a long time. Then we left.

Despite all this, Rob, James and I still talk, and I was keen to renew my acquaintance with 'the GP spot.' It was no more visibly infested with Giant Pittas than it had been three years earlier, but I felt a frisson of excitement just walking the short trail where we had come so close. Was the bird still in the area? Was it watching me as I worked the trails between the river crossings? The answers were unknowable, and merely added to the Giant Pitta's already immense mystique. *One day I will see one* I thought. And then it hit me like a slap in the face. That day needed to fall in the next eleven months or my mission was doomed to failure. Whose stupid idea was this anyway?

Currently, however, I was sitting pretty. I was one pitta ahead of schedule, and had three days during which I could please myself. It was time for a celebration. I stopped off at a roadside shack and purchased a *Bang-Bang Bar ('four tastes in one! Chocolate, caramel, wafer and crispy!')* and a can of indecently synthetic strawberry fizz. I secured forest permits after the requisite arm-waving and picture-drawing, and checked into accommodation just outside the park, the latter procedure including some bizarre reverse haggling by the owner: 'No! Not nine hundred, six hundred Baht! But as you are here for three days, five hundred Baht OK!' At last, some precious downtime. I perched nervously on a faded pink plastic chair, at least one of whose legs had seen distinctly better days, and gazed out over a stunning vista. A lake stretched out before me, its surface unbroken by a single ripple. The late afternoon haze blurred the distant hills, each successive range paler and less defined than the one before. At length I tore myself away, intending to brush on up my Thai pronunciation in order to procure dinner.

I spent the next day walking the dirt road that meanders through Kaeng Krachan, negotiating the three river crossings without any serious issues (one benefit of the recent dry weather). I stopped for lunch at the restaurant-with-no-food, choosing coffee from the varied menu. (Coffee, hot water, cold water.) Propelled into action by the caffeine, I coaxed my reluctant rental car up the rugged road that leads to the park's higher reaches. Arriving largely intact despite a few rough stretches of mountain road, the quiet solitude was a joy after the noisy crowds at Khao Yai. I strolled down the road in the sunshine, listening on the off chance for Rusty-naped Pitta, though not with any real expectation. The forest ravines are so steep and impenetrable here that even if I did hear one, seeing it would have been all but impossible. As the shadows began to lengthen, I drifted back down the hill, surprising a lone Lesser Mouse Deer as I departed. Mice Deer look like a bizarre scientific experiment made flesh. They are roughly the size of a Yorkshire Terrier with the body of a deer and the head of a mouse. Rich brown with black-and-white go-faster stripes down the side of the neck, they are impossibly cute and endearing.

As ever, I got lost in the dark on the way back; the poorer the neighbourhood, the less light sources, so that poverty, ironically enough, is revealed in a clearer light where the latter is least present. I ate another excellent rural Thai dinner in the restaurant next to my chalet, forgoing a meal in the establishment next door, which rejoiced, if its large hand-painted sign was to be believed, in the name of *The Restaurant Breakfast Lunch Dinner.* As I wiped the sweat from my brow and pressed my cold glass of beer to my forehead, I reflected on the day's highlights. Banks of tiny blue and white flowers. Huge flocks of iridescent butterflies that fluttered around my ankles as I passed, a technicolour snowstorm of wings and antennae. The assault of forest aromas: the tang of wild herbs, the thick, cloying perfume of unidentified epiphytes, and the rich stench of fresh elephant dung. Piles of the latter appeared on the road every morning, despite the animals themselves having melted away into the forest as only ten foot high pachyderms can. I had barely seen a soul all day, and was enjoying the solitude.

Friday the thirteenth got off to a flying start despite the date. A cracking male Blue Pitta showed up just beyond the first river crossing. I might have known I'd bump into one with zero effort having fought so hard for my prize at Khao Yai. Still *the journey is the quest* as I reminded myself.

A repeat coffee at the no-food-grill whiled away an hour as I waited for Kaeng Krachan's one-way, 'up-traffic hour' to arrive. Even if there had been food I doubt it would have been possible to order, since the entire complement of staff – five souls and a small dog – were all staring intently at the kung-fu soap opera unfolding above our heads via an ancient and precariously hung television set. There were groans when the credits rolled.

My coffee break was necessary because the road to the upper reaches of the park is so narrow that traffic can only run in one direction at any given time. As a result, a haphazard sentry system operates in an attempt to permit vehicles only to drive up the hill at the appointed hours. Of course bird-watchers are forever parking halfway up the hill, and then deciding they need to push on another couple of kilometres against the flow without even a cursory check of their watches. Which is fine until you meet a speeding 4x4 head-on at a blind corner.

Today at least, I was scrupulously law-abiding, and pulled up at the guardhouse at two o'clock on the dot. Once I had gained enough altitude to be up amongst the sub-montane species, I spent a couple of hours trawling for two birds I had missed on previous visits, the stripy, outsized Purple-naped Sunbird, a nectar-gatherer that rushes around as if it has already gathered rather too much sugar, and the bamboo-loving White-hooded Babbler, both of which gave themselves up after a brief tussle. The afternoon improved still further when I came across a Long-tailed Broadbill, a mid-sized sluggish bird of the mid-storey, whose sharply delineated yellows, greens and blues, as a friend of mine once put it, *always make them look as though they have just been freshly painted.'* I even met a couple of other birders, one of whom asked me if I'd *'heard about this nutter who is trying to see all the pittas in a single year.'* I nodded and introduced myself with a smile.

Returning to lower altitudes, I surprised a flock of Red Junglefowl, the true antecedent of the chicken. They look like chickens, they sound like chickens, and they would surely taste like chickens too if you could get your hands on them, but these are truly wild birds. They spend their days wandering the forests of Asia, and can regularly be heard crowing at dawn, an incongruous farmyard echo in the wilderness. Returning to civilisation, I checked the perimeters of the campsite for anything interesting. Birds were absent, so I settled for watching the camping fraternity at play. I marvelled at the precision with which a German father was marking out locations for his family's tent pegs, and noted just how much noise one man can make with a tin tray of ice cubes.

At dinner I was joined by my jet-skiing chalet-neighbours. I had first met the pair two days earlier, but they had disappeared off to Hua Hin. I had become convinced that they were covert CIA operatives, since they talked of 'clicks' instead of kilometres, were suspiciously well acquainted with 1970s US troop movements along the obscure upper reaches of the Mekong, and evaded my questions about what they did for a living.

They told me they were going shopping, but I had naively assumed they would return with a few vegetables, or perhaps the odd spare part for the jet-ski. Instead they returned with a gorgeous Thai girl who could not have been more than seventeen years old. I discreetly concentrated on savouring my spicy lake fish, lightly fried and shredded like crunchy cotton candy, combining with fresh-off-the-tree papaya and lethal bird's eye chillies in a winning whirl of textures and flavours. Doug, the younger of my fellow diners at fifty-two, patiently explained that he was building a house, and that the young Thai lady with him would be named as the majority owner of the property on the deeds, as required by Thai law. I nodded and smiled, but it wasn't my dinner that smelled fishy. I made my excuses and packed for Chiang Mai.

February fourteenth: a day for lovers everywhere, and since I love travel, a travel day for me. I needed to head north. The long drive back to Bangkok was enlivened by an advert in the back of a passing car for *The Lovely Pet Home and Eros Kennel.* Clearly Fido too was in for a great Valentines Day.

A couple of hours later I was barrelling through the outskirts of the historic city of Chiang Mai in my gleaming Toyota Behemoth 4x4, the myriad scooter riders weaving in my wake like angry bees around a bear's head. Shortly after dark I arrived at Malee's Nature Lovers' Bungalows, to be greeted by Malee herself, an amiable Thai lady who fussed over me to make sure everything was just so. It certainly was just so after a cold beer and a plate of home-cooked noodles.

The reason for my trek to northern Thailand was to visit a famous forest location known as Doi Chiang Dao in an attempt to find Rusty-naped Pitta. One of the hardest pittas to locate, Rusty-napes like to spend their time grubbing around in deep, dark ravines and grovelling in heavily vegetated gullies. I would become a gully sentinel, honing my ravine skills until I blended seamlessly into the dingiest corners of the forest.

Arriving in the dark, I found a sheltered spot overlooking a deep gully and waited. Five and a half hours later I was still waiting, and had seen little bar a few common understorey birds. I watched Pale-legged Leaf-warblers, tiny green forest sprites that announced their presence every few seconds with a fairy-bell *'tink.'* Streaked Wren-babblers, little ground-huggers striped in browns and blacks, crept rodent-like about the gullies. Asian Stubtails, also furtive ground-dwellers who would be better named *Asian No-tails,* completed the set. What I had not seen, nor even heard, was a Rusty-naped Pitta. During my first vigil I had perhaps seen only five or six individual birds in total, and a fidgety boredom was setting in.

The next couple of days involved a lot of gully-crouching. I varied my approach, sometimes sitting motionless in cover, at other times walking the trails at a snail's pace, and on occasion clambering along the more densely vegetated gullies in intrepid fashion, convinced at any moment that a cobra would rear up and end my pitta-hunting for good. I ventured as far as the Temple Gully, a wide dry river bed on the other side of the temple complex, but my efforts were in vain. The best I could claim after three days hard work was hearing a distant pitta calling for less than a minute at dawn.

On my fourth day, after a few hours working the Temple Gully, I almost stepped on a snake that wriggled ahead of me, zig-zagging across the stones with alarming speed, revealing a metre-long sinuous body. Having achieved a safe distance it froze, allowing me to admire the lime-green body and brown tail, the latter narrowly banded with black and buff stripes. Back at the accommodation I worked my way through Malee's self-assembled snake book, but my adversary was not there. It wasn't until much later when I found a corresponding picture on the Internet that I was finally able to identify the reptile as a Green Keelback *Rhabdophis nigrocinctus.* The accompanying text opined: 'Nothing is known about poisoning of humans. However the *Rhabdophis* species should generally be treated with care, because it is a rear-fanged snake. Therefore please refer to the recommendations on *Rhabdophis subminiatus...*' I clicked the *subminiatus* link. It read: 'Danger; Bites can lead to severe poisoning in humans and can cause kidney failure.' I decided not to look at any more pictures of snakes.

With an hour's daylight left before dusk I returned to the Nature Trail gulley, and walked the same short length of trail again, reaching the end of the pittas' supposed favourite area by the Fence Trail after six o'clock, and with the light fading fast. No joy. I sighed, despondent at yet another long pitta-less day, and unthinkingly stepped out onto the Fence Trail without checking the terrain first. Two large pittas, doubtless a pair, had been feeding in the open on the edge of the trail. (Note the use here of the past tense.) My stupidity in announcing my arrival with a size ten boot before checking the terrain had instantly flushed the shy duo into cover, and all I saw were two dark blobs exiting stage left in a hurry. Cursing my carelessness, I scanned the adjacent forest, but with little light left and the birds spooked I knew my chance was gone.

Had I had a scourge handy with which to whip myself I would surely have employed it on the walk back to Malee's. After all my years of pitta experience it was unforgiveable to forget the first lesson – *it ain't over 'til the fat pitta sings* – and I had blown a great chance to bag the Rusty-naped Pitta. Instead, I had experienced that most sickening of bird-watcher concepts, 'untickable views', and in the self-certifying bird-watcher's code of honour, UTVs are not enough. I knew exactly what the birds were, but I could not count them. The very phrase that ran through my mind over and over again during the next few hours, *there's nothing else they could have been,* in itself reinforced the decision I had reached at the time. UTV's. Not good enough.

Next morning I hid myself well up the Fence Trail so that I could watch the same spot from which I had flushed the pittas the night before. Nothing doing. I spent nine hours on the case, until my limbs were so stiff even the best traditional Thai massage would have struggled to restore me to health.

I was running out of time, and my fifth and final day dawned in unpromisingly chilly fashion. The unseasonal cold was confirmed by a passing monk whose standard shaven head was covered by a rather less traditional woollen beanie hat. Today I hid myself down-trail, a cunning ruse that proved no more successful than my previous tactics. I checked out and hit the road, and as I drove back to Chiang Mai, the realization hit me that with only six species on the board I had for the first time missed a really difficult pitta. The failure was not yet critical, since I could engineer another chance for Rusty-naped, but doubtless they would continue to be extremely tough to get to grips with. And what if the misses started to pile up? What then of my plans to write the story of the adventure?

Throughout the night I travelled from Chiang Mai to Bangkok, onward towards Manila, and finally, bleary-eyed, from Manila to Tuguegarao, a small town in northern Luzon. The year had started with a bang: the near-impossible Gurney's Pitta on the very first afternoon, Banded and Blue-winged Pittas in southern Thailand, Mangrove Pitta at the eleventh hour having missed it at the regular locale, the eminently missable Eared Pitta and the reluctant Blue Pitta in central Thailand. Everything had gone swimmingly. Suddenly however, I was confronted by the magnitude of the task in front of me, and by the spectre of potential failure. The wisdom of quitting my job, abandoning an industry in which I had worked so hard to establish a reputation over a twenty-year period suddenly seemed questionable to say the least. What the hell had I been I thinking?

Chapter 4

Missing in Action. Luzon, The Philippines

Down to earth with a bump. Not every landing can be perfect I suppose, and our connection with the cracked, pot-holed tarmac at Tuguegarao airport was rather more robust than the manual recommends. Still, it seemed that news of our impending arrival had been radioed ahead, and there was a huge welcoming committee arranged around the edge of the runway, complete with banners and smiling dignitaries. *How refreshing*, I thought to myself, *that eco-tourism has been so warmly embraced so far off the beaten track.* However, the assembled masses were there to greet a government minister, newly returned from political jousting in the big smoke on behalf of local interests. He was swept up by the mob, his gaudy Hawaiian shirt ensuring he remained visible amidst the throng.

We emerged into the bright Luzon sunshine, to be met by a smiling Aquilino Escobar, our guide for the five-day expedition up Mount Hamut in search of the endemic Whiskered Pitta. I had rendezvoused in Manila with the other expedition members, Brendan Sloan from the UK, and Scott Lin from Taiwan, accompanied by his assistant Wu Jian-Long. None of us had met prior to the trip, having convened via an oriental birds web forum, but all of us had some previous pitta form. Scott had the best record, having spent the last seven years working in Huben, Taiwan researching the Fairy Pitta. Wayne Hsu, a keen Taiwanese entomologist and birder was to have been the fifth member of our party, but he had failed to materialize at the airport.

After introductions to Aquilino's delightful daughter Quenilyn, we piled our equipment into his battered jeepney, our transport to the nearby village of Baliuag. *En route* however, we called in at Tuguegarao's market to stock up on expedition provisions. Tuguegarao may be a one-horse town (in fact we met the horse, labouring in front of a wooden charabanc which provided the local taxi service) but it does have a thriving market. The stalls were laden with exotic and unidentifiable fresh vegetables, dried salted fish, and a wide range of tropical fruits. A butcher's stand was rather less

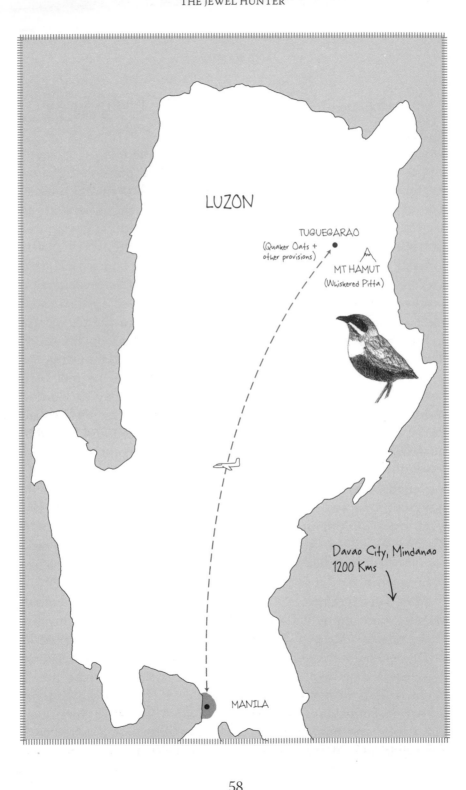

LUZON

TUGUEGARAO
(Quaker Oats +
other provisions)

MT HAMUT
(Whiskered Pitta)

Davao City, Mindanao
1200 Kms

MANILA

appealing, its contents resembling a particularly gory road accident.

I had never requisitioned for an expedition before and was a little out of my depth. How does one calculate the amount of rice one's crew will need for a five day yomp? Suddenly I was transported back to my schooldays, when I'd sat short-trousered and sweaty-palmed in a voluminous exam hall, staring hopelessly at a paper which read:

Five people climb a mountain. Each man is accompanied for five days by two porters and a goat. If the goat is a vegetarian, and each person will consume one eighth of his body weight in rice every second day, what is the gross domestic product of Spain? Marks will be given for showing your workings.

In any event, I decided that since Aquilino had put together many such expeditions, he would know the form.

'So Chris, what do you want to buy?'

'Erm, well, what do you usually take?'

'It depends on what people want to eat.'

'Mmm, of course. But there are some things that are always included?'

'Well Quaker Oats obviously...'

So we started with Quaker Oats, which were to provide us with our five a.m. fuel for the next few days. With hindsight I'm not sure I would go the porridge route every time, but we survived. Within twenty minutes we had an alarmingly full trolley that Aquilino had stacked with architectural precision, and we wove our way to the checkout. It was a long time since I had seen such an overstuffed supermarket trolley, and I glanced nervously around, half expecting *Supermarket Sweep's* Dale Winton to appear announcing I had lost the lot having taken ten seconds over the allotted time. We threw our impressive haul of orange juice powder, peanuts, rice, noodles, tins of sardines and the precious Quaker Oats into the back of the jeepney. After a quick sprint around the fresh vegetable stalls to ensure we wouldn't contract scurvy during our mountain sojourn we careered out of Tuguegarao, scattering a few of the less well-stowed provisions in our wake. As we rumbled down the high street I noticed a street urinal, *provided*, a notice read, *by the kind generosity of Brigadier Pensthorpe-Booth, 1967*. As an afterthought, a second smaller notice had been added beneath. *Men only.*

Once at Aquilino's house, a well-appointed wooden structure thirty minutes from town, we were cordially received by Mrs.

Aquilino and another gorgeous daughter Joy, who plied us with tea and biscuits. As I helped myself to a second ginger nut, my eyes ran along our host's bookshelves. One shelf included a volume celebrating Betty Boop, a first edition of *The Beginner's Guide to Trigonometry,* and a copy of *Birds of the Philippines,* the standard field guide for the archipelago. Next came a slim hardback, whose spine was decorated in gold, bearing the words, *The Healing Wonders of Herbs,* which in turn nestled alongside *An Insight on the Scriptures.* Eclectic to a fault. *The long winter nights,* I thought to myself, *must just fly by.*

Having resolved the financial details, figured out the total porter count required, and made plans for the morning, we adjourned to The Lorito, *the finest hotel,* the elaborate Baroque sign informed us, *in Tuguegarao.* Not to mention the only one. Nonetheless, they had cold beer and some unarguably fine fish, the latter awash with soy and ginger.

We woke at three a.m. and were clambering into the jeepney by four. After a prolonged allocation process dedicated to sorting out which porter was to carry what (an event that resembled a ramshackle tea dance at which all the dancers must swap partners at least twice) our human mules were ready. We set off up Mount Hamut, one of the larger peaks in northeastern Luzon's Sierra Madre range. Our progress was slowed by a morass of sticky mud, the result of heavy rain over the last three weeks. Our route took us through deforested agricultural fields along a succession of cattle runs, before we started to climb. I kept my eyes focussed on the ground, not daring to look ahead at the trail snaking off into the distance high above me. By eight a.m. the sun was beating down mercilessly from a dazzling blue sky, and for the next couple of hours we followed the trails up into the foothills, slipping and sliding our way inexorably higher. Clods of mud clung stubbornly to our boots weighing us down, and sweat stung our eyes and poured off us in rivulets, but we gradually made progress.

After two and a half hours we reached the forest edge, and the going really got tough. The gradient steepened, and the only path to the mountain's upper reaches led along narrow, quagmire corridors that sliced their way through the forests of razor grass. The latter is an organic embodiment of the paper cut, with a particular fondness for running along the back of the ear as you pass, leaving a neat incision to which sweat naturally gravitates. Our party suffered numerous falls, and by the end of the first couple of hours we resembled extras filming the horrors of trench warfare in the First World War. Only muddier.

Our team of porters made light work of the trying conditions, and were soon out of sight ahead, pausing only to smoke cigarettes and grin at our ineffectual exertions below as we approached the blue haze that marked their position. The only other evidence of our logistical team's existence was the beheaded snakes we encountered every now and then, each dispatched with a single stroke of a porter's machete. We picked up the lifeless bodies (having first made sure they were fully departed) marvelling at the bands of colour and rippling muscles beneath the smooth skin.

Despite such distractions, we succeeded in inching our way up the mountain, and five hours after leaving the village the advance party reached the river crossing, above which stood the famed 'Camp 1', our home for the night. Bamboo and tarpaulins had been erected and a fireplace constructed, and as we staggered into view some thirty minutes later, a pot of tea was on the go and everything was looking just dandy.

Apart from the weather that is. Having spent the whole climb dreaming of plunging into the cool depths of the river by the camp, we were now chilled by the montane air, and I shivered as a few outsize drops of rain splashed onto my head. Thirty seconds later the heavens opened. Undeterred, we flipped open our umbrellas and slithered our way up the hill to look for birds. The rain sheeted down and a strong wind sprang up, playfully slapping aside our umbrellas and ensuring we were well and truly inundated. We eventually abandoned our fruitless endeavour, returning to camp to wring out our clothes and pick leeches off our legs, shirts and boots.

Dinner – rice with tinned sardines – was a dismal affair, each of us lost in our own silent misery. Personally I was consumed with worries about the mission. My December deadline did not allow for entire legs to be defeated by the elements, and I dreaded having to return to Hamut if we did not find the Whiskered Pitta. I could not afford the time, nor to be frank the money to put together another expedition, and in any event I did not relish the idea of having to endure the climb all over again. This was certainly the hardest physical exercise I had undergone in thirty years of birding, and as

I shivered over a cup of coffee, dark thoughts engulfed me. What if it rained for the whole of our five days on the mountain? Would we die of exposure? Worse, would we fail to see any birds at all, let alone the pitta? In the three and a half hours since it had begun to pour we had seen one bird, an Elegant Tit (although this particular individual had been a rather soggy, inelegant tit.) Our prospects looked bleak.

In dense forest, birdsong is key, since hearing a bird is almost always the precursor to seeing one. If it rains hard, nothing sings (and even if it did you wouldn't be able to hear it). I hunkered down on the bamboo bench we had constructed and tried to keep out of the way of the worst of the rivers cascading off our tarpaulin roof. Whose idea had this expedition been in the first place? Which genius decided it would be possible to see all the species of pitta in a year? All it took was one set of adverse circumstances, one run of bad luck, and the whole thing would be derailed. Not for the first time I began to question my sanity; I could have been snug and warm in my office, firing off memos and tweaking Excel formulae. Instead of which I was freezing cold, soaking wet, and stuck halfway up a mountain in a remote part of the northern Philippines with leeches chewing on my lower limbs. Things were not going according to plan.

At around ten p.m., a note of cheer was introduced in the bedraggled form of our missing expedition member, Wayne. A long exchange in Mandarin followed, from which we managed to gather that Wayne had been forced to book a later flight and hence had missed our general rendezvous in Manila. Happily one of the porters had brought him up the mountain in the dark.

After a waterlogged night in my hastily erected tent, I woke before dawn and peered through the flysheet. It was still raining. I stumbled out into the camp and sloshed hopelessly around for a while until I found my boots. The grim task of draping wet clothes around my frame took a full ten minutes, by which time my teeth were chattering and my hands were shaking like a life-long dipsomaniac suddenly deprived of whisky. Breakfast – Quaker Oats in hot milk with a medically inadvisably quantity of sugar and garnished with mud – was hastily wolfed down, and we broke camp in record time.

I knew that Whiskered Pitta had been seen just above the lower camp, and had decided we would work the trails above Camp 1 for a few hours before continuing our ascent up the main trail. If all went smoothly, we could be at Camp 2 just below the summit before nightfall. By six a.m. the rain had eased considerably, and I began to entertain a glimmer of optimism. Within minutes we encountered that most joyous of rainforest sights, a mixed flock. Often in primary forest one can walk for hours and scarcely see a bird, until without warning a mixed species flock will appear. The transition from no birds at all to way too many to deal with is often instantaneous, and causes an adrenalin rush and panic in equal measure. In an instant the barren vegetation is transformed, and it seems as if every tree hosts a squeaking, chipping whirlwind of birds.

Just such a parade was now passing in front of us. First to emerge from the avian cornucopia were a few jaunty Blue-headed Fantails, which like so many of their family swung wildly from side to side, pivoting on their tiny feet as if nailed to the branch. Next up was a flock of burly Blackish Cuckooshrikes, which elbowed their way through the flock like bouncers clearing a path for a red carpet celebrity. The celebrity on this occasion was a White-lored Oriole, a scarce Philippine endemic, which in turn was shadowed by the undercover security patrol for the retinue, another endemic in the form of a Rufous Coucal. The coucal loitered furtively in the understorey, occasionally perching in a well-lit spot, its dark plumage suddenly glowing an intense orange, the light glinting off its lime-green bill.

All very distracting, but one thing was for sure; no pitta would ever join such an unruly mob. Strictly loners, pittas have far too much integrity to be caught associating with the forest hoi polloi. So we walked on, deeper into the forest, stepping as quietly as possible over dead branches and occasional patches of dry leaves that would instantly give our presence away via an unwelcome crack or a conspiratorial rustle. A couple of hours in and more in hope than expectation, I paused as always at a corner of the trail to scan the ground ahead with my binoculars. The proscribed sweep left and right yielded nothing as usual, and I stepped out into the centre of the trail. As I did so, I sensed a movement some twenty metres ahead, and a shape bounced out of cover to the edge of the trail where it paused in a gloomy recess. I instinctively knew what it was, and motioned to the others behind me to keep still. Raising my binoculars as slowly as I could manage in the mounting excitement, I bent my head to meet them, simultaneously flicking the focus wheel. The image in front of me fell into sharp relief, and what an image it was; a big, boisterous, bouncing ball of a bird, scarlet on the belly, with an iridescent blue back and a white moustache running from the bill-base towards the nape. Whiskered Pitta!

I swivelled round and whispered 'pitta!' to Scott who was a foot behind me, but he had already clocked the bird. There was panic in the ranks further back as the message was relayed, and just as I turned back for a second look the bird hopped off the trail and down the slope, disappearing into the forest as quickly as it had arrived. Of our group of six, only three of us had seen it. The euphoria was thus somewhat muted, but inwardly I sighed with relief. This early success was more than I could have hoped for, and freed me to enjoy the rest of our time on Hamut, all pressure having been removed by our rapid good fortune. One of the trickiest pitta species had been secured without really putting up a fight, and the mission was back on track. Best of all, I wouldn't have to wade knee-deep through treacly mud while getting slashed to pieces by razor grass. There would be no need to wrestle with Mt. Hamut for a second time.

There was still some further mountaineering to be negotiated however. The climb to Camp 2 was even steeper than yesterday, but the trails were drier, and we made good time. As we climbed, Aquilino told me how he used to hunt Wild Boar on the summit trail. His technique was simple; find a fruiting tree, then hide in it until the pigs arrive to graze on fallen fruit. Since there was no knowing when they would turn up, this involved sleeping in the branches of the tree for up to four days at a stretch. When the animals did finally show, all that was required was a silent repositioning, and then a single shot to dispatch the largest of the herd. The hardest part was getting the dead beast back down the mountain, larger specimens frequently weighing in at fifty kilos. With a market value somewhere around three dollars a kilo it was a tough way to earn a living, but a hundred and fifty US dollars is a lot of money in the Philippines. Aquilino simply shrugged when we expressed amazement that he had been able to shoulder a boar alone and carry it the eight hours back down to civilization.

After a few hours' climbing we reached a viewpoint, which afforded an amazing panorama over the forested valley to the north.

We drained the last of our drinking water and mopped the sweat from our brows while scanning the peaks opposite us, hoping for a glimpse of the mighty Philippine Eagle. This iconic bird (formerly known by the more graphic moniker 'Monkey-eating Eagle') is the national bird of the Philippines, and is one of the most endangered species on the planet. Years of logging, slash-and-burn agriculture and hunting have reduced the population to a tiny remnant within its former range, and it is now rarely seen. Certainly we didn't see it despite our vigil, but nonetheless we appreciated the respite from the rigours of ascending Hamut's slopes.

What goes up, it's said, *must come down*, and having reached the start of the summit trail we now forked off onto a tiny side-trail, descending a few hundred metres towards the sound of rushing water. Camp 2 was already in an advanced stage of construction in a spacious clearing next to the river. We collapsed gratefully onto the hastily constructed forest furniture and gulped down the proffered water. It tasted of the wood-smoke that had been used to purify it but was a blessing nevertheless. As darkness fell we sat around eating congealed spaghetti, and Scott and I discreetly toasted the pitta with rum and powdered orange, an ad hoc recipe that will no doubt become a staple in every bar in the Philippines. Even Aquilino was tempted to sample a snifter. It was his first drink, I discovered later with a pang of guilt, in twenty years. At least his return to the cocktail set was something special.

The next day dawned clear, and we headed up the summit trail before dawn in an attempt to find more pittas and other scarce birds of the high ridges. We had brief views of a Flame-breasted Fruit-dove, which clattered off through the forest with indecent haste, but nevertheless gave us a glorious glimpse of its orange crown and breast patch as it departed. A pair of delicate Citrine Canary-flycatchers charmed us as they hopped through the vegetation alongside the trail. Only four inches long, but with heads too big for their bodies, their googly eyes gave the impression of them being astonished by everything they encountered.

The highlight though, was the show put on by another Philippine bird that has been hunted almost to extinction. A deep, mournful *'woo-OOOH... woo-OOOH... woo-OOOH'* resonated around the upper reaches of the forest, and after a full thirty minutes of imitating the bird's call, a Luzon Bleeding-heart finally walked towards us through the forest and nervously crossed the trail. These shy forest pigeons get their name from the blood-red patch in the centre of their pearly-white breast, which makes them look as though they have been mortally wounded by hunters and are just tottering off to die in the leaf-litter. Even on remote Mt. Hamut they have largely been hunted out, and are now only found on the inaccessible upper slopes.

In the mid-afternoon Brendan headed out on his own to look for Philippine Eagle. We waved him off before continuing on our way. Birding our way up the ridge, we heard Cream-bellied and Yellow-breasted Fruit-doves, and found a rare Sooty Woodpecker and an engaging group of Luzon Striped-babblers. On the way back to camp we rested at the viewpoint, chatting about the day and being entertained by Aquilino's description of the forest people who lived below the ridge, a conversation prompted by the shouts of one of the tribes' members far below us in the valley. At dusk we returned to camp, and since the only figures visible around the fire were the porters, I wandered over to our tent to find Brendan. It was singularly unoccupied.

I hurried over to ask the porters whether they had seen him. After a lot of sign language and a frenetic picture-drawing session they realized what I was asking, and shook their heads; no-one had seen Brendan since first light when we had walked up to the ridge together. I sat down with Aquilino, whose worried expression was doing little to reassure me. Together we drew a trail map, and worked out where our lost colleague might have taken a wrong turn, and hence where he could conceivably be now. As we talked, I was jolted by a sickening realization. The shouts we had heard from the viewpoint were not those of a forest-dweller at all. They had been uttered by a different mouth, one belonging to an Irishman who was currently in more trouble than a haemophiliac at a vampire wedding. We assembled a search party, grabbed water, a whistle and lights, and breathlessly made our way back up the ridge trail. An hour later we were above the viewpoint, and after whistling and shouting, could just make out a faint bellowing in the distance.

'Aq-wah-leen-ooooh.'

It was Brendan, calling our guide's name, and he was a long, long way below us.

We scrambled to a point on the ridge directly above the source of the sound and hatched a plan. It was agreed that I would wait alone on the ridge to guide the party back up the mountain in the darkness, while Aquilino and his cohorts macheted their way straight down through the forest to try to access the valley trail below. They set off, causing a huge commotion as they hacked their way through the dense vegetation to intersect with the lower trail. As the minutes ticked by the sound of the party grew fainter and fainter, and I switched off my torch to conserve battery power. The darkness into which I was plunged was absolute. I could not see my hand in front of my face, and even walking a few yards along the trail without a light source was impossible.

I tried to recall how well Brendan had been equipped when we had last seen him. He had been carrying water as we all had, but this had doubtless long since been consumed. As far as I could remember he had not been carrying a GPS or a compass. We had parted at two p.m., and it was now almost nine at night; he had been missing for seven hours already. There were few large animals left in the forest capable of causing him any harm, although bumping into a group of wild pigs at night would be dangerous for sure. Far more terrible to contemplate was the possibility that in the darkness he could blunder into a hunter's trap, spring loaded and armed with a deadly sharpened bamboo stake, capable of killing a large Wild Boar at a stroke, or doing considerable damage to a lost, disorientated bird watcher

I banished such thoughts from my mind and focused on the shouts below me. The gaps between the rescue party's shouts and Brendan's responses were getting shorter. At length, the sounds stopped altogether. Either they had found him or the whole group was now dead...

After a tense thirty-minute wait I heard noises drifting up from way below the ridge, and I started shouting at regular intervals, peering at the luminous hands on my watch to calculate the timing. By nine-thirty I could hear the sounds of strenuous activity down-slope, and after a further fifteen minutes the rescue party appeared from behind a gnarled, twisted tree-trunk, filthy dirty but beaming and excited, like miners pulled alive from a pit disaster.

Brendan was in one piece. His flesh had been torn by the unforgiving rattan thorns and he had been savaged by leeches, but all major limbs were accounted for. Though he was largely intact in physical terms, his unplanned solo survival exercise had taken a toll. He had taken the wrong turning on the way back to camp, and struggled along a small trail that wound for miles down the valley. Having realized his mistake he'd tried to reorientate himself and had worked his way uphill off-trail. Still with no real idea of his whereabouts he had abandoned the idea, dropping back into the valley. As darkness fell he had simply lain down in the forest, having decided that his best chance of salvation was to wait until it got light.

We struggled back to camp, where a relieved group welcomed him back with smiles, food, a litre of smoky water and a stiff rum and powdered orange. He had cheated the Forest Gods and lived to tell the tale.

On our last day around the summit, I finally heard the sound I had been hoping to hear since our arrival; an owl-like *'Woo...hoo-hoo-hoo-hoo-hoogh',* proof positive that a Whiskered Pitta was not far away. I played a recording of the call, and the bird briefly responded before falling silent. Aquilino motioned for me to continue playing the recording, so we hid at the side of the trail while I kept the audio salvo going. The bird circled us, periodically giving a contact call; a short *'clerk'* as a New Yorker might pronounce it.*

Occasionally I glimpsed the crimson belly as the bird moved through the undergrowth, but one of our number had still not been able to connect. I whispered urgently, 'just watch the trail, nothing else, the bird will cross the trail.' Sure enough, the circuit brought the bird to the edge of the path, and it flipped across in a blur of colour. At last all of us had seen the bird, but there was more to come. The bird wheeled left and bounced towards us, re-emerging on the trail just yards from where we sat. It eyed a fallen log on the trail and, deciding that a few extra inches of height would help it to see off this pesky territorial interloper, promptly hopped onto the log and bounced along it. As it reached the far end it paused and turned in perfect profile, before finally returning to the thick cover at the side of the trail.

We all exhaled in unison, and exchanged a few silent high fives. Proper views of Whiskered Pitta for everybody. Firmly on the list. The only tragedy was that my camera had still not recovered from

---

* In fact exactly like Martha and the Muffins' 1980 hit *Echo Beach* where Martha Johnson sings 'My job is very boring I'm an office clerk.'

its soaking on the first day, and was emitting only the odd random, sickly click and whirr. No matter. The image was burned onto my retina forever in any case, and if others wanted to see the bird they would just have to climb the mountain as we had. Some things are better when they are exclusive, when getting there in the first place requires supreme effort. Pittas are often exceedingly difficult to see, which is why when you are allowed a brief interlude in their world you feel all the more privileged. Later in the day we debated how many people might have seen a Whiskered Pitta. A hundred? Two hundred? It was an elite club, and we were now all members. Our names were on the list and we were in. A huge queue of wannabees snaked back from the door outside, whilst we were inside with the pretty girls sipping cocktails. Life was sweet.

Having packed up, we worked our way slowly back down to Camp 1, admiring another shotgun-victim bleeding-heart on the way. The soundtrack that played us out came courtesy of a group of Coletos, prehistoric-looking birds decked out in black-and grey, with bizarre, pink, naked-skin faces. Their song is no more conventional than their appearance, an antiphonal collision of clicks, splutterings and failing telecommunications equipment. Played backwards. Aquilino paused at the forest edge to chat with a family of homesteaders, eking out a precarious existence here, a good four hours round trip from the nearest Wild Boar emporium. We reached Camp 1 without incident, and were seduced from our tents by the delicious aroma of fried chicken livers, okra in garlic and the ubiquitous rice.

Our last day saw us winding our way down through the foothills, denuded of forest and populated only by the odd flock of heavy-tressed sheep and an occasional goat. Under azure skies we stopped on the ridges periodically to glory in the panoramic views, the barren landscape rolling away to the distant shore, the sea beyond glinting in the afternoon sun, each successive wave beckoning us toward an inviting post-expedition dip.

As we wandered lower, Aquilino explained in faltering English that he had been a gold miner, but had seized the chance to take up professional guiding full-time as mining was just too dangerous. 'Only one pipe for air,' he shrugged, 'If it gets blocked...' His pregnant pause left me in no doubt that accidents had frequently occurred. Climbing Hamut a few times a year, no matter how strenuous, was a soft life by comparison.

Back at Aquilino's house in Baliuag we sprawled in a muddied heap, chugging down restorative bottles of coke before our extended entourage posed for group photos. In a few short days our mutual suffering had generated a real community spirit, and we were truly sorry to say our last goodbyes and climb aboard the jeepney for the journey back to Tuguegarao. As we drove along the back roads, the huge wheels of our vehicle helpfully crushed corn that had been laid out to take advantage of passing traffic. We gazed at gangs of workers in the fields, all of whom paused from their labours, flashing dazzling smiles and waving as we trundled by. Just as in rural Thailand, there is a genuine air of contentment in the Philippines despite the grinding poverty, and an innate friendliness seems common to the entire nation. Reunited with the Lorita Hotel, we wrecked our rooms while attempting to get our kit clean. A final dinner with Aquilino and his family followed, during which I was persuaded to try a local dish of stir-fried bitter gourd (which is basically a courgette with an attitude problem). Only an uninspiring native cuisine can prevent the Filipinos from taking over as the top tourist destination in southeast Asia.

Chapter 5

Jeepneys and Jeopardy. Mindanao, The Philippines

Having waved off Scott and Wu who were returning to Taiwan, there was time before our flight south to walk the streets of Tuguegarao, though the intense heat curtailed our ambition after a few blocks. We peered into dimly lit billiard halls and dodged the motorcycle taxis with their misfiring engines. We skirted around Chicken Corner, where buxom, leather-faced women kept their poultry charges out of the road with a periodic nudge of the boot. By eight a.m. the Internet cafés were crammed full of school kids playing pre-school video games. A large banner had been erected in an office window. *Wanted: Sales Representative, Graduate of BS Information Technology.* Now that's telling it like it is.

The Philippines would wither and die without music. Hotel lobbies worldwide would fall eerily silent, bereft of their shiny Filipino cover bands grinning their way through *Una Paloma Blanca* and *Knowing Me, Knowing You*. I was reminded of a Cebu Air flight I had taken a few years earlier. It was Valentines Day, and the in-flight speaker system had been commandeered by the chief air host, who announced an airborne karaoke competition to find the most romantic singer. First prize; a baseball cap. I swear the nose of the plane dropped due to the ensuing stampede to sign up. Suspended only for a brief period of turbulence somewhere over Quezon City, a fifty-year-old man won with his themed rendition of *The Wind beneath my Wings*. He proudly wore his baseball cap for the remainder of the journey.

Sadly today's journey on flight PR19 to Davao City, the capital of Mindanao, was less cheerful, our every need ignored by a surly, scowling air hostess named, with a winning sense of irony on the part of her parents, Charisma Reyes. I must confess I had some previous experience of the vagaries of Filipino names. On my very first business trip to the Philippines, I had met our company's local distributor. The proprietor was a charming gentleman who ran a big musical instrument and professional audio distribution business.

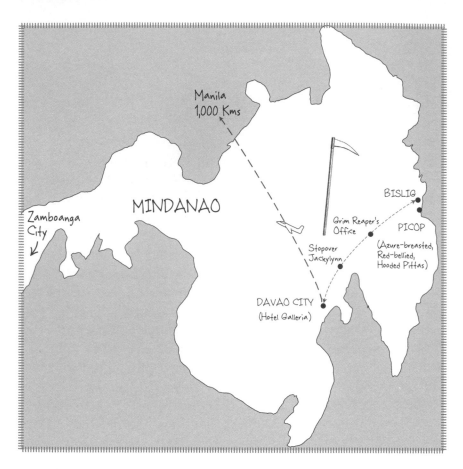

Before our first meeting I had been brought to the office to meet the team. The young salesman to my left introduced himself. 'Hi,' he said, 'my name is Bing.' I shook his hand, and turned to his colleague, who countered with, 'I'm Bong, pleased to meet you.' The temptation to reply with the riposte, 'Bong? James Bong?' was almost overwhelming, but I reined myself in. The next two members of the team got to their feet and shook my hand. Their names, they assured me, were Jyg and Dodo. I feigned a coughing fit. Two more new business associates handed over their cards, from which I learned that the team also boasted a Ding and a Dong. When his turn came, the newest member of the team at the end of the line stood up. 'Hi' he said, 'my name is Ding-Dong.' He looked at the floor and shuffled his feet, before adding wearily, 'like the bell.' That left only the boss's assistant, who, it transpired, was inexplicably named Eric. What on earth were you thinking Mr. and Mrs. Gomez?

Brendan, Wayne and I were met by Zardo Goring, our Passepartout for the next stage of the mission. We drove through a wet and windy evening towards our destination. The town of Bislig on Mindanao's east coast is a safe distance from the island's southwest peninsula, parts of which remain a stronghold for the Abu Sayaaf group of Muslim extremists. Noting with pioneering satisfaction the Mindanao travel advisories put in place by most western nations is one thing, but I could not afford to spend three months of my year being held captive in some dingy cell while the UK government refused to cave in to ransom demands. The opportunities for adding pittas from behind bars would be distinctly limited.

We arrived at the Paper Country Inn – a venue that looked as tired as we felt – shortly before midnight. In the sanctuary of my room I poured a shot of local *Tanduay Dark Rhum*. It was bright orange. Still, you couldn't tell once it was mixed with coke. I crashed out in my rickety bed, and slept the sleep of the dead. I woke at four, escaping from dreams in which I was pursued by Imelda Marcos screaming 'where are my shoes, infidel?' Whatever artificial colouring the Filipinos put in their rum was clearly starting to have an effect.

The Seventh Seal – not in this instance the classic Ingmar Bergman movie nor a Biblical revelation but the name of our jeepney – was parked just three feet from the frayed awning that jutted out above the hotel foyer. The torrential rain from Hamut had followed us south, and we got thoroughly soaked. We shook hands with our driver, and with his erstwhile assistant 'Hugh' (or possibly 'You!') The latter's duties included reaffixing hubcaps with a large metal hammer, guiding us through the more treacherous flooded stretches of what passed for roads around the 'Paper Industry Corporation of the Philippines' estate, and shouting directions during reversing manoeuvres. These consisted of a long series of *'atras, atras, atras'* end-stopped with *'oops!'* In addition, Hugh was the main axe-wielder when our way was blocked by a tree fall. His English was limited, but it seemed that his personal lexicon featured the most bizarre componentry, and our days were punctuated with a succession of short, explanatory utterances. We passed a rough-hewn square of mud with rusting iron hoops at either end. Hugh looked serious, before summarizing.

'Basketball court.'

We nodded sagely.

For the next five days our reduced group planned to traipse around the few pockets of forest that remained standing on former PICOP land. Zardo our guide had previously worked as the head of security at PICOP, who at their peak had employed fourteen thousand people. In the early days following the company's inception, Bislig was a backwater town. Then in 1952 PICOP built one of southeast Asia's largest paper mills there, and its operations drove the development of the town, which rapidly became the Caraga region's third largest city.

For fifty years Bislig ruled supreme as the Paper Capital of the Philippines, contributing in no small part to the ninety-seven percent deforestation of the archipelago. However, the company in later years pursued a strategy of selective logging, taking out only the largest and most valuable trees, allowing the forest to regenerate and thus continue as a sustainable resource. Following a complete logging ban introduced by the Philippine government in 2003, the PICOP logging concession naturally came to an end, and so too did their careful protection of their assets. As a result, hundreds of illegal squatters moved in to the forest, and, encouraged by shady timber merchants, proceeded to lay waste to everything they could reach with a chainsaw. Partial logging was replaced by clear-felling for agriculture, and by a supreme irony the logging ban thus accelerated the rate of deforestation in Mindanao.

I last visited the site nine years earlier, and the destruction since was enough to make a man weep. Only tiny isolated tracts of lowland forest remained intact, and we witnessed huge trucks piled high with relatively young trees chewing up the dirt roads every time we entered the area. That the logging is illegal is simple to establish, since *all* logging is now illegal in the Philippines. The local contractors were taking no chances, and had evolved a cunning strategy so that their activities remained undetected; they spirited the logs away from the site under cover of darkness. Genius! Now no-one will know what they're up to.

The sad fact is that the repatriation of families from Luzon is being spearheaded by the very government that introduced the logging ban in the first place. One can hardly blame the families if, on arrival, they try to squeeze a living from the land by removing the forest that prevents them from farming. The few timber dollars they make in the process do not go amiss either of course. There are a number of endemic birds whose range is limited to the southern Philippines: Black-headed Tailorbird, Mindanao Miniature-babbler, Mindanao Broadbill, Mindanao Hornbill, Blue-capped Kingfisher. Once PICOP and the two or three other remaining fragments of forest are gone, they too will be gone, for there will literally be nowhere left for them to live. One of the species for which time appears to be running out is the bird I had come to see, the Azure-breasted Pitta. There are now just two main sites at which it is possible to find the bird, PICOP is one, and Rajah Sikatuna National Park on the nearby island of Bohol is the other.

Churning through the brown floodwaters we passed numerous wooden shacks built by the newly arrived settlers, suspended on stilts to defeat tropical storms. The smarter houses boasted a communal living room, and one we passed was crammed full of kids gathered round a flickering TV set. We encountered children wherever we went, who would variously point, open-mouthed, at the foreign devils, wave so vigorously that their entire body would shake to and fro, or stare sullenly. Even the kind of glare that seemed to say 'I will stab you shortly' was inevitably followed by a beaming smile once you engaged them. We took photos of many of the families, showing them the digital images that invariably produced awestruck and delighted responses. For many of the kids it was perhaps the first time they had seen their own image.

Our jeepney had a two-foot clearance that allowed us to navigate the terrible roads, mulched by the passage of so many overloaded logging trucks, but our daily progress was slow and bone-jarring. The most comfortable ride was to be had by looping a sweat towel over the internal roof rail and strap-hanging like a London commuter. The driver had a four foot long, three inch high mirror above the windscreen allowing us to see his brow, furrowed with concentration, at all times. Below this mirrored strip was a multi-coloured crocheted banner stretching from one side of the cab to the other. These are common in Filipino truck cabs, and usually decorated with biblical verses. Ours was brusque and to the point: *God Help Us.* The remainder of the cab was decorated with ancient penguin stickers, their colour long since blanched, but flippered silhouettes still forlornly in evidence.

From time to time as we headed deeper into the estate we came across a tree fall, whereupon we broke out the axes and stripped to the waist, our amateur work party clearing a passage. During one of these exercises I cut a finger, and our driver proffered a magic balm. 'Will stop bleeding,' he said with a toothy grin. The contents of the small phial appeared to consist largely of engine oil. Nevertheless, coagulation ensued. Vignettes of Filipino village life faded in and out: *We are child-friendly* was daubed on the end gable of a makeshift school; close by a homestead boasting only a washing line and a billiard table; family groups waved as we drove by, their only shelter from the unceasing rain provided by large banana leaves plucked from the roadside.

Our destination was Road 42. All roads had been given numbers by the PICOP authorities, but there were no signs and we were glad to have Zardo along to navigate. Upon reaching one of the last remaining forest fragments we spilled out into the road and were soon birding under umbrellas along a side-trail. A little way up-slope we hit a small mixed flock that solely contained scarce species, as if they were all hanging out together swapping tips on how to remain extant. At the front of the flock was a diminutive olive-green bird, a Naked-faced Spiderhunter, whose name is comic enough but whose flight call is a rather accurate rendition of what my father would have dubbed a 'Bronx cheer'. Close behind was a pair of Philippine Leafbirds, a species that I knew had never been photographed in the field, and I managed to fire off a record shot. Their name is supremely apposite; when I finally got back to the UK and edited the picture it took me five minutes to find the bird in the image, such is their resemblance to the foliage in which they spend their days.

Further down the valley we heard a distinctive, ringing, three-note whistle, and after coaxing Zardo's battered cassette player into life we finally pulled in the source of the sound, a Celestial Monarch. It's a truly stunning bird which, when shopping for plumage, clearly could not decide between cerulean and cobalt blue, and so came away with plenty of both. This individual proved to be a male, his head adorned with an extraordinary crest, which can be raised like a punk's mohican when excited. Our bird, however, remained calm throughout proceedings, its crest laid flat on its back, thus resembling an ageing hippy who couldn't face trimming the remnant tresses of his rebellious youth. It was a great find, and I was delighted to finally catch up with this rare species, a bird I had long wanted to see.

Our excitement was dampened only by the showers that plagued us all morning. They intensified, becoming one long, continuous downpour, and after sitting on a log using giant leaves for cover, we eventually beat a retreat to the jeepney. We reached the vehicle and cowered inside while the rain hammered out a thunderous tattoo on the roof.

The monarch was a major result, but really hadn't helped. There were three species of pitta to be seen at PICOP, Azure-breasted, Hooded and Red-bellied, and so far we had not had a sniff of any of them. I nibbled disinterestedly at a club sandwich (composed, it seemed, of the requisite three layers, but with contents largely unidentifiable) and devised a Plan B. We drove to another section of forest next to a decrepit shack, but there was little activity. I amused myself by feeding the attendant scrawny kittens and mangy-looking baby chickens the leftovers from lunch. The cats fought over the pieces, mewling and tumbling over the tidbits of stringy meat and stale bread, although they were apparently not hungry enough to risk the dilapidated slices of gherkin, which they briefly licked before turning up their noses in disgust.

After another skeleton-rattling ride back to town we made ourselves look as close to presentable as is possible after weeks on the road, and dropped into the restaurant to order dinner for an hour hence, a wise precaution in Mindanao. I had become as picky as the gherkin-refusenik kittens had been, and decided to forgo the 'Chicken Bonanza.'

I opted for a pre-prandial shower, and went into battle with the ancient waterworks that lurked in the bathroom. I reached for the shower dial. It refused to budge, but it did give me an electric shock. I gave it a sharp encouraging nudge with my knee and received another shock for my trouble. Gingerly I poked the showerhead setting with a plastic biro while standing on a rubber bath mat, and succeed in moving it from 'lukewarm' to 'hot'. After a deft drop kick to the water-flow control, something stirred deep in the bowels of the hotel, and water finally emerged into the shower cubicle. Sadly it emerged in a spray of scalding water jetting out against the wall via a fiendishly positioned nozzle. Cold water meanwhile continued to gush over my naked body. I reached round to re-route the flow and received another shock for my pains. I retreated, placed the plastic water scoop under the stream of hot water and started soaping myself in earnest.

With my eyes full of soap I kicked over the nearly full water scoop, accidentally touching the metal shower pillar as I did so. It sent a not insignificant voltage down my left side. After a long wait for the scoop to refill, I was finally able to tip a cascade of hot water over my head.

I towelled off and poured myself a hard-won rum and coke. I collected my laundry from the front desk staff, who explained that it was 'not dry.' No shit. Nothing in Bislig is dry. I doubt whether anything in the history of the town has ever been truly free of moisture. Frankly that they ever managed to make paper here at all borders on the miraculous. At least the watermarks would have been easy to achieve.

The appointed hour for dinner drew nigh, and we adjourned to the dimly lit restaurant. Wayne our resident entomologist had already built up a fine collection of weevils, captured by shaking foliage from which the unfortunate bugs had neatly rained down into his upturned umbrella. We paused to admire the collection. Variously spotted and striped in pastel greens, blues and pinks, they looked like the kind of hard sweets left at the bottom of the bag after all the decent dolly mixtures have been snaffled. Our lacklustre meal was enlivened by a discussion of Islam and whether all world religions lead to war in the end. We called it a night and crashed out.

The next day we started early and headed to a site known as The Quarry. It was dispiritingly quiet. At length Zardo suggested we try another spot, so we drove into the hills, pulling up at a well-hidden stone trail. We walked in silence down the trail, and at length heard what I had been hoping for, the unmistakable, angry 'wark-wark-wark-wark-wark' of an Azure-breasted Pitta. I stalked our quarry inch by painstaking inch, and was immensely gratified when it flew past me and landed in the sub-canopy. We sneaked towards it, and after a few minutes were able to locate it calling amongst a mass of bamboo struts. Job done, and the eighth pitta bagged.

I had seen the species a decade earlier, also at PICOP, while birding with a fellow UK birder. On that occasion we had simply walked into the forest on our first day and bumped into an Azure-breasted Pitta perched up on an open branch. Ridiculously easy. The bird had given up without even a token fight, and where, we had asked each other, was the fun in that? Birding is basically pacifist hunting, and there is, after all, little fun in hunting if the animal in question trots up to you and lies at your feet. The bird had proceeded to sing its head off in full view for thirty minutes, and was still going as we left. 'A disgrace to its tribe,' as my colleague so damningly put it at the time. This time the bird was a little less accommodating, but even so, I was able to snatch some photos against the light. Despite the less than optimal conditions, the images revealed a gorgeous creature. The turquoise breast and flanks, a scarlet-and-black belly, iridescent green upperparts, and a black cowl wrapped around the head combined to stunning effect. With its white chin and throat, it resembled a public schoolboy who has applied the starch to his Eton collar a little too liberally.

This was the bird I had come to Mindanao to find. As a southern Philippine endemic, it is found nowhere else in the world. Miss the bird here, and I would need to return later in the year, or go to Bohol just to the north. But such worries were behind me now, the bird was under the belt, and only a sense of macho propriety prevented me from skipping back down the trail. I greeted the others with a jaunty but manly wave, my sense of achievement matched only by Wayne, who had found what he thought could possibly be a bug species new to science. We marvelled at the insect, whose back was covered in some kind of strange white substance, as if it had been spattered with egg-whites whipped into peaks. We named the find on the spot, and the Philippine Meringue-backed Weevil officially joined the vast ranks of the world's invertebrates.

Another day, another dawn start, and it was still pouring with rain. I contemplated stopping off to order an ark. By the time we arrived at PICOP the downpour was easing, and we stopped to spotlight a curious night bird, a Philippine Frogmouth. Like most frogmouths it looked socially inept and singularly unhappy. We were unable to ascertain whether we had somehow committed an unforgivable frogmouth *faux pas*, or whether the bird had simply been unable to hunt all night due to the bad weather.

Either way we were buoyed by this early success. As we walked back to the jeepney with the first glimmer of light appearing on the horizon, I heard a sound emanating from the dense forest just behind us, a rhythmical, hoarse and almost mechanical *'whirp whirp.'* The paired notes were regularly repeated every five or six seconds. I had heard this sound before, in Malaysia and also right here at PICOP, and I instantly recognized the source. It was the sound of a Hooded Pitta, and it was less than ten metres away.

79

Despite the bird's proximity, I didn't fancy my chances. The forest looked deeply uninviting, a twisted tangle of lianas, lethal rattan and tree roots jutting out at every angle. I had no option. I was going in.

Hooded Pitta is one of the species for which it pays to go 'off trail', since they typically call from the most thickly vegetated areas of the understorey, and rarely respond to imitations of their voice, except to sing endlessly from hidden spots in the forest's darkest recesses. However, they are rather approachable in pitta terms (which is to say that if you could somehow dig a tunnel and pop up right next to the bird, you'd have a chance of a view.) I crept into the forest, contorting my limbs to noiselessly negotiate obstacles. I got close to the pitta, whose call was now bursting forth from a spot just a couple of metres in front of me. Time and again however, just when it seemed I'd enjoy killer views of the bird on its song-post, it effortlessly wove a flight-path through the impenetrable vegetation and started to call from another hidden perch.

I repeated the process, and each time was rewarded only with a blur of colour. After an age, I finally managed to catch a better glimpse; a flash of red and green on the undercarriage, a blaze of white in the wing and a sooty black head were all visible as it streaked through a gap. Not stellar views but views nonetheless. Species number nine had fallen, and my first month was still not over. I contemplated doing the English football fan thing, running round with my shirt over my head, but a swift glance at my confined surroundings made me realize that this would end in tears. I settled for a faintly ridiculous jig on the spot instead and was pleased with my own idiocy.

We returned to the quarry and worked the area of woodland up to the edge of a huge flood that blocked access to the primary forest beyond. Frustratingly, the forest beyond the water looked in great condition. Zardo asked the inhabitants of the nearest house if they knew any way to get around the flood. Option one was to take the ferry, but the boat in question looked distinctly unseaworthy. Besides, there was nobody to man it. Luckily the lady of the house knew of a logging trail, and after following her convoluted instructions we found our way to the trailhead to pursue option two.

The trail proved difficult to follow, heavily vegetated with numerous tree falls and formidable blocks of razor-sharp granite. We struggled along, slipping and sliding as we worked our way around the deep water, discovering a little too late that it was certainly an active logging trail. An enormous hardwood came crashing down less than fifty metres from us, a sobering and depressing experience, but happily not a fatal one. Yet another reminder, as if any were needed, that this particular forest's days were definitely numbered. After an hour's titanic struggle we emerged into daylight at the far end of the trail, and onto a wonderfully flat dirt road with nothing worse than a stubbed toe to show for our pioneering. Enthusiastically we set about finding the trickier forest birds.

After a couple of hours we heard a soft but intense 'Wooooooaaaaargh-wo-oh', like a rooster doing warm-up exercises. Red-bellied Pitta. Small but perfectly formed, this bird is a real gem, and as a bonus, birds on the Philippine islands of Mindanao and Palawan are of an endemic race, the nominate form, *Pitta erythrogaster erythrogaster*. We called the bird in, and it responded strongly, coming within four or five metres. We could not, however, see it, though it could clearly see us. Nevertheless, it was only a matter of time before we saw it, since it was super-responsive. And then it rained again. A proper, full-on, tropical stair-rods affair that pummelled us for twenty minutes. The bird had slipped away, and our chance had gone. Or had it?

So often in the past when I had thought that a pitta had disappeared for sure, it popped up close by just when I least expected. I counselled caution, and we sat tight and waited. Fifteen minutes later the bird called again, in exactly the same spot. We crawled on our bellies to a spot further up the trail, and after a further half an hour I caught sight of the little tinker, scurrying across the trail like a scarlet rat. For the next hour the bird played hide and seek with us, always keeping one step ahead, and in the end it outsmarted us by flying across a flood. We didn't actually see it do this of course; one minute it was between us and the water on one side, and the next it was calling from beyond the far bank. Perhaps it had snorkelled across? The others grew tired of the pursuit, and I was happy enough having added another pitta to the growing tally, though the views could have been better. Still, it was on the all-important list.

The next day we returned to the same area. I was determined to outwit the Red-bellied Pitta, and I wanted to photograph it. We took the same rough trail in, confident of our route now that we were logging trail veterans. Whether through lack of sleep or compensating for my bruised toe, I had been feeling slightly off-kilter all morning, more mountain gorilla than mountain goat. As we edged along an angled section of the overgrown trail I put my weight-bearing foot on a small, wet tree-root, and my foot skidded sideways. I fell heavily, and as my full weight came down on my arm I felt one of the many sharp limestone boulders slice through my skin.

My shout alerted the others. I struggled to sit up, dazed by the impact, and stared down at my arm. I could see right inside, to the tangly bits. Bits that should definitely be on the inside were on the outside. Blood was liberally spattered over my left side, and dripped onto my shoe. Zardo hailed me.

'You OK?'

'Er, no not really.'

He strode over and inspected the deep wound, grimaced and disappeared into the forest. Brendan came to my aid, kneeling by my side to assess the damage. I looked up at him, hoping that in my shocked state I was overestimating the severity of the wound. He inspected the gash.

'Jesus that looks bad.'

Wayne joined us. 'You know, I always say that apart from a snake bite a serious fall on a trail is just about the worst thing that can happen.'

So much for my companions' bedside manner. I took another look at the gaping hole in my arm, felt instantly woozy, and vowed not to do it again.

Zardo re-appeared with a length of creeper and rapidly set about proving his jungle credentials. First he popped open a bottle of iodine and with a perfunctory 'this will hurt' sloshed it onto the jagged chasm where my skin used to be. Once my body had been retrieved from the canopy he peeled a banana, and laid the inside of the peel over the wound.

'Inside the banana is sterile,' he said sternly. Obvious when you think about it. Next he took my sweat towel and wound it tightly around the banana skin, tucking it in on itself. Lastly he tied the creeper around the towel to act as a tourniquet, and to keep the towel in place. I was impressed.

We had almost completed the trail, so we persevered to the far end and sat on the road taking stock. I could still use my binoculars with my right hand, and the pain was bearable if I kept my left arm in the Napoleon position across my chest. We were at least an hour from the vehicle, and two hours drive from a hospital. What to do? There was only one answer. We went to find the Red-bellied Pitta.

The others wandered off to amuse themselves up the extended trail, while Zardo and I hunted for pittas along the first couple of kilometres. After a lot of trawling and a few false starts, we heard the Red-bellied Pitta's voice. This time it was on the opposite side of a small valley, the ideal position, since if it came in across the valley we would surely see it as it approached. I coaxed another pitta call from the iPod, and within a few minutes I picked it up at long range. During the next ten minutes, even though we knew exactly where it was coming from and where it would end up, we had only the briefest of glimpses on two occasions. Then, without warning, it materialized right in front of us. If it came much closer there was a very real danger I would bleed on it. Skulking behind a thick, fallen tree-trunk, it peered up at us. I played one more call, and the bird streaked by, perching a couple of metres off the ground behind us. I swivelled round in slow motion, raised my camera cautiously so as not to spook the bird, focused and let fly. The motor drive whirred, and the bird sat still, flicking its wings nervously but for just long enough. I had my picture, not completely free of interfering foliage, but good enough, a frame-filler. Success!

By now it was early afternoon, and I was starting to feel undeniably odd. I motioned to Zardo that I needed to get to a hospital. We looked at the damage again, and to our mutual alarm, noted that my arm had swollen to twice its normal size. We bandaged up the carnage as best we could, and started back down the trail, with me on autopilot, staggering like a one-legged sailor in a force ten. After an hour's unsteady progress we had made it back to the vehicle, and Zardo cracked open a phial of antibiotic, which he tipped directly into the wound. The swollen bloodied remnants of my inner forearm frothed with a thick and disgusting pink mucus. I crawled up the rear steps and passed out in the back of the jeepney.

We jolted our way down PICOP's deeply rutted roads, heading back to what passes for civilization in eastern Mindanao. Our jarring passage set off the bleeding again, and the journey seemed to go on forever. By the time we reached the hospital I looked and felt terrible. Zardo propped me up and led me into the emergency room, where to my relief we were greeted with bright efficiency by a doctor and an orderly. They even spoke English, which was a bonus. My Tagalog is poor at the best of times, and this was certainly not the best of times.

The doctor, a charming lady in her forties, fired questions at Zardo. How had the injury occurred? Was the incision made by metal? What time had the incident taken place? And why on earth had it taken so long to bring me to hospital? Zardo mumbled something about us being well up a trail in the back of beyond, and winked conspiratorially at me. The doctor sighed, rolled her eyes, and gave us a ticking off for being so irresponsible. She used my full name, 'Christopher' not 'Chris' for this process, which by some spooky clairvoyant coincidence was exactly what my mother used to call me when I was in trouble during my formative years. I dealt with this as most men will by hiding behind my fringe and shuffling about in a fit of adolescent embarrassment. I briefly entertained the idea of showing the doctor my picture of the Red-bellied Pitta by way of justification, but the expression on her face made me think better of it.

The orderly approached me with a tray full of what appeared to be mediaeval instruments of torture. He smiled an executioner's smile.

'Your arm is a mess. I have to clean it first. I'm afraid it will hurt.'

I watched him go to work, cleaning the lurid mixture of banana skin, pink antibiotic powder and ragged human tissue with remarkable dexterity. Despite his gentle ministrations he was right; it hurt like hell. After sterilizing the affected area he stuck a large needle into my arm on either side of the gash, and after suggesting I lie down for a few minutes, went off to fetch materials to stitch me back together.

The anaesthetic did its work, and I felt the strange sensation of the two halves of my arm being pulled back together as each stitch was completed. I was also rather enjoying the spectacle of pink elephants circling round my head which it seemed had been provided as a distraction. Zardo was helpfully taking pictures at the far end of the operating table and giggling. After a tetanus shot I was allowed to depart to the cashier's office to settle my account, and from there it was but a few uncertain steps out into the fresh air. Just ten minutes more to the hotel and I could lie down and close my eyes. Bliss.

The jeepney had chosen this very moment to give up the ghost. Our driver and Joey (neither 'Hugh' nor 'You!' as it had turned out) were lying under the engine, surrounded by a collection of filthy vintage engine parts that may well have once belonged to a tractor or possibly a trolleybus. Joey beamed at me.

'No problem! Five minutes!'

An hour later I wandered out to the main road and slumped down on the verge. As my eyes started to close, I became aware of a large dark bird bearing a striking resemblance to a Pterodactyl, comprised of bits of broken, black umbrella. My first thought was that the anaesthetic was even better than I'd thought, but I snapped out of it as I realized what was circling above the treetops. It was a frigatebird. More precisely, an adult female Lesser Frigatebird. It landed out of sight in the canopy of a large broad-leaved tree on the hill above the hospital. A second bird then appeared, but this individual had a ginger head, a sure sign that it was a juvenile.

I staggered back to the jeepney and grabbed my camera, but by the time I was ready to shoot, the birds had settled into their nest and were no longer visible. I scribbled a few notes to make sure that I remembered the birds' plumage details correctly, aware that frigatebird specific identification is by no means straightforward. Zardo confirmed that he had never seen any species of frigatebird in Bislig in the forty years he'd lived in the town. I had found a first for Bislig, and strong evidence that the birds had bred on the mainland, a highly unusual occurrence for a species whose normal home-building takes place on a remote outcrop somewhere offshore. Great news! Clearly I should fall over more often; hospital car parks would become the new biodiversity hotspots, and my reputation would be assured. We celebrated our clean sweep of PICOP's pittas, the frigatebird and my survival that night with the least inedible dish on the Paper Country Inn's menu, Chicken Calderata. Tomorrow was a travel day, so we could relax, while up front our driver did all the hard work, cheating death on our behalf.

Mindanaon drivers are unquestionably highly skilled. It's just that their skills do not necessarily have anything to do with driving. They can probably rustle up five-star cuisine from a few random ingredients, knit imaginative toy animals for their kids from cast-off socks, and recite all the words from *Bohemian Rhapsody* from start to finish.*

---

* Including the tricky bits about a bloke called Bismillah and someone putting aside a devil for someone else.

Nonetheless, despite two flat tyres (the second blow-out fortuitously occurring directly opposite a garage promising *vulcanization services and much much more*) our driver did us proud, and we finally limped into the outskirts of Davao by mid-evening. We had long since tired of counting the tiny roadside stalls selling single mints, sugary twisted rusks, and cigarette lighters which double as eyebrow trimmers for the unwary. The allure of the greengrocers' shops, with their highly polished, artfully constructed grapefruit pyramids had worn thin. Even the food and drink establishments, rejoicing in names such as *'Stopover Jackylynn'* (which I think was a Dexy's Midnight Runners' song title in the eighties) *'Up Town'* and *'Hot Legs'* had failed to win us over as potential patrons.

Davao's streets were enveloped in a mini maelstrom, the dust swirling like green marsh gas in the harsh glare of the streetlights. *A real pea-souper to be sure.* I suddenly felt homesick, and longed for a discarded fish and chip paper to be whisked down Oxford Street before sticking itself immovably to my shin. The traffic ground to a halt, and we were besieged by salesmen dangling bags of oranges in front of our noses. As citrus hawkers go, they were relentless and determined. The lady in the front seat, to whom we had graciously given a lift owing to a family emergency, made a few half-hearted attempts to swat the fruit away, before finally giving in. At least her hospitalized sister would not go short of Vitamin C.

Following a brief tour of a few of Davao City's less salubrious neighbourhoods, we finally located the Hotel Galleria, whose illuminated legend positioned front and centre promised loving attention. *Like a mother to a child, our staff does worry about you.* Given that I had been wearing the same mud-spattered trousers for the best part of a month, I can't say I blamed them. Miraculously, their capitalist instincts triumphed over any sartorial reservations they may have been harbouring, and the doorman greeted me fondly.

'Hello Sir, I am your good friend.'

In time-honoured middle-class fashion, I instantly began to worry that I should have washed behind my ears. Given the driving on the way here, clean underpants in case of an accident would also have been prudent. Should I have brought a gift, or at least a bottle of wine?

We hit the town in search of a restaurant, and since we were in the Philippines, there was really only one option. We ate Vietnamese.

Having ordered freshly made vegetarian spring rolls and some kind of stir-fried concoction involving a large amount of lemongrass and mint, I washed down my painkillers with another swig of beer, and took stock of the year to date. I was into double figures, having seen ten species of pitta in record time. I had missed only one so far, the troublesome Rusty-naped in the ravines of northern Thailand, and could still squeeze in a second bite at that particular cherry. I had cheated death on the trail at PICOP (and had even managed to escape the worst of the doctor's censure for my tardy attendance by telling her that I was writing a book and would make her famous). I had then repeated the trick on Mindanao's roads, where the potential harvest is so great that the grim reaper is rumoured to have set up a permanent office.

There was no doubt about it: I was ahead of the game.

Chapter 6

The Swimming Pool Trail. Southern Vietnam

A beanpole figure bore down on me across the Ho Chi Minh airport concourse. 'Hello Chris! Welcome to Vietnam!'

I had met Richard Craik in Hanoi some years earlier, when he had helped find a driver to get me in and out of Cuc Phuong forest, a few hours' drive south of Vietnam's capital city. Now I was here in Ho Chi Minh, struggling with my bags and with my arm in a sling, but basically in one piece. 'You've been in the wars,' Richard noted sympathetically. I smiled sheepishly and waved my right arm. 'I can still lift my binoculars with this one.'

I had breezed through Vietnamese immigration *('Ah. From Manchester! You United or City?')* and with a similar lack of hold-ups, Richard drove us into town. On the way we exchanged global bird information at top speed. I declined the offer of lunch, having been royally fed on my flights from Davao to Manila and Manila to HCMC.

In any case, this was no time for food, we had urgent business to attend to. Foremost in my mind was the need to catch up on news of the Blue-rumped Pittas at Cat Tien National Park, my home for the next few days. Richard had visited recently, and told me that the Largerstoemia Trail was the best bet. *Would I be able to find it OK?* I wasn't even sure that I could spell it OK, but Richard assured me that the forest wardens knew the trail well and would point me in the right direction. We rendezvoused with my driver, a necessary luxury in Vietnam since it's still not possible for foreigners to rent cars in the country. Khanh spoke no English, but greeted me with a smile that threatened to split his face in two, and off we went, navigating our way through a sea of motorbikes.

We hit Highway One, and I was reacquainted with the comedy potential of the Vietnamese language. This, after all, is a country whose currency is called the *Dong*. As a teenager, like other English kids of the same era, I was exposed to the saucy seaside postcard humour of the Carry On movies, which left an indelible mark. Even now, I have only to mention to my girlfriend that I'm going to put

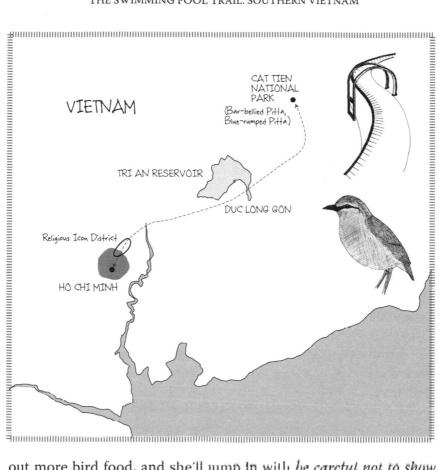

out more bird food, and she'll jump in with *be careful not to show your nuts to the neighbours* before collapsing into fits of innuendo-induced giggles. Sid James has much to answer for. We drove through the Ho Chi Minh suburbs, and I racked up a fine succession of business names: *Duc Lap, Minh Thi, Hai Phat* and so on, but it was the smutty ones that resonated most nostalgically. How could one fail to do business with enterprises bearing the moniker *To Coc*, or better still *Phuc Long*? Why *Carry on up the Mekong* never saw the light of day is beyond me. Within the space of a few short miles though, even my puerile sense of humour was satiated, and having figured out our intended route on the map, I slumped back in my seat and settled down for a serious session of world-watching.

To my mind, one of the true joys of travelling in a foreign country is the number of unexpected sights, sounds and experiences that crop up. I first visited Ho Chi Minh on business in the 1990s, and had spent an hour over dinner outlining my company's products to a potential business partner, a Vietnamese entrepreneur named Vu Quang who spoke no English. Luckily for both of us, his son Vu Bao was studying medicine in the US and was roped in as translator for the evening. After an exhaustive explanation of my company's activities and the respective boons of each of our products, I petitioned Vu Bao to ask his father if there was anything else he would like to know.

The older man considered for a while, and then issued his request to his son. There was a pause, during which the younger man's eyelashes flickered with embarrassment.

'Really, any question is OK' I chipped in, smiling encouragingly.

'My father would like to know...' Vu Bao said slowly, '...why German people don't use toothpicks.'

I thought myself well prepared to answer any question, had brushed up on the technical merits of our key products, and was wholly *au fait* with the commercial potential of the brand. But this question fired in from well beyond left field had me flummoxed.

Nor are such incidents limited to chance remarks. I had once tried to explain to Ian, an ex-pat colleague in Asia, the kind of random travel-trivia that I found so thrilling, the bizarre contradictions that arise from a collision of cultures. At length, the penny dropped.

'Like this place you mean,' he volunteered, with an airy wave of his hand around the Beijing airport bar.

'How do you mean?' I asked.

'It's a no smoking bar sponsored by Marlbro.'

Well exactly.

We drove through a series of grubby districts housing state-run industries dominated by rusting cranes, lumberyards and container depots, before crossing the Dong Nai River. The latter provided a brief vignette of the tourist Vietnam, with its traditional boats steered by pilots in conical straw hats. I could point out that the national headwear in Vietnam makes people look as though they are wearing lampshades, but that would be a bit rich coming from an Englishman whose countrymen regularly wear business hats that resemble inverted washbowls. Not to mention the national guards at Buckingham Palace who each appear to have a Coypu mounted just above their nose.

Vietnamese policemen stood at major intersections dressed in fetching pale orange uniforms with crimson epaulettes, and peaked caps with a single gold star. The latter suggested that I was a guest in what is still an avowedly communist state, though may simply have indicated that they were candidates for 'cadet of the month.' I smiled at their formality, contrasting with my own new found freedom.

Finally, I mused, I was doing what I had dreamed of for so long. No longer a pipe dream fading over the years, whittled down by tax demands and long hours in the office. No more need to network with people you wished would meet a violent end, but at whom you smiled. The thought of escape for many people is fleetingly blissful, but as it recedes, increasingly bitter. Here I was just south of Trang Bom, free to wonder why one moped rider doesn't have a face mask when all his cohorts do. Did he just forget to take it to work with him? Was it lost in a high-speed overtaking manoeuvre? Or was he just a paid up member of the live fast, die young, have a beautiful (if grubby-faced) corpse brigade?

Judging by the evidence I saw before me, a man could indeed find freedom in Vietnam. The freedom to mount a purple cockerel statue on the roof and not have people castigate you. The freedom to have dinner on the street wearing polka-dot pyjamas. How I longed to do that in central London. It would certainly stop the traffic. I passed another dusty, animal-themed, hinterland store, which sold only deer statues, each painted a garish shade of yellow. The roof decoration race hereabouts was clearly intense. *So, Mr. Cockerel-on-the-roof,* I imagined his newly deer-furnished neighbour crowing, *not so cocky now eh?*

We reached a district hosting small private businesses, and I contemplated just how many ornate funeral caskets could be sold in such a poor area. With seven vendors in two blocks, we were clearly passing through the neighbourhood of death.

The funereal trappings gave way to the religious statue zone, where Jesus and the Virgin Mary perched on a pole to advertise the wares of one particular emporium. One rather grand house had a top of the range Jesus model with sunbeams firing out of the anointed one's head. The church next door, in contrast, had no adornments at all. A block along, we passed an immense statue of Jesus with the sunbeam thing going on, and with the addition of a pair of doves on either side. The folks next door were the proud owners of another Jesus-and-Madonna combo. Both with halos. The latter figure's grandeur was somewhat compromised by a stout, once-cream poodle that had paused to urinate on Jesus' robes.

We under-took one last humungous container truck, scattering pedestrians and mopedists into the gutter. (Incidentally for those who are curious, I can confirm that there is no specific motorbike district. Everyone in Vietnam sells motorbikes.) Swerving around the last in a long series of dead dogs (*come to Vietnam, where the dogs are flat and tasty!*) we skirted a final, outlier gravestone store, before the traffic started to thin out. Tiny islands of greenery started to bleed in between the industrial compounds, until trees started to appear. Admittedly they were arrayed in neat rows, serried ranks of monocultural poplars with immaculately symmetrical corridors of light between them, beyond which trucks on a parallel road flickered as they passed, bit-part players in some ancient Lumière Brothers' feature. But they were trees nonetheless.

As we drifted into the countryside, I set about changing the dressings on my injured arm, which had been giving me a few problems. The pain was manageable only when the lower half of my arm was roughly upright, and was thus most comfortable laid diagonally across my chest with my left hand clutching my right shoulder. From certain angles I resembled a tin-pot Latin America dictator executing a newly invented salute. I determined to make the best of this affectation, and added a five-finger wiggle-wave that seemed to amuse and alarm the passers-by in equal measure. I was probably setting back the local tourist industry by at least a decade. The next village, Gia Kiem was populated by a singular lady pedestrian, resplendent in a pair of orange-and-black Mandarin-print silk trousers that would go down a storm in The Drapers Arms in Islington. I made a mental note to track down the source.

We pulled over to stock up on provisions. Shamefully I ignored the bags of fresh local produce displayed outside: dried tamarinds, glutinous sticky rice, and mandarin oranges, each with a single, perfect, bright green leaf attached. Mindful of an early trip to Thailand when, in a spirit of adventurousness, I had allowed my hosts to purchase the snacks with the result that I spent two days picking shreds of dried cuttlefish out of my teeth, I took charge and rushed headlong into the air-conditioned interior. I bought Malaysian dark rum, a litre bottle of coke, and a large packet of strawberry Oreo cookies. Synthetic, imported, and known quantities all.

Over a cup of coffee strong enough to keep a small army alert for a month, my driver and I compared scars (motorbike accident versus trail fall). I was the clear winner in the freshness stakes, and there was no doubt that Khanh was victorious in terms of scale, a livid scar running from his wrist to his elbow, legacy of a crash a few years earlier. We continued our journey, turning off Highway One, slicing our way through stands of towering bamboo and undernourished shrubs. It was the end of the dry season, and everything was coated in a thick layer of dust. Withered banana leaves lined the roadside, so desiccated, brittle and blackened I was sure they would crackle and fall apart at the slightest touch.

We cut across the southeast corner of the huge Tri An reservoir, but as expected it was a hundred percent duckless. (In Vietnamese, *Duc Long Gon*.) A fisherman paddled his rough wooden boat towards a distant lakeside shack-on-stilts, a baby crawling in the prow. An entire village appeared to be living within two metres of the waterline, and considerably closer to the breadline. A pig stared forlornly from its cage strapped to the back of a motorbike trailer, cognisant of the fact that his ride was destined to be a one-way trip. We passed through another tiny town whose youth squatted in cinderblock internet gaming dens, staring fixedly at the screen, their hands white-knuckle tense, toes curled in a rictus against their flip-flops. I looked up at one such establishment's entrance sign. It was called *Kaka-net*. Kenneth Williams, this country needs you. *These wan, callow young people should be out in the fresh air*, I thought to myself, *buying inflatable rhinos-on-sticks* (choice of colours available) *or working their statue stonemason apprenticeships*. Or perhaps they should have been out playing with the fluorescent orange bird-shaped kites that filled the skies in these parts, a sad reminder that most of the flesh-and-feather birds they replaced had ended up in the pot.

I cheered myself with the thought that I was headed for an oasis. Nam Bai Cat Tien is an impeccably run reserve, staffed by a team of wardens who care about the avian and animal charges that flourish under their protection, a state that is all too rare in southeast Asia.

We passed the last thatched-roof, hammock-strewn cafés with their chipped, glass-fronted food displays, their unidentifiable contents slowly congealing in the heat, and reached the end of the road. I grabbed my bag, thanked Khanh profusely, and paid the ferryman, who for a couple of dollars whisked me across the river into Cat Tien. My forest shack booking for one person/four nights had transmogrified into one for four people/one night, but a little one-armed gesticulating and note-scribbling sorted things out. I went to war on the wildlife population in my room (several million mosquitoes, one frog and an unnervingly large spider) but let the geckos be. I've learned over the years that geckos are our friends. They are quite capable of eating their own body weight in insects in a single night, and thus are a useful ally to have around. After all, it's a jungle out there.

I prepared the sacred libation. The Malaysian rum duly measured out (noticeably less orange than the Filipino version, an unpretentious little number with not much in the way of a complex follow through but perfectly palatable) I cradled my chipped plastic glass in both hands and considered the challenge ahead. Three full days and one extra morning to work the forest, two pittas to find.

I figured that the numerous and delightfully responsive Bar-bellied Pittas should not prove too difficult, since their over-enthusiastic territorial behaviour means that one can catch a glimpse of them as they come hurtling at you across the forest floor. But then there was the shy and potentially awkward Blue-rumped Pitta to be considered. A taciturn creature, the Blue-rump keeps itself to itself, occasionally muttering a woefully soft and abrupt *'powwk.'* Or (when overexcited on a Friday night out with the lads) a fractionally louder but almost equally terse *'wheerp.'*

Blue-rumped Pittas and I had some prior history. I spent four days at *Cuc Phuong* in northern Vietnam in 2007 being run ragged by them, and in the end only managed to see one by scaling a vertical limestone cliff. I didn't fancy my chances of connecting in three short days, since this early in the year they would be even less talkative than usual. I was up against it, and if I missed Blue-rumped here, I'd be forced to return to Vietnam in May. More expenditure, more hours of my life irretrievably lost in the Vietnamese embassy in London, and another week at least to squeeze into a tight schedule. I didn't have the time, and I certainly didn't have the money. I couldn't afford to fail.

The first day did not go well. I walked the Largerstroemia trail. Twice. In both directions. I saw lots of Largerstroemias (enormous hardwood trees with pock-marked bark, textured like hand-beaten pots on a coppersmith's last). I did not, however, see any pittas. The next day my luck changed, and at dawn I heard a Bar-bellied Pitta close by.

'*Kwa-wee-waaah;*' a noise like a squeaky toy that has just been trodden on.

I sat motionless, checking every inch of the forest floor for movement. The bird called again, closer this time, and I caught the faintest hint of movement in my peripheral vision. I homed in on the spot, but the bird had already moved. Then a clearer movement, already ten yards to the right, and a blurred splash of colour, half-hidden behind a tangle of evergreen shrubs. The bird called again, before sneaking across to the next patch of cover. I had it.

Bar-bellied is perhaps the most subtly beautiful of all the pittas, a vision in pastel blues and greens, with fine black and yellow bars on the flanks. And this individual was recklessly, wonderfully careless. It crept onward, dappled by shards of sunlight that had somehow found their way through the canopy above, and I was able to predict where it would next be visible. I had outmanoeuvred the enemy, and as the shutter clicked I knew I had my precious image. The Bar-bellied Pitta had fallen. Species number eleven was metaphorically nailed to a trophy plaque on my drawing room wall.

The rest of the day was spent hunting Blue-rumps, and though I heard one distantly in forest well up the road, I was never within a country mile of securing a view. While searching, I saw four more Bar-bellied Pittas and heard others. Had these ebullient, brash, boastful pittas driven the unassuming Blue-rumps out of the best territories? Or were the Blue-rumps lurking in the deepest recesses of the forest? I knew that Blue-rumps were in the habit of calling once and then shutting up indefinitely. Ten minutes after hearing one call, the bird could be a hundred metres away in the forest and thus one hundred percent invisible, or it could be standing just behind your heel and still one hundred percent invisible. There was just no way of knowing. Were birds responding to tape and coming in silently? Or were they steadfastly ignoring their pursuer and going about their daily business of tearing the heads off earthworms?

I personally believe Blue-rumped Pittas are able to travel through space-time. Or perhaps they dig tunnels underground with tiny, pitta-sized shovels in order to move around the forest undetected. After twelve long hours in the field however, I was no nearer being able to solve such mysteries. It was all very frustrating. I meandered back down the main jeep track, watching the nest-building activities of a pair of Black-and-red Broadbills, a species that appears to be made of deep purple velvet. They were hard at work, gripping bundles of tiny sticks in their wide-based bills, which shone a luminous blue. Flights of Red-rumped Swallows and *Treron* green-pigeons drifted overhead towards their roost sites, framed against a sunset that glowed the deepest shade of pink.

In the evening I adjourned to the forest lodge canteen, ordering food randomly from the menu in what was unquestionably poor Vietnamese. Spicy catfish was on the menu, but was unavailable. Since I didn't fancy the pigs trotters, I settled for something approximating to chicken.

I struck up a conversation with a couple of fellow diners, two Dutch birders Hans and Mario, who were as well qualified in the insane bird-geek department as I was. They were supremely well organised, as all Dutch birders seem to be. They had lists of all the birds they wanted to see, and were up to date with the very latest splits decreed by the scientific fraternity. They were also tooled up with audio clips of every creature they might conceivably encounter, and we compared bird-songs, to the bemusement of the non-birding patrons around us. They introduced me to a quiet but friendly Californian, Troy Shortell. Troy was birding his way around the hotspots of Asia after quitting his high-powered job as a major US corporation's 'Man in China.' He dug out pictures of his three daughters, and we 'oohed' and 'aahed' over his gorgeous girls. We learned that the girls' names had been chosen after consultation with a professional Chinese namer, an authority who had given one of the girls a moniker that translated as *'the swallow that soars at dawn.'* There is, it seems, no area of a birder's life into which avian influence may not creep...but we had to admit, it was a beautiful name.

Ignoring the hilariously dubbed B-movie playing on the cobwebbed TV set in the corner, we talked late into the evening. We traded backgrounds, swapped tales of close encounters with snakes, but mostly compared our respective world lists. Who had seen the killer species that would grip the others off? Who had dipped on ridiculously easy birds and must therefore be publicly humiliated? Who had still not seen the commonest of the flameback woodpeckers (that would be Mario) and thus must be teased mercilessly for the rest of the night... Such are the means by which birders' class structures are defined.

Before giving up the day job. The author as a fresh-faced youth on
his first business trip to Kuala Lumpur, Malaysia.

London snow on the first day of the mission, February 2nd.

The Emerald Pool, Khao Nor Chuchi, S. Thailand.

A Blyth's Frogmouth with gravy on its shirt-front.

The only Gurney's Pitta that's easy to see at Khao Nor Chuchi.

Yothin Meekao wearing a gift from the author;
a London Marathon winner's medal.

Lesser Mouse Deer, Kaeng Krachan
(Yorkshire Terrier not available for size comparison).

The 'precious downtime' view at Kaeng Krachan, C. Thailand.

The gully that was home for five days at Doi Chiang Dao, N. Thailand.
Note the complete absence of Rusty-naped Pittas.

Spirit House, Doi Chiang Dao, N. Thailand.
I reversed the rental car into it, thus bringing bad luck.

A smiling Aquilino Escobar, Tuguegarao Airport, Luzon, N. Philippines.

The victorious Mt Hamut team (L-R middle row: Joy Escobar, Brendan Sloan, Aquilino, Scott Lin, Quenilyn Escobar (kneeling), CG, Wu Jian-Long, Wayne Hsu).

Camp 2, Mt Hamut, N. Luzon.

The view from the ridge, Mt Hamut.

Zardo Goring, PICOP, Mindanao, S. Philippines.

The illegal logging continues at PICOP
(Note the mid-size trees, all the large hardwoods already having been felled).

Our jeepney, 'The Seventh Seal' at PICOP…

…with 'God Help Us' and penguin sticker interior décor.

The Vietnam crew at Cat Tien NP.
(L-R: CG, Troy Shortell, Hans Meijer, Mario Renden)

The ferry across to Cat Tien, S. Vietnam.

The Keeper of the Grove, Mawphlang, NE India. Where the tea comes from.

Golden Bush-robin sporting
Bladerunner eye makeup, Lumswer
Sacred Grove, NE India.

Ibisbill, briefly abandoning
its disguise as a boulder.
Nameri, NE India

Indian Elephant coming to investigate the jeep, Kaziranga, NE India.

The White-winged Duck at Nameri. Very rare, very farmyard…

The elusive Rail-babbler, showing off its balloons at Taman Negara,
Peninsular Malaysia.

My three new friends had hired a jeep to ferry them up to Heaven's Rapids ten miles to the north at dawn the following day, and they ganged up on me in an attempt to persuade me to go. It would mean one precious pitta-hunting morning wasted, and would heap greater pressure on finding the Blue-rump in the twenty-four hours that remained, but I was tempted. They continued to torment me, painting a scenario in which I would spend two days looking for the damn pitta and see nothing. They would return, relating thrilling tales of how they had scored both of the park's specialities, the extremely scarce Orange-necked Partridge *and* the equally endangered Pale-headed Woodpecker. The pressure grew too great, and their sales talk too sweet. I caved in and agreed to meet them at HQ at first light.

I woke at four, my slumber disturbed by some kind of moth-beast with clacking wing-beats. Pulling on damp trousers, I donned my head-torch and stuck my head outside to examine the laundered sock collection that I had hung out on the front porch in a foolish attempt to dry it overnight. It was still soaking wet, and had been commandeered by a stick insect. Still sleep-drugged, I idly wondered what would happen to a stick insect if you gave it a massage. Venturing into the bathroom, I discovered it had flooded during the night. I turned on the cold water tap, delighted to register not even the faintest electric shock, shooed the gecko out of the wash basin, and removed the ants from my toothbrush.

At Cat Tien's administrative centre Troy, Hans and Mario were already in the jeep, and I squeezed in, jamming my knees against the restraining bar to avoid an earlier-than-planned, involuntary exit. We sped up to Heaven's Rapids, scattering blizzards of butterflies from roadside pools and almost mowing down a strutting flock of Siamese Fireback pheasants. In no time at all we were walking slowly through the bamboo, scanning for movement as we went.

A few minutes in we hit a big bird wave, and spent a happy hour combing through the flock, picking out gems amongst the commoner birds. Dusky Broadbills thumped around overhead. Their pied plumage and aggressive demeanour made me think of nightclub bouncers flexing their muscles before the punters arrive. Metallic-winged Sunbirds flashed to and fro, their iridescent plumage catching the sunlight. An Emerald Dove belted past us down the trail, a blaze of wine-pink and green, late for some unmissable appointment.

An array of woodpeckers shuffled their way up and down the huge Largerstroemias, chiselling through the papery bark to winkle out juicy morsels. We picked out two Laced Woodpeckers, a pair of massive White-bellieds, a female Heart-spotted, a tiny Grey-capped, and a dowdy Rufous Woodpecker. To Mario's delight we also found a Common Flameback, the trash woodpecker we had teased him about the night before. After a panicky description of which bough the beast was inching along, Mario got onto it, and a typically forthright exhibition of Dutch joy followed our collective congratulations. This was, in birder's parlance, certainly a *tart's tick*, but it was a tick nonetheless; a new bird for Mario's life list.

The one woodpecker missing from the woodchippers' ball was of course, the very one we had come to see: the rare and retiring Pale-headed Woodpecker. This was no surprise, for we knew the bird was unlikely to join a mixed flock, preferring to spend its days in solitary fashion amongst the denser clumps of bamboo. However, we did not have long to wait. I played audio a hundred yards further up the trail, and a Pale-headed came screaming in, screeching at us and demanding to know where we had hidden his rival. We managed a few brief flight views, piecing together an image of a dark rufous woodpecker with a sickly, yellow-green face and a pale bill, before the animated 'pecker disappeared back the way he had come. The bird activity dropped off as the temperature started to climb, and by nine a.m. it was scorching hot. The partridges failed to put in an appearance, but we passed the time photographing butterflies, and snickering at the antics of a Grey-cheeked Tit-babbler. The long walk back was enlivened by the appearance of two Tickell's Blue-flycatchers, and by Troy's rapid trouser removal to remove a particularly adventurous leech. As we approached the jeep track we relaxed and reflected on a good morning's work. A female White-throated Rock-thrush, a scarce bird anywhere, rounded things off nicely, and we climbed back on board well pleased with our excursion, despite the total lack of pittas.

Back at the canteen, an hour spent dawdling over lunch allowed me to consider my options, and I began to fret. Troy, Hans and Mario left to go in search of a Green Peafowl in the grasslands to the south, and even though I had never seen a peafowl, I could ill afford to spend any more time on anything except the pitta. I had less than twenty-four hours left to find a Blue-rump, and so far had failed to get anywhere near one. Things were looking bleak, and I began to regret my headstrong decision to accompany the others, thereby wantonly wasting the whole of one of my precious mornings. How could I have been so reckless? Despondent, I struck up a conversation with one of the local guides, who listened patiently before throwing me a lifeline. A Belgian bird-watcher had reported seeing a Blue-rump ten days ago on the trail by the rubbish tip. I scribbled down directions, thanked the guide, and hot-footed it to the dump.

I should at this juncture reiterate that bird-watchers are used to looking for birds in the world's least appetising locations. Landfill sites for flocks of wintering gulls, derelict bomb-damaged buildings for breeding Black Redstarts, even sewage works, which are invariably the best place to find congregations of wading birds; all are grist to the bird-nerd's mill. I once went birding with a group of fellow twitchers in an immense 'water treatment facility' in Arizona, where we watched a flock of Wilson's Phalaropes, a delicate American wader. It was blowing a gale, and brown scum from the settling beds whipped against our legs, flecking us with brown froth until our group resembled an unsavoury cappuccino. The stench was indescribable. As we left the plant, one of the ladies in the group volunteered that she had never been birding in such a disgusting place in her entire life. One of the young birders looked at her curiously.

'But...a flock of Wilson's...in breeding plumage...'

He allowed his sentence to hang in the air, the clear implication being that it was the lady in question who had lost her marbles, not the rest of us who had just spent an hour being plastered with shit in order to stare through our telescopes at a few distant birds we had all seen before.

At the dump the last of the day's rotting refuse had just been loaded onto the fire. It reeked in that sickening, over-ripe manner that only vegetable scrapings and discarded pig fat left to stew in the tropical heat for a few hours can reek. I wrapped my sweat towel around my face and pressed on. I played pitta calls. I checked every corner of the dump, the nearby pig pen and the trash forest around them. Nothing. I cursed the guide who had sent me up this blind alley, and headed back to the main jeep track. There was no decent habitat here either, just trash bamboo and rattan scrub. Surely no self-respecting pitta would be caught dead in forest like this. Nonetheless, as I trudged back to the HQ, I thought I might as well play the odd bit of audio, just in case any adolescent pittas had wandered across to the poor side of town. Fifty metres up the track, I pulled out my portable speaker and let rip. To my utter astonishment a Blue-rumped Pitta immediately called, and from a spot not far in from the forest edge. I looked at the cover in front of me; dense, impenetrable, with nothing even resembling a trail to grant me access.

I crawled on my hands and knees through the rattan, silently cursing every barbed thorn as it tore flesh from my neck and arms. I selected the younger more supple branches and delicately snapped each one to forge a way, figuring that young green growths would make less noise. After twenty minutes I had covered thirty metres of ground, and could see clear forest floor in front of me, lightly carpeted with dropped bamboo leaves. I hid behind a rattan bush and played a single snippet of audio. Again, the pitta called back, 'cowk', almost imperceptibly soft and even more truncated than usual, but I knew it was close. What to do? I knew playing further imitations of the bird's call was likely to be fruitless, and may even drive the pitta away. If I moved, the bird would surely see me and vanish. So I waited. And then I waited some more. After which, I executed the immaculate strategy of waiting a bit longer.

Forty minutes went by. The pain in my crossed legs grew, and I was desperate to scratch my nose. My arms ached from holding my binoculars just below my chin, so that if the bird appeared it would require the absolute minimum of movement to bring the lenses up to my eyes. The leeches had found me, but I let them inch their way up my legs unmolested. Mosquitoes buzzed joyfully around my head. I ignored them all, and sat unmoving in an uncomfortable, sweaty, but I hoped, largely invisible heap on the forest floor.

Thunder rumbled above my head. It must be past four, time for the daily downpour. The pitta may well have been half a mile away by now, but as far as I was concerned the forest rangers would have to come and pick up my sun-bleached remains in a month's time. It had become a battle of wills, and I was not about to give in. Just as I started to question my new tactics, I sensed a presence close by on my right hand side. My eyes flicked to the spot, and found only gently swaying bamboo, teased into movement by the wind that presaged the coming rain. A sixth sense kicked in though, and told me something else, something animal, was there. My eyes told me otherwise, but I knew I was right.

From behind the rattan clump, a plump little bird emerged with a silent bound. It turned its head towards me, apparently as astonished to see me as I was to see it. I instantly knew what it was. I had seen this same rotund little animal in Cuc Phuong two years earlier, and the delicate combination of cobalt blue nape, lime-green back and warm orange underparts belonged to only one creature on earth. It was a Blue-rumped Pitta. I slowly moved my Leicas up to my eyes. A neat dark line ran through the eye, curving downwards latterly as it stretched towards the nape. The cheeks were fawn-coloured, dusted with pink, the bill blackish, paler at the tip. The legs were strikingly pale, the feet a similar shade, claws tightly gripping the leaf-litter beneath. I smiled, and perhaps this tiny facial movement persuaded the bird I was not to be trusted. It swivelled through 180°, and in a single bound, disappeared back behind the clump.

I was undeterred. There was no escape route the bird could take without me seeing it. The rattan clump in which it had taken shelter was isolated, the forest floor clearly visible on either side. Whichever way it went I would see it leave. I waited for another ten minutes. The bird did not reappear. I crawled in on hands and knees, holding my breath, the sweat dripping off my nose. I slithered beneath the thorn bushes and right up to the clump, until I was so close I could smell the rank soil in which it had taken root. Nothing. Incredulous, I peered round the back of the bush. It did not seem possible, but there was no doubting the facts. The pitta had done a bunk. I parted the stems of the shrub, just in case the bird had somehow hidden between them. Still nothing. I sat back on my haunches and tried to figure it out. The only possibility was that the bird had calculated the angle of retreat necessary to keep the tiny shrub between us at all times, and had absconded into the forest some ten metres behind. It demonstrated an animal intelligence and spatial awareness I thought unlikely in a bird blessed with such a small skull. Staggering.

Nonetheless, that one lax moment in which the bird had decided to stray into view was etched into my memory. After days of fruitless scanning, a manoeuvre executed with military precision had paid off, and I had my prize. I had spent hours hunting in pristine, primary rainforest, while all the time it seemed, the Blue-rumps were hugging the road, subsisting in trash forest just yards from the park staff going about their everyday business. I'd invested an immense amount of time in trawling the decent habitat, while the pittas sniggered behind my back in the dross. I felt like a private dick who'd scoured the city looking for a missing person in the finest hotels, when the fugitive was holed up in a dive bar on the wrong side of the tracks. Typical.

I swaggered back out of the forest down the newly created trail that I had worked so hard to fashion. I decided that the trail needed a name, but first I needed to attend to the pressing matter of finding shelter. Lightning crackled above me, and it began to rain with a vengeance. In seconds I was thoroughly soaked, and I ran for cover in the disused lido opposite. Sheltering under the eaves, I gazed at the elemental power of the storm. I wrote *BLUE-RUMPED PITTA!* in capitals in my notebook. And then underlined it. I drew a really poor picture of it in the top corner. I talked to the large toad hopping enthusiastically along the tessellated interior of the empty swimming pool, commenting happily on the downpour and how great it was that it was raining hard enough to corrugate the tops of our heads. The toad croaked his agreement before continuing on his way, despatching a few of the less observant water beetles as he went.

The rain showed no sign of abating, and I was in a state. My trousers were moulded around my legs, water ran into my boots. A bloated leech fed on my neck. I pulled it off, blood running freely down onto my shoulder as the anti-coagulant excreted by the little darling went to work. My phone, saturated to its core, was stuck in an endless reboot cycle, its main board doubtless shorted in numerous places. My iPod Touch, the vital piece of kit for playing imitations of birds' calls to bring them into view, had switched itself off and refused to be resuscitated.

I made a dash for the canteen, and squelched up the steps waving my one good arm. The heavily pregnant proprietress giggled at my drenched, bloodied appearance, but brought the celebratory beer without delay, and admired the picture of the Blue-rumped Pitta in my field guide.

'You see pitta?' she enquired.

'Damn right,' I said. 'On the Swimming Pool Trail.'

Chapter 7

One Cup of Tea? Northeast India

The mechanic sucked his teeth.

'Costya' he sang, before launching into a technical explanation of how the bearings were shot, and how the diffuser that fed air from the Wankel rotary engine to the carburettor was heavily corroded and needing replacing. Or something like that. My week in England was turning out to be considerably more expensive than I had hoped, but I needed that precious piece of paper embossed with the letters 'M.O.T.' I nodded my assent and went in search of tea while the work was completed.

I had spent a busy few days updating the pittasworld blog, replacing my rain-washed iPod, catching up on correspondence, reminding my long-suffering girlfriend what I looked like, and boring my friends into a stupor with slide shows of the birds I had seen. But I was already restless to be back in the rainforest, and the days were slipping by. So it was that twenty-four hours later I found myself immersed in the chaos outside the international airport terminal in India's capital city, New Delhi.

I had forty-five minutes to get to the domestic terminal, a journey that I had been warned would take at least an hour. In the end I managed to share a taxi with a posh adolescent who had just completed a three-month 'Grand Tour' of India, and an Irish lady who worked for Pepsi and was on her way to visit a bottling plant in Guangdong, China. We swapped experiences as our heroic, moustachioed driver wove in and out of the jams, dodging trucks, mopeds and cows, his rear-view mirror religious icons swinging as we lurched around the corners. He deposited us in a dusty heap right outside the terminal, and I shouted hurried thanks over my shoulder as I sprinted to the check-in desk with minutes to spare. The clerk looked at my ticket, looked at the clock, glanced up at my sweaty, fretting face and flipped a boarding card across the desk towards me.

'You'd better hurry' he said. 'The flight closes in four minutes.'

I stopped to buy a bottle of water on the way to the gate, a delay

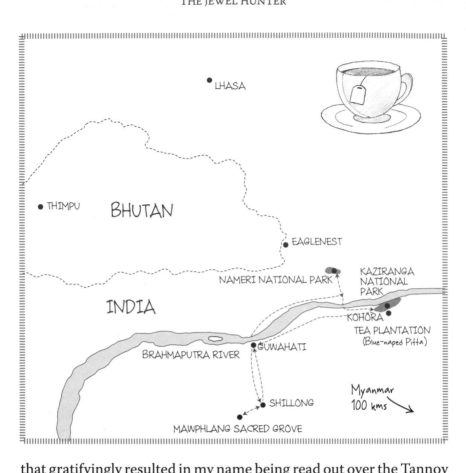

that gratifyingly resulted in my name being read out over the Tannoy as a straggler. The security check was not the most thorough (if you can't find a litre bottle of water with those machines perhaps it's time for an upgrade?) but the staff were at least aware that the flight was about to depart, and bundled me onto a bus, which grumbled its way across the apron, delivering me to the plane seconds before they closed the doors. I had made it, and would be able to rendezvous with my driver in Guwahati as planned. Had I missed the flight, I would have been stuck in Delhi overnight, and subsequently would have had no way to get to Kaziranga. We flew east, and two hours later touched down at Guwahati's ramshackle airport in the state of Assam. Where the tea comes from.

India is big, really big. It covers a mind-boggling 3·3 million square kilometres, which places it second on the list in Asian terms; only China is bigger. It also comes second to China in population terms, with a scant billion or so souls crammed between its borders.

Actually a billion is a rounded estimate, the true figure is one billion, sixty five million and change, so by rounding down I excluded a section of the populace roughly equivalent to the population of the UK. Large parts of the country are given over to agricultural production, and tea is the most important plantation crop. India is the world's single largest producer of the stuff, which means there are a lot of plantations. Many of them are in hill forest where the production of other crops is uneconomical, but the fertile edges of the Brahmaputra floodplains are also ideal for tea farming. As a result, the state of Assam is one of the cornerstones of India's domination of the world's tea markets.

So why the brief digression into economic geography? Well as an Englishman, I thought I knew a thing or two about this most revered of hot beverages before I went out to India. Now I know that I am not worthy to hold the non-business end of the Assam people's tea strainer. It's common knowledge that the Chinese invented the stuff roughly one billion years BC, but really, the Indians are the ones who have perfected the tea-making process. Tea in Assam is a religion. Make no mistake, these people know what they are about. They are tea-ninjas. As a UK Northerner I pride myself on being a genetic recipient of the finest tea-preparing skills. In my house when I were a lad, our Mam would serve the tea, and essential techniques were passed down through t' generations. So in a spirit of proselytizing fervour, here's the (tea) scoop:

A list of important things to consider when making a proper British cup of tea

- *As with most of the culinary arts, ingredients are important. Use fresh water, not stuff that has been lying in the kettle for three days. Likewise, use good quality tea. At all costs, avoid the no-brand, super-cheap, size-of-a-house boxes from your local supermarket. You may as well use sawdust. I recommend also avoiding the following:*
  Earl Grey. Girls' tea that stinks of lavender. Dreadful stuff.
  Lapsang Souchong a.k.a. 'Chinese Porky Tea.'
  Peppermint. A crime against humanity.
  Sencha. Sounds like 'Ganja' and looks a bit like it too.
  Apparently.

- *Always use a teapot. Making tea for one directly into the mug simply won't do. Like you and me, tea needs space to breathe. Indulge it.*

- *Make sure the water is truly boiling (not boiled) before allowing it to come into contact with the tea. If the water is not 100°C when it hits the tea, flavour will not be released from the leaves.*

- *Put the tea into the pot. Add the water to the tea, not the tea to the water.*

- *NEVER put the milk in first, see note above re: temperature. For heaven's sake, is this the first time you've been allowed to handle the sacred leaf?*

- *If forced at gunpoint to use a tea bag rather than the real thing, never, ever, cause the tea to release flavour by jiggling it about (a process referred to by a former colleague as 'disco dancing the bag.') Tea is too important to be hurried or mistreated. Show some respect.*

- *Leave the tea in the pot for two to five minutes depending how strong you like it. Don't overdo it though. 'Stewing' is a capital offence.*

- *Once the tea has been poured out, serve immediately. Don't leave the tea in the pot and then use up the dregs half an hour later. That's just plain dirty my friend, and besides, the tea will be bitter beyond belief.*

- *Don't forget the chocolate Hobnobs. Or at a pinch, e.g. during wartime rationing, Jammy Dodgers. If you're in an Asian rainforest, strawberry Oreos are an acceptable substitute.*

Assam is almost as far north as you can go in India before it stops being India and starts being Bhutan or Tibet, and is almost as far east as you can go before it starts being Myanmar. Only Arunachal Pradesh is more remote, and I would be travelling to the southern edge of the latter state during the next few days. First however,

---

Footnote: Never, ever, order a cup of tea in America, it will only make you unhappy. The US is the only nation to have gone from primitivism to technology without ever learning how to make tea.

we had to get to the town of Kohora. Having loaded my gear into the jeep, Basu and Hoon who were to alternate as my drivers and companions for the next eight days fired up the engine, and we joined the cavalcade of trucks heading east.

As darkness fell we crossed the mighty Brahmaputra, following the river through Mangaldai, Kharupati, Dhekiajuli. Each successive village was a study in miniature chaos, with cows wandering freely about the streets and the occasional truck lying prone on its side gasping its last, its cargo scattered across the road like a slain oxen's guts. Out in the countryside the darkness was absolute, and the scenery emerged piecemeal from the dust-filled night, looming in front of us before disappearing back into the swirling void. I stared out at the gaily painted trucks, each bearing public safety messages on their mudflaps. *Use your horn!* (as if anyone in India needed any encouragement) and (on the overtaking side) *Good Luck!*

Driving is a dangerous game in India. It's a little known fact that Darwin came up with the central 'survival of the fittest' tenet of his theory of evolution after studying the rush hour in Delhi. I noted down the details of the numerous road safety signs dotted along Assam's highways: *No race, no hell. Don't gossip, let him drive. Don't mix sleeping and driving. No hurry, no worry.* Effective but rather lacking in imagination I felt, and I began to dream up my own. *Drive with care, be goat-aware. Slow down now, holy cow. Speed through town, upside-down.* And (the potentially seminal) *Roadkill winner: chicken dinner.* The last one admittedly may need a little work.

Every now and then, barefoot children materialised out of the darkness, guiding their animals back home by administering a sharp smack on the rump with a homemade switch. A few were overseen by groups of ladies in sequinned saris, glimmering like fish under moonlight. As we neared Tezpur we had to brake sharply to avoid two domesticated elephants in the road, their monstrous derrières swaying beneath their cargo of bamboo.

We stopped off for sticky-sweet tea and aromatic samosas at a roadside teahouse, the walls emblazoned with hand-painted motifs, each featuring a snarling Tiger. Back on the road and with an hour to go, Basu and Hoon decided some entertainment was in order, and blasted me with a compilation CD relayed by the in-bus stereo system. The favoured style appeared to be something of a cultural hybrid. Imagine The Pussycat Dolls' *Don't you wish your girlfriend was hot like me* meets Hindi dance music and you're halfway there. As we drove through the night, I noticed a building belonging to the 'Forest Beat Officer.' He's presumably the guy who puts the dance mixes together.

After a six hour journey we arrived in Kohora late in the evening, and I lost no time in beating a path to the reception area at the Jupuri Ghar Lodge, an up-and-coming if budget establishment just south of the Kaziranga National Park. As I unpacked my things I studied a notice outlining the rules of the house, most of which concerned themselves with decorous behaviour. Another banned the use of firearms while under the influence of alcohol. One less thing to worry about then.

The staff had waited patiently for my arrival and served dinner on the patio, a fine selection of curried meats, vegetable side dishes and naan breads. I had lost seven kilos during the mission so far, and it seemed entirely possible that I would put them all back on during my brief stay in India. The primary house rule soon became glaringly evident: *do not, under any circumstances, try to do anything for yourself.* Even readjusting the tableware in some minor way would bring a waiter scurrying over to check that everything was just so. As someone who has lived in London for the last ten years, I found this level of attentive and considerate service to be vaguely terrifying, since even something as simple as obtaining a glass of water in a London restaurant may best be achieved by poking a hole in the roof during a downpour.

Hoon was there to meet me at first light the next morning, and our destination was, where else, a tea plantation. Specifically the neatly manicured environs of the Kaziranga Tea Plantation, twenty minutes drive south of the park itself. The lone species I had come all this way to find was the Blue-naped Pitta, and it was one of what I had dubbed 'The Big Five.' These were the pittas that were the hardest to see, but were also the ones that were possible to locate in only a very narrow time-window. In most cases, this was because they were impossible to find when not calling, and thus needed to be seen during the month prior to the start of their breeding season. During this period, males would be calling frequently to defend their territories and to attract potential mates. I knew that the Blue-naped Pitta was just such a bird, and that if I didn't find it in late March/early April, my quest to see all the species in a year would be over almost before it had begun.

During my time in India, I met a local guide named Rafiq, who had been showing people birds in Assam and the neighbouring states of Meghalaya and Nagaland for a number of years. I asked him how many times he had seen Blue-naped Pitta outside the pre-breeding season period. He thought for a while, rubbing the back of his head to assist the cogitative process, before eventually responding.

'Never.'

No pressure then. I had arranged with Hoon that I would spend my entire stay looking for the pitta if necessary, but that if I were lucky enough to see it quickly I would travel around to see other birds. If I was to avoid spending an inordinate amount of my time in India lost in a sea of tea bushes, I needed to find the bird pronto.

The three best places to find a Blue-naped Pitta in Assam are the Tea Gardens, a remnant area of woodland known as Panbari Forest, and the eastern sector of the Kaziranga National Park itself. The latter site is highly unreliable, since visitors are not allowed out of the jeeps for fear of being killed by one of the many wild animals that roam around the flood plains. Elephants pose by far the greatest danger, followed by Water Buffalo and, famously, the Tigers. The Panbari Forest was a good spot, but the fact that the cover throughout was extremely dense and the pittas low density lessened the likelihood of a sighting. The Tea Gardens were by far my best shot, so my search began there.

Pittas and tea may seem like an unlikely combination; most pittas after all live in primary rainforest. Blue-napes, however, like bamboo, and at Kaziranga the tea estate is surrounded on all sides by steep-sided, bamboo-filled, leech-infested ravines. It's always bloody ravines. I thought of my unsuccessful vigil in Thailand. My heart sank at the thought of another extended stay in boggy, snake-riddled ditches. The odd spot of ravine-dwelling seemed inevitable, but I had been assured that the pittas would come out of the ravines to feed beneath the tea bushes. It all sounded rather civilised. Perhaps to complete the picture I should have asked for some cucumber sandwiches with the crusts removed.

As I cleared the top of the ridge at the entrance to the plantation however, it immediately became clear that seeing the birds in the tea or anywhere else was going to be no picnic. The tea-bushes were so tightly packed together that it was impossible for the most part to force a way between them. Hence they offered one hundred percent cover to any small creatures sheltering beneath. The crop stretched away to the horizon. Only three or four paths led through the entire estate. The one ray of hope was that every fifty metres or so, a narrow channel had been cut through the tea to allow the teams of ladies who pick the crop to gain access to the leaves that were ready for harvest. I knew though, that Blue-napes had a wicked reputation as extreme skulkers, and that the chances of catching one in the act of nipping across one of these open channels were slim. I had my work cut out.

Hoon and I had walked no more than ten yards when we heard a pitta, and the volume of its call clearly indicated that it was not very far away. We dropped to the floor to make sure we were less of a threat to the bird, if by some miracle it should be out in the open further up the path. Our prone position also facilitated an unobstructed view of the sub-tea terrain. *This is clearly the required technique,* I thought to myself. The tea bushes were knee-high, green-topped and wiry, their gnarled and twisted tiny trunks surprisingly sturdy. Since tea bushes have little vegetation at ground level, one could see in for a few metres under the foliage. If I could just persuade a pitta to come within range... We waited in silence for thirty minutes, but the bird fell silent and never materialised. We played the tape. The pitta ignored us. Over the next six hours we heard another pitta on the other side of the path, and a third calling from one of the ravines further up. A fourth called from the opposite ravine, and a fifth way off in the distance. We never came close to seeing any of them. The bird's unaccommodating reputation began to seem thoroughly justified.

After another immense curry lunch, we stopped off at the Panbari forest, but a cold front had swept in, and the unceasing rain and surprisingly fresh breeze put paid to any hopes we might have entertained of finding a pitta at the site. We drove back to the Tea Gardens and returned to the fray. An hour before dusk a bird began calling from a ravine close to the estate entrance. We played it cautiously, lying on our bellies under the tea bushes. The bird appeared responsive. After half an hour's work though, the bird suddenly stopped calling. We peered out above the tea and were met by the sight of a slightly embarrassed Indian gentleman wearing binoculars.

'Oh. Um, Hi. Sorry.'

It was Hoon's colleague Rafiq, with a group of British and American birders in tow. They had, through no fault of their own, ruined our painstaking stalk, holing it irrevocably below the water line and simultaneously blowing us well and truly out of the water. Our chance was gone. I know Gandhi said, 'violence will not solve anything', but I will lay good money that he hadn't just dipped a Blue-naped Pitta. I fumed quietly, but in my heart of hearts I knew it was nobody's fault. Rafiq and his group were targeting the same bird, and we had been invisible beneath the tea. It was just one of those things. By now dusk was sweeping in, and we abandoned the chase for the day. *C'est la guerre*, some things are just not meant to be. Back at the Jupuri I moodily pushed curry around my plate, hoping against hope that my only chance had not gone.

Before dawn the next day, I was in position lying under the tea, listening to the querulous *'ooh-weep?'* call of the pitta, but getting no closer to actually seeing one. Things were improving though. I had learnt the previous day that approaching a calling bird directly was hopeless. What was required was a more oblique angle of attack. The key was to locate a bird, move fifty metres along a gully, hide in a spot with a clear view, and only then play tape. This strategy was an improvement, and in front of me at the edge of the tea I could just make out a low strut of bamboo that was quite obviously bearing the weight of a pitta. I could see it vibrating each time the bird called! Still, however, the bird would not show. My quarry escaped again, and I emerged from the gully more frustrated than ever.

Behind me in the distance, I could hear a second bird calling, but I could not place the exact location. It seemed neither to be in the near gully nor in the next one on the far side of the crop. As I approached I realized why; the call was coming from a spot slap bang in the middle of the tea. I crept towards the bird, bent double in my efforts to remain unnoticed. I reached a spot twenty metres shy of the bird, where two of the tea-pickers' channels met the main path in a 'V.' The bird was calling from a spot between the two channels. All I had to do was stay put at the apex, and whichever way the bird went I would see it. I lay on my belly in the dirt to ensure a clear line of sight and waited. The bird continued to call, and every fifteen minutes or so I would 'tickle the tape' to keep the bird interested. Suddenly I became aware of a new clod of earth in the left hand channel that had not been present a moment earlier.

I slowly raised my binoculars, and there, at the edge of the channel keeping absolutely still, was a Blue-naped Pitta. A relatively sober-coloured species, it sported a flush of pale orange on the cheeks, a green shawl wrapped around the back, and a delicate peach wash on the underparts. As it scanned for danger, the bird turned its head away from me, and I could clearly see the cobalt blue patch on the back of the head, extending down to the top of the mantle. The bird turned to look at me before disappearing into the tea beyond the channel. After a further ten minutes the bird re-emerged, and once again paused in the channel to weigh up the situation. This time I was ready with my camera in position, and I managed to fire off three photos before the bird hopped back into cover and disappeared for good.

I lay on my back in the mud and waved my arms and legs in the air, to the astonishment of the gaggle of tea-pickers who chose that very moment to walk past me. I rolled over onto my side and greeted them with a grin. They increased their pace and continued on their way, laughing and discussing the mad antics of foreigners as they went. Pitta number thirteen, unlucky for some, was on the scoreboard, and in record time. The first of The Big Five was out of the way, and I heaved a sigh of relief. I strode back to the vehicle, woke the snoozing Hoon, and gleefully waved my camera at him.

The Brahmaputra floodplains are a green buffer, India's last fecund stand against the encroaching barren lands to the north. On a clear day you can see the snow-capped peaks of the Bhutanese mountains, massive and mysterious in the distance. As I surveyed the scene in front of me I vowed that one day I would get there. After all, it's not every country whose government has substituted the standard measure of GDP for the more enlightened concept of 'Gross Domestic Happiness.' Bhutan is however, an inordinately expensive country to visit, and many bird-watchers opt instead to visit India's Eaglenest resort, which nestles in the hills just east of the Bhutanese border. Eaglenest is home to a newly discovered species, the Bugun Liocichla, which still sounds to me like a Czech post-punk band. I didn't have enough time to mount an expedition to Eaglenest, but I remain in thrall to the Himalayas. I'll be back.

Since I had succeeded relatively quickly with the pitta, I decided to visit the Kaziranga National Park. Wedged between the tea belt to the south and the semi-deserts to the north are thousands of birds and animals, beneficiaries of the Brahmaputra's largesse. The seasonal flooding that occurs annually has created a fabulously rich habitat. Added to this is the fact that the region bestrides three overlapping biogeographical provinces, the Indomalayan (south Asian) Palaearctic (European, north Asian) and Afrotropical (African). Throw a mix of altitudes and a variable climate into the equation and you have the perfect recipe for biodiversity. Within the park's nine hundred and thirty square kilometres, almost five hundred species of bird have been recorded.

Occasionally in Assam, one comes across the odd hint of former colonial times. I had taken tea with a local English teacher who was keen to hear from a real Englishman the correct way to pronounce the word *bath*. I solemnly taught him the northern way, insisting that he instruct his students to keep the vowel as short as possible, to rhyme with 'math' not 'calf'. (I fully intend to return to his schoolroom in a year's time to check that the entire class has mastered the first verse of *On Ilkley Moor Bar T'at*.)

On a couple of excursions I came across lovingly maintained Mock Tudor shacks, a wayward echo of the old country. The strongest reminder of the British Empire's former influence however, is the endless bureaucracy. The Kaziranga Park HQ itself is filled with tottering piles of mildewed ledgers occupying an entire wall. I sneaked a look at one of them: *Tiger Deaths 1980–2000*. It was a worryingly fat file.

Having collected our pre-requisite armed guard, sorted out our permits, and waited for the inevitable receipts to be written out longhand and formally presented, we drove our open-top jeep along the dirt road into the park along the central range. The park's wide-open plains are more reminiscent of Africa than southeast Asia. Rhinoceros lumbered across the horizon, their immense horns shimmering in the heat haze. Herds of Sambar and Barking Deer grazed the open areas, while Water Buffalo waded thigh-high in the swamps. Periodically the jeep lurched to a halt, affording me the opportunity to stare out at whitewashed Great Egrets and fuzz-feathered Woolly-necked Storks. Bald-headed, brute-ugly adjutants strode about, looking for trouble. These skinheads of the heron world are blessed with obscene nude neck pouches, which they are able to distend and inflate at will to impress lady adjutants. The larger and rarer of the two species, the inspirationally named Greater

Adjutant (someone was up all night on that one) even appears to have a spatter of matted blood on its forehead, as if freshly emerged from a pub brawl.

As we returned towards dusk, we stopped to search for one of the park's star avian attractions, which I knew had been seen earlier in the day on an area of burnt-over ground close to the entrance gate. After an hour's diligent scanning, I spotted the bird at long range, strutting through the blackened grass; a male Bengal Florican. Floricans are essentially supermodel turkeys. The males are jet-black with white wings. Long-legged and lithe, they strut about the plains, but their true exhibitionist nature is not evident until the breeding season comes around. Since they live in tall grasslands and stand less than a metre tall, they have evolved a logical yet spectacular display. They leap ten metres into the air above the grass, where they hover, showing off the dazzling white of their quivering wings, then slowly float groundwards while they wait for applause. Sadly, such grandiose romantic gestures were conspicuous only by their absence on the evening of our visit, but at least we were graced by this rare and endangered bird's presence.

Having seen the pitta, the rest of my pencilled-in itinerary could now be confirmed, and our next port of call was Nameri, a park perched on the very edge of Arunachal Pradesh, some two hours' drive to the northwest across the Brahmaputra. After the usual formalities, an armed guard was assigned to us, and he cradled his ancient rifle to his breast, the business end resting on one of his two gold braid epaulettes. I gave his weapon the once over; it had seen about as much action as the ladies toilet at a Masonic lodge. However, less than an hour into our bush-walk we had cause to be grateful for his protection. Turning a corner, we ran into a she-elephant with a young calf. The calf was close to us, its parent a little further away, and the mother was visibly anxious. I noted with some concern her agitated ear-flapping, a sure-fire sign that she was unhappy with our unannounced presence. The guard shooed the youngster back in her direction, and mercifully the baby turned tail and ran towards his mother. Our guard shouted at the larger animal, brandishing his rifle and raising his hands above his head. She backed away, the stand off averted. I asked our protector what would have happened if the baby had continued past us, placing us between him and his mother. He raised an eye-brow but did not respond.

Our first stop at Nameri was a small group of unprepossessing muddy pools. We were here to look for one bird in particular, the White-winged Duck, a highly endangered species whose population now numbers less than two hundred and fifty individuals on the entire planet. Nameri boasts a population of no less than seventy individuals, a huge percentage of the world population. And we were in luck. The very first pond we tried hosted a wary female swimming through the reeds. I crawled on my hands and knees through the tall grass, praying that I wouldn't put my hand on a snake in the process, and managed to snatch a couple of photographs of this rare creature. Admittedly with its blotchy head and neck, bulbous red eye and broad orange bill, it resembles an in-bred farmyard duck, but despite its domesticated appearance it is a global rarity and we accorded it the respect it deserved. A little later we were treated to a close-range fly-by, which afforded us views of the extensive white blaze on the forewing for which the bird is named. Checking the visitor's book over a swift lunch of okra in mustard, sour curd with molasses and Bombay potato, it became clear just how fortuitous our view had been. Many visitors had spent a week or more looking for the birds, often in vain.

After a brief, curry-induced nap, I donned my water wings and embarked on a dinghy safari down the Nameri River. A strong headwind ripping up the river meant that my position wedged in the prow of the boat ensured I got a thorough soaking, but at least I wasn't doing the hard work paddling. Two strapping young men from the lodge were sat at the back labouring away to keep us out of the worst of the rapids. My aim was to find the Ibisbill, a bizarre wading bird that spends its life searching for edible morsels on shingle deltas. Ibisbills are devilishly hard to pick out from their pebbled surroundings. They are painted in a soft, dove grey and their rounded body profile blends in perfectly with the small boulders strewn around their river bed home. That is, until they turn in profile, when the long, decurved, red bill gives the game away.

After a couple of hours scanning, we picked out a bird feeding at the edge of a fast-flowing stretch, and had wonderful views as it bobbed nervously at the river's edge before flying past us to the far bank. We also chanced upon a Great Thick-knee, another evolutionary freak, which sports an over-developed black and banana-yellow bill, and a lizard's staring, pale green eye. Crested Kingfishers and Pallas's

Fish-eagles completed the cast that entertained me during a restful afternoon. Having returned to the eco-lodge at Nameri, I chatted to the owner, Ranesh. He was virtually an honorary Brit., having been raised, he proudly informed me, as a devout reader of *The Beano* comic. He regaled me with stories of his stay with elephant expert Mark Shand in Knightsbridge, the smartest of London's upscale neighbourhoods. Mr. Shand is the brother of HRH The Duchess of Cornwall Camilla Parker-Bowles, who in turn is the wife of Prince Charles, first in line to the British throne. Ranesh had clearly relished his time partying in the 1980s with various minor royals at the swish London nightclub *Atticus*. I would pass on the gossip, only MI5 would have me shot.

On the way back to Kohora, Hoon and Basu drew my attention to the fact that not a drop of tea had passed our lips during the entire day. Hoon politely whispered 'one cup of tea?' and I nodded my agreement. We drew up outside a suitable establishment, *The Modak Sweets Centre* on the Bhalukpong Road in Balipara, squeezed ourselves around a tiny table at the back of the store, and ordered tea for three. To general hilarity I photographed and studied the wall-mounted menu. How to choose between *cham cham* and *malai cham cham*? Was the *vegetable choop* good today? How special, exactly, would the *special sabjee* be, and would I survive a portion of the emetic-sounding *mewa barfee*? We settled for a mixed plate of sweets, which arrived in short order, a rainbow of pastel pinks, greens and yellows. Tea was served from the pot, and consumed with much appreciative lip-smacking.

Paintings of Hindu Gods jostled for space on the walls, festooned with multi-coloured paper garlands. Each time the overworked fan mounted above the counter swung in our direction thick clouds of incense billowed towards us. The son of the owner proudly posed for photographs amidst the tottering towers of biscuits and sandbagged stocks of rice, after checking that all was in order with regard to his neatly trimmed pencil moustache. We learnt a little of the family history. Why, I wondered, had such a dapper individual abandoned the fertile plains of south India for a flyblown, back-of-beyond town like Balipara? Was he a fugitive from justice? Or was his migration the result of an unhappy love affair? I was unable to ascertain the answer, despite the cultural exchanges that followed. I discovered that a single red spot on a lady's forehead means that she is a married woman, and the proprietors of the Modak Sweets Centre learned the finer points of White-winged Duck identification.

The lives of both parties suitably enriched, we waved our goodbyes and trundled back through the darkness into the Jupuri Ghar's waiting embrace, via the usual collection of near-death transit incidents. The prayer flags that lined the path to the restaurant fluttered their greeting, leading the way to another repast worthy of a maharajah. Once again there was enough food to satisfy not only an Indian prince, but most of his retinue to boot. Despite sneaking hefty portions to the attendant group of luminous-eyed, skinny kittens who watched my every mouthful, I was defeated. I said goodbye to Hoon before staggering back to the chalet to lie down. Struggling to digest the mountain of food now squeezing itself through my digestive system, the peristaltic process was accompanied by alarmingly loud rumblings and seismic gastric activity.

At first light, Basu the Bengali and I climbed into the cab of our truck and headed west. We followed the course of the Brahmaputra back towards Guwahati, before turning south and winding our way up into the hills. Our destination was Shillong, a transit town up on the plateau, headquarters of the East Khasi Hills District and home to a different set of montane birds. Not far out of Kohora as we rounded a sharp curve Basu pointed ahead. A truck sprawled on its side, axles indecently exposed, a sea of broken glass strewn across the tarmac. A body lay by the side of the road, swaddled in an inappropriately gaudy tartan blanket. Basu, his English almost as limited as my Hindi, looked serious for a moment and raised a single finger.

'One dead' he said. Indeed, the blanket was drawn up all the way over the poor unfortunate ex-driver's head, and we silently paid our respects as we passed. If only the departed had spent a little time reading Ghandi's sayings, he would have known that *there is more to life than to increase its speed.* The road safety sign's words bounced unspoken around my head, *no hurry, no worry.* An involuntary shiver ran through me. How slender the thread that ties us to this world.

We crossed out of Jorhat and into Nagaon division, rumbling past raffia houses splashed with pink and green, past dimly lit roadside temples, through whose doors one could occasionally make out the wraith-like figures of the sadhus prostrate in prayer, their sweat-matted dreadlocks cascading over ochre-coloured robes. The local landscape was dotted with teams working ploughshares, whilst others hacked at the clods of dry earth with primitive hoes. The tea-pickers' in their rainbow saris resembled a host of multi-coloured beetles working their way around the edges of the crop. Bus passengers waited in that quintessential Asian-peasant pose, squatting in the dust, hunched over their heels.

The single leitmotif that binds the drama of the Indian landscape together is the bicycle. Most of the countless thousands we encountered were the standard issue: dark green, with a fully enclosed chain guard and a silver bell. Not the last word in racing kit perhaps, but functional, *a comfortable ride, a reliable companion* as the ad. legend ran. All were equipped with a rear pannier to transport just-lathed table legs, bundles of okra, relatives etc. There appeared to be little customization (*Pimp my Bike!* An Indian TV series waiting to happen) but just occasionally we would pass one with plastic flower garlands woven through the spokes, a pair of Catherine wheels in motion.

Cycle rickshaws were more grandly decorated, their panels emblazoned with idyllic pastoral scenes, red Ferraris, proud army cadets firing pistols, Hindu monkey gods and preening pop stars. Needless to say, all had their permit number and license details neatly displayed, as required. God's own billion-piece dynamic jigsaw slid seamlessly in and out of the traffic. The hulking commercial trucks were also personalized with lines of icons along their side-panels: peacocks, stars, flags, eagles, horses. Only a few were plain, decoration presumably vetoed by teams of grey, corporate killjoys. A few scrawny mutts were always in evidence, defying death on the roads by a matter of inches, pausing now and then to add their own personal signature to wheels and mudflaps. Most dogs here are flat. If they are not flat they are young. The canine life expectancy is that life will be irredeemably hard, and then you'll die.

People were everywhere, spilling over into the rivers to do their ablutions and laundry, sometimes both in worrying proximity. As we eased our way out into the suburbs again, the bustling city receded into the distance behind us, and life proceeded at a gentler pace. Pink water hyacinths carpeted each home's personal reservoir, and the goat-per-capita ratio started to climb. We stopped for one cup of tea at the Dhaba Highway Café. I shuffled the condiments – water, salt and chillies – and watched the cook shaping chapattis, slapping them into shape in a skilful, noisy process that provided its own applause. At Sonipar we turned south and entered Meghalaya. The belching coke works' chimneys ensured that everything smelled of smoke and was slathered in a layer of thick red dust.

I was a boy again, transported back to the mining villages of north Wales where my grandmother lived, where the town toiled in the shadow of the slagheap, where it always rained, and where everything was closed on Sundays for Chapel, including the mouths of the local populace. At nearby Bersham I had leaned over the edge of the weir and experienced one of my formative bird-watching moments; learning to tell the difference between Grey and Yellow Wagtails. I learnt that Grey Wagtails live near Wrexham, Wales in February, and Yellow Wagtails do not. The latter are still in sunny west Africa, not storm-lashed north Wales, rendering identification a formality. Nevertheless, I studied the minutiae, and became aware that Greys have longer tails, and that their yellow colouration is restricted to a small patch on the undertail-coverts. Now, almost thirty-five years later, I was travelling through another smoky landscape, but one that differed in almost every other detail.

After a chicken biryani lunch we climbed up the switchbacks, our jeep, the grandly named 'Ambassador Nova,' wheezing its way up the steeper sections like an asthmatic bullock. As we passed through Nongpoh and gained altitude we hastily pulled on jackets as we stopped to breathe in the sharp, clean air of the pine forests.

Shillong is a military town in the Khasi Hills, three hours drive south of Guwahati. Ex-patriots' property was handed over in 1971, but a few diehards stayed on and now passed their time making cherry brandy. This doubtless came in handy to calm the nerves; the whole town seemed in grave danger of sliding down into the valley without any assistance from the regular earthquakes. I checked into the Tripura Castle Guesthouse, whose inner courtyard is panelled with badly faded black and white photos dating from the halcyon days of the Raj: various royal palaces, teams of players relaxing post-polo, and so forth. Doubtless there's one of folks taking Tiffin after a spot of croquet somewhere too.

On arrival I shared a beer with the officer for 'The Northeast Today.' He was on good terms with the King's son, whose house abuts the guesthouse. The young royal's passion is saving stray dogs from a flattening on the streets, a laudable aim, although I felt less kindly towards his endeavours at three a.m. as yet another volley of barks disturbed my slumbers. My journalist friend entertained me with stories of tourist kidnappings in Manipur a few years earlier, and I filed away a mental note to leave the state off any future itineraries.

The people here looked very different from those down on the plains: broad-faced, almost Mongolian in appearance, with a pronounced Chinese influence somewhere back in their distant heritage. All manner of ethnic influences had been stirred into the local pot it seemed. Most were swaddled in colourful blankets as protection against the cold, and the sleeping babies firmly tied on top of the passing trucks' cargoes were well wrapped up.

My first morning in the Shillong area had been earmarked for a visit to the Mawphlang Sacred Grove, a remnant area of forest which had been protected for hundreds of years by the local animists, whose religious beliefs included the idea that when one dies, one's spirit takes the form of a bird. Hence killing a bird, or destroying its habitat is just about the most serious crime one can commit. My kind of religion, where do I sign? We arrived at the locked gate that barred the entrance to the forest. A brief salvo on the jeep's horn brought The Keeper of the Grove scurrying over. He appeared to be several hundred years old, and was in grave danger of tripping over the bottom of his trousers, which were several sizes too big for him. His crumpled, moss green suit was firmly tied at the waist with string, and atop his grizzled head sat a creased purple beanie hat, which bore all the hallmarks of having been recently slept in. A stylish pair of sunglasses finished off the ensemble. He looked like John Belushi's grandfather after a particularly gruelling family party on the Blues Brothers set.

Having crossed the gatekeeper's palm with silver we bumped our way across the hillside before sliding to a halt at the entrance to the grove, which looked every bit as ancient and phantasmagorical as its guardian. I strolled between the twisted trunks with as much nonchalance as I could muster, but in truth it was an eerie place, and every twig-crack beneath my feet and leaf-rustle above my head made me jump. There were certainly birds here though, and I quickly located my target, a tiny lime-green and slate-grey tail-less ground-dweller, the Grey-bellied Tesia. It grovelled furtively around in the undergrowth looking for all the world like a mini-pitta. An ideal substitute, I decided, in the absence of the real thing in this part of India. After five happy hours wandering through this fantastical landscape, I had notched up an impressive species list.

Lunch was a dingy affair at the most abject restaurant in which I have ever had the misfortune to set foot. In the previous village we had seen a sign that urged us to *discover a new lifestyle – hygienic tasty food.* This eaterie was clearly not the place. There were no menus, for the simple reason that there was no choice; seldom has the phrase *'the dish of the day'* been so literally applied. The waiter briefly broke off from a shouting match with his wife to inform us in a charmless fashion that today's dish was 'Chow', presumably as in *Mein* but quite possibly as in *huahua.* The gritty pork with which the rice was laced was served separately, and each mouthful contained the recommended daily intake of saturated fat for a small town. We ate in silence, cowed into submission by the shrieking TV soap opera that blared unwatched in the background. On the way out I stupidly glanced into the kitchen and bitterly wished I hadn't. A group of rats was circling the cooker, presumably on a protest march demanding cleaner working conditions. We didn't leave a tip.

Tea o'clock came early at three, the divine beverage served in microfilm-thin plastic cups that became unworkably supple when holding hot liquid. Juggling and mostly wearing our tea, we began conversing with the owner of the Duwan Sing Syiem Bridge Café on the Cherrapunji road, who spoke English and helpfully advised us of another sacred grove close by. A guide was dispatched to ride with us and show us the way, and after settling our five rupee bill (roughly $0 US) we quickly located the tiny strip of forest. I wandered around the site, probably the first birder ever to set foot in the place, and in a couple of hours had seen both White-cheeked Partridge, a decidedly scarce and elusive northeast game-bird, and a stunning Golden Bush-robin.

The latter, I can confirm, does exactly what it says on the tin. It's a robin, it lives in a bush, and it's unquestionably golden. It also has a neat little highwayman's mask that gives it a darkly sexy allure, like the Daryl Hannah character *Pris* in Blade Runner, which works for me. I suppose it's understandable that the bird's most attractive feature is not included in its name. *Lesser Highwayman-masked Golden Bush-robin* would be a little unwieldy. Mind you, the recently discovered Cachar Wedge-billed Wren-babbler's name sports twenty-eight letters and is one of the longest English names of any bird in the world, so who's to say? At the opposite extreme are the Hawaiian name for the Gannet and the Japanese name for the Cormorant, which are *A* and *U* respectively. (My gift to you for your next trivia quiz, though admittedly of limited use to Scrabble fans.) Having charted the unknown grove by scribbling an entirely undecipherable map in the back of my notebook, we slipped back into Shillong under cover of darkness, to rejoin the baying hounds at the Tripura.

A last morning working the Old Guahati Road turned up a few more local specialities, before Basu deposited me at the airport. I slept all the way back to Delhi, thus minimizing my frustration at travelling in entirely the wrong direction due to the vagaries of the airline industry's arcane flight routings. I crawled onto my flight to Kuala Lumpur, exhausted by eight days of dawn-to-dusk birding. It had all been worthwhile however. The Blue-naped Pitta, a significant mission milestone was mine, and now a new set of challenges lay ahead. I was heading for one of the biggest unbroken tracts of rainforest in southeast Asia, Taman Negara in Malaysia, where I had a date with a Garnet Pitta.

Chapter 8

Rusty's Return. Peninsular Malaysia

'What the hell have you done to your arm?'

The unmistakable plangent tones of a Londoner rang out across the clearing, accompanied by raucous laughter.

'Dr Catsis and Dr Mears I presume' I replied with as much dignity as I could manage, and the three of us shook hands and slapped backs with a vigour that only British people who haven't seen each other in a while can muster.

I showed off my wound to my countrymen, which though healing well, still looked horrendous. While discussing our respective plans back in England at the start of the year it became apparent that we'd be in Malaysia at the same time, and so had decided to join forces. Mike and Andy had reached Taman Negara twenty-four hours ahead of me, and had already been ferreting around in the forest, finding rare birds with which to royally piss me off. They had already scored a few minor successes, but worryingly they had not heard a pitta so far.

Still, it was early days, and I had a whole week at Taman Negara to track down the one pitta that would be new for the year. TN is in fact home to five species of pitta – Hooded, Blue-winged, Banded, Giant and Garnet – but I had already seen the first three, and I stubbornly refused to believe in the existence of the fourth, which if it existed at all was only present in extremely low densities in Peninsular Malaysia. So realistically that left only one pitta to find, the small but perfectly formed Garnet. I knew they were relatively common in the park, and figured that finding one should be like falling off a log. Preferably in a less literal way than I had managed in Mindanao.

Taman Negara is huge. It occupies four thousand three hundred and forty-three square kilometres, and is estimated to be a hundred and thirty million years old. That's even older than Kirk Douglas. The park list boasts over three hundred and fifty species of bird, more than half of the Malaysian total, and unlike some other rainforest reserves I might mention (Khao Nor Chuchi take a

bow) hosts considerably more than one individual of each type. Malaysian Tapir, Sumatran Rhinoceros and other rare animals lurk in its depths. There are even a few Malayan Sun Bears, Leopards and Tigers (at least sixteen individuals of which were recorded by camera traps in 2001). Which means there's a minute chance you might actually get eaten while looking for pittas. A sobering thought, but at least you'd die in a blaze of publicity. It even has a riverine beach with a swimming area, Lubok Simpon. The vast majority of the park however, is a muddy, snake-filled, rain-sodden, leech-infested, mozzie-fest. In a word: paradise.

I had cruised from Kuala Lumpur to Taman Negara in style, courtesy of a Mr. Vela and his magic taxi. On the way he updated me regarding the recent Malaysian election.

'The new Prime Minister is a nice guy,' he insisted, 'but his wife does not have love in her eyes.' In similarly forthright style, he initiated me in the ways of local religion. 'See this picture? That's a Malaysian Hindu holy man, Guru Agatthiyar. He's the tallest God in the world. Well I reckon if you're going to worship a God you may as well go for a big one.'

On arrival I had rented a lovely wooden chalet, a little piece of Switzerland transported to southeast Asia. There was, admittedly, no air conditioning, but a sturdy little fan going hell for leather in one corner helped me to keep my cool. The bungalow was also missing a small pane of glass that could easily have functioned as a portal for all the world's mosquitoes. I sprayed the frame with hundred percent DEET and hoped for the best.

Having settled in, I put on my lowland rainforest combat gear. Firstly, a pair of climate-controlled pants (an inspired Christmas present from my girlfriend's mother). The world's grubbiest trousers followed, equipped with both thigh and leg pockets for storing bird notebooks, mosquito repellent, tissue paper (for lens cleaning) spare audio cable, camera accessories, three pens, trail map and money for the ferryman. Next came a long-sleeved shirt that covered almost all my exposed flesh to keep bugs at bay. My feet were protected both by cotton socks and by my indispensible leech-proof socks. The latter are a life-changing marvel. They look as though they have been constructed out of old flour bags, and are worn over regular socks and tied at the knee. They're effective, but you do look as if you've had two prosthetic limbs fitted. (One's gait is similar too, if you tie the drawstrings too tight and cut off the circulation.) They do however mean that you get to concentrate on hunting down birds rather than spending all day worrying about leeches and repeatedly removing your boots to winkle out the more determined of the little bloodsuckers. Lastly, I donned my trusty baseball cap, tweaking the peak until it sat at a suitably jaunty angle, and threaded a sweat towel through my belt loop. All that remained was to load myself up like a beast of burden with binoculars, camera, telephoto lens and flash-gun, GPS, an umbrella to fend off the inevitable afternoon downpour, a litre of water and sufficient birders' tapas to get through the day. Finally I was ready to stagger out into the forest. If I wasn't fit when I saw my first pitta, I'd be fit by the time I'd seen the last. Or possibly dead.

A list of birders' tapas dishes

- *Hello Kitty Lonely God potato twists*
- *Maple syrup sponge cake*
- *Dried cranberries. In those clever re-sealable bags*
- *Compressed Japanese Nori Seaweed*
- *Strawberry Oreos*
- *Salted peanuts. Especially the wasabi-covered ones*
- *Snickers bars*
- *Tong Garden Snek Parti (peas and nuts again)*
- *Nips (effectively peanut M and M's with a 'Carry On' name)*
- *Mentos Sour Mix sweets (similar to heroin only more addictive)*
- *Dried cuttlefish (last resort only)*

I met Andy and Mike down at the river's edge and we enjoyed a delicious, fiery lunch at one of the floating restaurants. In fact the only thing wrong with these establishments is that the owners often have cause to roll out the most terrifying couplet in the English language: *no beer.* Happily, from here it's only a one minute boat ride across the Tembeling river (drop your fare into the plastic box marked *Hello. One Ringgit per person. Pay now. Here. OK, let's go*) and after a stiff climb up a steep set of wooden steps you're in the glamorous Mutiara resort where the posh people stay. And which has a bar. And beer that's served in glasses that have been in the fridge all day. Unhappily, however, a small Tiger beer is the equivalent of roughly one hundred US dollars (OK, it's actually only $6 US, but still pricey) so during our stay we restricted our intake to one per night.

If you should accidentally take the wrong path that leads away from the bar, you're soon on the trail that leads up the east bank of the Tahan River. From here you can walk for sixty kilometres or more into some of the richest forest in Asia. It is, quite simply, awe-inspiring. The only problem is you have to walk back too, and the trails are far from flat. Add to this the fact that your pudgy, flaccid body will be undergoing a work out conducted in intense, sapping eighty-percent-plus humidity, and you have the recipe for long and extremely tiring days. But the best birds live in the deepest forest. 'You don't see great birds in your living room' and all that. Go visit, you won't regret it.

Our first afternoon was uneventful. Hot and sticky, high on insects, and for the most part, low on birds. Except that is, for one great moment on a trail known as The Swamp Loop. (It's called this because it loops round a swamp. See? Birding is easy.) We were hot, sweaty and tired after tramping around and seeing bugger all, but were stopped in our tracks by one of the most beautiful sounds in the natural world. A single, pure, monotone whistle that fades out slowly, as if its owner had lost his train of thought mid-way through. It belongs to a mythical creature, one that has been known to make grown men cry like babies, gnash their teeth, and rent their hair in a frankly biblical manner, such is its legendary allure and its simultaneous ability to elude detection. For this is the song of the Rail-babbler.

Some birds, like the Peacock, have specialised feathers; iridescent tails that are fanned seductively in display, extended neck plumes that flicker and float in the sunlight, beckoning the female toward an embrace. The Rail-babbler appears poorly endowed in this department. Some birds, like the Golden Orioles, possess dazzling plumage with which to wow their potential partners. Nothing so ostentatious for the orangey-brown Rail-babbler. (The closest it comes to a burst of feather colour is a pair of thick stripes, one black, one white, which run backwards from the eye. They look like something an over zealous am-dram make-up artist might fashion for the queen in a production of *Anthony and Cleopatra*.) Some birds like the Nightingale thrill with their songs, mellifluous melodies that tear at the heartstrings. The Rail-babbler, as already outlined, restricts itself to a single note. A few adventurous species have evolved amazing display flights employing loop-de-loops and other aeronautical feats. The Rail-babbler settles for walking on the ground, pausing occasionally on a decaying log to bow low, inverting its body like a banana. But, and it is one of the biggest *buts* in all creation, it has a secret weapon in the wooing war. It has built-in balloons. Balloons that inflate on the sides of its neck every time it whistles. Purple balloons that gradually turn bright blue as they swell to their maximum size… It's a neat trick. If I had a pair of those I'd be in bed by ten every night. And I would not be alone.

Unfortunately, Rail-babblers live in dense, swampy forest, and can be devilishly difficult to find. Even if they whistle right in front of you, you can whistle Dixie if you think you're going to see them. It was this very same whistle that we had heard just a few yards off the swamp trail. We sat, we whistled, we waited. The Rail-babbler whistled back, and glided to and fro, sneaking invisibly through the shadows. And then a remarkable thing happened. It walked out from behind a fallen log, and stalked towards us on its skinny, ridiculously long legs. It stopped, whistled again, and performed a brief balloon dance of lurve, before melting back into the forest.

As cabaret goes, pretty unbeatable. We whistled furiously for an encore, but the show was over, and the temperamental artiste could not be tempted back onto the stage. We walked back to the HQ, and sat in the bar with our tiny, indescribably precious beers, discussing this aberration. Clearly the bird was not injured, it had not exhibited any obvious signs of mental illness, and yet it had given itself up remarkably easily. We shrugged our shoulders, clinked our glasses (being careful not to spill a drop) and drank a toast to the Rail-babbler. *Eupetes macrocerus;* truly a remarkable creature.

Our beers all too quickly drained, we prepared for the next onslaught. The worst thing about being a bird-watcher is that even when it's dark, your work is not done. Phil Hansbro, whom we were to meet at Taman Negara a couple of days later has summed it up best.

'I just want to see all the owls. Every last one of the f*cking things. Then I won't have to go out in the forest at night any more.'

But the sad truth was that we were far from having seen every last one of Malaysia's f*cking owls. So we went night-birding.

There are two extreme forms of bird-watching which, when the layman hears about them, are usually greeted with incredulous laughter. The first is seawatching. This involves lines of bird-watchers lying on a storm-lashed cliff top on some desolate peninsula, staring miles out to sea through their telescopes, waiting for something to fly past. It's called 'seawatching', I secretly suspect, because there are often no birds present. Vast expanses of sea are typically all that you get to watch. This activity must, at all costs, be performed under atrocious conditions. If it's sunny and warm with a gentle zephyr tickling your cheek, the seabirds will be five miles offshore and you won't see anything. In fact, if you can see anything at all through your telescope, which will in all probability be ruined after copious amounts of sea-water have seeped into its every orifice, conditions are too fair for any decent seabird to be seen dead near the British coast. The problem is that once in a blue moon a spectacularly rare seabird like a Black-browed Albatross or a Madeiran Storm-petrel does show up, and only those who are there at the time get to see it. It flies past, disappears over the horizon, and is gone forever. In any event, for birders seawatching is the primary source of frustration, despair and premature death.

Night-birding, in my book, comes a close second. The concept is simple; some birds are diurnal. They feed during the day, you see them, they sleep at night. Which, in my humble opinion, is the way things should have been ordained for all the winged creatures. Sadly, the universe is more complicated than this, and for some reason that I cannot fathom, has not been tailored according to my personal requirements. Hence birders have, since time immemorial, been trekking into rainforests, hostile environments even during daylight hours, stumbling around in the black of night armed only with a tape recorder and a spotlight, whose batteries can be relied upon to fail at the critical moment. This lack of illumination usually coincides with one reaching the point most geographically remote from wherever one happens to be sleeping.

The theoretical technique is then to play an audio clip of whichever night-bird you wish to see, and the bird will fly in to repel this new, unseen usurper. The tiny problem with this theory is obvious: it's too bloody dark to see anything flying anywhere. Expert night-birders have evolved a kind of sixth sense, which tells them when a rare owl (designed, let us not forget, for silent flight) has landed close by. They whisk round, snap on their several-billion-candle-power portable lamp, and unerringly pick out said owl in the beam. This, as you may have guessed, has rarely been my experience. I do not have the sixth sense described above, and in the forest at night, I have to confess that the regular five are functioning somewhat below par. The usual outcomes in my case are:

- *It rains (and thus all self-respecting night-birds are tucked up snug and warm in a tree cavity).*

- *Owls hoot and nightjars sing joyfully but inaccessibly from the other side of an impenetrable swamp, delighting in my increasing irascibility.*

- *Some tiny Scops-owl (the size of a garden pea, give or take, and indistinguishable from any other kinds of Scops-owl without the aid of a syringe and a well-equipped DNA laboratory) does in fact come sneaking in, before spending half an hour calling innocently from the canopy right above my head, hopelessly obscured by several hundredweight of sturdy branches.*

Then there is the technique of 'going in.' Once again, the theory runs smoothly enough. The bird calls close by. You stroll into the forest, get very close and then shine a torch on it. You get great views, and everyone goes home happy. The reality is inevitably somewhat different. You trip over the moment you leave the trail, get inextricably caught up in thorn bushes, and brush against slimy and/or spiky things and have an attack of the heebie-jeebies. You see something move that you convince yourself must have been the owl, only for a bat to shit inconveniently on your head. Only then, when you are well and truly panic-stricken, do you realise that you have absolutely no idea in which direction the trail lies. You may think this an exaggeration, but I know any number of birders who will be only too happy to relate tales of their night of terror lost in the jungle, how they had to feed off morsels of stale food that had lodged in their beard the previous day etc.

None of which of course dissuaded me for a second from rushing back into the jungle on my first night at Taman Negara. I really needed to see a Large Frogmouth. It's one of the biggest of the Asian frogmouths, and is spectacularly whiskery. This is why, despite my best intentions, I found myself post-beer, deep in the forest at night, sweat trickling down my neck, heart beating dangerously fast, and with an audio clip cued up and ready to go on my iPod.

'*Ooo-wuuurgh!... Ooo-wuuurgh!*' The incalculably strange song of the frogmouth rang out through the heavy air. And for the second time in twenty-four hours, I was to be rocked back on my heels. A Large Frogmouth immediately started calling, flew in to my recording, and perched in full view on the liana just a few feet above us. It turned its head to and fro, allowing us to capture an impressive range of images for posterity. It called while we watched, inflating its throat as it did so, vibrating a set of whiskers of which any sea captain would have been proud. It swivelled round on the branch, granting us full access to every last detail of its plumage.

And then it departed as swiftly as it had come, keen to gape that ludicrous mouth and snaffle a few of the jungle's winged beasts, to assuage the ravenous hunger that presumably takes hold of you if you spend all day immobile and camouflaged in a tree hole.

We couldn't believe our luck, and knowing we were on a roll, cued up Oriental Bay-owl. It called. Distantly. For ages. We cued up Reddish Scops-owl. It hooted from the other side of the river. We tried Sunda Scops-owl and there was no response. In all we stood there for a further two hours and saw absolutely nothing. Unless you count the odd bat that is, a couple of which tried inconveniently to shit on our heads.

We trudged back through the mud to HQ, crossed the river (*Hello. One Ringgit per person. Pay now* etc.) and clambered up the steps to a tiny shack to buy water for the next day. I browsed the wares, my pidgin Malaysian improving all the time. I added a new gem to my lexicon, discovering that the Malay for *Barbie Lookalike* is *Bah-bee Lookeelike*. Travel truly does broaden the vocabulary, if not the mind. As we exited the store, we heard a soft, falling call.

'*Whoouw*.'

Three paces to the right under the canopy of a small tree was a Reddish Scops-owl, perched in the open and beautifully illuminated in our spotlight. We were surrounded by buildings, twenty metres from our chalets, on the 'wrong' side of the river, surrounded by open, trash-habitat country. The bird had presumably flown across the river from the primary forest in which we had been searching, and doubtless would return there at any moment. What an incredibly fortuitous one-off!

The owl called all night right outside our accommodation and kept us awake.

Entertaining though our nocturnal activities were, they were unlikely to produce a pitta. (Although others have stumbled across roosting pittas by torchlight at night, so it wasn't beyond the bounds of possibility.) Having not even heard any species of pitta in the Kuala Tahan HQ area during the whole of the previous day, we decided to head for pastures new. The previous evening we had met the supremely helpful Mr. May, who owned a boat. He was keen to ferry us up and down the Tembeling River for a fee, so we had arranged to meet him half an hour before dawn by the floating restaurants.

Andy, Mike and I stumbled, bleary-eyed onto the tiny craft that rocked alarmingly from side to side as we found our seats, before puttering downriver for thirty minutes. The breeze caused by our passage was delightfully cool, and we were fully awake by the time we disembarked at the rough-hewn jetty that jutted out from the opposite bank. The trail here, I knew, led through lush forest, perfect for a Garnet Pitta. Avian activity was high during the first couple of hours after first light, always the best time of day in primary forest, and we split up to maximize coverage. One of my favourite birds made an appearance, an Asian Green Broadbill. As a boy I had turned a page of John Gooders' avian encyclopedia *Bird Families of the World* to be confronted by a full-page portrait of this luminous green creature, glowing in the rainforest gloom. It had taken my breath away as a child, and still does whenever I encounter the species today.

In a noisy mixed flock I chanced upon a White-necked Babbler, a new bird for me, and the flock also contained a pair of Fluffy-backed Tit-babblers, whose behaviour is as delightful as their name. They do indeed have fluffy backs, raising their dorsal feathers when excited, but the most charming aspect of Fluffy-backed Tit-babbler married life is that males and females cuddle up together, pressing their bodies tightly against one another on a single branch while duetting. When was the last time you saw that at a karaoke night?

An hour later I bumped into Mike. We compared notes, but the news was dispiriting; neither of us had heard a pitta call, despite the perfect habitat and our early start. Together, we worked a side trail that led to a cave known as *Gua Telinga*, famed for its vast population of Fruit Bats. It's also home to Cave Racer Snakes that prey on the bats. I am not at all keen on confined spaces, and not particularly fond of snakes either. Hence *caves with snakes in* sit somewhere near the bottom of my 'must visit locations' list. However, the trail that leads to the caves had proved productive in the past, and we walked slowly, listening carefully to the birdsong drifting out of the forest around us. As we did so, I became aware of a single, clear whistle, very like the Rail-babbler's song but fractionally upslurred and abruptly end-stopped. I signalled excitedly to Mike, recognizing this as the song of the Garnet Pitta. We crept back up the trail in the direction of the sound, but the source seemed to shift as we moved. True to form, the pitta's location proved difficult to pinpoint.

Wherever the sound was coming from, it was clearly some way from the trail. There seemed to be absolutely no way through the wall of impenetrable forest that loomed before us. We exchanged despairing glances. Mike had never seen the species before, so was just as keen as I was to see the bird, but we both knew that the way to see Garnets was to locate the bird and then silently 'go in' after it, since the species is rarely lured close to imitations of its song. After a brief whispered confab we agreed that this was not the one to pursue, and started to walk away.

Ten metres down the trail I stopped, and turned on my heel.

'Mike, I know it looks impossible, but we might not even hear another Garnet all week. Last time I came to Taman Negara we went in for one bird, and it was the only bird we saw or heard in seven full days' birding.' We examined the jungle again, and decided we simply had to give it a go.

Forty minutes later we were extremely hot, profusely sweaty, scratched to pieces and almost certainly lost. We had snapped off twigs to mark our way, but the difficulty in precisely locating the pitta, combined with areas of forest that were simply impassable, meant that of necessity our route had been circuitous. The good news was that the pitta was still calling, and compared to when we had first picked it up, the sound was now incredibly loud. We could hear the slightly rasping, throaty quality to the song, and the slight variation in pitch had become more apparent. We were close. Casting aside all thoughts of having to live on berries and rainwater for the rest of my life, I focused on the pursuit. After a little more high-stepping over creepers, ducking under fallen branches, and twisting around complex root systems we had reached a fractionally more open area that afforded reasonable views into the sub-canopy. We scanned diligently with our binoculars, desperately trying to track down the hidden songster, but to no avail. Until, that is, Mike took a cautious step forward to change his viewing angle, and suddenly whispered, 'I've got it.' After a few seconds of minute gesticulations and whispered instructions, I too had the bird. It was indeed a Garnet Pitta, and it was just three metres in front of us in the canopy.

Garnet is one of my favourite pittas. It is rather small, about fifteen centimetres from the tip of its bill to the end of its dainty toes. Named for a precious gemstone, its plumage does not disappoint; largely scarlet below and dark blue above, with an incredible azure patch on the wing. The subspecies here in Malaysia, *coccinea*, has delicate red scaling on the blue breast, and like all races it has a broad black band through the eyes. It's a simply exquisite creature, and we were thrilled to be watching this individual, singing its heart out just above our heads. Although Garnets, like most pittas, spend a good deal of their lives hopping about on the forest floor, they often ascend to the canopy or sub-canopy to sing, so that they have a better view of what their potential rivals are up to. Unlike most pittas, they are tolerant of human presence, so long as that presence is silent and moves slowly, with no sudden movements. Mike and I spent a minute or two manoeuvering ourselves with infinite care into a better position, before I lined up my camera. I checked one or two images, and they were fabulous, well lit frame-fillers. On a couple of occasions, I raised my camera too quickly in the excitement, and the bird flipped across to another branch, emitting a startlingly loud 'crack' as it flew. So far as I can establish, this sound, whether vocal or mechanical, is not documented in the literature, but is presumably a defence against predators.

After a truly awe-inspiring audience, we silently picked our way back through the tangled vegetation and via a few unplanned detours, managed to relocate the trail. We brushed the bugs out of our hair, squeezed the rattan thorns from our flesh, removed the leeches from our boots, and congratulated each other on our good fortune at having shared such privileged views. Pitta number fourteen had been well and truly bagged, and I was walking on air. Whilst not being one of the species that I had imagined would give me the most trouble, nonetheless I had struggled to see the bird on my previous visit to Malaysia, and I knew that Taman Negara was by far my best chance to connect with the bird. It was certainly not a given; I knew a number of people who had spent a fortnight or longer in Malaysia, and who had come away empty-handed. Now it was a done deal. Either my technique was hot, or my luck was in, or a little of both. The single beer that awaited me at the Mutiara resort that evening would taste all the sweeter.

We sat out the heat of the day at the floating restaurants, and sucked down one fresh lime juice after another in a vain attempt to replace the copious amount of liquid fleeing our bodies via every pore, and to combat the spicier components that had peppered our lunch plates.

Our post-prandial snooze was interrupted by a rumbustious figure striding towards us. 'G'day, you birders?' he enquired brightly, with a robust twang and choice of introductory vocabulary that identified him immediately as an Australian. We nodded with what we hoped was a decent show of grave British reserve.

'Great,' came the reply, and the stranger pulled up a chair, swinging it round in a broad arc that had other diners ducking for cover, before sitting with splayed legs against its upright back. The assault continued.

'What've you seen then? Mind if I get some info.?'

As Englishmen we were taken aback at the stranger's forcefulness and direct, no-nonsense approach. I mean, our families had never met. We had not been formerly introduced. We did not even know this rocket-fuelled interloper's name. Surely there was a law against this sort of thing?

The last mystery at least was swiftly dealt with.

'Name's Phil, Phil Hansbro' the stranger said, thrusting a large mitt in our direction and scattering the remnants of lunch. In the space of about twenty seconds we learnt that Phil was originally from Leeds, had been living in Australia for a few years, was a lecturer in microbiology, and was in Malaysia to round up any stray, unsuspecting Kuala Lumpur university students who might not have a good enough reason to avoid continuing their studies in New South Wales.

I didn't fancy their chances. Leeds plus Australia, that most explosive of cultural cocktails, would make mincemeat of them. I suppressed an involuntary shudder at the carnage about to be unleashed in the nation's capital. The academic business at hand, we were brusquely informed, was not due to start until the weekend, which gave our new friend enough time to grab a couple of days in the forest. Phil whipped out his notebook, and waved it at us.

'Here's what I need to see.'

He lobbed it accurately across the table, and under guidance we flipped to the familiarly detailed list that had been scrawled in the back pages.

'Ones with the stars are the ones I need. Other stuff'd just be nice to see.'

We warmed to the task. After all, it was a list and we were birders, so this was home territory. We passed on our sightings, and Phil furiously scribbled down the details.

The information download was interrupted by the arrival of Keir, an uncharacteristically quiet, shaven-headed New Yorker whom we had met the previous day. He was a dead ringer for the actor John Malkovich, but today his appearance was even more arresting than usual, despite the strong competition from the Australo-Brit sat next to us. Gone was the calm demeanour that had so impressed us the previous day. Keir was soaked in sweat, and a slightly crazed expression played around his features. His eyes burned rather brightly, and he had the whiff of the evangelical about him. His hands were shaking slightly, and he gripped the bottle of coke he had just purchased a little too tightly.

'Oh my God it's good to be alive,' he started, before dissolving into a maniacal giggle. 'I thought about writing a farewell note to my girlfriend and family and everything...'

Once we had persuaded him to sit down, the details of what had happened to so radically change Keir's character began to unfold. He had been birding downriver in an area near the Blau and Yong Hides. Having heard a Garnet Pitta call, he had gone way off-trail to look for it, and after hunting around for an hour had realized that he was lost. Not just marginally off-track, but properly, hopelessly disorientated, cast adrift in the endless ocean of greenery that make up Taman Negara's forests. Once off the trail, one tree looks very much like another, and the dense foliage prevents one being able to sight even the most prominent of landmarks. Keir had been carrying neither compass nor GPS, and was equipped with only the most rudimentary trail map. He had already eaten all the food he had been carrying, and was dangerously low on drinking water. He was, as Phil so elegantly put it, 'pretty much f*cked.'

As Keir consumed an impressive quantity of water in a bid to rehydrate, the whole sorry tale came out, all except the dénouement, which in his heightened state of sensory excitement, he completely omitted to mention.

'So how did you escape?' I ventured at length. It transpired that he had found a small clearing deep in the forest, had constructed his own sundial out of twigs, and waited. After an hour, the sundial's shadow had moved, allowing Keir to confirm his suspicion as to which direction was east. He had then ploughed through the forest for an hour or two, until he had emerged onto the north bank of the Tembeling River. From there he had managed to re-find the trail, and had walked all the way back to the HQ. In all, he had been out in the wilderness for seven hours. We stared at him in admiration. Englishmen, with the honourable exception of Sir Ranulph Fiennes (whom I personally expect to be unmasked as a German travelling incognito at any moment) are sometimes prone to flap in a crisis. Keir the American had stayed calm, and in an unrivalled show of ingenuity, had engineered a method of escape using bush-craft logic that was truly inspiring. We slapped him on the back and welcomed him back to civilization. He scampered off to get cleaned up, still exuding the zeal of a newborn unable to believe he's made it into the world.

Over the next few days, we covered as many trails as we could, casting our net wide in an attempt to see as many of the scarcer lowland species as possible. Garnet Pittas proved to be in full song; we heard them daily and saw two more individuals after protracted exercises in stalking off-trail. Banded, Blue-winged and Hooded Pittas were all patiently hunted down and, where possible, photographed.

We pioneered up-river, taking a boat to the derelict and deserted Trenggan resort and walked all the way to the remote Kumbang hide. We tracked down two more irrationally co-operative Rail-babblers. Three of these arch-skulkers seen in a week! What on earth was going on? We virtually had to kick a Great Argus, Malaysia's monumental pheasant species, off the Jenet Muda trail, walking right up to this usually shy and retiring behemoth of a game-bird with its outlandishly long train as it refused to budge from its dancing ground. Andy and I had brief views of a pair of Malayan Peacock-pheasants, although Mike missed out on a view and rechristened them with an obscene moniker that has no place in a family volume such as this. We homed in on a rare Cinnamon-rumped Trogon, perched unobtrusively in the understorey and somehow managing to disguise its crimson underparts. Buff-necked and Olive-backed Woodpeckers both made an appearance, and we called in a scarce Rufous-collared Kingfisher. A distant Rufous-tailed Shama was similarly sociable, and we even managed to flush a small covey of Crested Partridges as we ran for cover in the midst of a fierce rainstorm.

The best bird of all though, cropped up in a truly unexpected manner. After a long hike up towards the Tabing Hide, I had decided to try for one of the Banded Pittas that had been tormenting me by calling unseen from the furthest corners of the forest. Ever the optimist, I had made up my mind that nothing was going to stop me from photographing one. Having located a bird giving its distinctive whirring *'kirrr'* call, I spent an hour stalking it, but it steadfastly resisted giving itself up. At times I was no more than a metre or two from its hiding place, but it refused to offer anything but the most fleeting of glimpses. After a long struggle, I caught sight of a movement ahead, and the bird flew up and perched on an isolated branch that looped across the trail. *At last,* I thought, *it's decided to behave.*

I slowly raised my binoculars, but instead of a Banded Pitta, there, in perfect profile and in full view, stood a Chestnut-capped Thrush. This bird belongs to a clandestine group of thrushes in the *Zoothera* genus, and all are highly sought after by bird-watchers. Almost all are good-looking, and most are rare and infuriatingly difficult to observe. I had played the song of this species on many occasions in a number of southeast Asia's lowland forests in an attempt to locate one and lure it into view, but had never had so much as a squeak in response. Now, without any focused effort on my part, one was sat in front of me in plain view, nervously looking around and deciding on its next move.

It was a peach of a bird: slate-grey on the back, white below with heavy black spotting on the flanks, and with a solid black patch on the chin, throat and breast. The crown and nape as the name suggests were deep chestnut, and the wing-coverts sported two broad, crescentic white bars. I watched it for a few seconds, stunned into inaction, and before I knew it, the bird had dropped into an area of short cover at the side of the trail. I backed off and waited for a few minutes, but the bird did not reappear. I checked my watch. There was an hour of daylight left and I figured I could reach the others in a ten-minute sprint.

I hurtled down the trail, the humidity causing me to gasp with the effort of ascending the steeper sections, and finally reached the beach at Lubok Simpon, startling the others as I burst out of the jungle. Mike, Andy and Keir were relaxing with their boots off while waiting for the regular Blue-banded Kingfisher to streak by. An explanation tumbled breathlessly from my lips.

'Stalking...Banded Pitta... disappeared...replaced...Chestnut-capped Thrush.'

I gesticulated wildly up-river, while the others rapidly grabbed their belongings, and we high-tailed it back in the direction of the thrush. We stopped just short of the site and scanned, acutely aware of the species' reputation as a shy and retiring bird. We stood rooted to the spot until it got dark, but the bird did not reappear. My joy at chancing upon such a gem was tempered by the fact that my companions had missed it, but even so I relayed the full story from the comfort of the Mutiara's bar that night.

At dawn the following day we were back in position. During a two-hour vigil, Andy enjoyed a brief, obscured view, but by the time he had described the precise location, the bird had dropped back into hiding. In the evening we returned, and Phil Hansbro had a fleeting view of the bird on the trail, less than ten metres from the spot in which I had first seen it. Despite further attempts, Mike, Keir, and others who had heard the news were never to catch up with the thrush, a crushing disappointment. I felt for them, but there was no denying either my unbridled joy at finally seeing a bird that had eluded me for the best part of two decades. Seeing the pitta was a relief, but seeing a Chestnut-capped Thrush was a massive and unexpected bonus.

Once again, despite meticulous planning and research, the forest had surprised me, as it so often had in the past. Which is, I think, the essential untamable beauty of rainforest. No two days are ever the same, and no amount of advance calculations will generate exactly the result you expect. There will always be moments of random joy, and equally days of unforeseen despair at a target species' inexplicable failure to show up as instructed. In essence, that is why bird-watching, like any hunting, is such a thrill. No matter how skilful you become, how honed your technique, it's all so uncertain.

Our time at Taman Negara had come to an end. We reluctantly packed, savoured our last mouthful of chocolate and banana pancake courtesy of our friends at the floating restaurant, and drove south. I had triumphed over the obstacles that stood between me and the one species of pitta I needed to find in the Malaysian lowlands, but an altogether more daunting task now waited for me in the mountains.

As Mike drove us to the former colonial resort of Fraser's Hill, I reflected on the job in hand and discussed tactics with Andy. I had failed to find a Rusty-naped Pitta during five days in northern

Thailand earlier in the year. Now I had just four short days to track one down in the steep-sided ravines that snake around the upper elevations of Fraser's Hill. One thing I knew for sure; it was not going to be easy.

The proprietress of the Shahzan Inn at Fraser's Hill wrinkled her brow in amusement. We were negotiating hard, and had already secured a mid-week discount due to the fact that Fraser's Hill is primarily a weekend retreat for the rich denizens of KL, two hours to the south. Our silver-tongued charms eventually won the day, and we got a room for three for the price of a double. With packed breakfasts thrown in. (Not literally thrown into the room you understand. That would create an unholy mess, not least because the processed cheese sandwiches would stick to the counterpanes and the oranges would roll under the beds and be difficult to retrieve.) We celebrated our capitalist expertise in the only way we knew how. We dressed down and went birding.

I had been to Fraser's Hill seven years earlier, and had seen Rusty-naped Pitta briefly in flight on a precarious but long-established path known as the Bishop Trail. Fraser's Hill is named after Louis James Fraser, a Scottish tin-miner, colonial adventurer and fortune hunter. Described by Sir George Maxwell as 'a slightly built little man with a thin grey beard, and appearing between fifty and sixty years old,' he was by all accounts an enigmatic and colourful character. Fraser was rumoured to run an opium and gambling den frequented by miners in the Pahang Hills. In the early 1900s, Fraser vanished without a trace, and to this day it is not known what became of him. (Stoners of the world, let that be a lesson to you all.) The story of the Bishop trail is that while holidaying at the site in 1917, C.J. Ferguson-Davie, then Bishop of Singapore, together with his colleague A.B. Champion, the Chaplain of Selangor, went trekking to find Fraser's Bungalow up in the hills. The bishop employed local labourers to make a bridle path from his residence, a cottage named 'The Retreat' and later renamed 'Bishop House', and this same narrow, undulating trail still exists today. After winding its way through the hills for three kilometres, the Bishop Trail morphs into the Maxwell Trail, named for Sir George Maxwell, Chief Secretary of the Federated Malay States, whom in 1920 took a keen interest in the development of Fraser's Hill. Workers are said to have used the trail to gain access to Whittington Bungalows to listen to First World War news on the hill resort's only radio set.

I was more interested in natural history than ancient history, and I knew that the first few hundred metres of this trail were a famous site for Rusty-naped Pitta. This was my best chance finally to overcome what had emerged as something of a stumbling block in my mission. We parked up and I hunted around in the long grass for the trailhead. A helpful local wandered up to me and asked what I was doing.

'I'm looking for the Bishop Trail' I told him. He cocked his head on one side and weighed me up.

'You were here some time ago?' he said enquiringly. 'They closed this section five years ago. The trail now starts behind the Bishop's House up the road.'

I thanked him for his assistance, and we motored up to the spot. I recognized it immediately as the old secondary entrance that led downhill to bisect the old trail halfway along. We clomped down the steps and found the end of the old trail on our left, cluttered with signs that read *Access prohibited. No entry under any circumstances.* So, like generations of birders before us, we went in. The trail had clearly not been used for a while, and was thickly choked with vegetation. Less than a hundred yards in, we reached a stream crossing littered with major tree falls. Beyond we could see a continuation of the obstacle course on the far side. It seemed impossible to get down the trail, let alone see anything from it. We turned around and went back to the new trail to discuss our options.

I was extremely concerned. The one place I was relying on to host a Rusty-naped Pitta was no longer accessible, and April was the optimum time to find the birds, since they would be calling ahead of the breeding season which coincided with the onset of the monsoon rains in May. If I missed the bird here my best chance would be gone, and I would have to rely on finding a bird later in the year without it calling. This, I already knew from bitter experience, was going to be phenomenally difficult. I mentally ran through the few retail outlets at Fraser's Hill. None of them, as far as I could recall, sold machetes. We would simply have to try other places until we found a co-operative Rusty-nape, and hope for the best. I thought back to the Chestnut-capped Thrush, and the birder's uncertainty principle. What goes around had most certainly come around, and with a vengeance.

There was nothing for it but to work the rest of the Bishop Trail, a path I had trodden before, and where I had trawled repeatedly and unsuccessfully for Rusty-naped Pitta in the past. We worked the trail, bumping into a scurrying group of Malaysian Partridges as we rounded a particularly sharp corner. This was a recently split species, and a new bird for all of us. At least the day was not a total write-off. With an hour of daylight left, we reached a narrow stream bed that crossed the trail as it ran near-vertically down the mountain-side. I thought I sensed a movement, and we played our tape of Rusty-naped Pitta's call.

'Chom-WIT!...Chom-WIT!'

The call reverberated around the valley as I snapped off the tape, and I was gratified to hear a bird respond above us. We were standing on the trail in full view, so we scuttled into cover and hid our bulky frames as best we could. The bird continued to call, and it was coming closer. A couple of minutes more, and the call was almost deafening.

The bird crossed the trail. To be precise, it crossed the trail about a metre from where we had been standing, and from which vantage point we would have had an incredible view had we stayed put. By pure ill luck our new position did not allow a view of the bird's crossing point, but it seemed not to matter. The song was by now even louder, and we frantically craned our necks for a glimpse of the bird. I could tell that the bird was extremely close, and had taken up residence behind a large fallen tree trunk directly opposite us. It had stopped moving, and after a further minute or so of calling fell silent. I pondered the timeless dilemma. Should we rush it and hope for a flight view? Or stay put in the hope it would re-cross the trail in a more favourable spot? We elected to pursue caution, since our chances of moving without sending the bird bouncing off unseen through the forest seemed slim at best. We waited and waited, but the bird did not appear. Finally, our patience exhausted, we crept up to the fallen tree and peered behind it. The bird had gone. It had obviously been able to see us even if we could not see it, and had clearly found the sight of three sweaty bird-watchers a less than appealing proposition. We had blown it.

Still, I figured, we knew where the bird was, and it was without doubt an extremely responsive individual. This was a major bonus, for Rusty-napes have an unpleasant reputation for refusing to respond to imitations of their song. All we had to do was to go back to the same place before dawn the next morning, pick a spot with a better view of the immediate surroundings, and play tape, right?

Wrong. The three of us were back in position just before first light, and waited for the pitta to start singing, as it surely would, at dawn. It never did. We played tape. No response. We waited in silence for an hour, just in case the bird came in silently. It remained conspicuous only by its absence. I was baffled. I knew for certain that a Rusty-naped Pitta was on territory within a hundred metres of where we stood. It had come in strongly to tape the previous evening. And now, at what should be the absolute peak of calling activity, early morning at the best time of year, it professed a profound disinterest in our fake rival male on its home turf. There was only possible conclusion; this was one canny bird. It had heard the tape, come in to have a look, realized we were jerking its chain, and made a mental note not to get suckered by the same punch twice. Pretty damn smart. For the next three hours we trawled the entire trail, playing short bursts of what we hoped were pitta-friendly tape every two hundred metres or so. We saw and heard nothing. Fraser's Hill appeared to be no more densely populated with pittas than Essex is with intellectuals. Not good. Not good at all.

We gave up the unequal struggle and decided to try our luck at the Telekom Loop on the other side of The Hill. The Loop is a circular road encircling the enormous radar mast that dominates the landscape at Fraser's. Andy had information from a friendly bird tour leader who had heard a Rusty-naped Pitta 'in the second gully along going clockwise' a couple of years earlier. It was a long shot, but our list of options was shorter than Hannibal Lecter's Christmas card list.

We found the ravine and played tape. *Nada*. We backtracked and tried the previous gully, and then walked up the hill to try the next one. Same negative result. We walked slowly up the loop road, birding as we went and trawling with audio every few hundred metres. As the day warmed up, activity was starting to diminish, and it looked like our hunt for a new pitta would have to wait until the following morning.

And then, just as we were on the point of giving up, we heard a response. We crept to the edge of the ravine and after each picking a spot with some kind of view of the leaf-litter below us, knelt down. I had chosen a position surrounded by dense forest, but which was blessed with a single, narrow corridor of visibility extending almost down to the ravine floor. I figured that if the pitta tracked laterally along the side of the ravine, it would have to pass through the gap at some point. I triggered two seconds of audio, and the bird called a couple more times before falling silent. This hiatus might signal that the bird was no longer interested, but I was sure that it sent a different message; the bird was on the move. I pre-focused my binoculars at a likely range and held my breath.

The pitta called again. Closer, definitely closer, and no longer buried deep in the bottom of the ravine. Another bout of silence, then that same explosive *'chom-WIT!'* There was a hint of a movement just to the right of my gap, before a strapping Rusty-naped Pitta bounced right into the middle of the space and paused, surveying its surroundings.

'I have it,' I whispered to Mike and Andy, describing as best I could where it was. The bird looked up-slope, stared directly at me for a second, and then bounded on behind the wall of vegetation to my left. Andy scored a reasonable view as it continued to work round us, circling the tape, keeping superbly well hidden as it flashed through the forest.

My six and a half days of searching had finally paid off with a glorious, three-second view of the whole bird. As pittas go, it was a bit of a bruiser, a powerful physical presence packed into a chunky frame. Bull-chested and broad-headed, it was for the most part peachy-orange, with an olive green back and a dark line behind the eye. I thought of my Assam bird. This Rusty-nape was a darker, more butch version of a Blue-nape that has been spent too long on the sun-bed. Despite the species' intelligence and guile, its wily and at times downright sneaky manoeuvering, I had finally managed to stay one bounce ahead. It had led me a merry dance, but now victory was mine. I had notched up my fifteenth species for the year, and a wave of relief swept over me. The way ahead had cleared, and the mission was back on track.

That evening we opened the bottle of wine for which we had scoured Malaysia. We had managed to track down a Chinese liquor vendor in a dingy backstreet in some faceless little town *en route* to Fraser's Hill, having figured out that after the Taman Negara beer drought we had better stock up. When I eyed up a litre bottle of Thai rum, the pretty girl behind the counter (in what must surely have constituted a first in Chinese trading) had down-sold me to a more modest bottle. *'Have you drunk this one before? If not I recommend the smaller one'*. It was a shame too, as the rum turned out to be pretty damn good. Better at any rate than the bottle of wine, which Mike's connoisseur's palate was unable to tolerate. We finished off the last of the beer too, so by the time Phil Hansbro rocked up, fresh from harvesting new students in KL, we were already strangers to absolute sobriety. He too came carrying an armful of beers, which scarcely improved matters. We updated Phil in a rather rambling fashion on our antics, and presented him with the map we had prepared, which carefully detailed the whereabouts of the key species we knew he'd want to see.

We spent the next couple of days birding from dawn 'til dusk, finding another Rusty-naped Pitta along the way, which only Andy saw well. I had a fine view of its nether regions as it hopped off the end of an obscured branch an inch or two off the ground. All three of us had blip views of the same bird as it hopped behind a massive hardwood tree. We lined up our optics on the other side of the tree and waited for it to emerge. It never did. How it could have known that we would all be in a position to get a good look if it took three more hops is beyond me. Just like Cat Tien's Blue-rumped Pittas, Rusty-napes have an uncanny ability to use cover to their advantage, calculating the angles between themselves and their potential voyeurs, using whatever items of vegetation will most effectively screen them. If they were shoplifters I would not want to run a retail store in Rustyville.

We dropped down to The Gap, an area of forest below Fraser's Hill that holds a different set of lower altitude species. Mike and I succeeded in seeing the incredibly skulking Marbled Wren-babbler which no-one had seen at The Gap in recent times, and we all enjoyed the Blyth's Hawk-eagle that soared above us, as strikingly pied as Postman Pat's cat and considerably larger. On our last day we got into the spirit of things and worked our way through Phil's list of birds that would be new for him. Although all our Rusty-naped Pittas had already learned not to show their faces when we tried each of them in turn, we had nonetheless made a sizeable dent in the list by the time we had to leave for the airport. After wishing Phil the best of luck in tracking down a Rusty-nape to call his own, we swung down the hill and on to Kuala Lumpur.

Arriving at the airport we realized that I had made a tiny miscalculation. Andy's ticket was fine, but mine was a problem.

Although I was booked on the right flight at the right time, I had made my booking for the following day. Happily the cheerful Malaysia Airlines staff was able to make the necessary adjustments for a small fee, and I scrambled to the gate just in time to make the flight. As we cruised south towards Jakarta, I chatted to Andy about our success. He was as giddy as I was, despite having seen Rusty-naped Pitta before. His previous views had been so poor that he considered them to have been untickable. Thus he had not felt able to include the bird on his world list. Now however, he would be able to place an indelible mark next to the bird's name. Rusty-naped Pitta, on the list at last. We discussed our respective impending adventures. Andy would visit Gunung Gede and Halimun National Park in western Java, whilst I had planned a pioneering raid on southwestern Sumatra.

By the time the lights of Jakarta started to wink far below us, we were both fast asleep, and I was already dreaming of the next milestone to be passed on my journey.

Chapter 9

The *Toktor* Will See You Now.
Southwest Sumatra

I whiled away the day, catching up on sleep and taking care of a few chores, before decamping to the airport transit hotel. Late in the evening, I managed to hook up with the urbane Troy Shortell, whom I had met at Cat Tien a few weeks earlier. Our local fixer Roman duly showed up and we swapped wads of Rupiah for airline tickets and a detailed itinerary, before tippling rum and cokes and crashing out ahead of our early flight the following morning.

We were making for the Indonesian island of Sumatra (that's the big, westernmost one. See Singapore up there? Down a bit and left). Our flight was mercifully short – just thirty-five minutes in the clutches of Sriwijaya Air – and delightfully uneventful. The flight cruised in to land on a slippery runway at Bandar Lampung Airport on Sumatra's south coast. The tail end of the wet season was still doing its work, and our bags were distinctly damp as we dragged them off the clattering carousel.

Although geographically close, Bandar Lampung felt light years away from the frenzied hustle and bustle of Jakarta's busy streets. Even here in the big city, one could feel Sumatra's distinctly laid-back vibe. Although it's the second largest of Indonesia's many islands, the population here is a mere thirty-nine million people, spread thinly along its seventeen hundred kilometre length. Much of the southeast is permanently flooded, and we planned to visit Way Kambas to look for water-birds, but before that we were heading for the rugged mountains of the southwest. Our first destination was Way Titias, an area of dense jungle near Liwa, after which we would climb into an area known locally as *Danau Ranau*, a range of mountains overlooking a spectacular lake in an old volcanic crater.

Our scowling but efficient driver waved us impatiently into an ancient jeep, and we sluiced through the quiet, impoverished suburbs. Five hours later we rolled up outside a modest house and were introduced to our guides, the irrepressibly cheeky Toni, and the serious, considered Gamal.

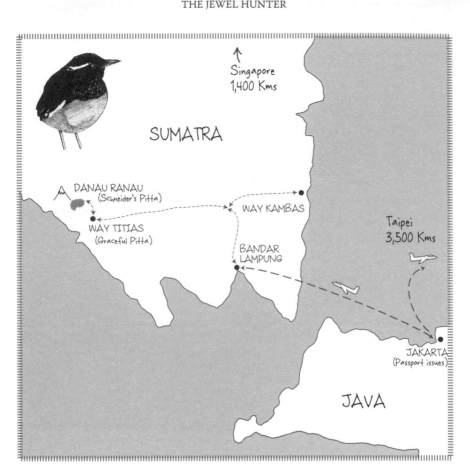

We had come to remote, southwestern Sumatra for three specific reasons:

- *To find the island's two endemic pittas: Graceful and Schneider's.*

- *To hunt for the* Toktor, *the recently rediscovered Sumatran Ground-cuckoo.*

- *To look for rare game birds that have long since been hunted out in many of Asia's more accessible forest sites.*

The *Toktor* was thought to be extinct until 1997, when the species was rediscovered. There had then been no subsequent sightings until 2007, when a captive bird was discovered in a bird market in Sumatra. The story, as far as we could glean from our limited Bahasa, was that the local salesman, the aforementioned Toni, had introduced an enquiring ornithologist to his colleague, Gamal the bird-catcher. The latter had brought the same scientist to Way Titias, where he habitually caught the birds. Using his knowledge of the birds' calls and his hunting skills, polished by years of bird-catching for food and profit, Gamal had been able to locate the birds, and the rest is history.

Toni's family entertained us, his three shy children chasing a rather less shy kitten around the room, the kitten in turn pursuing a flock of cheeping chicks. Toni's two elder daughters, though barely of school age, were already wearing Malaysian-style Muslim headscarves, the eldest daughter's just failing to cover the *Hello Kitty* motif that peeped out from the front of her jacket.

Times change. I knew that in the seventh century, Sumatra had been the epicentre of the Buddhist kingdom of Srivijaya. A Hindu empire was founded in the eighth century, before Islam was introduced by Arab traders in the thirteenth century. Within three hundred years Islam had spread across the island to become the dominant religion, a state of affairs that perseveres to the present day. Quite when Hello Kitty got involved is less clear, but it's a welcome if eclectic addition. We gratefully accepted the offer of coffee, and as a storm raged overhead, had our first impromptu Bahasa Indonesian lesson, learning to count to five. The crib notes I had brought with me advised that Bahasa has no tenses, and that verbs are not conjugated; my kind of language.

Eventually the downpour abated, and we strapped on our packs and slithered and sloshed our way up to Gamal's house in the nearby village of Landos. In contrast to Toni's place which boasted two electric light bulbs, Gamal's house did not have any *listrik*, but we were made to feel very welcome. After a candlelit dinner of crunchy pork, noodles and a seemingly inexhaustible supply of prawn crackers, we spent a restless night on the wooden floor of Gamal's living room. I woke early, and spent a few minutes quietly chanting '*tagu, dua, tiga, empat, lima*' under my breath, determined not to lapse into Bahasa innumeracy. My homework completed, I slapped Troy awake, packed up my kit, and greeted our newly arrived crew, Habzi the forest ranger, Bambang the cook's assistant and our two porters.

We set off on the trek into Way Titias. The site itself is not particularly high at only eleven hundred metres above sea level, but the tough access trail switchbacks up and down over a succession of minor hills, before plunging down into the valley, where seven river crossings wait to be negotiated. Initially we tried to keep our boots dry by hopping from boulder to boulder, but stable footholds were hard to come by and we soon abandoned the attempt, wading through the thigh-high waters. Each crossing became deeper and more perilous, and Gamal took great delight in pointing out where previous pioneers had come to grief, illustrating each tale of woe with elaborate hand gestures, like a particularly macabre game of charades. *'Here is where Richard Thomas broke his finger!... This is the place where Nick Brickle had his cheek pierced by a bamboo stave!'* I was just waiting for *'this is the very spot where Henry was impaled on a Wild Boar's tusks and tossed into the canopy'*, but mercifully it seemed the injuries sustained over the years had been relatively minor.

We paused at regular intervals for the porters to smoke, and Troy and I would pass the time by calming the trussed live chicken we had brought with us. Troy turned out to be an expert Chicken Whisperer (now there's a movie sequel just crying out to be made. I can see Robert Redford now, manfully clutching an untamed bantam and murmuring sweet nothings into its feathery ear). I settled for feeding the unfortunate bird with chocolate wafers. Whilst I maintained publicly that my motives were pure ('every condemned man deserves a last meal') I was secretly determined to enjoy a Mexican-style *Mole Poblano* for supper. After one such smoke-stop we became aware of a commotion ahead of us, and Toni came rushing past us in the opposite direction, chortling to himself and shouting *'ayam, ayam!'* It seemed that in the post-nicotine rush, someone had left the chicken two crossings back. It was swiftly retrieved, and was soon safely tucked under our guide's arm once more. Along the way a few birds showed up to keep us amused. Tiny Blue-eared Kingfishers zipped past us at the river crossings while a Sunda Forktail bobbed and pirouetted at the water's edge. But the star of the show was a female Sumatran Trogon sitting motionless in the canopy, staring down at us out of huge, blue-rimmed eyes.

The history of this attractive, colourful bird is somewhat convoluted, but I shall attempt to unravel. As the name suggests, the Sumatran Trogon, more formally known to the scientific fraternity as *Apalharpactes mackloti*, is endemic to Sumatra. Until the early noughties, this was considered to be the same species as Javan Trogon (now *Apalharpactes reinwardtii*) and the pair was collectively known as 'Blue-tailed Trogon'. (This was in itself pretty confusing since there was already a Blue-tailed Trogon in South America, now known as White-eyed Trogon or Choco Trogon, *Trogon comptus*. Still following? Do please try to stay awake.) Anyway, in 2002 a couple of esteemed taxonomic experts, Messrs. Collar and van Balen, pointed out that males of the Sumatran race had a maroon-coloured rump, unlike their Javan cousins. They further observed that the females of the two species showed small differences in wing-panel colour and pattern. The birds in Sumatra also boasted at least one vocalization (a throaty *'wih-wih-weeugh-ah'*, with the last two notes lower) quite different from that of Javan birds. And none of them, on account of their short stubby wings and sedentary nature, had ever visited South America.

All of which meant that after due deliberation, the speciating powers-that-be duly pronounced, and the Sumatran birds were given full specific status. Quite right too for such a good-looking bird, and reason enough to justify a visit to Way Titias. You should definitely go there. Tomorrow. It will be hard work physically, and you'll get wet now and then, but it is way more fun than the office. And you have a very good chance of seeing the trogon for yourself. (In Sumatra I mean, not in your office. That's pretty unlikely, and if you claim to have seen one near the filing cabinet people are going to give you funny looks.)

There is much to know about trogons. I am reliably informed that the word *trogon* comes from the Greek meaning *nibbler*, a reference to the trogon family's habitual gnawing of tree bark in order to create nest holes. The family is the only group of animals in the world with a heterodactyl toe arrangement (toes 3 and 4 point forwards whilst toes 1 and 2 point backwards). Which doubtless means they are forever being invited to dinner parties and then when everyone has had a few, are routinely asked to take their shoes off so that the diners can check out their bizarre extremities. If trogons wear shoes at all, which on reflection is perhaps doubtful. Can you imagine sitting in a branch of a Clark's shoe shop and patiently explaining to the assistant that you have two toes that point forward and two back? Even if they could deal with the shock they'd be out of your size as always.

Strange-toed or no, the trogon was a new bird for me, and I attacked the trail with renewed enthusiasm. Having crossed the final river, we slowly wound our way up into the higher hills. Fending off

Tiger Leeches, enormous yellow-and-black spiders and numerous ticks we made good progress, and at last sat on top of the ridge, listening to a distant Large Hawk-cuckoo's hypnotic 'brain-fever' song. After a final descent down a treacherous incline, we reached the riverside clearing where we would build our camp. Satisfied with the facilities (running water. Erm, that's it) we did our best to construct a home-away-from-home out of nine bamboo struts and a large blue tarpaulin. As we sat back and reviewed the result of our labours, we were pretty pleased with ourselves. Ray Mears would have wept with envy.

A list of advantages for urban-dwellers living in the jungle

• *Surrounded by nature in all its fecund glory*

• *Pittas on your doorstep*

• *No need to purchase expensive residents' parking permits*

• *Minimal danger of being woken at 4am by drunken revellers*

• *Relatively low numbers of Jehovah's Witnesses and/or local government election candidates at your door*

• *Next door's dog completely inaudible*

• *Total lack of access to chocolate and red wine = guaranteed weight loss*

• *Fine dining (Chicken Mole Poblano)*

• *It gets dark early, so plenty of time to brush up on your Bahasa*

• *River-bathing free and only two metres from camp*

• *Chance to play 'who's got the biggest leech?' Every night*

• *Generation of an endless fund of macho 'roughing it' stories with which to amaze and amuse your friends*

• *What doesn't kill you makes you stronger*

Now that we were here, the scale of our task became apparent. The forest was dense, and criss-crossed by extremely steep-sided ravines through which passage was all but impossible. There was but one decent trail leading up the hill from the camp. Accessing anywhere else in the forest would be very tough, necessitating copious amounts of machete-work, and no small exertion of energy. It was important that we stayed out of harm's way here. Falling sick or getting injured would be no laughing matter, with no facilities, only a basic first-aid kit, and a long and difficult slog to get back to civilization. These realizations left me in a sombre mood as we ascended the slope above camp.

An hour or so above the river, Gamal suddenly froze in his tracks and hissed, *'Toktor!'* We crept towards the sound, a chilling series of primaeval, high-pitched wails, and hid ourselves behind a tree, squatting on our haunches to minimize our profile. Tracking the sound, we realized that the ground-cuckoo was moving through the jungle, and it was soon directly below us, deep in a ravine. It switched from its primary song and began to make a remarkable series of aspirated sounds, *'puussh... puussh... puussh'*, like an idling steam train taking on water. For half an hour the *Toktor* was never more than a few metres below us, but it remained stubbornly hidden, until at length it slunk deeper into the forest. We were crestfallen. To have been so close to this mythical creature, this living fossil, and not to have seen it was bitterly disappointing.

Gamal's eyesight and hunter's instincts were unerring. If a bird could be eaten or sold he could find it, and he knew many of the local species' vocalizations, even if he did not know their names in English. We asked Gamal questions in our faltering Bahasa over an excellent supper of salted fish, sambal, and our former companion, the chicken (not, in fact cooked Mexican-style, but stir-fried with fragrant lemongrass and ginger). He told us that catching a ground-cuckoo had usually taken him three to five days, and that each bird would sell for thirty-five thousand Rupiah; roughly $3 US, not exactly a fortune. Once he discovered that he could earn ten times that figure *per diem* guiding bird-watchers through the forest, his hunting days were over, and he had been only too happy to join the developing world's growing band of poachers-turned-eco-guides. We reflected on this fact as we prepared for a night in the forest. Our payments, despite being filtered through a travel company in Jakarta, were helping to save the Sumatran forest and its inhabitants. Perhaps our obsession with Asia's birds and animals was finally serving some useful purpose. We slept well, secure in the knowledge that we were one small part of a sustainable solution.

At dawn we worked our way back up the hill above the camp, but our contact with the ground-cuckoo was limited to a single bird heard at long range. Ten hours of hard work produced a few good endemic species, but no *Toktor*. It did, however, produce a pitta.

Late morning, I heard a single-note whistle, indistinguishable to my ears from the Garnet Pittas I had been hearing at Taman Negara in Malaysia. Gamal was dismissive. *'Burung jauh jauh'* he said, indicating that the bird was a long way off, and gesticulating at the mass of foliage cloaking the steep slope below us. He sat down for a smoke, the pungent aroma of his *Gudung Garam* clove cigarette drifting through the forest, thick and sweet. Buoyed by my recent Malaysian experiences however, I decided that I couldn't let this opportunity go to waste. I half-clambered, half-fell down the slope. Lying in a heap at the bottom, I listened acutely to the whistle, which was now considerably closer. Gamal followed, keen as ever to prevent one of his charges from getting into trouble. I gave him a clandestine thumbs-up and whistled to the pitta, which immediately responded.

Within five minutes, the bird was almost at my feet, though still buried in a substantial thicket. One final whistle drove it over the edge, and it emerged into a tiny hole in the vegetation, scurrying about like a hyperactive mouse. As soon as it appeared out of the gloom it caught sight of me, performed a rapid *volte-face*, and scuttled back into the understorey. A three-second view, but enough to identify it. Graceful Pitta was on the list. Despite the brevity of our meeting, in those few precious seconds I had already fallen hard for Graceful Pitta. A vision in scarlet and black, with an iridescent blue arc curving backwards from the eye and a matching azure blaze on the edge of the wing, it was poetry in motion.

Troy and Gamal joined me at the base of the slope, and we spent half an hour trying to coax the pitta back into view, but it was having none of it. We returned to the trail and resumed our climb, working our way steadily up into the higher reaches of the forest. Tiny Rufous-browed Flycatchers called from cover, occasionally popping into view and showing off their smart white gorgets. A Cream-striped Bulbul shrieked at us from the canopy, a member of the dowdiest tribe of birds on the entire planet, but a scarce Sumatran endemic nonetheless. Just before dusk, we heard a pair of Long-billed Partridges duetting, the male and female's calls becoming ever more inextricably intertwined as they approached their ecstatic crescendo. Troy and Gamal were ahead of me, and saw the birds as they disappeared over the ridge, but I was too late even to glimpse a departing tail feather. I was gutted. This is a bird that has not been seen in most of its range for at least a decade, and even here in Indonesia they remain a very rare bird. Still, only I had managed to clap eyes on the pitta, and I would not have traded places for all the salted fish in Liwa. Number sixteen for the year. I was at the halfway point already with time in hand.

The next day was a carbon copy of the previous one, except that this time we did not even hear a ground-cuckoo, nor any pittas. I did, however, catch up with the same pair of Long-billed Partridges, and after a painstaking stalk across a steep slope just before dusk, I had a brief view of the singing female at point blank range, before the pair exploded from our feet and flew up into the canopy. The highlight of the day though, was provided by another gallinaceous bird. High on the hill we walked a seldom-travelled animal trail, where a male Salvadori's Pheasant sauntered across in front of us, its iridescent blue-black plumage and bare crimson facial skin catching the light. This rare bird lives only in the lower montane forests of Sumatra, and has been seen by very few people. Happily that limited band now included us amongst their number.

Gamal was becoming increasingly worried by our continuing failure to locate the *Toktor*, and was leading us through ever more inhospitable terrain. We scrambled through steep ravines, forded forest streams, and struggled along barely navigable trails. On our last morning, we were negotiating one such trail when Gamal stopped dead in his tracks, pointing his machete forwards. I thought he must finally have found the ground-cuckoo, but as he turned the look on his face quashed my hopes in an instant. Instead of the delighted expression I had expected to see, his face was a mask of fear. His next move took me by surprise. He turned and belted past me, whispering 'Bruin' as he ran. In the space in front of me I saw the cause of his concern. A large black shape was lumbering towards me, the unmistakable silhouette of a Malayan Sun Bear.

I struggled for an instant to remember what one should do when confronted by a large carnivorous animal with extremely long, razor-sharp claws. I considered the available evidence. The experienced hunter armed with our only weapon had just legged it in the opposite direction. I elected to follow, sprinting past a startled Troy and shouting, 'Bear. Run!', over my shoulder. We crashed a little way down the trail before veering off to hide behind a fallen tree in a panting, gasping pile. The bear continued on down the trail, ignoring us. Troy was disappointed not to have had a chance to take a photograph. I was simply relieved to have escaped with enough limbs to be able to shoot future photographs.

After one last extreme but futile attempt to locate the *Toktor*, we broke camp and hoisted our belongings onto our backs. As we started back up the trail we were caught in the heaviest rain I have ever experienced, and the torrent continued all the way back to Landos. The river crossings became an altogether more dangerous proposition, and we struggled through the swirling waters, repeatedly slipping over and getting thoroughly drenched. Habzi, our trusty forest ranger led the way enveloped in a fetching pale blue set of waterproofs, surging ahead like an inelegant dolphin.

By the time we made it back to Gamal's house, every inch of me was soaked, and to peals of laughter I laid my possessions out across our guide's living room floor. My passport was ruined, and despite drying each page individually with tissue paper, it was a sorry mess. My notebook, full of precious behavioural notes, GPS co-ordinates, and identification points was beyond repair. After a community effort to propel Habzi on his motorbike in a roughly upright manner, we squelched back into Liwa. We squeezed into the jeep and eventually made it to the Permata hotel. We failed in our quest to find a place to do laundry, but I remained upbeat, looking forward to spending a night in a real bed, unaccompanied by numerous smaller members of the forest fauna. After dinner Troy hitched a ride to the neighbouring town on the back of a motorbike, and returned carrying cans of Guinness and Bintang beer. He shouted to me through the wall of our adjacent rooms.

'What are you up to, want a beer?'

I responded that I was sitting on the toilet. He apologized for the intrusion, but I told him not to worry.

'I've been here for fifteen minutes. I'm not actually using the facilities. I'm just enjoying the sensation of sitting on a real toilet.'

Our jungle living had clearly taken its toll.

The first part of our journey to *Danau Ranau* passed without incident; two hours in the bus, followed by a restful hour crossing the lake on a gaily painted wooden ferry boat. We spread our steaming clothes out on deck while we basked in the sunshine and tried to restore our trench-feet to some semblance of good health. Ahead of us was an exacting six-hour climb up into the forest's dark interior. Our route would take us up through acres of coffee plantations, where once virgin forest must have stood.

After five hours of backbreaking work, broken only by a cup of coffee at a relief hut, we reached a small bamboo bench that signalled our arrival at the viewpoint. And what a view; we gazed out over the placid waters of the volcanic lake far below us, discussing its weirdly regular shore. To our left lay a remote plateau accessible only on foot, where dinosaurs doubtless still roamed. To our right, unbroken forest stretched all the way to the horizon. We sat enjoying the breeze and the spring sunshine. It felt good to be alive. More particularly, it felt good to have survived the tough ascent. Our guides had not been exaggerating; we really were going to earn our birds here. Toni nudged my elbow, indicating the trail twisting out of sight above us.

'*Sekarang itu medapat berbahaya.*'

I translated slowly in my head. 'Now it gets dangerous.'

He inclined his arm steeply upwards and raised an eyebrow. The real climb had not yet begun.

Toni was right. The next hour or so was phenomenally demanding. At times we were crawling on all fours, on other occasions hauling our tired bodies up inch by inch, using the trailside trees as leverage. The inclines were so steep that a direct assault proved impossible, and we had to zigzag our way across the slopes, completing one traverse after another. Covering even the smallest distance seemed to take an age. My under-utilized muscles, every sinew taut, were taxed to the maximum. I reminded myself continually that I had come here of my own free will, that I was paying for the privilege, and that flocks of Schneider's Pittas would be waiting to greet us at the summit. Most of all though, I reminded myself that the agony would be over at any minute. After one final spurt we reached the summit. Even our youthful porters looked ashen-faced, exhausted by lugging twenty kilos a man up these unforgiving gradients. We had made it, and with not a single man down.

From the *puncak* (summit) it was only a few hundred metres to a sheltered clearing in the forest, and mercifully it was downhill all the way. We forded the river at the bottom of the escarpment and pitched camp. I whittled three missing tent pegs and scraped off the moss that encrusted the impressive forest furniture assembled by the last party to venture this far. I bathed in the river and settled down under a tarpaulin. After a restorative Milo and the ubiquitous dinner of rice, noodles and vegetables, we towelled the evening drizzle from our hair, crawled into our sleeping bags and slept like babies.

Awake at four a.m. I dressed and checked the clearing, breathing in the forest air and listening for the calls of the Dusky Woodcock that I felt sure would be display-flighting overhead. Nothing but insect noise. We struggled back up the hill towards the *puncak*, and as it started to get light, listened to the forest waking up. A Red-headed Trogon called away to our right, a measured, '*taup-taup-taup-taup-taup*', probably the first ever recorded at this rarely visited site. A pair of Sumatran (Grey-breasted) Partridges cranked up their increasingly frenzied duet on a distant peak, while Temminck's Sunbirds and Orange-bellied Flowerpeckers tittered and chipped in the canopy above our heads. I filtered out these extraneous noises as I strained to pick out the sound we had come so far to hear; the distinctive, querulous '*coo-er-woo?*' of the Schneider's Pitta. At length, our patience was rewarded, and we heard a pitta calling way off in the distance. I cued up the iPod and played back a single phrase of the call. Within seconds, a pitta responded, a second bird, and less than fifty metres behind us. Troy, Gamal and I exchanged glances, eyebrows raised sky-high, and crept surreptitiously into a hiding place behind a large tree-trunk. I re-played our tape lure, and the bird again responded, closer still. We sat in silence on the forest floor, ignoring the mosquitoes that whined about our ears and praying that the ticks would find the insect repellent distasteful.

I carefully raised my binoculars to eye-level and scanned the terrain, my body taut with anticipation, alert to the slightest movement. Before long a shadow moved through the low evergreen undergrowth at the edge of my field of vision. I slowly swung my head in the direction of the movement. At first I saw nothing, but after a few seconds, there was the movement again, this time a little further to the left. I swung my optics further left, found a tiny gap in the cover, and waited. A shape materialized, a familiar, hunched profile on stout legs set well to the back of the body. *Schneider's Pitta*. The bird moved around us in a circle, eating up the ground, but always staying in cover. As it circled, it closed on us, eventually coming in behind us as pittas so often do, approaching to within a few feet. It surveyed us from within a thicket, paused to remove a bug from its breast feathers, and called again, the sound shockingly loud at such close proximity; '*COO-ER-WOO?*'

I mentally mapped out the detail of this mythical bird, a species seen by only a handful of people in modern times. It's endemic to the mountains of western Sumatra, and was first discovered in the latter part of the nineteenth century. Specimens were collected between 1914 and 1936, but the bird then went missing, not being seen for fifty-two years until its rediscovery in 1988. It's a stunning-looking creature, with a bright orange head. A thick, jagged black line runs down the side of the neck behind the eye, as if it had tried to apply eyeliner while running for a bus. The nape, mantle and tail are deep, iridescent blue, whilst the breast and belly are suffused a sumptuous peachy-buff. The legs, sturdy in common with most of the pitta family, are nonetheless a delicate shade of fingernail-pink. In short, a vision of loveliness, and standing just yards away from us at improbably close range.

The sound of Troy's motor-drive awoke me from my trance, and I grinned in triumph as I too cued up my camera, twisting in slow motion to avoid making any obvious movements. Despite our considerable care the bird moved off, having decided that we posed no threat to its ownership of this patch of prime forest real estate. All we could do was track the diminishing call as the bird bounced off about its business. Muted post-hunt celebrations followed. We had found one of the world's rarest and most elusive pittas, and had been privileged to see the bird at close quarters. For a few fleeting moments, it had even perched in the open. My decision to shun the regular bird-tourist site, Gunung Kerinci a few hundred kilometres to the north, had been well and truly vindicated. Although birders had beaten a well-worn path to Kerinci for years, I knew that many had failed to find Schneider's Pitta there, despite searching for days on the mountain slopes. I knew that the population at Kerinci was now greatly reduced, deforestation having forced the birds up to higher and higher altitudes. At Danau Ranau, if our initial experience was anything to go by, the population remained healthy and the birds responsive. What a result. A major mission obstacle had been overcome, and I strolled along the trail in a state of elation, grinning like a fool.

A little further up the hill we came across a tiny clearing, and rested for a while, continuing to listen for birdsong. Before long, we heard a tell-tale, monotone call, the purest sine-wave whistle imaginable, with an almost imperceptible upslurred final flourish. Somewhere in the tangle of lianas and low shrubs in front of us a Graceful Pitta was setting the boundaries of its territory. We crouched as low as we could and whistled back. The pitta responded, and after a protracted, whistled exchange, this tiny gem of a bird flipped into view, eventually perching on a low branch in the gloom of a well-vegetated gully. It sat there whistling and blinking nervously, its whole body puffed up with the effort of calling, neck stretched upward, like a tiny dog howling at the moon.

One of the smallest of the *Pittidae*, Graceful Pitta is also one of the cutest, with a maroon breast, scarlet belly and flashing azure-blue wing panel. A matching set of fine, iridescent sky-blue head plumes project backwards from the eye, extending a short way beyond the rear crown to form a set of miniscule 'horns'. This was a proper view, so much more satisfying than my brief encounter at Way Titias. I managed to snatch a few photographs as the bird circled us, and after a couple of circuits we left it in peace. Emerging from the clearing onto the trail we marvelled at our good fortune. In three hours we had seen and photographed Sumatra's two endemic pittas within a few hundred yards of each other. I looked at Troy, suddenly consumed with the seriousness of the moment.

'We need to name this spot. Log it properly I mean. So that others can find it.'

Troy thought for a moment. 'How about 'Graceland'?

So Graceland it was. We solemnly carved the site's new name into the wooden shelter opposite the glade with the tip of a machete, and stood back to admire our handiwork. Not bad for a couple of city boys with limited carpentry skills.

We worked our way back towards camp, and stumbled across a mixed species flock that sucked us into the forest and off the trail. An hour sped by as we picked off the commoner species, calling to each other periodically as we found something of interest. Trawling through the flock I came across a medium-sized bird perched motionless in the canopy. I mentally flicked through the likely candidates and drew a blank. The bird had pale purple cheeks, a brick red throat, and a curious bare pink patch around the eye.

Asian Green Broadbill, Taman Negara, Peninsular Malaysia.
As close as I could get to replicating the shot that inspired me as a child.

A view from the High Pines Trail,
Fraser's Hill, Peninsular Malaysia.

Dusky Langur at dusk,
Fraser's Hill.

A good omen for our chances of Rusty-naped Pitta at Fraser's Hill.

The luxurious camp at Way Titias, SW Sumatra.

The SW Sumatra Team (L-R: Gamal, Bambang, Toni, Habzi).

Passport ruination while leaving Way Titias, SW Sumatra.

'Everything I own is wet.' Gamal's house, Way Titias.

The lake at Danau Ranau, SW Sumatra. Swimming not recommended.

Bukit Pogong: 'Area Poxai Hadji Number One', Danau Ranau.

'Cochoacochoacochoa!' Danau Ranau.

A Sumatran Trogon bashfully hiding its heterodactyl toes at Way Titias.

The beautiful Taiwanese east coast N. of Tienhsiang.

A male Collared Bush-robin, Anmashan, Taiwan.

The view from the pass at Hehuanshan, Taiwan.

'This'll be the place then.' Fairy Pitta Guest House sign, Huben, Taiwan.

The real Mikado, Anmashan.

The forested banks of the Kinabatangan River, Sabah, Borneo.
Where the Giant Pitta lives.

Chico the Storm's Stork, hanging out by the restaurant, Kinabatangan.

The smallest elephant in the world. For once not playing football,
Kinabatangan.

'The Karl Malden of the monkey world'
Proboscis Monkey, Kinabatangan, Sabah.

'The Sweetest Sting'. A scorpion lurking on Kit's trousers,
Kinabatangan, Sabah.

Orang-utan, Borneo Rainforest Lodge, Sabah.

A leech enjoying the author, BRL, Sabah.

Wallace's Flying Frog. 'Dapper is too small a word.' BRL, Sabah.

Rafflesia keithii, The Corpse Flower in bloom, Poring Hot Springs, Sabah.

A young Red Leaf Monkey, BRL, Sabah.

Early morning light, The Coffin Trail, BRL, Sabah.

'What *is* this?' I murmured to no-one in particular. I studied the bird again, realizing with mounting excitement that whatever it was, I had not seen it before. 'Hey Troy, what the HELL is this bird?' Startled by my bemused tone, Troy hurried over and located the bird. A torrent of colourful language ensued, followed by a scarcely coherent babble. 'Cochoa!It'sthecochoa!Cochoacochoacochoa!'

Of course! The penny dropped. Troy was right, it was another of Indonesia's enigmatic avian jewels, a Sumatran Cochoa. It was a real prize, a bird in pursuit of which my companion had spent many days trudging up and down the mountain at Kerinci. Despite his efforts, the cochoa had remained hidden. Until now. We hastily photographed the bird to confirm the record, aware this was only the second time the bird had been documented in southwest Sumatra. The record shot secured, an unseemly scramble ensued as we struggled to find a spot less unobstructed by foliage. The bird did not move, casting the odd baleful glance in our direction, but otherwise ignoring us completely. From our new position we could clearly see the lilac wing panels, tail and matching cap, and we took shot after shot to preserve the details for posterity. Studying my efforts in the viewfinder I knew these were the best photographs ever obtained of this mythical bird; our amazing day had improved still further. Eventually the flock moved on and pulled the cochoa with it, leaving us to celebrate in the leaf-litter. I endeavoured to explain to Gamal in my best pidgin Bahasa that this was an important bird, that it would bring more bird-watchers to the site. '*Uang besar!*' Big money!

Back at the camp we huddled around our cameras' viewfinders and showed the cook, the porters and the forest warden our exciting discovery. We had been in the field for just six hours, but we had already seen the *pitta besar*, the *pitta kecil*, and now the cochoa. We could have lain around camp for the next three days and the trip would still have been an enormous success. Sadly, however, chilling out after a major success is not the way a birder's brain is wired. The logic runs thus: *we have seen some great birds in a short space of time. Clearly, the forest here has some fabulous creatures lurking in the shadows. We need to get out there and find the rest of them while there's still time.* Our initial success simply meant that for the rest of our time at Danau Ranau we were condemned to work harder than ever.

The afternoon was inevitably something of an anti-climax. We did manage to find a Sunda Treepie, a handsome, long-tailed beast dressed in sombre greys and browns. A couple of Wreathed Hornbills launched themselves into clear skies, drawing attention with their familiar nasal honking, their specially adapted wings whistling rhythmically like a swan's as they cruised majestically overhead.

As dusk fell we retreated to the camp, where Toni had been hard at work rustling up the world's spiciest tofu. We drank tea to quench the fire, spitting out the bolder bugs that endlessly invaded our makeshift dinner table, and flicking the scarier specimens back into the forest. Although the insect assault was unceasing, I was aware that *we* were the out of place organisms in this environment. Human beings have not evolved to co-exist comfortably in the rainforest, and it's invariably a struggle to stay fit and healthy in what is an alien environment. Over the years I have grown to love it, and to tolerate the hardships and irritations that are part and parcel of forest living, but I must admit that I checked every morning that the zipper on my flysheet was as snugly fitted to the ground as possible. Even so, the final sweep before flicking off my head torch beam at night often revealed something objectionable requiring removal in order to ensure a good night's sleep. Biting flies? I'm sorry to say that my eco-friendliness is not boundless, and they were summarily dispatched. Spiders with big, fat abdomens? Cast out into the darkness. Being close to nature is all well and good, but there are limits.

The next day we knew we were in for a rough ride. *Danau Ranau* is also home to the *Poxai Hadji*, the Sumatran Laughingthrush, *Garrulax bicolor*. The laugher is a little-known, high altitude species that had recently been discovered hiding on Sumatra's uppermost mountain ridges. We had brought a *Poxai Hadji* specialist with us, a man whose real name is Uyung but who had earned the nickname 'Hacking Billy' for his uncanny ability to sprint up near vertical slopes while wielding a machete to fashion a trail through even the densest *Rhododendron* thickets. We trekked north for a few hours, picking our way through smouldering fields cleared for coffee production, the hacked remains of uprooted tree stumps blocking our path. The sight was horrific; pristine forest clear-felled, gone forever. The scene that remained resembled a First World War battlefield, pock-marked with craters, a desolate, muddy wasteland.

Having negotiated the desecration we arrived at the foot of a steep slope. Uyung yomped ahead, while Troy, Toni, Gamal and I gamely but ineffectually tried to keep up with him.

After an hour or so of crawling on all fours I had reeled in Uyung slightly, and was fifty metres ahead of the others, Gamal as ever dawdling at the back to make sure we didn't get into any unnecessary scrapes. A shout rippled up from below.

'Hey, we've found a snake, you want to come and look at it?'

I surveyed the sheer drop below me and decided I didn't want to negotiate the same energy-sapping stretch of trail again. I figured by the time I got down there the snake would have slithered off into the undergrowth, never to be seen again. I sat down on the trail to take a breather and waited for Troy, Toni and Gamal to catch up with me.

Troy emerged first, grinning and waving his camera in my direction.

'I found a pit viper. I think it's a Sumatran Pit Viper.'

I enquired as to the circumstances.

'I put my foot down and the bloody thing reared up at me out of the shadows!'

I looked at the viewfinder and saw the face of a bright green snake roughly three feet long staring back at me. The reptile was clearly agitated, coiled and ready to strike.

'You said it was in the shadows? This photo was taken in bright sunshine.'

'Mmm. Well…Toni decided it would be a much better photograph if the snake was well-lit.' He paused and looked thoughtful. 'So he flicked it with a stick.'

I looked at Troy intently, the smile wiped from my face.

'With a stick.' I repeated slowly. 'And exactly how long was this… stick?'

Troy thought for a while longer. 'Not long enough.'

Discussing the incident later we agreed that Toni was probably unaware of the level of danger to which his actions had exposed him. Had he been bitten (which had clearly been a strong possibility – this is, after all, a snake that can strike up to twenty feet) he may not have lived to tell the tale. We were at least six hours' walk from the lake. Add an hour for the boat ride, and four or five hours to get to the hospital in Bandar Lampung, and you have to figure it might all have been over bar the funeral casket. Still, it was a pretty photograph.

We continued the slog up the east face of *Bukit Pogong*, until we had reached what our guide assured us was *Area Poxai Hadji Number One.* Uyung had spent the last two hours whistling an imitation of the bird's call, but to no avail. Now we had arrived at laughingthrush central. Uyung whistled until blue in the face, but we heard not a squeak in response. The *Poxai Hadjis* (or as Troy had begun referring to them, the *Poxy Hoaxies*) were clearly elsewhere for the day. We did, however, hear a rhythmical song that I didn't initially recognize. Troy and I had spent an hour the previous night assiduously making a list of all the birds that occur at Kerinci, but which had not yet been recorded this far south. One of those species was Rusty-breasted Wren-babbler, and the timbre and pattern of the song we were now hearing was a wren-babbler for sure. We were up at 1700 m, high enough for Rusty-breasted, so I dialled up the song and let rip. The wren-babbler played hard to get, working his way around us and always under cover, but eventually popped its head out of a dense clump. The first record for the species at the site, and confirmation of a five hundred kilometre southerly range extension. Pioneering stuff.

We returned to our forest guardians and mimed the story of our success. Uyung did a funky little dance to the undeniably tuneful wren-babbler song that cracked us all up. We pointed at the species in our field guide, and explained in broken Bahasa that this was a new species for Danau Ranau. The southern side of the mountain was as yet untouched by coffee production, and we paused to catch our breath and admire the view, gazing out over pristine forest, an immense swathe of green as far as the eye could see. A pair of Black-capped White-eyes flirted with our attention for a while, and an Indigo Flycatcher sparkled in the gloom as the mists rolled in, but the trail ahead looked impenetrable and we reluctantly decided that even Uyung's immaculate hacking skills would be no match for the *Rhododendron* forest that blocked our way. The laughingthrush had won, but our fatigue was such that we were past caring.

After a perilous descent, happily completed without a repeat pit viper encounter, we stopped for a coffee at the plantation shack, as close to the source as coffee can be. It was rich but bitter, earthily fragrant but heavily populated with course grounds that stuck between the teeth. The snaggle-toothed plantation owner tried on my stinking boots, several sizes too big for him, and clowned around to general hilarity, before his comic turn was interrupted by the arrival of his son, who effortlessly slipped an immense sack of coffee beans from his shoulder. Troy waved in greeting, and wandered over to the sack. To our mutual astonishment, he could barely lift it. We asked how much the family would receive when they sold the sackful of beans, which must have weighed at least a couple of hundred kilos. The answer when it came was as obscene as it was ludicrous.

'Oh, about a dollar and a half.'

We picked our way back through bonfires and devastated trees, resting for a while in an isolated patch of mature woodland. We watched a family party of Pin-tailed Parrotfinches cavorting amongst a pile of fallen branches, the handsome male changing colour at every turn, first deepest blue, then vivid green, then crimson. After a few more hours' exhausting scramble through the mud we finally made it back to camp. Dinner was enlivened with a spot of community singing, coaxed forth by the two swigs of beer we each enjoyed courtesy of the small can of Bintang we had smuggled up the hill. As night fell we explained to our guides that we would not be returning tomorrow to look once more for the elusive laughingthrushes, preferring instead to spend our last full day trawling for new birds in the forest around the camp. Since so few people had worked the area, I felt sure we could make further exciting discoveries. It turned out to be a good call.

As dawn broke we were already up and out on the trail, fortified by a hot mug of Milo and a bellyful of *nasi goreng*. Reaching 'Graceland' we heard a Lesser Shortwing, and when we showed Gamal the picture in the field guide he shook his head to indicate his unfamiliarity with this skulking species. Never able to resist a challenge we tape-lured the bird in, and were gratified with the response. This delicate bird, a distant relative of the European Robin, worked around us in an ever-tightening circle, eventually coming within a few inches of Gamal's left boot, much to the latter's delight.

A little further up the trail Troy flushed a mystery bird, and shouted that from his brief glimpse he thought it could possibly have been the woodcock. I dived into the trailside grasses that towered above my head and struggled through to the other side, only to be confronted with a near-vertical slope. I managed to claw my way up it, but there was no sign of the fleeing woodcock. Returning to the trail I found the others whispering to each other and pointing at a hole in a tree a few metres away.

'Not woodcock,' Troy mouthed. 'Owl!'

Sure enough, I could just make out a shape deep in the shadows. It was indeed an owl, and it appeared to be on a nest. Through binoculars I could make out a bold white 'V' on the bird's face, the apex of which met just above the bill. The remainder of the head was strikingly dark. It was a small owl, some kind of *Otus* scops-owl for sure, but which species showed that distinctive face pattern? We were perplexed. Neither Mountain Scops-owl nor Sunda Scops-owl should show such a strong facial contrast, but those species were the only small owls known from southwest Sumatra. 'Could it,' I pondered aloud, 'be a Rajah Scops?' We peered at Troy's viewfinder, and studied both the owl and the eggs, which Habzi had briefly held aloft for Troy to photograph. Certainly we thought that Rajah Scops-owl was the best fit, and subsequent research confirmed our suspicions. Another new find for the site, and the first time the species' nest-site and eggs had ever been seen or photographed.

We trawled unsuccessfully for Schneider's Pitta. Clearly the bird we had seen previously in this area had already become familiar with our tape and was no longer taken in by such cheap tricks, but as I played the cut I noticed Uyung doing his funky James Brown routine again. I looked at him quizzically, and he grinned, repeating the jig. Suddenly it clicked; Uyung had heard another Rusty-breasted Wren-babbler close by. We duly brought the bird in and enjoyed views far superior to those we had fought for the previous day. Before the morning was over we had seen two more, and I realized that every time I played the Schneider's Pitta tape, the wren-babblers would start up again. I listened critically to the Schneider's cut, and there in the background was the song of the wren-babbler, faint but unmistakable. We were bringing them in without even realizing it. So our bird yesterday was not, it seemed, an isolated individual. The number of singing individuals suggested that the species was common at the site. It was simply that nobody had ever searched for them before.

In the afternoon we walked the trail below camp, finally connecting with another Danau Ranau speciality, the Sunda Laughingthrush, not the laugher we really wanted, but a good bird nonetheless. A vigil at the forest edge produced, as hoped, a couple of fly-over Sumatran

Green-pigeons, and we sat around on the tree stumps amongst the coffee enjoying the sights and sounds of the forest residents going about their business. A Large Hawk-cuckoo sang its endless 'brain-fever' song in the distance, the acoustic cousin of that monotonous, ascending refrain used to crank up the atmosphere at ice hockey games. Wreathed Hornbills honked conversationally across the valley. A troupe of Mitred Leaf Monkeys screamed furiously at a snake they had discovered sliding through the grass beneath them. A second Graceful Pitta showed beautifully, allowing us enough time to fire off a few more photographs as it perched close by in the undergrowth. Just before dusk we heard a new Schneider's Pitta close to the trail. We crept towards it, and after a tense few minutes were rewarded with brief views as it scuttled furtively to and fro behind a fallen log just yards from where we stood, a fitting end to another good day.

The next morning was our last, and after packing up the camp we spent a couple of hours walking through the forest beyond the river. We had blip views of our third and last Schneider's Pitta, and I recognized the high-pitched tinkling of a bird I had last heard in Malaysia a few weeks earlier. The song belonged to a male Rufous-chested Flycatcher, and we managed to photograph this tiny red, black and white bird in the understorey, yet another species new to the site, and another Sumatran range extension.

After a sticky yomp back down the mountain we crashed out on the lakeshore to await the arrival of the boat. I could not resist a quick swim in the perfect symmetry of the volcanic crater, although evidence that the jetty was used as the village toilet meant that I kept my head out of the water and brought my aquatic activities to a premature end. Averting our eyes in gentlemanly fashion from the unfeasibly beautiful, sarong-clad maidens who had materialized at the water's edge to do the week's laundry, we clambered aboard the boat and stretched out on the warm gangplanks. We used the return trip to get our clothes dry, sprawling out on the roof of the boat while compiling a species list to leave with Gamal and the guys for future reference.

A rain-lashed six hour journey to Way Kambas in Sumatra's southeastern corner tested our patience, but as we stared glassy-eyed at the countryside sliding by, Troy's iPod soundtrack soothed and comforted us: Jeff Buckley, The Flaming Lips, Massive Attack, Buddy Guy. Diversity to celebrate diversity.

Sumatra is in a bad way. Deforestation is wreaking havoc on this amazing island. For now at least, a few large tracts of forest remain, and we had been privileged for a few days to share in some of their least-known riches: sun-bears, cochoas, pit vipers and a host of birds. As an endemic, Graceful Pitta had been a vital component of our success. Most satisfying for me though, was the lost avian jewel we had teased out of the forest three days earlier; Schneider's Pitta. I had found that most enthralling truant of the forest floor, the pitta that went AWOL for over half a century.

Chapter 10

The Eight Colour Bird. Taiwan

Jakarta airport's security x-ray machine was out of action. Nobody frisked me. Numerous passengers loaded down with metalwork passed unchallenged through the arms-detection devices, sending the machines into a frenzy of beeping. My baggage label was carelessly hand-written. In pencil. No-one batted an eyelid, waving through *bona fide* passengers and potential terrorists alike with a generous *laissez faire* attitude and a winning smile.

The severe interrogation I subsequently underwent at the hands of the Indonesian border officials thus came as something of a shock. I managed to extricate myself from the firm grasp of a team of officers, all of whom appeared unhappy with my paperwork. They brandished my passport. *Where was my entry stamp?* I pointed to the faint green smudge that adorned page seven, while explaining, to universal disbelief, that it had been washed away during a Sumatran downpour. I was on the point of chiding them for using cheap ink in the first place, then thought better of it. They passed me along to a more senior lady.

'Your passport is very wet.'

'Everything I own is very wet.'

She dragged me off to a small office. A fleshy half-walrus, half-human figure in military uniform sat slumped behind an enormous desk, his rolls of belly fat squashed together on the wooden fascia like a python's coils. He glanced at the passport before looking up at me.

'Well Christopher,' he said at length, 'what went wrong?'

I was about to explain that ground-cuckoos are shy creatures and almost impossible to see. Instead I mumbled something about a rainstorm and a river in flood and smiled feebly. My interrogator sighed and barked an order. After a further brief interview it was decided I was foolish rather than dangerous, and after a stern ticking off I was released, with strict instructions to a.) avoid swimming in rivers with important documents in future and b.) obtain a new passport as soon as I got back to the UK. I breathed a sigh of relief.

169

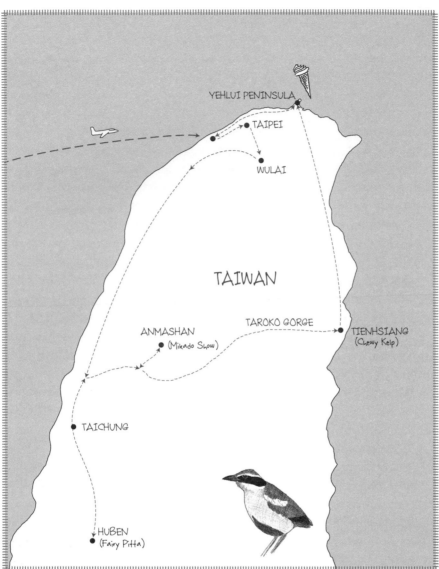

Not only would a couple of weeks in a Jakarta jail not have been much fun, more importantly it would have put a serious dent in my Fairy Pitta plans. Chastened, I fled as a free man along the corridor to Gate D3.

Five hours later I landed in the early evening at Taipei's Taoyuan International Airport. I waltzed my way through an efficient rental car handover *(we're not in Sumatra any more Toto…)* a process that was conducted entirely in sign language. I didn't understand a single word of the renter's Mandarin, and I am equally sure that my every English word was beyond him. Undaunted, we completed our transaction, and after three signatures and a handshake I had my vehicle. I drove off into the night, navigating with one of the five maps that the man from VIP Car Hire had thrust through the car window at the last moment. I nosed my way through downtown Taipei, miraculously managed to connect with Roosevelt Road, and ploughed southward, heading towards Wulai. By eleven, the lights of the town twinkled before me, and I pulled up outside a spa hotel. After another session of international charades I claimed my room, bumping into a sixty year-old cleaning lady clutching a mop.

'Wa, hello! You so handsome!' she said, in something approaching the Queen's English.

I had the feeling I was going to like Taiwan.

The island's original name, *Ilha Formosa*, reflects both its original discovery by the intrepid Portuguese in the sixteenth century, and its outstanding natural beauty. *(Ilha Formosa is Portuguese for beautiful island.)* The little I had seen during my moonlit journey up into the hills suggested it was an appropriate soubriquet. In my current state, however, I was highly likely to pollute any local beauty in the immediate vicinity. I rolled my ball of mud-caked, blood-stained clothes into the bath, and left the shower running while I mixed a medicinal rum and coke.

The room was equipped with hot water, soft, neatly folded towels, shampoo, a dressing gown and a proper bed with plump, inviting pillows. In the corner stood an immense, gleaming TV set that screened both HBO movies in English and the BBC News. I was particularly pleased with the latter, having developed over the years (via enforced exposure in a thousand hotel rooms) a lifelong aversion to CNN, on account of their inability to allot more than twenty seconds to any given item of news. That and their habit of juxtaposing a report on a mudslide in the Philippines that has killed a hundred souls with a piece on a skateboarding cat in Idaho. The batteries in the TV remote control worked. There were FOUR electrical sockets, all of which functioned perfectly and none of which were hanging off the wall.

I stripped off and lay on the bed, sipping my rum through a complimentary straw and giggling hysterically. This was the life. I decided before drifting off into a blissfully deep sleep that I would definitely NOT be getting up at dawn to start my search for Taiwanese endemics. I had plenty of time so long as the Fairy Pitta played ball, and it had been a long and exhausting road trip. I would get up at eight, lie in the bath for an hour, and then partake of a leisurely breakfast. After that I might venture out for a stroll, perhaps take in a little local scenery.

The song of a Taiwanese Whistling-thrush woke me at five. I attempted to unglue my eyes, and struggled to the window. The thrush was in full flow, but out of view. I sighed, pulled on a pair of semi-dry trousers and a t-shirt, and walked barefoot to the end of the building. The thrush flew up and perched in full view on the hotel wall. As I moved round so that the light would be behind me, I clocked a movement on the hotel roof. It was a Taiwan Magpie, a potentially tricky Taiwanese endemic and the bird I had come to Wulai to find. I gave up the unequal struggle, laced up my boots and went birding.

It was a beautiful, sunlit May day, and spring had most definitely arrived in Taiwan. Wulai is a charming spa town, tucked along the edge of a spectacular natural gorge. A river rushes through the canyon, and I wandered along it for a few hours, striking out on trails when I found them. I wound my way up lush valleys, pausing to perch now and then on the boulders that dotted the river's edge and take in the views. Birds were shy but plentiful, and over the course of a few relaxed hours I found Taiwan Scimitar-babblers, more Magpies, a Taiwan Barbet and heaps of whistling-thrushes. Plumbeous Water-redstarts disported at the water's edge, and Grey-cheeked Fulvettas of the local *morrisonia* race peered at me, their huge eye-rings giving them the air of an old science professor glaring disapprovingly at an errant student.

It was all very lovely, but after a contemplative morning the urgency of my mission began to weigh on my conscience once more. *I was not here to enjoy myself*, a voice in my head repeated, *I was here to find a pitta*. I stopped off at Wulai's Seven-Eleven for provisions, and over breakfast watched two ladies on a stationary scooter fussing over an obese, tan-and-white rabbit wedged between them. The reluctant pet struggled to free itself from its imprisonment. Other ladies, I noted, were scootering more rapidly, their dogs enjoying some brisk exercise alongside. It occurred to me that if the rabbit had adhered to a similar regime, maybe it wouldn't have grown so fat in the first place. I pointed the rental car west and drove to the village of Huben, huddled in the hills just inland of Taiwan's west coast. Taiwan is home to most of the world's remaining Fairy Pittas, whose population, following the all too familiar tale of lowland deforestation, now numbers only three to five thousand pairs. Within Taiwan, Huben is the epicentre of pitta activity, and I had a date with Mr. Ruey-Shing Lin Ph.D., an Associate Research Fellow who worked for the Endemic Species Research Institute. 'Scott' Lin had been researching the Fairy Pitta for the last seven years, and had been a member of my Mt. Hamut expedition earlier in the year when we had collectively triumphed in finding the Whiskered Pitta. Scott had kindly offered to meet me in Huben, and to show me his charges.

I eased my way out of the traffic on Highway One and headed inland, finding Huben village without too many problems, thanks in part to the huge Fairy Pitta mural painted on a wall at the edge of the village. Finding the Fairy Pitta Guesthouse itself however, proved more tricky. My first attempt succeeded only in confusing a local householder and infuriating her dogs. My second took me into a dimly lit parlour illuminated solely by flickering red lanterns, where two elderly and rather Confucian gentlemen graciously received me. I presented my passport, which seemed to be the source of some amusement, although I was unable to ascertain whether their mirth was caused by the passport photo or the document's sodden, post-Sumatran condition. When I opened my field guide and showed them the picture of the Fairy Pitta they laughed even harder, and shuffled out into the shabby courtyard, gesticulating in the direction of a small garden a little way up the road. Third time lucky. I belatedly noticed a second, smaller mural on a low wall. Daubed in bright colours was a cartoon depiction of a bird. A speech bubble billowed out from its beak: *Hello, I am Fairy Pitta. How are you?* This'll be the place then.

Two matronly ladies stood by the ornamental border. I waved and they ushered me in. It seemed I was expected. They fussed over me, bringing tea and two sticky lumps of dough, convinced that I must be hungry after my long journey. I sampled the first before discreetly feeding the second to the blue-eyed husky loitering with intent beneath the table, the animal in question having temporarily suspended his vicious attacks on any neighbourhood mutts that had the temerity to stray onto his turf. Presently two girls arrived and sat down at the table, explaining in faltering English that Scott sent his apologies having been unavoidably called away. He would not now arrive in Huben until the following afternoon.

Stowing my bag in one of the guesthouse's basic rooms, I headed for the hills, intent on at least locating a calling pitta. The forest fragments were distressed and had been invaded by dense stands of tall bamboo, which proved to be the favoured habitat for the vast majority of Taiwan's mosquito population. Happily malaria is not present on the island, but my attempts to get inside the forest were thwarted by squadrons of the little biters, and stopping in one spot for more than a second or two was unbearable; not an environment conducive to finding pittas.

I beat a retreat, and cursed my stupidity in not stopping off to replenish my supplies of repellent, exhausted after ten tough days in Sumatran forests. Happily, the guesthouse sold glass phials containing some sort of natural repellent, which proved to be a life-saver. I cruised around the neighbourhood, and having found a likely spot, pulled out my iPod intending to trawl for any territorial birds close by.

At this point I made a rather unfortunate discovery; before leaving England, I'd forgotten to copy my Fairy Pitta mp3 file across to my iPod. In a panic I checked my back-up iPod, and found it similarly deficient. As oversights go, it was a pretty big one, and I upbraided myself for my poor planning. I sat back and considered my options. I could bypass technology altogether and whistle the pitta's call myself. I also had the alarm call of Blue-winged Pitta, and since Blue-winged is arguably the pitta species with which Fairy Pitta is most closely allied, I figured that it might well provoke a response from the resident birds in an emergency. I drove around for a while, whistling hopefully (or rather, judging by the lack of response, hopelessly). After four hours of surveying suitable habitat I had not even heard a Fairy Pitta. I was starting to become a little concerned.

I spent a restless night tossing and turning, plagued by the thought that such a basic planning error now threatened to de-rail my mission at a stroke. Fairy Pitta was one of the 'Big Five' critical species that I had prioritized while sketching out my year-plan. The window of opportunity for seeing the species was relatively narrow, and I knew that if I missed the birds when they were calling before they settled down to breed I could kiss goodbye to any hopes of seeing the species for the rest of the year. Scott had already told me that once birds are breeding they become almost impossible to see. In addition, despite an immense amount of effort the scientific fraternity has to date still been unable to pinpoint the exact whereabouts of the Fairy Pitta's wintering grounds. There are zero ringing recoveries of Fairy Pitta outside of the breeding season, and less than ten sight records of birds that have finished their post-breeding migration. If I missed the birds at Huben, my year would effectively be over before it had really got going. No wonder I slept badly.

I was on the road before dawn, heading into the stands of bamboo north of the village and praying that the pittas would be calling at first light. Scott had warned me in advance that they had been late in arriving this year, and that fewer birds than usual had returned to the breeding grounds. During the first three hours' search I didn't hear a single pitta, and was starting to despair. Where were they? Why were they not vocalizing? I parked the car close to another forest clump, and as I reached into the back to pick up my binoculars I froze.

'Phweu-werp, weurgh.'

A throaty, rising whistle was clearly audible, and its source did not sound very far away.

'Phweu-werp, weurgh.'

It was definitely the pitta, although the second half of the call was curiously truncated compared to the recordings I'd heard. I crawled on my belly to the edge of the forest, and scanned the forest floor that sloped up and away in front of me. The bird stopped calling, and a further ten minutes of silent, stationary scanning proved fruitless. Had the bird seen me already? Since pitta-hunting is essentially a war between hunter and bird, and since in war the high ground is everything, I decided that I needed to be at the top of the slope looking down, not, as was currently the case, at the bottom looking up. As noiselessly as possible I crawled up the slope, dragging myself upwards in slow motion using the smaller saplings for leverage, contorting my limbs in order to edge through the denser thickets without disturbing the foliage.

After fifteen minutes work sweat was dripping off my nose, but I had established a good position, largely hidden but with a clear view of the slope opposite. I waited a few more minutes, but still no sound came from the opposite side of the valley. I reached for my audio equipment and, at a glacial pace, cued up a recording. I played a single cut of Blue-winged's alarm call at the lowest volume I could manage. Within seconds the Fairy Pitta called back, and, hearing no further response from its *faux* 'rival', settled into a determined routine of calling, one phrase repeated every twenty seconds or so. I tried to pinpoint the sound. One thing was for sure; it was getting louder. The bird was unquestionably coming in to check things out. I held my breath for what felt like an eternity while scanning the leaf-litter, establishing a mental image of the bird in my mind and then searching only for those colours that were exclusive to the bird. It was an approach that I had used before, and which had often yielded results. Eliminating all the myriad greens and browns of typical forest allows the mind to pick out anything non-standard with considerable acuity. Find the colour, find the bird.

After a few excruciating minutes, my strategy paid off. A tiny flash of blue, semi-obscured behind a tree root, betrayed the pitta's presence. I knew instantly what this colour was; the shining sky-blue of the wing-covert panel. A few seconds more and I could make out the broad black stripe through the eye and the warm chestnut tones of the crown, neatly bisected by a thin dark chocolate line. A whitish supercilium above the eye completed the pattern. The bird hopped a few centimetres closer, dainty, feminine, moving with an almost balletic grace. Now I could clearly see the dark, matte green of the back, and as it turned to hop up-slope, the butter-buff breast and belly and the crimson vent. The Mandarin name had it right: *Ba-se-niao;* Eight Colour Bird.

My midnight terrors suddenly seemed foolish. The anger I had directed at my poor preparation was forgotten, and a warm wave of elation washed over me. Close by the village, and after only a few hours of searching, the bird was in the bag. It seemed that those childhood tales were true. Fairies really did live at the bottom of the garden.

I concentrated on keeping still, and tried to note every detail as the bird bounced ever closer. It had still not seen me, but was closing fast. How would it react when it finally realized I was watching? The answer was not long in coming. The bird rounded a thicket, and reached an open area of forest floor. It stopped and stared straight at me. My muscles tensed, and I ached with the effort of keeping still. The pitta cocked its head slightly, apparently weighing up the pros and cons of proceeding. But no; a pink leg shot out, and it gave its ear a thorough scratch. Feathers were fluffed out and shaken, before the tiny body swelled and the bird called again. It changed tack and bounced a little further down the slope, keeping one beady on me the whole time in case I should start to act up. Having established what it considered to be a safe distance between us it continued to circle me, using the available cover skilfully, pausing occasionally to press a small stone or low bough into service as a song-post.

I noticed that the bird had already been caught by the research team, a fact revealed by the colour rings it bore on both of its uncharacteristically spindly legs. I made a careful note of the arrangement: *left leg ringed white at the top of the tarsus, green at the base, right leg ringed silver (metal ring) at the top, red at the base.* I wondered whether the bird had been ringed during a previous season. Had it already been seen this year, or would my sighting actually contribute something useful to the research project? Where had it spent the intervening months? The latter question remained unanswered, but at least I had logged one tiny piece of meaningful data. It could be used to help analyse whether individual pittas returned to the same breeding sites year in, year out, or whether they shifted territories from one year to the next in response to local conditions or competition from other birds.

For the next fifteen minutes the bird hopped about in the general vicinity, alternating bouts of feeding with brief spells of preening and general feather maintenance. As it became accustomed to my presence I allowed myself the luxury of an occasional movement, and risked the odd photograph. As is often the way with pittas, the first flash was greeted with a nervous twitch, but subsequently the bird would ignore the flash altogether, as if accepting this sudden burst of light as just one more natural phenomenon. After a final bout of calling the pitta melted back into the forest, and I could at last ease the searing pain that comes with kneeling with one's full weight on the soles of the feet. I removed my boots, and rubbed my toes in an attempt to encourage some vestige of blood to return to the extremities, all the while sporting a grin that a Cheshire Cat would have envied. The pitta scoreboard clicked over. Eighteen with a bullet, and just in time for a late breakfast.

I made my way back to the Fairy Pitta guesthouse, and ordered tea and dough. The research girls arrived, back from marking out forest plots, and timidly enquired whether I had managed to hear a pitta. By way of response I turned my camera around and, to a series of gratifyingly loud gasps, brandished the best of my photographs that just happened to be cued up and zoomed in. No-one likes a smart-arse, but at that precise moment I couldn't have cared less.

Scott returned from his research meetings in Nantou a couple of hours later, and over coffee and fried rice at *Billy's* in nearby Linnei I relayed the detail of my successful morning. After lunch I scribbled out the colour ring information, and Scott hurried off to check the records, returning a few moments later to tell me that the bird I had seen was a returning adult female. She had been ringed the previous year, and had not yet been seen during the current breeding season. My scientific contribution was valid!

Scott asked if I'd like to visit a Fairy Pitta nest-site in the afternoon. I jumped at the chance, and we drove west to one of the plots. We visited two nest-sites, but sadly the birds were absent in both cases. At the second site we waited at a safe distance for a while, but the birds did not return.

'The nest isn't complete yet,' Scott advised. 'The male and female build it together, and they often take the afternoon off to feed.'

We checked another prospective location, but again drew a blank. I was beginning to realize how truly fortunate I had been in the early morning to locate a singing bird. We spent the evening sitting out in the guesthouse garden, rigorously following my self-administered healthy eating regime. Scott provided the papaya and I supplied the rum and coke. My host continued my education, explaining that the strange calls echoing overhead were the sound of the rarely seen Slaty-legged Crake, a crepuscular species that lives in the depths of the forest. For reasons best known to themselves, these crakes have a 'roding' display flight. Biology has thus decreed they must spend their nights flying round and round in circles in the darkness, declaring the boundary of their territory to any other Slaty-legged Crakes that might be listening.

One of the critical gambles of my pitta year involved trying to guess in advance how many days each pitta would require to track it down. Since I could not afford to buy open-ended flexible air tickets, in each case I had to guesstimate how much of a fight each species would put up, and then allow enough days to find the bird, including an affordable safety margin. The downside to this strategy was that if I got it wrong I was stuck in a particular location with a few spare days on my hands. The upside was the same. Having seen the Fairy Pitta with only the odd minor hiccup, I was now at liberty for a few days. I had prepared for such an eventuality, and with Scott's help figured out the best route to Anmashan, one of the island's most scenic mountain locations, and home to most of Taiwan's endemic birds. I jotted down a few directions, marked squiggles on the map in the vain hope that I would be able to decipher them later, and retired for the night.

In the event, the road to Anmashan proved easy to find, though it ran for forty-three tortuously twisting kilometres, winding ever higher into the hills. It was one of those beautiful spring days when the sky seemed bigger than the standard issue, where every natural detail was somehow crisper, unnaturally sharpened. I stopped off frequently along the way as a series of perfect picture postcard views unfolded. Ranges of crumpled hills stretched away into the distance, each tumbling pile a slightly lighter shade of blue than its nearer neighbour. Wisps of cloud snaked along the valleys like carelessly discarded mink stoles. Usawa Cane and Silvergrass dotted the grassier areas, and Dark-spotted Cherry trees clung tenaciously to the remoter ridges. I nibbled another Seven-Eleven cuttlefish slice and inhaled deeply, glorying in the scents of pines and gentians.

Bird-watching in mountain forest is all about the mixed flocks. It's possible to wander for an hour registering barely a flutter in the canopy above, but eventually a chorus of chips, twitters and squeaks will drift through the lifeless silence. As the sounds get louder it can still be difficult to locate the source, until suddenly the flock appears and all hell breaks loose. A madcap flurry of activity follows, with a huge number of different species passing by, until with a final flick of a wing and twitch of a tail, the whole cacophonous ensemble disappears as swiftly as it arrived.

I encountered four such flocks during my first afternoon on the mountain, and each experience was as exhilarating as it was initially bewildering. Taiwan Yuhinas were staple members, their rufous crests flicked up like gelled psychobilly quiffs. Irrepressible Taiwan Liocichlas hopped animatedly in the undergrowth, chattering amongst themselves, while inquisitive White-eared Sibias repeated their cheery 'swisswisswiss-sweeeoo!' wolf-whistles. Occasionally, something less expected would show up in a flock, a group of furtive Taiwan Barwings perhaps, skulking in the shadows on the way to a gang-fight, or a gaggle of garrulous Rufous-crowned Laughingthrushes gliding from one tree to the next on stiff, outstretched wings. Or perhaps a Flamecrest or two would drop by, the males, as their name suggests, looking like they'd held their heads too close to an open fire.

After a long but productive day I rolled to a halt outside the visitors' centre and booked a log cabin in the woods. I squeaked into the last serving of dinner at a minute to seven, but after a selection of dubious Taiwanese delights – watery rice gruel, slimy bamboo shoots and some stiff, aged sardines – I wondered whether my luck had been good or bad. Since I was dining alone I was promptly adopted by two local ladies, Julie and Veronica. The former was a chatterbox student working as a gopher at the centre, the latter a quiet refugee doctor whose English name, she told me, had been inspired by a heroine in a Paulo Coelho novel. After six years of medical school and a year working in a Taipei hospital she had summoned up the courage to tell her parents that she had done her filial duty, hated being a doctor, and was off travelling while she decided what to do with her life. I delicately enquired whether her parents had accepted her decision.

'Yes they have', she said with a wry smile, 'but then again they had few options. I told them either they accept it or I'd emigrate to New Zealand and they'd never see me again.'

I complimented her on her negotiating skills as I pushed a particularly rigid sardine around my plate. I explained that I too was a fugitive from reality, and outlined my plans for the next day. Since Veronica was also at Anmashan in pursuit of our feathered friends, we agreed to meet up at six the next morning so that I could drive us up to the higher reaches.

After a freezing cold night during which my life was saved by the provision of an electric blanket, we rendezvoused as arranged in the garden behind the canteen, pausing for a few minutes so that I could photograph a Eurasian Scaly Thrush before driving a few kilometres up-slope. My breath condensed in the chill morning air, and I was glad of the ancient, battle-scarred coat I had remembered to pack. Our destination was KM 46.8, a famous stakeout for one of Anmashan's most spectacular and elusive species, the resplendent Mikado Pheasant.

I must admit that I have no idea how the Mikado Pheasant came by its name. Is it because its severe expression and measured gait find echoes in the musical number *With Aspect Stern and Gloomy Stride* from the Act One finale of Gilbert and Sullivan's musical of the same name? Somehow I doubt it. Is it perhaps, because the elongated and undeniably glamorous tail feathers of the bird, when worn by Taiwanese aborigines, resemble the outlandish headgear featured in period productions of the piece? That seems a little far-fetched. It can hardly be a vocal reference though. Far from breaking into a swift rendition of the melody from the chorus of *Three Little Maids from School are We*, the best the pheasant can manage by way of a song is a shrill and rather tuneless strangled whistle.

The name's origin remains shrouded in mystery. The birds themselves, it has to be said, are uncooperative with regard to the matter. In fact they are famously uncooperative full stop. I had heard tales of pheasant fanciers spending days looking for these elusive, stately birds of the forest without success, and was expecting more of the same.

However pheasants, like pittas, are habitually contrarian, and as I pulled up at the pre-ordained spot at first light, a pair of Mikado Pheasants was sauntering around on the edge of the grass verge without a care in the world. They remained in full view not more than two feet from the road for the next hour, much to the delight of the growing throng of Taiwanese photographers, whose cameras' frantic clicks and whirrs sounded like a short-circuiting R2D2. So much for the form book.

After a happy hour spent digging out a reluctant Taiwan Shortwing from the gloomier corners of a particularly dense thicket, and having devoted a few minutes to admiration of an immaculate, freshly painted male Collared Bush-robin, I dropped Veronica back at the cabins. She had realized just in time that food did not figure in my plans for the day, and plumped for breakfast. I drove to the highest point of the mountain at the very end of the road and parked up.

I don't know what it is about geographical extremes, but I have always been drawn to them. When visiting Punta Arenas in southern Chile years earlier, I had felt an almost magnetic attraction to the continent's southernmost point. When wandering around western Ireland in the 1990s, I had naturally gravitated to Cape Clear at the island's extreme southwestern tip. Drop me off in the middle of nowhere and I will find my way to the edge of the world.

Language itself seems to suggest that I am not alone in wanting to be alone, that others share my predilection for the geographically remote. Compare the pejorative punch of phrases such as *the middle of nowhere* and *halfway house* with the rattling positivity of *cutting edge,* and *on top of the world.* True there's *out on a limb* and *lost in the backwoods* to be considered, but even the latter phrase for me suggests an untouched, forested wilderness jam-packed with gorgeous American wood warblers or rare Neotropical antpittas. The Spanish have a word, often employed as the name of a bar, *el rincon* which literally means *the corner,* but which implies a cozy nook, a comfortable snug hiding place. If I owned a drinking establishment its name would instead reflect my love of far off places, something like *The World's End* or *The Far Side of Mars.* On reflection, perhaps the latter wouldn't work; nobody wants to drink in a place with no atmosphere.

Maybe this attraction is simply bound up with that endless quest for exclusivity that so obsesses bird-watchers. Walk the extra mile, the implication is, and you are bound to see a bird that no-one else has seen. Rare birds are intrinsically worth more than common birds. This is clearly common sense. No-one points out pigeons in Trafalgar Square, but an Ostrich pecking in desultory fashion at the base of Nelson's column would be a talking point for sure. Twitchers talk about very rare, vagrant birds being 'unblocked' when they turn up after many years without being recorded. By the same token however, if the bird stays a few days affording a large number of fellow twitchers the same opportunity to travel and see it, the bird is said to have become 'devalued.' The mystique is tarnished, the allure gone. These emotions are felt by twitchers with an almost sexual ferocity. *What's the point of turning up at the pub with a pretty girl on your arm,* the logic runs, *if everyone else in the joint is already intimately acquainted with her favours?*

Anyway, back to geography. Gratifyingly I had reached the highest point of Anmashan, which if my elementary grasp of physics had not deserted me meant that the only way was down. This ought to be a good place to look for alpine species unwilling to sully themselves with a trip to the lower slopes. A quick mooch around confirmed that I had chosen wisely. A pair of Grey-headed

Bullfinches fed surreptitiously under a wooden viewing platform, usurped a moment later by a male Vinaceous Rosefinch, glowing in cerise and vermilion finery. I carefully noted the bullfinches' details, aware that the birds here were *owstoni*, subspecifically speaking. As a result, in common with many other Taiwanese taxa that may one day be split off as separate species, they merited extra attention. My potential armchair tick noted, I turned my attention to a small bird feeding in a distinctive manner on the edge of the wood below me. It swooped out in pursuit of insects before returning to its initial perch, the avian equivalent of an advanced yoyo trick. I instinctively knew it was a flycatcher, and the delicate peachy wash on the underparts contrasting with the cold, pencil-grey tones of the head told me that it was a Ferruginous Flycatcher, another new bird for the morning.

Hours passed but I barely noticed as I scurried along remote tracks clocking up sightings. I lurked by a large expanse of dense bushes in order to catch a glimpse of a singing Yellowish-bellied Bush-warbler. The song is extraordinary; like a tiny kettle coming to the boil, its high-pitched '*wheeee-wheeee-wheeee-wheeee*' whistle spirals higher still, until all the dogs in the neighbourhood come running to see what the fuss is about. Finally, after winding itself up into a frenzy, it exhales, winding down with a long descending trill, like a clockwork toy running out of steam. Anmashan's other bush-warbler, the Taiwanese, advertises its presence with a similarly upper register ditty, an infectious, percussive '*dee-dittiduh-dee-dittiduh-dee*', like a pixie jazz drummer setting a furious pace on the hi-hat before the rest of the band come in. (I must confess I don't know whether the pixie world reverberates to the complex cadences of jazz, but if it does it would surely sound like this.)

As the day wore on I started to run out of new species to chase, but one continued to elude me, and although I heard it on a couple of occasions it resolutely refused to put in an appearance. In the end I decided guerrilla tactics were required, so I crawled inside a bamboo thicket and cunningly lay on the ground for an hour waiting for a White-browed Bush-robin to hop by. I waited in vain. The bird continued to sing from ever more inaccessible corners of the bamboo, and after an age I gave up and settled for watching the Taiwanese at play. In the evening I stopped off for the second act of the Mikado Pheasant drama, where the same courting couple were billing and cooing at the side of the road. An even larger gaggle of photographers was arrayed across the road, peering out from behind their equipment, which stirred a fit of lens envy deep within me. The downward traffic was forced to stop, and a long line of motorists leaned out of their cars, pointing out the pheasants to their passengers. Quite the event.

In the evening I met up with my new friends in the canteen, who were horrified that I had spent the entire day out in the forest, fortified only by the end of a packet of chocolate Oreos and a few battered rice crackers, which after a week of riding around in my pockets had seen better days. On learning I was writing a book, Julie insisted I accompany her to the visitors' centre to meet with the manager, a meeting which was cordial but short on account of our almost total lack of compatible language.

In one of the resultant unavoidable long pauses, the resort boss thrust a coffee table book in my direction, a tome devoted to extolling the virtues of Taiwan's natural heritage. The book included a picture of a Canadian lady, and I recognized her as someone I had met at the BirdFair in England the previous summer, working on the *'Visit Taiwan'* booth. I pointed out the lady in question and explained to Julie that she had introduced me to a Taiwanese guide whose identity, after a struggle, I managed to remember. 'His name was…Simon Liao,' I said at last. At which point I heard a snigger, and from behind a screen a figure stood up.

'Nice to meet you again,' said the very same Simon Liao, at Anmashan with his client, a marine seismologist with an interest in birds. Simon introduced me to Bruce, whom, he explained, had just spent a month in the South China Sea studying the effects of earth tremors on marine mammals.

'And what are the effects?' I asked, recognizing this as a once-in-a-lifetime chance to answer such a burning question. Bruce smiled nervously, before admitting, 'I don't know, we couldn't find any.'

Simon and I traded bird information, and I discovered that the Golden Parrotbill I had seen on the way into the park on the previous day had been at an abnormally low altitude. I noted down this nugget, making a mental note to author a paper entitled *The effects of climate change on the altitudinal distribution of the Golden Parrotbill, Paradoxornis verreauxi*. I also discovered that the Scaly Thrush I had watched earlier in the day was a highly sought after bird, which belonged to a small, dark race (most probably the nominate *Zoothera dauma dauma*) that resides in the Taiwanese mountains. Taiwan also plays host in winter to migrant Scaly Thrushes of a different race, but these it seemed were always to be found in the lowlands, and the mountain birds would have nothing to do with these northern interlopers. Since the thrush was also the bird that Bruce most wanted to see, I scribbled directions so that they could try for the bird in the morning.

I strolled back to my cabin in the woods, admiring the artwork on the information signs at the edge of the path that urged me to *beware of poisonous snakes and wasps.* The light was beginning to fade. The tree frogs had taken over jazz duties from the bush-warblers, and were attempting a complicated woodblock concerto by an *avant garde* composer. The same authorities who had so assiduously warned me about the venomous denizens of the forest had also taken care of litter disposal, and each bin was monogrammed with a *Dancing Mama* logo featuring a maternal cartoon pig. It seemed that the traditional Japanese domination of rendering the ugliest animals cute via creative animation would not continue unopposed. Elsewhere in Taiwan I came across a *Gimi* water scoop bearing the image of a rosy-cheeked hippo in a pair of designer sunglasses. At any moment I expected to be confronted by a local brand featuring a snowboarding woodlouse.

Having reached my cabin, I sorted out my kit for the following day. The frogs having finished their set, the silence was all-encompassing, and I was lost in a contemplative reverie as I admired the contours of the distant peaks through the open door. After so many weeks away from home I was self-sufficient and used to life on my own. On my more remote travels, deprived of English-speaking conversational partners, there had been periods when I didn't speak for days on end. Loneliness or boredom was never an issue though. There was always something fresh and unexpected around every corner, a new bird to admire, or some startlingly beautiful scenery in which to wallow.

I thought about my old job, and the attritional wear and tear it had caused. I remembered meeting an old business contact from Chile, an eccentric Frenchman who had made his fortune buying bus stops from the government and then renting the sides of the same structures back to them for use as advertising space. I had not seen him for years, and when we did bump into each other by chance, he shocked me with his greeting. 'Oh, you got old!' It's the combined impact of tiny daily stresses that do the damage, the weight of the world bearing down. You go to bed as a fresh-faced youth and wake up grey-haired and careworn. The trick is to throw it off and make a run for it. It was working for me.

As I left Anmashan there was just time to make one final stop. I had failed to find the mountain's other star game bird, Swinhoe's Pheasant. Born in 1836 in Calcutta, Robert Swinhoe was a busy guy. An English naturalist by profession, he also worked as a consul in mainland China and Taiwan (then Formosa). He learned Mandarin and, being based in Hong Kong for a number of years, the local Hokkien dialect, and in 1856 had visited Taiwan. He discovered a number of southeast Asian birds, and a storm-petrel, an egret, a minivet and the pheasant in question are all named in his honour, along with a number of fish, mammals and invertebrates. He corresponded with Darwin, and even named a race of the Koklass Pheasant after the eminent biologist.

Swinhoe had found the pheasant during one of his subsequent trips to Taiwan, which was more than I had been able to do thus far. However, another top tip from Simon had me wending my way down the hill to a particular hairpin. Two cyclists and the ubiquitous huddle of photographers marked the spot, and we didn't have long to wait before the pheasant strutted out of the forest to feed on the verge. It was a male, and even more gaudily dressed than the Mikado had been; scarlet-faced, with a matching band on the shoulder, scalloped iridescent green on the wing-coverts, with blue crescents circling the base of the tail. The crown, back and ornate uppertail were pure white, as though a light dusting of snow had drifted across the bird's upper reaches as it slept. A fitting finale, I decided, to my time on Anmashan, and I saluted the bird as I headed back into the Taiwanese hinterlands.

The rest of my time on the island passed in a blur. I walked silently along the famous Blue Gate Trail above Wushe, negotiating the treacherously muddy trail in an effort to catch sight of nervous White-tailed Robins before they flushed. Later the same day it was not the incomparable views from the top of Hehuanshan that took my breath away so much as the lack of oxygen, in short supply here at around three thousand five hundred metres above sea level. I travelled onward, edging across the Wuling saddle, feeling my way along the very backbone of Taiwan, before plunging down into the abyss that is the Taroko Gorge.

The Gorge itself is so immense that it spans three counties, Hualien, Taichung and Nantou. Driving its entire length is not for the faint-hearted. Many have perished by failing to navigate safely around its endless curves, plummeting to a dramatic death in the river below. The remnants of wrecked vehicles visible below were a reminder of the dangers of losing concentration even for a moment. Hemmed in by marbled cliffs on either side, I negotiated my way through the Tunnel of Nine Turns, before finally emerging with some relief into Tienhsiang, where I spent the night at the wonderfully affordable youth activity centre hostel. The journey had been much longer than I had anticipated, and I was relieved to have made it in one piece and delighted to be able to order a pizza in the hostel restaurant. I even snaffled the last cold beer.

The culinary respite did not last long however. After struggling through the least digestible breakfast since Wulai (broad, chewy kelp and congee) I made it to the spectacular east coast. Crossing the Tai Lu Ge Bridge over the Liwu river, I looked down on the waters beneath me. They seemed to dance for joy, apparently excited that their long journey to reunite with the sea was almost at an end. A long but scenic drive took me north through the towns of Su-ao, Wujie and Jhuangwei, until I reached the Yehlui peninsula in the northeast, a popular day trip destination for Taipei's harassed urbanites massed some forty kilometres to the southwest. I had heard that Yehlui was one of Taiwan's migrant hotspots, attracting falls of birds grounded by adverse weather. However, my chances of any appreciable *vismig* were dashed by arriving on a beautiful sunlit Sunday afternoon with not a cloud in the sky. A quick glance around at my fellow trippers confirmed that I was, as usual, the only man present praying for a cold front and an easterly gale.

I did my best to blend in, adding an ice cream to my equipment list, but in truth my telescope and binoculars hindered my attempts to pass myself off as a regular tourist. I settled for watching a pair of Peregrine Falcons hunting off the tip of the peninsula (I had, needless to say, walked right to the very end as usual), and politely posed for photographs with the locals when asked. Such requests always came just at the moment when I had succeeded in painstakingly stalking the Grey-tailed Tattlers (not, as you might suppose, a touring folk band, but a flock of transient wading birds) that were picking their way along the foreshore. The tattlers were just about the only migrants I managed to find all afternoon, and eventually I gave up and checked in at a very fancy spa hotel in the hills, the only place which had a free room and where the staff could understand the strange, mud-spattered foreigner babbling at their reception desk. In my room I spread the disgusting contents of my rucksack out over the immaculate wooden floor, before cornering and subduing my socks and tossing them into the whirlpool bath. A delightful dinner for one followed, unmarred by any further kelp and congee incidents.

My time on Formosa had come to an end, and I was sorry to leave. The island had proved to be well named, its residents both delightfully welcoming and determinedly helpful, even when my best-sketched efforts to explain what I was up to had failed. Most importantly, the Fairy Pitta had co-operated, despite a few technical glitches. The mission was still on course, and the Eight Colour Bird was mine.

Chapter 11

Who's the Daddy? Sabah, Borneo

I had been to Malaysia on a number of previous occasions, but this trip was different. My forays into the relative familiarity of Peninsular or 'West' Malaysia had been to forests that were easily accessible from the capital Kuala Lumpur, where the ground was for the most part well-trodden and reassuringly well-known. This time I would visit Sabah in exotic 'East Malaysia.' I was bound for *Negeri di Bawah Bayu;* The Land Below the Wind.

For a change, I was not travelling alone. Over the last few years I had made a number of international trips with the same three companions. However, our self-styled 'Gang of Four' had been struggling to find a mutually convenient set of dates to visit Sabah, and it had just not come together. School holidays, work commitments, wedding anniversaries; somehow the fates had always conspired to prevent us from setting foot on Bornean soil. I choose the word advisedly, for Sabah had assumed an almost religious significance in my mind. Perhaps it was because I knew that large tracts of pristine rainforest still survived there. Maybe it was the possibility of seeing the Karl Malden of the primate kingdom, the Proboscis Monkey. But in my heart of hearts I knew neither of these things were responsible for Sabah having planted a seed of desire in my soul. Sabah's irresistible allure had claimed me the first time I saw the region described as *the centre of the pitta universe.* A monomaniacal intensity shared only by Homer Simpson when encountering donuts had consumed me, and I had vowed to get there by hook or by crook.

My pitta year declared, the stars magically aligned; I was on my way. Not only that, but my three long-standing friends, Bob, Kit and Graham, veterans of many gruelling international trips and hectic Norfolk bird-races, would be coming with me. Since I was already somewhat overwhelmed with logistical organization for the year, Rob Hutchinson, an old friend who runs a company called Birdtour Asia had offered to sort out the details and to guide us, and within a week, everything was set.

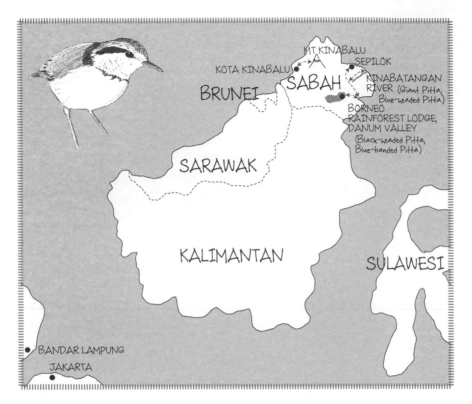

Rob and his business partner James had been immensely helpful the previous year when I was doing my research to calculate whether seeing all the pittas in a calendar year was really possible. The three of us had sat down on a baking hot day in Rutland and started to assemble the pieces of the jigsaw. As we worked through each species, Sabah was suggested as the best option for not just one or two pitta species, but an incredible five. And there was more; I knew that Sabah was by far the best place to look for my arch-nemesis, the species I felt sure would tear the wheels off my mission in a hurry; the mythical Giant Pitta.

A little background on the latter; we are talking now about a bird that any number of the world's top bird-watchers have never even heard, let alone seen. Of those who have heard the bird's soft, eerie whistle, only a small proportion have been able to find the source in its densely vegetated forest home. It's the kind of species that birders talk about around the campfire after a long day in the field. The Giant Pitta makes Rusty-naped Pitta look like a gregarious, outgoing, 'see 'em everyday in my back yard' kinda bird. It is an enigma. I had spent years searching for the species in Thailand and West Malaysia, and had never really come close to seeing one, with the single, honourable Kaeng Krachan exception outlined in Chapter 3. On that occasion James and Rob had shown me a picture they had somehow just managed to take of the only female Giant Pitta in the park, pretending it was a run of the mill 'mystery photo.' I had missed that bird by only a few minutes, and at the time I remember thinking, *that was my moment.* I still felt the same way; that fleeting half-chance had come and gone before I knew it, and now it was entirely possible I would never set eyes on the beast. Still, I reasoned that if Rob, who knew Sabah well, could help me to locate a Giant Pitta after all this time, what better way to heal the wound? He certainly wouldn't hurt our chances. I might even finally forgive him.

The five of us had put together an itinerary that would fling us to Sabah's furthest corners. Our itinerary included the home of the Orang-utan, Sepilok, in the northeast of the territory, the Kinabatangan River just to the south that flows out into the Sulu Sea (after which, Star Trek fans, the show's Mr. Sulu was named) and the Borneo Rainforest Lodge in the fabled Danum Valley Conservation Area. We would then fly west, spending time at Poring Hot Springs, dropping into the Rafflesia Reserve in the Banjaran Crocker mountain range, before ascending to the montane forest that cloaks the foothills of the mighty Mount Kinabalu. I had pored over my map of Sabah for months before travelling, and the dribbles of saliva are probably still visible to this day. I couldn't wait to get off the plane and get started.

First, however, we had to get there. Like most remote places, the key to Sabah's unspoiled natural riches lies in the very fact that it is not easy to get to. If one could simply wait for a bus, or stick out one's thumb and magically arrive, the loggers would have clear-felled the entire island long ago. So we had to take a series of flights involving aircraft of ever-dwindling dimensions to get to our destination. London to Kuala Lumpur, KL to Kota Kinabalu, KK to Sandakan. My compatriots chatted or slept the whole way, whilst I drummed my fingers on the arm of my seat and stared out of the window, anxious to arrive. When at last we tumbled out onto the tarmac at Sandakan, I had already had my fill of air travel, as we'd devoted more than one whole day of our short lives just to get to the island of dreams. Having picked out Rob's smiling face in the arrivals hall, we were now but a short bus ride from Nirvana. And in the battle of excitement versus exhaustion, adrenalin was proving to be the decisive factor.

There was enough daylight left for a quick jaunt along Sepilok's canopy walkway, and we raced to get started, mis-tying shoelaces and forgetting vital pieces of kit in our eagerness. After what seemed like an age we were ready, and were soon taking the first swaying steps on the walkway, our unsteady progress further threatened by a loud crash in the branches to our left. It was an Orang-utan; improbably huge, impossibly orange, and incredibly human.

The 'man of the woods' beat a hasty retreat, but already we had fallen under Sabah's spell. All around us the sights and sounds of primary forest were assaulting our senses, and we began to tune in to our surroundings. An angry chittering above us revealed the presence of a Prevost's Squirrel, a handsome beast described in black, white and ginger, all stripes and attitude. Although it was mid-afternoon, hotter than hell and stickier than melted toffee, birds were still in evidence. I knew that our chances of connecting with a pitta in the afternoon were slim, but it was still great to be out in the forest again, and activity was all around us. A Slender-billed Crow rowed lazily past, wings characteristically never rising above the horizontal, its familiar death rattle of a voice matching the funereal plumage. In West Malaysia this is a scarce bird, but here these forest undertakers are everywhere, never short of work to do in the endless cycle of life and death, birth and decay. Collared Kingfishers fizzed from one branch to the next, stopping so abruptly they seemed to vibrate from the impact. A Rufous-bellied Eagle drifted over, all magisterial arrogance, effortlessly regal. Long-tailed Parakeets, shockingly out of place to our European eyes, squabbled over pieces of fruit, screeching complaints at one another.

Diverting though these scenes were, we had a particular quarry in mind. Sepilok is the best place in the world to see a bird that is as astonishing as it is unique; the Bornean Bristlehead. The size of a small crow, its body is similarly dark, the colour of aged coal dust. Its head, on the other hand, is a riot of colour, being for the most part bright crimson, with a pollen-yellow patch plastered across the crown. The bill is black and swollen at the base, and there is an echo of the dominant head colour in the matching pair of red gaiters at the top of the legs, as if the bird were wearing an obscenely small pair of cycling shorts. Its vocal repertoire consists of pairs of upslurred, querulous whistles, and raucous, atonal caterwauls. For such a remarkable bird it is often inexplicably difficult to track down, yet within an hour of arriving we were following one as it clumped through the canopy. One of the trickiest Bornean endemics had fallen on our very first excursion.

As dusk closed in, the rippling, melancholic whistle of another species of kingfisher – this time the much rarer Rufous-collared – drew our attention. After a brief foray down a side-trail, we managed to tease the bird into view, where it sat motionless for a while, chiding us for disturbing its twilight song. Graham was especially pleased; this was a species he had talked about endlessly, and was one of the birds on his 'most wanted in Asia' list. I had tormented him with close-up photographs of the one I had seen at Taman Negara earlier in the year, and here in Sabah he had gripped back in no uncertain terms. That evening, the level of excitement in camp was palpable, and over the inevitable rum and cokes (Sarawak's own Peng Guan distillery brand, founded by the *Soon* family – as in *soon you'll wish you hadn't opened that bottle*) we chattered about what dawn would bring. Forest is always liveliest during the first few hours of daylight, and despite our weariness, we had trouble getting off to sleep, excited as children on Christmas Eve.

As is so often the way, our heightened expectations weighed on what turned out to be a disappointing morning. True, we did find a small group of endemic Bornean Black Magpies. We also picked off other new birds, including Bold-striped Tit-babblers (another near-endemic) and a Jerdon's Baza, a scarce species of raptor. By noon, however, we had seen little else bar a Red-bearded Bee-eater, a pair of beefy White-bellied Woodpeckers, and some commoner Asian species. I was inconsolable, since we had heard a calling Black-headed Pitta but been unable to locate it. We had 'gone in' off the trail and had crept through the forest keeping a keen eye out for snakes and scorpions. Nonetheless, our collective stealth had not been enough to prevent the bird from seeing us, and after toying with us for a while it stopped calling and stayed hidden in the depths of the forest. An inauspicious start. Would this be the only Black-headed we heard in Sabah? Had my chance come and gone? I was starting to think it might have been better to have come to Sabah alone, convinced that with five us on the trail together we would frighten off every pitta we came across, despite our silent approach work.

We headed to Sukau, the jumping-off point for Kinabatangan, stopping off at the Gomantong Caves, home to a couple of million bats, two well-fed Bat Hawks, and an incredible number of swiftlets. Two of the four species present, the Black-nest and Edible-nest Swiftlets, are so similar in appearance that the only way to be sure which is which is to follow their fluttering, erratic flight until they land on their respective nests. If the nest is milky white, the bird is an Edible-nest, the species whose hardened saliva is harvested and consumed with gusto by gourmets across China and beyond. The soup is incredibly expensive, not least because collecting the nests can only be done once annually after the birds have bred, and because collection is an extremely dangerous business. The Swiftleteers clamber a hundred metres or more up swaying, rickety ladders that look as though they themselves might be held together with little more than swiftlet spit and a few threadbare twists of twine. They then knock the nests from the roof of the cave, before swivelling into a new position and working on the neighbouring nest. I looked up awestruck at the roof of the cave far above my head, and an involuntary shiver ran down my spine as I imagined the scene.

Not that our current troglodyte existence deep in the heart of the cave was particularly comfortable, even in the absence of imminent Swiftleteer plummeting incidents. The echolocation of the bats and the high pitched, miniature screams of the swiftlets twisted together in the echoing recesses of the caves, reverberating and bouncing off every exposed rocky surface and setting my teeth on edge. The towers of guano built up over the years reeked, and it was hard to inhale without an immediate and unavoidable gag reflex kicking in. Mildewed moss hung limply from the walls, whilst foetid water dripped and seeped through every fault and fissure. The floor beneath our feet was impossibly slippery, but handrails had thoughtfully been provided. None of us availed ourselves of this steadying influence however, since one glance revealed that their every surface was liberally covered in enormous cockroaches. My gaze drifted to the floor of the cave, which seemed to twist and roll like a gentle sea. It was a seething mass of roiling, filth-caked cockroaches, literally billions of them, squirming, fighting, mating. In the darker crevices, strange crustacean-like creatures lurked, all spiny, waving antennae and skeletal fishbone carcasses, withdrawing further into the gloom whenever we shone a light in their direction. Had Dante had the opportunity to visit, his *Inferno* may well have featured another level. Emerging out into the daylight, we attempted to clear our mouths and noses of the acid bile that had accumulated. Was there not a neat and tidy sewage farm close by we could have visited instead? Bird-watching; stupid bloody hobby.

By the time we reached the quay at Sukau it was witheringly hot, and we were grateful for the shade offered by the rickety shelter at the river's margin. Once the boat arrived and our luggage had been loaded, we set off up-river, the breeze wicking the sweat from our foreheads and purging the last vestiges of cave-stench from our clothes. As we approached the lodge that was to be our home for the next few nights, we could see in the distance a figure crossing the butterscotch, mud-drenched waters of the river. Drawing closer, the outline of the figure came into sharp focus, and we were astonished to find that the mystery swimmer was a Proboscis Monkey. Our course brought us close to the animal, and as we passed it slowed, turning its pendulous, swollen-tipped nose in our direction. Water dripped from the end, and individual droplets clung to every wrinkle on the animal's remarkable, scrotal cheeks. Its face seemed overwhelmed by flesh, like a crash-diet pig whose coarse-haired skin no longer fitted. Baggy double eyelids, an old man's thinning beard, a tufty crop of raw-ginger, mother-cut hair set low on the forehead, and deep-set wrinkles cutting from the corner of each eye completed an exceptional set of features. The monkey swam on, until much to our amazement it leapt vertically out of the deep water and hauled itself up onto an overhanging branch. We broke out into spontaneous applause. Karl Malden could never have done that. Not even in his prime as the star in the first series of *The Streets of San Francisco*. Which is why Michael Douglas got the gig to play KM's younger partner I suppose.

We tethered the boat to the River Camp's jetty and clambered out, avoiding a curiously crumpled oil drum whose significance would be revealed the following day. Accepting bottles of water, we were introduced to our host, the inimitable Robert Chong. He fixed me with a steely yet mischievous gaze, and sat down to chat.

'So you're the pitta man?' he said.

I confirmed I was one and the same, and Robert explained the lie of the land.

'Well we have Blue-headed Pittas here, shouldn't present too much of a problem. Black-headed is here, but easier to see at Danum Valley. We have Hoodeds, but they are thin on the ground, you might hear them, but Blue-banded isn't here.'

'And Giant...?' I ventured, hardly daring to ask the question.

Robert grimaced. 'It's here, but rare. We did have one close to the compound a few years ago, but I haven't seen them for a while. I did hear one a couple of weeks ago though. We'll cruise by that way in the boat tomorrow and see if we can hear the call.'

Robert is a legend; experienced, knowledgeable, eccentric and funny, and I had paid close attention to his mini-briefing. Especially the words *I did hear one a couple of weeks ago...* My heart skipped a beat, and I felt my pulse rate increase. The Giant Pitta was here. Within a couple of kilometres of the spot in which we were currently sitting. I had to physically restrain myself from giving in to the desire to fling myself into the river and start swimming upstream to the nearest patch of forest to start the search. But patience was required. Danum Valley, I knew, was our best chance to connect with the bird. Giant Pitta was rare at Kinabatangan. *Nobody sees the bird here*, I counselled myself silently. *Be patient.*

In contrast with many rainforest locations, looking for Kinabatangan's birds and animals is a relatively peaceful pastime. You walk to the jetty, pausing on your way to bid good morning to Chico, the camp's resident Storm's Stork. Birders are fond of passing on detailed directions to one another to facilitate finding special birds. *From the church with the crooked spire, take the minor road that runs southwest through open farmland. After three kilometres take the left fork and park by a stile with a piece of blue wool tied to it. The birds are feeding in the* Pittosporum *in the furthest corner of the onion field.* That kind of thing. Directions for Chico, to be frank, would be simpler. *Have breakfast on the verandah. Look by the kitchen door.*

Before six a.m. we were breakfasted, kitted out and standing on the jetty. While we waited for the boat to be made ready, we quizzed Robert about the electrified fence surrounding the compound.

'It's rarely needed', he confided, 'but occasionally the Bornean Pygmy Elephants wander by and they have caused trouble in the past. We've distracted them of late by leaving an oil drum out so they can play football. The only problem is that when they get bored with the game they squash the can underfoot, so we need regular replacements.' A mystery solved.

We cast off and puttered upstream against the current, eddies swirling like boiling toffee beneath the keel. Wrinkled and Helmeted Hornbills glided from one side of the river to the other, the latter's ungainly bodies and extended tail-feathers lending them a most undignified flight profile. Storm-ripped kites, with tatters of cloth flapping at their extremities, they seemed to struggle to stay in the air. The Wrinkled Hornbills' loud, guttural grunts announced their presence long before we saw them, and were invariably followed by their distinctive, whistling wing-beats as they hurled themselves across gaps in the canopy. Just occasionally we would find one perched up, the jet-black body contrasting with the orange neck, white chin, and blue facial skin. A large, protuberant casque jutted out above the base of their outsize, red-and-yellow bills. Hornbills are always a majestic sight, and they are true forest frugivores, their presence here an indicator that the habitat remained in good shape.

We spent a pleasant day drifting along the river, watching White-chested Babblers fussing along the water line and craning our necks to follow Grey-headed Fish-eagles as they soared overhead. As the day drew towards a close, there was just time to try our luck along a quieter section of the river. Robert guided the boatman to the spot, and once again we killed the spluttering motor and waited. Within minutes, a distinctive sound drifted out of the forest. It was a sound I had waited my whole life to hear. A long, drawn-out, melancholy whistle that initially rose in pitch, before fading as it fell.

'*Wheeeoooooooowwh.*'

The sound turned the droplets of sweat on my neck to ice. I knew that only one creature on God's earth made a sound like this, and that creature was the Giant Pitta. The call was slightly higher-pitched than the recording I had played thousands of times and committed to memory, which made me think that perhaps this bird was a female. Rob and I exchanged glances, and the boat was silently paddled to shore.

Having dumped all extraneous kit, we crept into the forest in single file, our every sense sharpened, like a military patrol that has just heard a twig snap. We knelt down in the mud, with Robert Chong and our boatman considerately hanging back. We waited and listened. Nothing. And then, after what seemed like an age, there it was again, the same lovelorn, breathy, hopeless whistle, a miniature steam-train swan song. I offered up a silent prayer to any deity I thought might be listening. I could not claim to have lived the perfect life, but surely it was not too much to ask…The whistle came again, forty metres ahead on the right, and we risked creeping forward to a spot that gave better views across the forest floor. If the bird came within range here, we would at least stand a chance of seeing it before it saw us.

Giant Pittas, despite their rather bull-chested stature, have an enviable reputation for being able to flit ghost-like through the forest without leaving a trace. They are will-o'-the-wisps, ephemeral though undeniably portly wraiths able to drift unseen through a parallel dimension. They carry at all times invisibility cloaks, jaunting belts and all the other time traveller paraphernalia, and can undoubtedly slip through worm holes in space-time when necessary. Indeed, until this very moment I had doubted they existed at all, having traipsed an immeasurable distance in their wake, checking every thicket and vegetative hiding hole, whistling in the dark, and never hearing even the briefest of responses. Until now.

Rob triggered a single whistle from his iPod. A second answering whistle, slightly deeper this time, immediately sounded to our left. A male! The female called again in response, and we snapped off the tape. This, I knew, was the perfect situation. We were between a pair of Giant Pittas, and both birds believed that a second male had come between them. Surely one or other would come to investigate this intruder in order to cement their pair bond?

We did not have to wait long. A shadow flickered against a low bush not five metres to our right. Again; a second ripple of movement, a few inches to the left, and again. I scanned frantically with my binoculars, desperate to locate the bird. I knew exactly where the movement had been and in which direction the bird had moved, and I scanned further left in readiness. I had learned from bitter experience that pittas can move over ground faster than you might imagine, and if you focus your gaze on the last place in which you saw a movement, chances are they will already have flicked behind the next available cover. The trick, just as when photographing birds, is to get inside their head and second-guess their next move before they make it.

The theory of this 'behaviour imaging' was sound – of that much I was sure – but would it work in practice? This was, after all, a Giant Pitta, the grand Pooh-Bah of non-cooperation, who tore up form books for fun. The rules of the game may well have changed, the laws of the known universe would not necessarily apply. I waited, focussed, hyper-alert, ready. The shadow twitched darkly in deep cover, and a classic pitta movement followed, a hunch-necked, clandestine bounce, a dissident drawing her shawl more tightly about her head, hiding her face from authority. At the extremity of my binocular vision I could see a gap, and I watched it intently, my napalm stare torching stray twigs and leaves, eliminating all except the single space that constituted my only chance.

The gap disappeared. I suppressed a gasp as the space was blocked by a sandy, mini-rugby-ball of a body. In the penumbra, I could just discern the outline of a massive steel-grey bill, and at the opposite end, a light blue flash of a tail. After so many years of pain, so many empty-handed failures, my brain stubbornly refused to register the creature I was now watching, but there was no denying the reality. There in front of me stood an impossible vision, my nemesis unpicked; a female Giant Pitta.

I'd had the foresight to balance my camera on my knee, and I slowly lifted it to my eye and fired a single shot, not daring to use flash for fear that I would commit the ultimate crime, flushing the bird before the others had seen it. I need not have worried. The pitta bounced on, its heft guaranteeing that everyone picked up on the movement and had at least partial views. The bird changed direction, alarmed perhaps by its close proximity to the spot where we cowered, terrified of moving lest we reveal our presence and scare it off for good. The shadow melted back into the forest, blurring back into the darkness like cigarette smoke in night air.

I became aware of a movement ahead, and caught a glimpse of Rob's boot as he stepped silently over an awkward root. I circled round him, and after a few agonizing Tai Chi moments had him in my sights. That deeper whistle again; the male was calling close by. A defiant series of whistles followed, and I knew that the male was likely to stay on his perch for a few seconds, even if he was cognisant of our hiding place. I crawled forward on my belly, twisting myself ivy-like around a convenient trunk. I scanned the foliage; greens and browns, tans and ochres, dappled leaves and moss-scarred boughs, until suddenly, there it was – a misplaced bolt of blue, three feet off the ground. Male Giant Pitta.

I contorted my aching limbs still further until I could see almost the whole bird. As the pitta called I could see the chest inflate, distending the breast feathers slightly, before falling again like a deflating balloon. As the bird looked around, the short, bristled chin feathers shook. The shards of light that had made it through the forest canopy ricocheted off the surface of the bird's gleaming orb of an eye.

It was so close that I felt the impact of the sheer, bull-headed, barrel-bodied bulk. I could see the tip of the upper mandible extending fractionally beyond the lower half of the bill. The cheek feathers were edged in black, scaled like a reptile. The silken back, electric blue, hummed with colour, each feather shaft invisible, overcome by the intensity of the sheen. A fountain of black streamed out from behind the eye, arcing down towards the neck, separated from the ragged black necklace by a single sliver of silver, an archduke's tufted badge of office. The thick legs were fault-barred, gnarled like the ancient wood from which they appeared to grow. It was in every sense a vital bird; massive, thrilling, defiantly in the moment.

The Giant Pitta stretched its neck upward and froze, its face hidden in shadow. Despite the vibrant colour and the extraordinary scale of the bird, had we walked the trail with the pitta in this position we would never have noticed it. A shape-shifter, chimeric despite its heft, born of the earth and yet somehow not of it. It was everything I had dreamed of, and now I was terror-stricken that it would leave before I had been able to fully take in its arrival. But the bird sat on, motionless, allowed us a minute longer in its presence, before it dropped to the ground and disappeared into the gathering gloom. I never saw it once it hit the floor. A twitch of the magician's cloak and it was gone.

We picked our way back through the twisted trunks, which I was sure had closed ranks since our arrival. Now they threatened to hold us prisoner, to drag us down and suffocate us in the stinking mire. Despite their attempts to snare us, to cage us as alien curiosities for the forest's entertainment, we managed to regroup, and crawled back to the boat. Nobody said much. Each of us was lost in thought, replaying the movie in our minds.

I tried to fix every detail in my head, but by the time we reached camp, the footage had already become grainy. The images jerked and danced, like re-runs of family holidays on flickering ciné film years after the event, faces blurred, fuzzy at the edges. Graham handed me one of his trademark, super-strength rum and cokes, a local brand, *The Legacy of British Borneo.* He clinked my glass.

'Hey, what's up?' he said, 'you don't seem as delighted as I thought you'd be to finally lay the ghost to rest?'

I smiled, and reflected that he was right.

It was more complicated than that though. I *was* delighted, and a warm glow of success was indeed spreading from my core to my every extremity. There was relief too. What was undoubtedly the toughest part of my mission had been completed, the most insurmountable obstacle overcome. But in a strange way I felt bereft too. A part of the hunter in me had wanted the biggest stag of them all to get away without a shot being fired. As it was we had stalked and won, the virtual kill had been executed with unlikely speed and unseemly efficiency, and the body was now laid out, inert on the slab of our collective experience. None of us would ever again see a Giant Pitta for the first time. We owned a small part of the bird now, and things could not be the way they were. The burden lay heavy on our shoulders, and a single tick on a set of obscure lists stacked on a dusty bookshelf did not seem enough of a prize for such a bird. Surely at the very least, a system should be designed whereby such birds count double, or tenfold? How could a mythical beast like this be equivalent to a dowdy prinia or a streaky pipit, whose names we would forget within weeks of first seeing them? It simply wasn't right.

There was no denying the significance of the achievement though. Pitta number nineteen, the behemoth, the daddy of them all, was on the board. The Giant Pitta had fallen, and was swinging from my hunter's belt.

A list of the top ten Sabah birds seen by us that other birders would give their right arm to see.

1 *Giant Pitta*

2 *Giant Pitta*

3 *Giant Pitta*

4 *Giant Pitta*

5 *Giant Pitta*

6 *Giant Pitta*

7 *Giant Pitta*

8 *Giant Pitta*

9 *Giant Pitta*

10 *Giant Pitta*

After a few beers and a leisurely dinner, we took turns on scorpion watch and drank the remainder of the rum. We replayed the afternoon's events in a hundred different ways, arguing over the minutiae and reminiscing over other great days. In the last thirty years we had all enjoyed any number of fabulous moments in the field, but today's was up there with the very best.

Still in reflective mood, I mused on why I had become so obsessed with pittas in the first place. At its root was the whole adolescent male collecting fetish; the search for the missing football card, the elusive first-day cover stamp that will complete the set. Not just any old stamp will do, though; the one you really want is the one no one else has. Exclusivity is the key ingredient. At a deeper level, bird-watching is a kind of sanitised hunting. At its heart, it is predatory, carnivorous, red in tooth and claw, and nowhere does this become more apparent than in the rainforest. Within this uncivilised other world, the most supremely hostile environment on the planet, the greatest challenge is to stalk the shyest creatures on the forest floor. To see them before they see you. To achieve a clean kill. It's no coincidence that the verb applied to the act of taking a photograph is *to shoot.*

I realized early on quite how primal the whole bird-watching business is. In South America, I required my girlfriend (the same woman who is now, in a feat of patience and tolerance unequalled anywhere in the universe, my wife) to wade waist deep through an Andean melt-water river. I'd felt this was necessary in order to ensure that she got up close and personal with a Diademed Sandpiper-plover. It is true that this bizarre high altitude wading bird is one of the most sought after birds in the world, but it's equally true that my other half didn't care two hoots whether she saw it or not. I was well aware of this fact, but it remained extremely important to me that she saw the bird, and saw it well. Over a placatory dinner at the venerable O'Higgins Hotel in Valparaiso that evening, we had discussed why I had cared so much. It was, I had realized, simply the hunter-gatherer gene working overtime. It was no good just killing the mammoth, I had to drag the damn thing back to the cave and present it to my mate.

The rest of my mania is pure logic. What are the shyest and most beautiful birds on the rainforest floor? No contest; the pittas rule supreme. They say you never forget your first pitta, and it's certainly true in my case: a Noisy Pitta on Mount Whitfield in Cairns Australia, on the morning of the twenty-fourth of September 1995. I can still feel the hairs on the back of my neck standing up when I heard its distant whistle, the adrenalin rush when it finally, hesitantly, bounced onto the trail behind me and stood there weighing me up, a riot of colour packed into a tiny frame. Only I had seen it. No one else was there to share the moment. A life-long love affair was born.

The next day we dropped anchor in a quiet backwater, and listened to the sounds around us. The forest was alive with activity in the cool of the early morning. The strident complaints of a pair of Ashy Tailorbirds, the mesmeric, soporific cooing of Emerald Doves and the thin, repetitive melody of Malaysian Blue-flycatchers all reached our ears. A snuffling Bearded Pig distracted us for a while, quietly rooting out morsels from the dank earth, but my attention was caught by an altogether more emphatic sound, a short, whirring 'pe-wheeoorrr', interspersed with a trisyllabic 'hooweooow' Cherokee war-cry. The timbre reminded me of the Banded Pittas I had seen before in Malaysia, soft but insistent, beseeching one to pay attention. I knew this new song well, having played a recording of it many times over the previous months. It was the song of the Blue-headed Pitta.

We loosely moored the boat to the opposite bank, crouched low in the stern and played the tape. The pitta's call grew louder. We waited in silence, bodies tensed, binoculars an inch below our eyes. We had to be sure if the bird reappeared we didn't startle it with a sudden jerk of our optics towards our faces. The minutes dragged, time slowed by our urgent desire to catch a glimpse of our quarry in the dense forest cover. After what seemed like a lifetime, I caught a sudden movement on the opposite side of the river, and then another, as the bird hopped between two tree trunks, culminating in a tiny bounce onto a crooked liana. There it was.

Despite our best efforts to stay silent, an audible gasp went up from the occupants of the boat, such was the pitta's shocking beauty. First to catch the eye was a brilliant cobalt blue cap that glowed as if internally lit, set off by the tar-black face below. An arrowhead of white cut across the throat. The back seemed to change colour depending on the bird's angle, at one moment deep chestnut, the next a darker ruby-red. A snow-white flash ran the length of the wing, and tiny silver streaks flecked the mantle. The deep sapphire breast and flanks burned with an intensity for which the artist Yves Klein would have killed when searching for his ultimate blue.

The bird continued to call from its perch for a minute or so, allowing us to take in every ounce of its loveliness. I was close enough to note the washed-out pink of its toenails, the tiny mud-spatters across the base of the bill where it had been probing in the rich, moist leaf-litter on the forest floor. This jewel of a bird had been entombed in the darkness, had dug itself out of the filth and decay of the forest floor, to emerge, glittering, into the early morning light. It was vitality encapsulated, its tiny frame unable to contain the energy within. It stood with feet slightly splayed, as if primed to explode into action at any moment, bobbing with nervous excitement every few seconds. All too soon, despite our audio chicanery, the pitta figured out that we posed no threat to its territorial dominance, and in a single movement turned and dropped into the mulch. Our brief audience was over, and I had a new favourite. I collapsed back into the boat and finally allowed myself to breath once more, my palms damp, my heart beating against my ribs. This must be love.

We drifted on into the heat of the day, admiring the dextrous high-wire skills of the Long-tailed Macaques as they crossed from one side of the tributary to the other without the aid of a safety net. As the morning wore on, the heat sucked the life from the forest, and the early shift was replaced by the droning cicadas and a billion other unidentifiable insects. We beat a retreat back to camp and I dozed fitfully on my bunk for a couple of hours, disturbed at intervals by new rivulets of sweat that tickled me awake. The humidity sat like a sandbag on my lungs, the smallest movement requiring a monumental effort.

As the afternoon cooled we reassembled to don leech socks and apply suntan cream and DEET-heavy mosquito repellent. Kit called us over to admire his trousers. Whilst his unique fashion sense was something to which we had all become attuned over the years, this still seemed somewhat narcissistic. As we approached he pointed cautiously at his left knee. There in the khaki folds, sat a tiny, immaculate scorpion. It seemed to be carved out of polished chocolate, promising the sweetest sting. It did not move a muscle, secure in the knowledge that the cotton valleys on either side of its sculpted carapace would keep it safe. And so they did for a while, until a deft flick sent it over the balcony rail and down into the mud.

Our afternoon cruise was enlivened by a close encounter with the world's smallest pachyderms, the footballing Bornean Pygmy

Elephants we had heard so much about from Robert. The group we found feeding at the river's edge had enough members to make up two complete teams with a couple of substitutes per side. We drifted at a respectable distance; though relatively diminutive for an elephant they are still potentially dangerous animals. Their teamwork extended to applying muscled grey shoulders to the buttock of the animal in front as they fought to drag their lumbering bodies up through the thigh-deep mud and onto *terra firma*. Occasionally an elephant on the bank would reach too far for a particularly succulent stick of bamboo, and would topple over into the river, sending waves in our direction that threatened to tip us into the water.

Nor was this to be the last endangered animal sighting of the day. A night-time spotlighting cruise brought views of a Flat-headed Cat, a rarely seen nocturnal feline padding silently along the river bank. The perfect pet it was decided; a tabby you can park your beer on without fear of spillage. Our attempts to spotlight a calling Oriental Bay-owl came to naught, but while probing every last possible perch we did find another bird roosting quietly on an exposed twig; a Hooded Pitta. I had already seen the nominate race *sordida* earlier in the year in Mindanao, but this individual was of one of the black-crowned races, *mulleri*, and photographing it was an easy task, since like most roosting birds it was determined to keep perfectly still to avoid detection. Although the combination of lime-green body, blue wing-coverts and scarlet belly were as delicious as usual, this individual appeared moribund. Bare skin was peeping through the feathering at the base of the bill, its breast-feathers were torn and matted, and mosquitoes were feeding rapaciously around its ankles. We quickly snapped off the light and left it to suffer in peace.

One key Kinabatangan target remained. Having missed the bizarre Sumatran Ground-cuckoo in Indonesia, I was exceedingly keen to wipe away that painful memory by tracking down the *Toktor's* cousin in Sabah, the equally alien Bornean Ground-cuckoo. In between pitta-hunting sessions we had already devoted a few hours to searching for this most enigmatic of Sabah's mysteries. Anchoring the boat in suitably remote stretches of river we played the ground-cuckoo's call – a deep, booming 'oo-wo-ok-oooh... oo-wo-ok-oooh' – which reverberated across the turbid, muddy waters. Despite our intensive efforts however, our overtures had remained unanswered. After a couple of days' work we were a little dispirited, oppressed even, by the constant repetition of the resonant call.

On our last morning we tried a spot where Rob had seen the bird in the past, and after some time, we could at last make out the sound we had been straining to hear. From way in the distance came a faint echo of the call, and our pilot skilfully manoeuvred the boat into a tiny bay where the vegetation was fractionally less impenetrable. Our overactive imaginations convinced us that the sound was growing louder, and after a few minutes it proved to be so. There was no doubt; the bird was being inexorably drawn towards us.

We hunkered down in the boat and waited. A few minutes more, and the call was louder still, less than a hundred metres away. All of a sudden there was a commotion on the bank, and the outlandish creature hopped into view on a low branch. A prehistoric dinosaur of a bird, it had clearly bred with some kind of extra terrestrial being at some point in its convoluted lineage. If Hanna-Barbera's Road Runner bred with a Peacock, and the resultant offspring then crossbred with a Star Wars extra, the third generation freak might resemble the sight that now presented itself before our disbelieving eyes. The bird ducked nervously in the shadows, a rangy, long-legged beast with bare blue facial skin set in a coal-black head. Its rainbow back shimmered green, blue and violet all at once. A long, slightly shambolic tail, over-endowed with feathers, trailed behind. Black and yellow tiger-stripes were emblazoned across the underparts, and a pair of yellow-ochre legs long enough to grace a Milanese catwalk propped up the whole ensemble. The bird surveyed us warily from its lair, before haughtily dismissing us as unworthy of its attention, and departed as quickly as it had arrived. So astonishing was its appearance that it seemed to leave a ghost of its image in the spot where it had stood, and we all continued to gaze at the recently vacated space, stunned into believing this bizarre animal was still present. If you doubt the impact a ground-cuckoo's appearance can create, just invite one to a cocktail party and see how quickly the room falls silent. You may want to keep an eye on the canapés too, although personally if a ground-cuckoo wants the last vol-au-vent I'd think twice about standing in its way.

Once we were sure the bird had left, and having allowed sufficient time to ensure the imprint of its freakish majesty was firmly established in our minds, we cast off and drifted back downriver to the lodge, the atmosphere on the boat now transformed into one of celebration and levity. It was time to party, our complete lack of vol-au-vents notwithstanding. A riotous lunch ensued, our fellow diners bemused by our giggling antics, before the time came to bid farewell to Robert and his staff. After one last restful river trip, we moored up at the quay where our chariot stood idling in the road, ready to whisk us to our next location. The mythical Danum Valley awaited.

Chapter 12

The Famous Five. Sabah, Borneo

I'd dreamt of setting foot on Danum's hallowed turf for years. After a long, uncomfortable journey through a tropical downpour, we finally drew up outside the lodge, stumbling around in the blackness of the Bornean night.

Borneo Rainforest Lodge is a fancy affair. It is the ultimate fantasy tree-house, whose every wooden balustrade has been varnished and polished until it shines. Comfortable couches are artfully positioned to give the best view of the rainforest, and once you sink into their depths it's impossible to summon up the willpower to extricate yourself.

Sabah is the scene of a delightful culinary collision of Chinese, Bruneian, Malay and Indian influences. No need in this part of Malaysia at least to settle for fried rice – *nasi goreng* – three times a day. The nightly buffet groaned under the weight of a *smorgasbord* of fragrant curries, including my favourite, juicy Beef Rendang served with *lemang* glutinous rice cakes. Even if I could have ignored this and the vast array of western dishes so considerately provided by our hosts, there was no way I could have made it past the tureen of *sambal udang*, chock-full of succulent prawns frolicking in a sea of chillies, shallots, tamarind and tomatoes. If by some miracle I could have body-swerved around this temptation, the Sarawak *laksa* would have got me, lassoing me by the nose as it wafted garlic, galangal, lemongrass, coconut milk and the unmistakable odour of belacan prawn paste in my direction. Sinful desserts beckoned too, intent on our dietary downfall, and we were unable to resist. The bread-and-butter pudding in particular, laced with spiced raisins, wreaked untold damage on our waistlines. At breakfast the onslaught continued in the form of Roti Canai, great circles of roasted unleavened bread, served sweet or savoury with a glass of thick, sugary coffee.

It crossed my mind that after this sybaritic overindulgence, there was a distinct possibility that we might not be able to fit onto the trails at all. We didn't have far to walk to find ourselves in prime

Birding the main entrance track at dusk, BRL, Sabah.

'The Gang of Four' sheltering from the daily downpour, Mt Kinabalu
(L-R: Bob Harris, Kit Britten, Graham Hogan, CG).

A Colugo pretending to be a canopy handbag, BRL, Sabah.

The upper Liwagu Trail, Mt Kinabalu, Sabah.

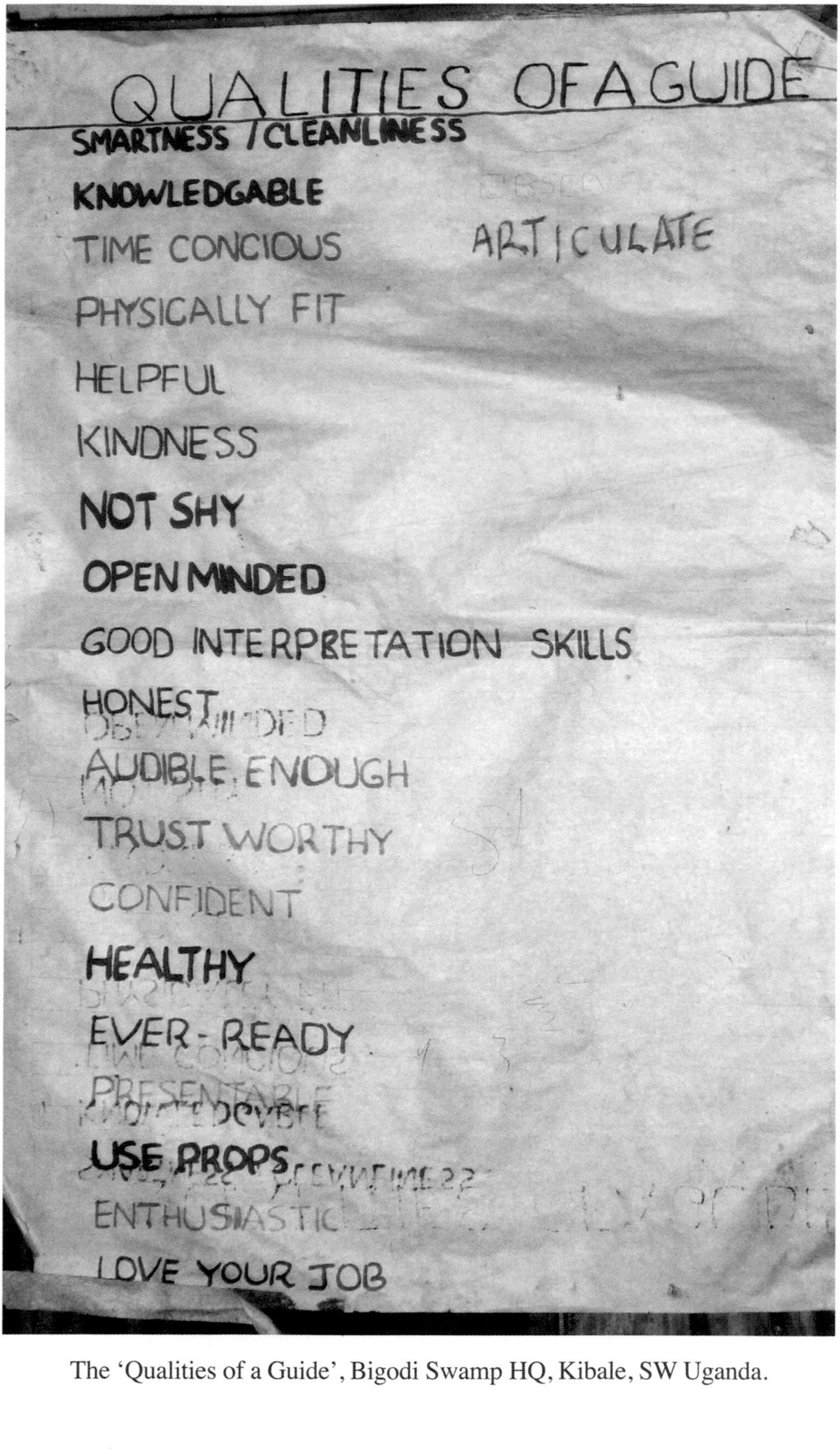

The 'Qualities of a Guide', Bigodi Swamp HQ, Kibale, SW Uganda.

Early morning at Lake Mburo, SW Uganda.

The fabulous Finfoot at Lake Mburo. This is a male.

Bigodi Women's Group sign at Kibale, SW Uganda.
Note Green-breasted Pitta top right.

L'Hoest's Monkey, Bwindi, SW Uganda.

Gerald T, for once not watching a Green-breasted Pitta, Kibale, SW Uganda.

The main road at Kibale, SW Uganda.

The swamp at Ruhizha, Bwindi, SW Uganda.

Blue lagoon, Peleng, Indonesia.

The Peleng crew (L-R: Maleso, Theo Henoch, Labi).

Peleng Tarsier, Kokolomboi, W. Peleng. About to do the pinball thing.

The High Street, Kokolomboi, W. Peleng,
showing washbowl headwear and chicken coop.

Probably the first photo ever taken of Sula Scrubfowl, E. Peleng.
Now we know who ate all the pies.

A Wagler's Pit Viper thinking about
biting the author, Tangkoko, Sulawesi.

A daytime Barking Owl on Halmahera, Indonesia.

Wallace's Standardwing, 'the lovechild of ET and Liberace', Halmahera.

Blue seas and volcanoes between Ternate and Sidangoli, off Halmahera.

Jalak bali, the Bali Starling, Bali Barat.

Dry forest, evening, Bali Barat.

The mysterious Mr Klau and the moustachioed Nimus, Flores.

The author having lost a few kilos after a bout of dysentery, Flores, Indonesia.

A Flores Hawk-eagle at two kilometre range.

Mountain village, W. Flores.

habitat however. The lodge squats in a tract of primary rainforest that threatens to overrun it at any moment. Probing tendrils curl in an orgy of repossession around the raised walkways connecting the HQ to the chalets. Wild pigs snuffle around the bins. Snakes wrap themselves around the rustic banisters. Bugs the size of pigeons mob the flickering oil lamps at night, the creepy-crawlies here being outsize, but not necessarily outside. Imposing Rhinoceros Beetles, Giant Green Grasshoppers, immense Rajah Brookes Birdwing butterflies, all appear overfed, overweight and over here. In the evenings too, the whickering cries of unseen animals drift across the balconies, causing the assembled ecotourists to pause, fork aloft, as they graze.

We had work to do at Danum. Kinabatangan had been an unqualified success, but there still remained three additional pittas to find in Sabah. All three were present at Danum, and all were endemic, a fact which had been playing on my mind. Were I to miss any one of them, there would be nothing for it but to return to Sabah later in the year and try again. The wet season might well make that impossible, and budget would certainly be an issue, for BRL's delights cost considerably more than the low-grade accommodation I was used to. Our next destination was Mount Kinabalu, where we would spend our time at higher altitudes, and where the air was too thin for most pittas' taste. Besides, even here in the lowlands, the pittas might well be impossible to find at another season if they had ceased calling, having finished their breeding cycle. A return visit could all too easily be marked only by an unproductive tramp around silent forests, the pittas secreted behind a wall of vegetation, taciturnly going about their business far from the prying eyes of an Englishman on a lunatic mission. The stakes were high, and the pressure unrelenting. I simply had to find all three birds in the short time available.

The first morning the five of us ventured out along a perilous, leech-infested track near the entrance gate known as the Tekala Trail. We lost a hard-fought duel with a Blue-banded Pitta that refused to show itself, a major disappointment. I knew that Blue-banded, a relatively low-density pitta in population terms, was eminently missable. The commoner Black-headed Pitta was equally uncooperative, and despite an epic pursuit off-trail through the most rattan-infested section of forest in which I have ever had the misfortunate to be incarcerated, the mischievous sprite always managed to stay a few hops ahead of me. I sat defeated on the forest floor, deftly flicking leeches off my lower regions, as I listened to the bird's whistles retreating into the distance. Each dwindling note seemed designed to mock my bumbling, flat-footed, city slicker ineptitude. For four hours after dawn we sweated and stalked, crept and cajoled, but without success. It looked like it was going to be one of those days.

Birding in tropical environments can be a frustrating business. There are times when, despite Herculean efforts, one sees very little. Tempers can fray as the difficult conditions, long hours and close confinement threaten the collective companionship and put an end to the bonhomie engendered by a common goal. Over the years, our 'Gang of Four' had evolved ways to ensure that things never got out of hand. Frequently it was the quietest of our quartet who would come to the rescue. Bob's puns were legendary. A labourer balancing a logging instrument across his crown in Peru had prompted the observation, 'I bet he's got a saw head.' On another occasion elsewhere in South America, our transport was on the point of being engulfed by a herd of cattle heading for their evening feed. 'We'd better get a move on', Bob had solemnly intoned, 'or we'll be here until the cows come home.' A group of tiny seabirds wheeling above a distant shoreline would inevitably be greeted with a swift rendition of *Thank Heaven for Little Gulls.* Folks in Watford evidently make their own entertainment.

Graham, being an architect by profession, is of a more sober bent, and hence settles for occasional fits of giggles, the most alarmingly protracted of which had occurred many years earlier at the edge of a marsh in northeast China. He had leant over to me and confided that he had a sure-fire identification method by which to pick out one of the elderly participants on our tour, *viz.* her habit of blinking repeatedly at lightning speed. This inexplicably sent both of us into paroxysms, much to the chagrin of the tour leader who was traversing the marsh for the umpteenth time in an attempt to show the ungrateful onlookers a particularly skulking Pechora Pipit.

As the youngest of my trio of companions, Kit's brand of humour is somewhat drier. In the 1990s we had been driving along a lonely road in Costa Rica when we passed an incredibly beautiful young girl, the epitome of taut womanhood, riding a pony. An entire busload of sex-starved bird-watchers had swivelled to a man, craning their necks to savour every last drop of lecherous potential. Pausing for effect, Kit surveyed the gaggle of malodorous, misshapen voyeurs before him, before pricking our conceit with two well-chosen words. 'Nice horse.'

Today however, such humour was impossible, silence being a prerequisite for finding the shyer wilderness residents. And so we stuck to our task, until we emerged onto a steep slope, the trail passing through an area of more open forest. We paused to scrape the clinging mud from our boots, and to check for any leeches boldly going where no leech had gone before.

A list of Bornean trail-talk subjects

• *Whether it would be possible to do a Dogtagnan-style version of the Mission Impossible theme voiced entirely by a Scottie Dog*

• *Leech bites*

• *Watford FC's greatest ever line-up*

• *Annual Sabah rainfall, and given that Eskimos allegedly have fifty words for 'snow', whether there is a precipitative equivalent in Borneo*

• *The name of that damned woman who sang 'I never promised you a Rose Garden'*

• *Whether one could eat an entire bowl of green sago without throwing up. (This was put to the test by Rob Hutchinson in an infamous bet at Kinabalu. It transpires that it can be done, but has the potential to be a mighty close-run thing)*

• *What trogons do when it rains*

Up-slope, our attention was caught by a distinctive alarm call. Although higher and of shorter duration than its close relatives in Thailand and Malaysia, I knew immediately that it was a Banded Pitta. The birds here are of particular taxonomic interest. They are of a different race, *schwaneri*, and they both look and sound subtly different from their more westerly congeners. The dominant plumage colour here is a vivid banana yellow, which engulfs the head and flows down the flanks and across the breast, threatening to wash over the reduced blue of the belly. These birds literally glow in the undergrowth, and in the relatively open forest favoured by this individual we had soon located it, perched up on a low branch and calling defiantly in defence of its territory.

Once everyone had seen the bird, Rob and I embarked on a military manoeuvre, inching forward on our elbows and bellies, cradling our cameras like marines protecting their weapons as they shimmy under low-strung barbed wire on the training ground. Our fieldcraft paid off, and we were soon clicking away, taking photo after photo of this breathtaking bird. Although I had already seen Banded Pittas in Thailand and Malaysia earlier in the year, I knew there was a good chance that *schwaneri* would soon be split, and accorded full specific status in its own right as 'Bornean Banded Pitta.' The spectre of having seen all the pittas only to have the goalposts moved after the fact filled me with dread, and I had vowed to make sure that I saw all the races of Banded Pitta come what may. Now the most difficult of them was out of the way, and I heaved a sigh of relief.

We left the bird in peace and crept back to the trail, bleeding profusely from the attentions of the leeches, which were clearly ecstatic that we had seen fit to join them on the forest floor. Leech socks do a great job at stopping the bloodsuckers' progress up the legs, but are of little use when you are lying full length in the dirt intent only on capturing the image of a bird that has rarely been photographed. In truth, we valued the evidence of the leeches' assault as a medal of honour, proof that we had suffered for our cause: the testosterone-fuelled, masochistic machismo of hunting.

After another sumptuous lunch that probably contributed little to the sharpening of our hunters' senses, we negotiated the main road. Following further heavy rain it was more of a quagmire than a thoroughfare, but we made it to a circular structure wrapped around an immense dipterocarp tree. This was BRL's famous canopy walkway, an altogether grander affair than the young pretender at Sepilok. Its suspended rope bridge allows a rare glimpse into the rarefied atmosphere of the uppermost level of forest life. A couple of leisurely hours followed, punctuated by occasional canopy-dweller appearances. Gold-whiskered and Red-throated Barbets churned out their monotonous songs from isolated snags, and a pair of Green Imperial-pigeons mooched lazily in a shady cluster. A clumsy Chestnut-breasted Malkoha seemed oddly out of place as it clomped about in the higher branches, while Silver-rumped Spinetails streaked by overhead, their streamlined, spool-shaped bodies the pinnacle of aerodynamic evolution. Spinetails have been clocked flying at over 175 kilometres per hour in level flight, a good contender for the title of 'world's fastest bird.'

Fascinating though the canopy is, pittas are rarely to be found there. So as the day wore on we wound our way back down a second swaying staircase and worked our way home. The forest is so good at Danum that dense evergreen habitat extends right up to the edge of the road, and at regular intervals I heard the monotone whistle of Black-headed Pittas at tantalizingly close range. Frustratingly, most were buried deep in impenetrable scrub. After rejecting two calling birds as being totally impossible to access, our party came across a third songster close to a vestigial trail that allowed us to squeeze into the forest, and we lost no time in hiding ourselves in the dense, tangled foliage.

We whistled to the pitta, imitating its simple territorial call, and the bird approached while remaining hidden. After a long wait, the bird's curiosity finally got the better of it, and it hopped onto a branch a few inches off the ground. I checked the head. Satisfyingly black, lacking any hint of Garnet Pitta's scarlet crown, and with only a narrow post-ocular blue streak to liven things up; a lightning bolt in the gloom. The rest of the bird was a riot of colour: maroon on the back shading into darkest blue; a cerulean blaze marking the edge of the wing; black-throated below, giving way to a bright red breast and belly. It's a dainty creature as pittas go, with large, loveable puppy-dog eyes, a small head and a petite body; the ballerina of the genus. Judging by the number of birds we had heard calling, the species was common at Danum, but this bird like all the others went out of its way to keep out of ours. It was forever skulking, using every last strand of vegetation to sustain the hide-and-seek, never perching in the open, always keeping something back, eager to maintain its mystique. I nodded my approval, issuing silent thanks as we crept back to the road after capturing a couple of partial images of the bird. The twenty-first species of pitta secured, and the fifth species of pitta in four days; a veritable purple patch.

However, a major challenge remained. We had to find a Blue-banded Pitta, another endemic which, if I failed to find it would require a return trip. Since early February I had been living a charmed life, having missed only Rusty-naped Pitta north of Chiang Mai in Thailand. Even then, I had subsequently managed to catch up with one at Fraser's Hill in Malaysia, thus avoiding expensive additional return trips. Surely my run of luck could not last the entire mission? I knew that Blue-banded Pittas were thin on the ground, even here in pitta-soaked Danum Valley, and as the following day dawned I was full of trepidation.

We inched our way forward in the dark, up the slick path that climbed the hillside across the river from the lodge. This was the infamous Coffin Trail, named, I surmised, for the boxes in which less hardy trekkers had been carried off the hill after one exertion too many. A rhyme from my childhood insinuated its way into my brain where it rattled round like a wayward marble. *It wasn't the cough that carried him off, it was the coffin they carried him off in.* In fact the trail takes its name from an ancient *Kadazandusun* burial site built into the side of a large hanging rock which thrusts up through the soft earth just east of the river. I focussed carefully on the few yards of trail immediately ahead, ignoring the steep incline that reared up dizzyingly in the distance in front of us. I rubbed the scar on my forearm, keen to avoid the kind of fall that had hospitalized me in the Philippines.

After a strenuous climb we reached the lookout point, and were immediately enveloped in a rolling bank of cloud that smothered everything beyond the immediate vicinity. So much for the view. We pressed on, stopping at regular intervals to play the pitta's call, straining to separate any response from the mêlée of insect noise. Nothing. If the pittas were here, they were not in vocal mood, and as the hours clicked by, I began to think that my luck had indeed run out. We negotiated the ribbon of trail around the head of the valley, before weaving our way back in the opposite direction, stopping off at *The Jacuzzi Pool* to wash our sweat-streaked faces.

Revitalized, we set off again, traversing a knife-edge track that cut its way laterally across a steep hillside. Mindful of the pitta's preference for slopes, my concentration levels ratcheted up a notch as we silently edged our way forward. Only a couple of hundred metres into this sloping section, a single whistle froze us in our tracks. A lonely monotone, clear and thrilling in its penny-whistle simplicity. *Like Black-headed Pitta or Garnet Pitta, but a little too long*, I thought to myself. *Perfectly flat, hollowed out, without Garnet's upslurred peroration. Higher-pitched and more certain than Black-headed's nervous, wavering whistles.* It had to be a Blue-banded.

We crouched down in the dirt. Another set of fluted notes floated towards us, source unseen. None of us dared move a muscle, exposed on the trail, denied the time we needed to secrete ourselves in the nearest foliage by the bird's proximity. The purity of the call made it impossible to locate accurately. We exchanged glances, each of us extending index fingers to indicate the direction from which we believed the sound might be emanating. The discrepancies were as embarrassing as they were depressing. How were we supposed to find the bird when we couldn't even agree in which direction we ought to look?

The minutes ticked by, and gradually we pieced together the bird's general locale. We could track its movement somewhere up on the bank above us. We signalled to each other, a platoon unified by a common purpose, one to lead, three to follow, one bringing up the rear to cover. We wormed our way forward into the forest, sheltering behind a convenient mud-bank fifty metres off the trail. The call was ahead of us, but the bird had moved deeper into cover. Despite our extreme caution, it had seen us, and it had not liked what it saw. I can't say I blamed it. After five days in the forest the sight and smell of our unshaven, ragged band of brothers would have put far larger creatures to flight.

We waited and waited, but the bird stayed resolutely hidden, delighting in its obscurity, wedded to the gloom and in no hurry to hit the trail to perform a hat and cane routine. Another thirty minutes dragged by, but despite careful scanning, we emerged back onto the trail empty-handed. The bird called no more. For the second time at Danum it had fought and won, denying us even a brief glimpse of a blue band. The only blue thing in the forest was our language at having missed out again, that and the endless sky above our heads, stretching cloudless into the distance. We'd got the blues all right, but not in the way we had intended. The failure weighed heavy on my shoulders, and I began to give in to that spiral of negativity that inevitably brings its own defeat.

A little way down-slope, I reached a corner where a tree fall jutted out, and as I rounded it, a pitta-shadow bounced off the trail. My heart was in my mouth, but as the bird paused and turned it revealed a primrose yellow curve above the eye. It was a Bornean Banded Pitta, the same species we had seen the previous day. Such is the fickleness of the birder, I cursed this individual, a bird I had been thrilled to find less than twenty-four hours earlier, railing unreasonably at its lambent beauty. Where all should have been red and blue, it was yellow and brown, where a single breast band should have curved round from one shoulder to the other, this bird sported a mass of black and yellow bars. We had seen one of Asia's more recalcitrant pitta species, and all I felt was a crushing disappointment. That and a twinge of guilt at my inability to rejoice in finding this difficult species, a bird that many people miss altogether, for the second time in as many days. We waited to see if this pitta would show again, but our advance along the trail had clearly flushed the bird, and it was doubtless now well down the hill, masked by the verdant vegetation.

As we waited, I heard a familiar ringing whistle behind us. As pittas so often do, the Blue-banded had watched us leave, and once the coast was clear, had once again set about defending his territory against all-comers. The Gods had offered us a second chance, and we needed no further invitation. We crept back up the hill, stopping just shy of a small ridge, behind which the bird was issuing its simple song. We whistled once and waited. The response came again, now a little further to the right. We whistled once more, and the echo came again, now closer. We edged off the trail and into cover, scanning the forest floor and the mid-storey. It was entirely possible that the bird, responding to our imitations, had ascended a metre or two in order to get a clearer view of proceedings. Such behaviour is common amongst the pittas when they sense a rival for their mate's affections close at hand, even amongst those species that habitually keep their feet on the ground. But there was no sign, no flash of colour, no tiny vibration of tail or bill as the bird called. Just a wall of greenery keeping us from our prize, every leaf and branch faultlessly fitting our expected image-map.

And then it happened; a fractional movement way back in the forest, so slight that I suspected at first that it might only be a figment of my fevered imagination. But then a second, more substantial shadow-twitch, and a third, and at last, that wonderful, familiar shape moving rapidly across the terrain which signals the impending arrival of a pitta. Suddenly the call was shockingly loud, and the bird was almost upon us. I hissed at the others to watch the trail, and unbelievably, the bird burst out of cover and paused for a few seconds at the edge of the path. I stared at it through my binoculars, revelling in every tiny fragment of detail. The scarlet crown and nape, breast and belly. The face delicately washed in faded orange. A thrillingly phosphorescent cobalt streak cascading down from above the eye to the back of the neck. A ragged breast band in the same colour, like paint spilling over the lip of a tin. A teal wash across the back, truncated by an iridescent exclamation mark of a tail. Astonishingly, breathtakingly beautiful, here it was, eyeing us suspiciously, calculating the angles, weighing the options.

The pitta took another hop forwards, and I took my chance with my camera. I focused as precisely as I dared, knowing that I had only a second or two before the bird moved away. I barely had enough time to fire off two shots before the bird bounded across the trail, hopped onto a low limb on the other side of the path, and with a single shrug of a wing, flipped effortlessly into the forest.

There are few happier sounds than a group of birders exhaling in unison after sharing a rare glimpse of a difficult pitta. We exchanged grins, shaking clenched fists in manic joy, all the tiny, mute gestures of repressed celebration. The bird continued to work through the forest, and since we knew its exact starting point and could figure out where it was headed, could track its trajectory as it circled around us, arcing surreptitiously, clockwise, streetwise, little lightning bolts of colour every now and then as parts of the bird became visible through the tangle of rattan and evergreen shrubbery, until at last it melted back into the forest, its solid presence once again whittled away to an airy whistle.

There really ought to be a post-pitta song that groups of bird-watchers can yodel as they head out of the forest after a successful hunt. Something with the *joie de vivre* of the Seven Dwarfs' *Hi-Ho* married with the bombastic glee of Queen's *We are the Champions*. With perhaps a *soupçon* of something classical and militaristic thrown in to reflect the stature of the glorious victors' homecoming.

A touch of *Shostakovich's Fifth* perhaps. Or Tchaikovsky's *1812 Overture.* With the cannons. As it was, we were forced to make do with Bob's rendition of *Thank Heaven for Little Gulls.*

That evening we celebrated over fake rum and cokes (the ersatz alcoholic content provided by a bottle of *Rafflesia Likeur* manufactured by Sunny Bear Trading, doubtless the origin of the phrase *a bear with a sore head).* I had to pinch myself to confirm the reality of our unlikely achievement. We had managed to find ALL of Sabah's pittas, and we had done it in just five days. We toasted Rob's experience and expertise, our own self-appointed status as 'The A-Team,' and Danum Valley as a whole. As the evening wore on I believe we may also have toasted Girls Aloud, The Queen Mother, Albert Tatlock off Coronation Street and some obscure members of Watford FC's reserve team. To be frank, recollections get a little hazy at this point, but everyone, we were sure, had helped in their own small way. We babbled incoherently to complete strangers and showed them pictures of the pittas on my laptop. They too, I could tell, were vicariously warmed by our success. You could see it in their smile, if not by the way they edged nervously towards the exits. The world was full of great places and Sabah was the best of the lot. Everyone and everything was unquestionably grand.

Our last full day at Danum was a relaxed affair. Another session on the main entrance trail and up on the canopy walkway produced great views of some cantankerous Black-throated Wren-babblers chuntering in the undergrowth, and a female Orange-backed Woodpecker undulating away over the treetops. One of our number risked their hard-won status as a committed conservationist by accepting Kit's ten dollar challenge to prove that leeches can, in fact, be bitten in half. I must confess that I was the first to try for the prize money, but found the combination of the wiry centre section and the slippery, writhing body too much to deal with. The eventual victor grasped the bloodsucker firmly at each end of its disgusting, wriggling torso before simply gnawing his way through the middle. Unsurprisingly, our winner reported that the little critters taste appalling. Still, a neat act of revenge we decided, all of us having suffered in a wide array of Asian forests at the hands of leeches. Not that leeches have hands *per se*, but you get the point.

As is the case at so many other bird-rich locations, the days are long at Danum. Pre-dawn starts are essential, and there's always another species to track down, another virgin trail to explore. When dusk falls it falls hard, and the black night is all-enveloping. After twelve hours in the field we were invariably exhausted, spattered with mud and blood and ready for a good rest. Darkness, however, does not spell an end to activities. It's just nature's way of confirming that it's officially time to go owling. We had already had some success in this department, having shone our spotlights inconsiderately into the faces of a Brown Wood-owl and a fine pair of Buffy Fish-owls. Sadly the latter species is not named for any striking resemblance to the pulchritudinous Sarah Michelle Gellar of *Buffy the Vampire-Slayer* fame, but instead is a rather more prosaic reference to the colour of the bird's underparts. (Come to think of it an owl with Sarah M.G.'s face stuck just above the beak would be a successfully frightening proposition.)

Even for the hardened birder however, Danum's night birds are overshadowed by its incredible complement of nocturnal mammals. During our time in Sabah we had already seen over thirty different species of mammal, including a Binturong (aka Bearcat), and that most highly sought-after of Bornean beasts, the Marbled Cat. A fine selection of amphibians had been topped by stellar, spotlit views of a Wallace's Flying Frog, owner of the world's stickiest feet, largest eye-to-headsize ratio, and a strikingly handsome lime-green jacket with yellow trim. *Dapper* is too small a word. After gazing in wonder at this fabulous creature I was briefly tempted to mount a second expedition to try to see all the world's frogs in a year. Right up to the point that I discovered there are at least five thousand kinds of frog, at which point my enthusiasm waned somewhat.

Our final night-drive excursion witnessed a hard-fought match between the Bornean and English spotlighting teams, the home side winning out in the end, courtesy of a Banded Palm Civet, a few Maroon Langurs, and a Colugo or Flying Lemur. The latter, we discovered, when sleeping upside-down suspended from a branch, has the singular ability to disguise itself as a lady's handbag accidentally left hanging in the canopy. Our feeble visitors' response consisted mainly of squirrels. Sadly, despite immense effort, we as the underdogs were unable to find a Bornean Clouded Leopard, which would surely have counted double as an away goal.

We admitted defeat and slunk back to the lodge knowing we had met our match.

After a final dawn foray, we struggled back down the entrance road in another downpour, our 4x4 careening its way through the deepening mud. A brief stop yielded a stately Great-billed Heron feeding at the river's edge, a final gift from the forest Gods. Our expectations on arriving at Danum had been sky-high, and it had certainly not disappointed. A couple of hours later we pulled up alongside the terminal building at Lahud Datu Airport and scurried for cover, the rain still coming down in stair rods. We swam for the shallow end of departures and prayed that the tide would be with us for take-off. Lahud Datu airport is about the size of a basketball court but rather less crowded. It is a little down at heel, though in an ill-advised attempt at grandeur, someone had commissioned the check-in desks to be hewn from fake green marble, to disturbing effect. As ever though, the unflappable ladies in traditional Malay dress who ran the café dispensed kind words and hot beverages in equal measure, the latter from ancient jars with hand-written labels. We took off and flew towards Mount Kinabalu, which, we were sure, would be drier and altogether more civilized. We could not have been more wrong.

Sabah is even more beautiful from the air. We passed over silver rivers that caught the light like strands of tinsel. Low-lying clouds cloaked the forested valleys, an irregular lattice broken only by Kinabalu's thrusting hulk, which burst through the cloud as if caught in the very act of eruption. The late afternoon sunshine glinted off knife-edge ridges and pyramidal peaks, tinting them gold. Sadly, even from this height the havoc that man has wrought was all too visible. Two-lane highways stitched through the forest like grey zippers. Countless plantation acres bore testament to the developed world's insatiable appetite for palm oil. As we came in to land a football match was in progress on the estuarine mudflats adjacent to the airport. The winners of the toss had no doubt elected to play with the tide, and judging by the waves lapping at the southern touchline, extra time seemed unlikely. Unless they sent on the subs.

At just short of four thousand one hundred metres, Mt. Kinabalu is Malaysia's tallest peak. Ranked twentieth in the list of the highest mountains in the world, it dominates the surrounding landscape. The massive granite extrusions that form the mountain's upper slopes are habitually cloaked in mist, the lower surrounding peaks breaching the omnipresent layers of cloud like Humpback Whales coming up for air. A massively biodiverse region, it supports at least eight hundred species of orchid, six hundred different ferns, a wealth of other flora including the huge, insectivorous *Nepenthes* pitcher plants, and over three hundred species of bird. It even has its own endemic, the charmingly if inaccurately named Friendly Bush-warbler, *Bradypterus accentor*. Less endearingly, it also plays host to the Kinabalu Giant Red Leech, whose size can be gauged from the fact that its staple diet is the Kinabalu Giant Earthworm. Tragically we failed to find either invertebrate. Kinabalu receives an average of over one hundred inches of rain per annum, and since our visit coincided with the southwest monsoon, most of it seemed to fall on us during our time on the mountain.

In the same way the peak itself is frequently obscured by stratocumulus clouds, so the origin of Kinabalu's name is lost in the mists of time. The most likely source is the Dusun phrase *'Aki Nabalu'* meaning *The Revered Place of the Dead*. Moss that grows amid the wind-scoured summit rocks is said by the indigenous Dusun guides to provide food for the spirits of their ancestors. Not a good spot in which to get stuck then. In the 1990s a group of British soldiers, close to death, were rescued after becoming stranded for more than three weeks in a deep chasm just below the Low's Peak summit. A Dusun legend tells of a dragon that guards the entrance to Low's Gully, which they regard as the resting place for the souls of the dead. Expeditions regularly took the precaution of sacrificing seven white chickens before departing, something the hapless army team had apparently overlooked. Such an easy thing to forget in the fevered atmosphere of pre-ascent preparations...

Most of those who ascend the peak set out from the Timpohon Gate near the National Park headquarters. Already here you are at 1,866 metres above sea level, while high above the Laban Rata Resthouse sits at 3,270 metres, a six-hour climb. The peak is three hours beyond, and the ascent is usually made in the dark so that climbers can enjoy the spectacular views from the summit before the clouds roll in late morning. Agusti Amador, winner of the 2008 International Climbathon, 'The World's Toughest Mountain Race' did it rather more quickly, completing the entire twenty-one kilometre round trip in an astonishing two hours, forty-four minutes and forty-

221

seven seconds. A sign below the gate reads, 'Sabah park regulations require that all persons intending to climb to the summit must be accompanied by a registered mountain guide.' The name of Señor Amador's guide was sadly not recorded for posterity. Tough gig.

Happily, the birds we had come to find at Kinabalu did not require a schlep to the summit. All could be found on the lower slopes between 1,000 and 2,500 m, and it was this lower montane zone that occupied our attention. Even so, as we worked the higher reaches of this zone, we caught occasional glimpses of huge slabs of black granite towering above us, exuding power and menace in equal measure. Just before dusk the sun regularly painted the underside of the clouds cerise and magenta, the landscape aflame like a Turner watercolour. For three days we walked the trails, a network of veins traversing the body of the mountain, each one blessed with an exotic-sounding name: *Mempening, Pandanus, Liwagu, Silau Silau.*

There are, for the most part, no pittas on Kinabalu, which you might think would limit my interest in the mountain. (Actually, this is not entirely true. There is a single record of Giant Pitta from Kinabalu, way above the upper limit of its usual altitudinal range, an extraordinary extra-limital record. It is thought that this individual was fleeing the Sumatran forest fires that now cause such massive disruption on an annual basis.) Short of flying to Sumatra ourselves and torching a large swath of forest, it seemed unlikely we would find a second Giant Pitta. Nonetheless, Kinabalu's mystery had grabbed me, and I was held in its dripping, misty thrall. Since we had seen all of Sabah's key pittas in record time, I was free to enjoy our days on these little-known slopes. The birds and animals here are inspirational, and we did our best to catch up with all the local specialities. And the local rum of course. *Golden Azak Wangi* from the Rajang Winery since you ask. Not for the faint-hearted.

Our observational efforts were rewarded with sightings of some of Kinabalu's special birds. The Friendly Bush-warbler led us a merry dance at Mesilau, before eventually coming in to our tape and scuttling around our feet like some ancient rodent throwback. At the Rafflesia Centre we set up our telescopes to watch a group of Fruit-hunters, school-uniform-grey birds with berry-stain-orange heads and black bibs, feeding on a crop of small green fruits. We quickly found two of the famous Whitehead's trio (not in fact an obscure jazz combo but three species named after their discoverer, John Whitehead. Though he died at only thirty-nine years old, he managed to discover at least nine bird species new to science, and somehow also found the time to turn up a Woolly Bat and a Spiny Rat.) Whitehead's Spiderhunter and Whitehead's Broadbill both came our way without too much of a struggle, but Mr. W's wily Trogon stayed silent and still amongst the abundant foliage, and it was not until our very last morning that we finally found one. To be more accurate, we found five, two pairs and a juvenile, in exactly the same spot we had searched so diligently during many hours over the preceding days. Sometimes I think birds do it on purpose, sitting there with their own tiny binoculars watching the watchers, freezing motionless as we approach before sticking out their tongues and making rude wing-gestures behind our backs after we have passed, oblivious to their presence. Then I take my medication and get a grip.

Halfway through our sojourn at Kinabalu we upped sticks and struck out on a day-trip to nearby Poring Hot Springs. Even the weather capitulated, being hot and never po(u)ring. After a long, arduous climb, we found the most difficult Asian Broadbill, this time a Hose's Broadbill, a riot of blue and green. The bird was an adult, tending a cute, luminous tennis ball of a juvenile which never moved a muscle in the hour we spent watching it. The species was named for Charles Hose, another eminent zoologist who contributed much to our understanding of Borneo's fauna. Although he lived longer than Whitehead, he too was no slouch, and despite devoting large periods of his life to anthropology, managed to find a few spare moments to devote to natural history. As a result, innumerable species still bear his name, including two frogs, an oriole, a pygmy shrew, a dolphin, two squirrels and a palm civet. (Anyone who can publish a serious natural history book entitled *The Field-Book of a Jungle-Wallah* gets my vote, though I wouldn't like to have been employed as his cleaner.)

Thrilled though we were to have tracked down the broadbill, it was not a bird that stole the show at Poring, but a flower. It has to be said that the list of flowers interesting enough to knock a stunning bird like Hose's Broadbill into second place is decidedly short, but then *Rafflesia keithii* is an exceptional bloom. This parasitic plant has the largest single flower in the world, measuring almost a metre across in a full-grown specimen. It attracts flies and carrion beetles by adopting the look and smell of rotting flesh, the truth of which quickly became evident when we visited the closely guarded site in July's stifling midday heat. The flower's charming local name is, for all too obvious reasons, *The Corpse Flower.* The colour scheme is deep orange, liberally spotted with flesh-pink. At its centre is a large round aperture, capacious enough for a family of Clangers to inhabit without ever having to evict the Soup Dragon. This rare, rainforest freak blooms only once every few years, and even then for only a few days. We were privileged indeed to see such a monster in its overpowering prime.

With the exception of our brief trip to Poring, our daily routine varied little. We rose painfully early, in order to take up positions on the mountain before first light. We'd stake out something massively tricky to see, like an Everett's Thrush (so rarely seen it barely exists at all) at the bottom of the Mempening Trail. We'd find it, scribble a few notes about it, retire to the edge of the forest and jump up and down a bit in a foolish manner, then walk a long way birding very seriously for a few hours and seeing very little, occasionally bumping into something amazing like a Bornean Stubtail or a Crimson-headed Partridge. All the while, the weather would be creeping up on us, sneakily drawing a dark grey veil over our heads when it thought we weren't looking. Suddenly it would rain in a vicious and frankly unprovoked manner for quite some time. (Once, the weather cut to the chase and it rained hard from before first light, which was just not cricket. That much is obvious I suppose, since if it had been cricket, rain would in any event have stopped play.)

As soon as it became clear that the morning rain was no trifling shower but a proper monsoonal event, we'd retire to the Liwagu restaurant where we sat outside under a humungous tarpaulin stretched across the balcony and watched forest-edge birds. This was quite possible in even the heaviest rain, since a number of species would crawl under the tarpaulin with us, looking even more bedraggled and pissed off than we were. This, we decided, was fair enough, since they did not seem to own a single umbrella between them, and since feathers can take an age to dry. One lunchtime, somewhere between indigestible spaghetti and weapons-grade chocolate cake, Rob noticed an Eyebrowed Jungle-flycatcher sheltering on a ground floor window-ledge, and sprinted out into the downpour in an attempt to record its song, hiding behind an adjacent wall to mask his approach. From our lofty vantage point we could see both him and the bird, and through a series of clandestine and thus wholly ineffective hand signals, attempted to explain that the bird was still present and that he should stick his mike round the corner. Scenes worthy of the Keystone Kops ensued, and the bird never did get recorded for posterity.

Our afternoon activities depended very much on the vagaries of the Bornean weather. Sometimes it would rain in earnest only for an hour, and thus we'd abandon the restaurant and head back to the trails. Some days it would rain until it got dark, and we would be forced to while away the hours drinking endless cups of tea, throwing cake at each other, and seeing how many of us could lie simultaneously on the outsize benches in the rest area. We would invent complex ruses to try to get our favourite waitress to come and serve us, all of which, you will be astonished to hear, failed miserably. Or we would sketch out new and ever more sadistic tiny torture instruments for the leech population.

In rare moments of seriousness between deluges, we would mount a round-the-clock watch for Mountain Serpent-eagle which remained conspicuous by its absence, one of only four seriously achievable Bornean endemics we missed.* Hardly a shock I suppose, given that raptors don't like the wet, and we only ever looked for it in the worst of the weather. No matter how skilfully we wielded our umbrellas, we would inevitably return to our digs soaked to the skin, but somehow warm rain is not too uncomfortable compared to being lashed by a freezing gale on some godforsaken English headland in November.

---

* Of these, one was a bulbul, the ginger stepchild of the bird world, over which no self-respecting birder would ever lose a wink of sleep. The second was a Pygmy White-eye, which is so small that it is almost invisible and thus scarcely counts according to the law of inconsequential mass. The other two were both raptors, which I decided many years ago I would no longer bother with, since my blanket inability to identify any of them made me unhappy. I have never regretted this decision for a moment, not least because in order to see raptors you need to look up, and in order to see pittas you need to look down. The pittas won.

A list of things to do in Bornean rainforest when it rains (with value rating)

Run five kilometres back to camp to fetch the umbrella
you forgot this morning *0*

Drink tea under cover and laugh at the monkeys' antics .. *10*

Organise leech races with Bob's foot as bait *5**

Shout, 'look at that big snake!' just as your companions
settle down for a snooze *10*

Disrupt an ant procession with a stick and watch
them bump into one another *10*

Debate whose brilliant idea it was to visit in the
wet season in the first place *7*

Re-enact the seminal scene from 'Singin' in the Rain.'
And make Graham do the Debbie Reynolds' role *8*

Discuss, again, why pittas don't call when it rains *3*

Make shelters out of banana leaves and tree bark *2*

Try to dry off optics with last scrap of dry clothing *1*

Get last scrap of dry clothing wet while trying to
dry off optics *0*

Body-surf along the trails *5***

Eventually the appointed departure hour arrived, and we retraced our steps back to the urban sprawl of Kota Kinabalu, Sabah's state capital. After one last session of urban bird-watching from a busy dual carriageway on the outskirts of town, it was time to leave. We flew home via Kuala Lumpur, spending a night at the airport's budget hotel, *The Tune Inn*, which is as close to a Japanese capsule hotel as porky western body dimensions allow. We had booked single rooms since that's all the hotel offered, and I'd had the foresight to order towels and eight hours air conditioning from the

---

* This is an average rating. It's less fun for Bob than for everyone else.
** Fun at the time, less so afterwards.

'optional extras' list. Tiger beers were only forty-four Malay Ringgits for a six-pack (£1.25 a time) and arrived in stylishly opaque, limited edition designer bottles. The beer inside tasted the same as usual, cold and massively welcome. We ordered a couple of rounds and sat out in the sticky night air, choosing our favourite Bornean birds and reminiscing about our amazing days in the field.

Our pitta haul was impressive, perhaps unprecedented; the whole damn Sabah set achieved in five days. With the year barely half done, twenty-two of the world's thirty-two pittas had already been herded into the corral, including the most unpredictable animal of the lot. It was time to head for the hills, and I had a particular set of hills in mind. I set a course for the heart of Africa.

Chapter 13

The Heart of Darkness. Southwest Uganda

Back in the summer of 2008 before starting my mission I made enquiries about finding the two African pitta species. I was particularly worried about how I might go about tracking down Green-breasted Pitta, one of the least known members of my target family. A number of people made helpful suggestions, but it soon became clear that little was known about the bird. Its display call remained unrecorded, and there wasn't a single reliable place in the entire world where the bird was regularly seen.

'The Democratic Republic of Congo is your best bet,' one authority assured me, adding as a post-script, 'though there is the small matter of a war going on at the moment. Highly unsafe there. Not recommended unless you can put together your own revolutionary force and arm them to the teeth. Even then I wouldn't book a return ticket if I was you.'

Hmm, maybe not Congo then. Gabon, Cameroon and northern Zaire were all mentioned, but I could not find anybody who had ever actually seen the species in any of those countries, nor who could recommend specific sites where the bird might occur.

Luckily, I had an ace up my sleeve. A few years earlier and purely by chance I met one of the leading lights of southern African birding, Jonathan Rossouw. He had called me in search of some recordings of Asian birds on a brief London stop-over, a hurried hiatus in his outrageously jet-set life. I had the species he needed, so he came over for supper and we drank too much wine while painstakingly copying recordings from my analogue gear to his. Jon had promised to assist whenever I needed help with African birds, so I called in the favour and wrote to ask for his advice. His response was not quite what I'd hoped for:

'*Those bloody African pittas are a nightmare... I have never seen Green-breasted, only heard a call that corresponded to the only known recording, which is probably of an immature bird. And that's despite four months spent scouring the forests of Uganda for my book, and a slew of tours there since, although my visits were not at the ideal season.*'

Otherwise good. Jonathan did however recommend two other possible sources of expert opinion, Dave Hoddinott and Adam Riley of Rockjumper Birding Tours. I followed the trail, and after a number of conversations with both gents, had something approaching a plan. Eastern DRC borders western Uganda, and in the extreme southwestern corner of Uganda lies a little-visited but largely intact area of pitta-habitat, the Kibale Forest. Further research unearthed the fact that a few bird-watchers had seen the pitta at Kibale, but it seemed hopelessly hit-and-miss. From the information I could piece together, one just turned up at Kibale and wandered aimlessly round the forest in the company of the chimp-trackers. (These monkey-stalwarts locate troupes of habituated chimps in order to show the animals under relatively safe and controlled conditions to the few tourists who venture this far from Kampala.)

The theory ran that if one spent enough time walking the habitat with enough people, eventually someone would wander close enough to a pitta to flush it. Since the forest was relatively open, one then stood a reasonable chance of at least seeing a bird in flight. I talked to as many people as I could who had been to Kibale. It was a pretty small group. All had devoted days to trying for the pitta. About one in three had succeeded. Not great odds, but the best I could get. I booked a return ticket to Kampala.

I'd allowed ten days at Kibale to give myself a reasonable chance of connecting with the pitta. Whilst I knew that the birds were highly unreliable, and that bumping into them was largely a matter of pure good fortune, I figured that in ten days one could do a lot of wandering about off-trail. Surely that would be enough time to randomly bump into a pitta?

Dave and Adam had recommended a local company to sort out logistics, Livingstone African Safaris. I contacted the owner Kalema Livingstone personally, explaining that I needed to get from Kampala to Kibale and back, and that I required somewhere affordable to stay. I also outlined my extremely vague itinerary. (Go to Kibale. Stay there until I found the pitta. Use any remaining time to visit as many sites as possible in southwest Uganda.) Livingstone was supremely efficient and in just a few days everything was arranged.

A week later I was on an Emirates flight bound for Entebbe airport, although *en route* I received a rather enthusiastic welcome from the transit police in Dubai. After a further brief stop in Addis Ababa (ah the joys of budget airline routings) I was on the final leg, and found myself sat next to a devout young Muslim gentleman who spent the first two hours of the flight surreptitiously checking his mobile phone and praying fervently. He had, he confided *sotto voce*, just been sequestered in Pakistan where he had been undergoing religious training. However, Afzal's relentless friendliness, combined with his ability to sleep soundly for long periods of the flight soon shamed my suspicions.

We landed smoothly at Entebbe, scene of the bloody hostage crisis in 1976, and in truth the airport looked as though it had not received much maintenance since. Entebbe itself was altogether more charming than Dubai. A little rough around the edges maybe, but erratic and individual, with not a Starbucks in sight. As I checked into Sophie's Motel just off the Bugonga Road I asked the receptionist whether it was safe to walk around the neighbourhood carrying my binoculars and telescope. She looked at me as though I were a few sandwiches short of a picnic, and nodded slowly.

'Of course, it's fine.'

Just to make sure she understood that I really was a mental case, I sought further confirmation.

'Even after dark?'

She looked bewildered and nodded again. Yes, even after dark it would be fine.

And so it proved; I received a universally warm welcome as I tracked down my first Ugandan species in Kampala's suburbs. Indeed, the only problem I encountered was that every time I set up my 'scope to look at something I would be surrounded by a group of school children, ladies carrying baskets of washing and motorbike taxi drivers, all clamouring for a look at the birds. The subsequent 'oohs' and 'ahs' and wide-eyed amazement at their first close-up views of the birds of their neighbourhood were enough to warm the cockles of any conservationist's heart. Gangly Eastern Grey Plantain-eaters, delicate Red-chested Sunbirds, twitchy Speckled Mousebirds– all were greeted with astonishment, and a whispered conversation in the local language, Luganda, would ensue. (I briefly felt bad about not being able to speak a word of Luganda. Right up to the moment I discovered it's one of more than fifteen hundred languages in the Niger-Congo linguistic family.) One lady insisted on inviting me into her back garden so that she could show me the pair of African Fish-eagles that nested there. Although the eagles were absent, we chatted while watching the antics of the energetic Meyer's Parrots, a chunky Double-toothed Barbet, and a pair of garrulous Crowned Hornbills.

One particularly curious on-looker summoned up the courage to speak to me, and asked in immaculate English, 'Sir, are you a journalist?' I replied in the negative, advising that I was but a humble ornithologist, which if anything deepened his bafflement as to exactly why this skinny white guy was loitering outside his picket fence. After a pleasant couple of hours during which I seemed to have met the vast majority of Entebbe's population, I picked my way back through the acrid, smouldering bonfires, followed the touchline of a bone-dry and far-from-level playing field, rounded the corner of the gaily painted primary school and, ignoring the entreaties of the motorbike taxi gang, strode back towards reception. After a prolonged negotiation I managed to persuade Sophies' restaurateur to part with a beer and a pitifully emaciated chicken, before settling down to decipher my scribbled afternoon notes. After a long struggle, I was able to figure out that the little brown job I had watched grubbing around inside a thicket was a Green-backed Bleating Warbler. And yes, since you ask, it does sound like a miniature sheep.

I must admit I am woefully ignorant about large parts of Africa (whose large parts, given the size of the whole, are considerably larger than others' large parts). Were some bureaucratic diplomat to brief me over the course of a consular dinner on the minutiae of inter-African cooperation, it's highly likely that I would inadvertently cause a full-scale internecine war before the ladies were asked to leave so that port could be served. I am prone to say *Zambia* where I mean *Zimbabwe*, to mix up my Malawis and my Mozambiques. Burundi, I am fairly sure, is one of those flour tortillas that are popular in Mexican cuisine. Ask me about Angola and I'll tell you he plays centre forward for Burnley. Togo and Benin? Hmm, let's see, types of Latin American dance? I do know all about Sierra Leone though. He's the Italian guy who directed Clint Eastwood in the archetypal spaghetti western, *A Fistful of Dollars.*

Bright and early next morning I met up with Robert Bahindi, who was to drive me across southern Uganda to Kibale. As we sped west I stared out of the window at the passing landscape. Cassia bushes were everywhere, huge yellow blooms competing for attention with the Forest Flame trees' shocks of colour. Papyrus swamps, head-high and then some, swayed gently in the breeze. Life in rural Uganda revolves around the few roads that cut through the vast acreage of bush. The village markets in the linear settlements were loaded with river fish, cassavas, plantains, mangoes and bananas. They were tended by women in rainbow skirts whose husbands wore lurid, loose-fitting shirts and Rasta-tricolor beanies. As we drove the ragged-edged roads that sliced through the thick, rust-red landscape we passed travellers in spiv-suits, miles from the nearest town bicycling who-knows-where. Most bikes featured twin punctures, or no tyres at all, and the panniers were invariably laden with jackfruit or other produce.

Robert had lived through the Idi Amin years, and relayed what he had witnessed first-hand. Amin, 'Conqueror of the Britiah Empire in Africa in General and Uganda in Particular' was a monstrous, despotic figure, and the agonies and indignities heaped upon the Ugandan people in the late 1970s are unimaginable. Huge numbers were murdered, perhaps as many as half a million in total. Villagers caught walking into town were forced by Amin's militia to eat their own sandals. Thousands were paid to convert to Islam, and then promptly converted back to Presbyterianism or Catholicism following Amin's eventual removal by Julius Nyerere's Tanzanian forces, armed in the end by re-diverted aid money from the UK government. A sobering history.

From Kampala we drove due west, through Mityana and Mubende, and on through Kyenjojo to Fort Portal, before performing the only manouevre in the entire three hundred kilometre journey, a left turn south to Kanyanchu. We sneaked down narrow corridors between the tea plantations, once British-owned, now the property of Asian conglomerates. After eight hours on the road, we finally slid to a halt in a muddy hollow at the edge of the forest just as the light was fading. A tall, elegant figure in sharp-creased khaki fatigues stood above us on a mud-bank, beaming down at me with a smile that would light up the darkest African night. In the safari company owner's manual, Chapter 1, *Deportment and Bush dress*, it simply says 'see Livingstone.' It was the man himself. I'm sorry to say that I did actually greet him with the words, 'Mr. Livingstone I presume,' an introduction that doubtless was as funny to Livingstone as repetitive jokes about my surname are to me. He took it in good part however, and having dispensed with social pleasantries we got down to the serious business at hand.

'I'm afraid I have some bad news.' Livingstone said, his suave tone suggesting perhaps that I would be required to dress for dinner. 'No word from Harriet.'

This was grave news indeed. Harriet was the crack chimp-tracker, the key to finding the pitta. Everyone I knew who had seen the bird had seen it with Harriet. I had been careful to ensure that she would personally co-ordinate the team of trackers we would work with to try and find the bird. Despite having made all the necessary arrangements something had clearly gone wrong, and now she had gone AWOL. My carefully laid plan lay in tatters before me.

Mystifyingly however, Livingstone was still smiling.

'I don't think it's going to be a problem though.'

I looked at him, confused as a butcher's dog on a Sunday.

'Linda and Jim are with me for a few days birding the southwest,' Livingstone said, waving his hand in the direction of the kindly looking American couple stood next to him. 'We've been birding at Kibale since before dawn and they've had rather a good day.' A mischievous smile flickered around Livingstone's broad, handsome features. Still puzzling over the mismatch between Livingstone's news and his mien, I shook the proffered hands and congratulated them on their good fortune.

'So what have you seen after all your hard work in the forest?' I enquired politely.

The answer came in a deep, calm, southern drawl, though I was more affected by the words themselves than by the accent in which they were delivered.

'Well we've seen a bunch of good birds. I think maybe the best though was the Green-breasted Pitta this morning.'

Jim spoke slowly and deliberately, delivering the news in a tone so level he could have been reciting their breakfast menu. I stared at them in what was doubtless a rather impolite manner. Linda took my silence as a signal to continue.

'We watched a male displaying just as it got light. He was bouncing away, up and down, in the canopy.' She smiled sweetly at me. 'Then, when the sun rose, the birds gradually worked their way lower and lower. In the end we followed one for a while as it fed on the forest floor.'

I became aware that my mouth was open. I snapped it shut and made a feeble stab at composure. My travel-fuddled brain refused to take in the full significance of the facts. I had just spent two full days getting here to look for a near-impossible bird, and the first people I randomly bump into are the guy who arranged my transport, and his two clients, all of whom have seen the very bird I have come so far to find.

I managed a spluttered response. 'Good views?'

'Oh yes,' Linda assured me, 'really marvellous. And such a beautiful bird.'

Another figure emerged from the shadows, smiling as enigmatically as Livingstone.

'This is Gerald T.,' Livingstone said by way of introduction. 'There are two Geralds here, but Gerald T.'s the one who knows Kibale's birds. He's one of the forest guides here, working for the UWA, the Uganda Wildlife Authority. Harriet has gone freelance now, so she's not the person on the spot in quite the same way as she used to be. Gerald, on the other hand, most certainly is.'

I shook Gerald's hand warmly, and very nearly forgot to let go.

'Congratulations on finding the pitta,' I offered, 'a great achievement, I only wish I'd been here a day earlier.'

'Don't worry,' came the nonchalant reply, 'we'll see it tomorrow.'

I fixed what I hope was a steely gaze on Gerald, a warning that this was not a subject for humour. But Gerald appeared entirely serious.

'Really,' he said, 'I'm sure we'll find the bird tomorrow so long as we get there before first light.'

I stared at him as if he'd announced that The Ark of the Covenant was stashed in a lock-up just down the road.

'There are at least three males calling in an area of forest beyond the HQ. It should be no problem to track them down again. We'll leave an hour before it gets light.'

There must be a catch. The site would turn out to be a long way beyond the HQ, accessible only via decrepit rope bridges strung across dizzyingly high canyons. Perhaps we would have to wade waist-deep through crocodile-infested swamps. Maybe in order to gain access to the site we would have to answer some inscrutable riddle posed by a wizened old man in a pointy hat. My brain was overrun by a million questions, but the only one I managed to spit out was, 'Is it a difficult trail?'

'Oh not at all. Thirty minutes easy walking.'

I looked over at Jim and Linda. They were nodding in agreement.

'Oh one thing though...'

Here it came, the killer twist I had known would arrive...

'You might want to bring a torch and a bottle of water.'

Livingstone beamed at me again.

'Good luck tomorrow. Gerald's the man now it seems. We've fallen on our feet.'

And with that he ushered Gerald, Jim and Linda back into their vehicle, and in a cloud of dust they were gone. I stood in the road, waving feebly like a slow child who has just met Santa Claus.

I checked into a luxurious bungalow at The Primate Lodge, and poured a rum and coke. What was going on? The pitta was supposed to be impossible to find. It had never been heard calling at Kibale, mainly because no-one knew what it sounded like. It was the proverbial needle in a haystack, and had threatened to come a close second to Giant Pitta as lead contender for the title of 'pitta most likely to trip me up during the mission.' Now it seemed that the bird's whereabouts were, after all, known. It called, if this evening's conversation was true, regular as clockwork prior to dawn, and all we had to do was undertake a far-from-arduous stroll out from HQ, locate a calling bird, and then wander over and look for a bouncy silhouette high above our heads in the treetops. To say I was incredulous would be putting it mildly. I simply didn't know what to make of it.

I did not sleep well. I was plagued by stress dreams in which I was naked on stage at the Albert Hall, expected to play a gig with a group of musicians, all of whom were intent on performing jazz-fusion numbers in F# with 15/8 time signatures. I was wide-awake at three a.m. I cleaned my boots, polished and re-polished my binoculars, and ran through my kit list innumerable times. I checked my torch batteries more often than was strictly necessary, and then worried that in so doing I might have run them down. I paced nervously around the chalet, counting off the minutes as the rendezvous hour approached.

I met up with Gerald T. at the edge of the forest, and together we walked through the trees in silence, starlight flickering through the branches, fitfully illuminating the trail as we hiked deeper into the forest. After half an hour or so we stopped, and I instantly became aware of a distant sound half a kilometre ahead. Surely this couldn't be...Gerald whispered, 'You hear it?' I did. A reverberant and curiously non-avian 'brrroit,' emanating from a spot somewhere high above and beyond us. Any doubts in my mind as to whether this really was the pitta were erased when I clicked my torch on, to be confronted by a grinning Gerald a few feet ahead of me. We inched our way towards the source, and the sound grew steadily louder. We crept forward, stealthy as commandos on a night raid, careful not to spook the bird calling above us. Wherever it was, it was moving. Having identified which massive tree it was calling from, I'd thread my way through the thorn-bushes towards it, only for the bird to start up again from a new song post behind me.

A second bird started calling, and then a third. We waited to confirm which individual had really got into its stride, and then made our way towards the sound once more. Same result. It was still pitch black, with the first hint of daylight barely visible above the horizon. We waited, crouching in the dirt, our breathing as slow as the coming of the dawn light. One bird had stopped calling already, and I was seized with the fear that the other two would also fall silent, stealing away in the darkness before I'd had a chance to locate them. The sound came again, deep, primaeval, lonely. This time it was shockingly close.

We moved to a more open spot where we could see the canopy unfolding above us. There, sixty feet up and framed against a sky imperceptibly shifting from black to blue, was a tiny, bouncing figure. One of Africa's most difficult and enigmatic birds, the Green-breasted Pitta was displaying above my head. Each time it called it jumped vertically into the air, bouncing roughly six inches above its perch, before landing back in the same spot. Each jump was accompanied by a flick of the wings, a choreographed move designed to show off a flash of white in the primary feathers. At the same time, the ultramarine tail was raised aloft, displaying the dazzling colour of the upperside and revealing a flash of scarlet belly. The head was dropped low, maximizing the impact of the pair of broad, golden stripes above the eye. These stripes extended beyond the nape, flaring and jutting out beyond the outline of the body, like Pegasus's winged feet. Between calls, the bird skittered, squirrel-like, along horizontal branches, until it found a new display perch that met with its approval, whereupon the whole dance was repeated. Each call from a rival male would set the group off again, each interacting with the others' energy. This was a communal display, an exploded lek in action, each member of the group whipping the others into a frenzy. So few people had ever witnessed this sight. I felt humbled and honoured to be present.

As the light improved, the birds worked ever lower. An hour after sunrise we watched one bird flight down to the floor. The forest here was relatively open, and we were able to surreptitiously follow the bird at a discreet distance, tracking its every move as it fed a few yards in front of us. Aware of our presence, it was nonetheless surprisingly tolerant, allowing us to shadow its movements so long as we remained quiet and still. On two occasions it hopped up onto a moss-cloaked log and peered quizzically back at us, before hopping further into the forest. For a few seconds it stood motionless, allowing me to take a series of photographs and admire its grandeur. The breast was indeed shining green, olive in shade but electrified in direct sunlight, sharply cut off at the lower edge; a sleek, buttoned-up dandy in an *outré* waistcoat. Individual covert feathers were broadly tipped the brightest, most luminous blue imaginable, a string of neon baubles glimmering and coruscating in the half-light. The whole of the belly and undertail was a rich, dipped-in-jam vermilion. A simply astonishing creature. Eventually our continued presence made the pitta skittish, and after a final few minutes it drifted further into the woodland depths and was lost to view. Our audience with a legend was over.

We retired to a suitable distance before Gerald and I high-fived. The pittas were stacking up, number twenty-three had been collected, and the mountain of those still to find was no longer as dauntingly high as it had appeared from the barren foothills back in February. The scales were tipping in my favour. However, I must confess that not for the first time during the mission a curious sense of loss was mixed in with the euphoria. A scintilla of the pitta's mystery had been consumed, something ineffable had been tamed, and it seemed as if in the process, the bird's colours had dimmed fractionally. My unseen pittas constituted a precious resource, and it was dwindling rapidly.

Perhaps, I thought to myself, this is how a hunter feels as he stares down at the limp body of his prey, stilled at his feet. There can only be one first time, and there would never be another first time for the Green-breasted Pitta and I. In a moment of pathetic fallacy a breeze stirred, sighing through the Ugandan trees. Maybe it was just the lack of sleep, or the claustrophobic effect of being hemmed in by so many twisted, moss-laden trunks, but I suddenly felt mortal and insignificant, and an involuntary shiver ran along the length of my spine.

Casting such existential musings aside, I hatched a plan to spend the rest of the day birding around Kibale, which held a number of birds that would be new for me. We walked slowly up the main dirt road through tall forest, just beyond the carved wooden chimpanzee that gazes down the entrance track to the Kanyanchu River Camp. Plain and Toro Olive Greenbuls teased us from the depths of the roadside shrubberies, their drab dowdy plumage and unobtrusive habits making identification a nightmare. A Grey Parrot, charcoal-grey with a scarlet tail, heaped raucous abuse on us from above, before exploding like a newly lit firework from the canopy. A Yellow-spotted Barbet stomped about above us in shoes that were clearly several sizes too big. Further up the road, a Cassin's Grey Flycatcher flitted nervously around the river's edge, flicking from overhanging branch to mid-stream rock and back again, a soft, dove-grey acrobat performing for our pleasure.

Monkeys were everywhere. Overdressed Red Colobus shrieked and hollered forty metres up, alternately flashing black and chestnut, a gang of deranged scientists having a bad hair day. The ubiquitous Olive Baboons on the other hand, strutted boldly across the road in front of us, daring a confrontation, baring their fearsome teeth and naked bottoms in equal measure. A dense mat of doormat-coarse, grizzled fur, with a bare protuberance jutting out at either end, they looked like the victims of a pair of monkey union barbers forced to down tools by an industrial dispute. We even chanced upon a single, long-limbed Chimpanzee, a gawky, jug-eared adolescent, wary and agile high amongst the leaves, its mobile, expressive features hauntingly human.

By the end of the day my new bird tally was higher even than our monkey count, and I was ready for a rum and coke and a lie-down. First though, I needed to confer with Livingstone and confirm my plans for the next eight days. My unflappable host took my unexpectedly clear diary in his stride and promised to make arrangements. Within an hour he had set up a whirlwind tour of the southwest, taking in Queen Elizabeth (the National Park not the dead monarch) Bwindi Impenetrable Forest National Park (three sites, separated by approximately eighty kilometres: Buhoma, The Neck and Ruhizha) and Lake Mburo. I thanked him profusely, grateful for his ability to fashion the experience of a lifetime at the drop of a hat.

For the first time in days I could relax. I was at liberty in Africa, and having relocated to cheaper accommodation, was now the proud occupant of a comfortable tent in which to sleep. I was to dine on marinated, char-grilled gazelle, and exotic fruits whose pulp proved far easier to digest than their names were to pronounce. I even had time to figure out the finer points of that boon to bush sanitation, the drop toilet.

Early next morning I met up with Samuel, who was to guide me around the Bigodi Community Swamp. Most communities have Centres, Policing or Mini-buses. This being Uganda, Bigodi on Kibale's western perimeter had a swamp. Whilst it sounded unlikely, the positive results were visible for all to see. The swamp's wildlife was protected, and income from guiding fees and handicraft sales had already allowed construction of a school and a health clinic. Samuel was polite and punctual. While completing the inevitable paperwork I realized why. On the back of the HQ door was a sign outlining the prerequisite *qualities of a guide.* Amongst the more obvious desired facets *(smart/clean, knowledgeable, trustworthy, physically fit)* I noticed *audible enough,* plus the intriguing suggestion to *use props.* I wondered what the day might bring, and made a mental note to look out for Venn diagrams and flip-top charts.

Props, in the end, turned out to be superfluous to our needs. We found African Blue-flycatcher without the aid of cardboard models, and picked up Red-headed Malimbe, Grey Kestrel, Speckle-breasted Woodpecker, Red-bellied Paradise-flycatcher and Yellow-throated Tinkerbird, all without the need to resort to either laser pointers or PowerPoint presentations. We heard our main quarry, the ever-elusive White-spotted Flufftail, a tiny marsh-dwelling rail with a chestnut head and breast and a body spotted with white polka dots, but unsurprisingly it remained invisible in the papyrus. I have yet to see a single member of this super-skulking family, and do not plan a mission to see all the flufftails in a year any time soon. Seeing them all in the same century would be enough of a challenge.

All too soon our time ran out, and Robert and I hit the road, driving south via Kasese, then crossing the equator (cue cheesy tourist photo opportunity) to Queen Elizabeth. A night at a brand new lodge overlooking the Kazinga Channel seemed likely to provide a few quintessential safari experiences. By the time we reached the national park we were covered from head to foot in a fine film of red dust thrown up by passing trucks. We pulled over beside the Kazinga Channel that flows between Lake Edward to the west and Lake George to the east just as the light started to fade. Beneath a crimson sky we watched a flock of a hundred Pied Kingfishers, black and white bullets that fizzed into the water all around us. They were so strangely set afire by the dying rays of the sun that I half expected a hiss and a wisp of smoke as they smacked into the water.

The lodge in which I was to stay was the sister establishment of my temporary home in Kibale, and I had strict instructions to seek out the manager Rubin, and to assure him that his staff at Kibale were 'working hard and pushing harder.' My brand new room featured an outside shower, cunningly fashioned in a mosaic of local shale, the sturdy granite walls protecting one's modesty from hippos' prying eyes (and more to the point, teeth). Hot water was provided by a staff member who carried it in a barrel on his back across the camp, before ascending a wrought-iron ladder and pouring his load into a feeder tank suspended four metres up. One did not bathe, so much as take on water in the manner of an old-fashioned steam train. Everyone was wonderfully welcoming, and I wished I could have stayed for more than just a single night in this haven.

Our destination at dawn the following day was the northern sector of the Maramagambo Forest. Not for me the wild open plains of the savannah, the vast herds of Wildebeest stalked by prides of Lions hiding in the long grass. Why would one waste time on that kind of spectacle when there was a host of small, dowdy birds waiting to be identified in impenetrable forest just ten kilometres away? We wandered through Maramagambo's silent woods, and for an hour saw absolutely nothing. We visited the famous bat cave, allegedly home to an immense, smug and ludicrously well-fed Rock Python, but saw neither bats nor snake, though it was hard to miss the sound and more particularly the smell of the former wafted up from deep within the bowels of the cave. The python was clearly secreted within, doubtless sleeping off another gargantuan meal of roast bat. We were accompanied as usual by an armed escort, a gentleman of advanced years with a rifle that made him seem a spring chicken by comparison. If we'd been attacked by a large carnivore, I suppose we might at a push have killed it by accident when the gun-barrel exploded. Certainly the weapon did not appear to have seen any action since being purchased from the Boers somewhere on the Transvaal, back when the continent was still cooling.

After a slow start, our morning went well. Not only were we not gored to death by an irascible Buffalo, we also succeeded in finding a number of Maramagambo's avian specialities. Two Red-tailed Ant-thrushes, sleek and rufous ground-dwellers, paid us a brief visit, and a closely related White-tailed Ant-thrush also swooped past us, co-operatively showing off its white tail-corners. A pair of

Scaly-breasted Illadopsis, confident of their camouflage, grubbed furtively through the undergrowth making a beeline for our feet, only veering off at the last moment having decided our toes looked like trouble. We even found a lone Shining Blue Kingfisher, which appeared to be the first record for the forest.

And then it was on to Buhoma, a long drive which allowed fleeting glimpses of a whole series of vignettes of Ugandan life: A shop in the village of Kihiihi, festooned with billowing traditional clothing, *khangas* for the ladies and *khampala jumpas* for the men, the traditional designs giving a nod to both Aboriginal and Cherokee aesthetics. In Butogota, a design agency featuring *real, talented designers*, jostling cheek by jowl with the *God's Mercy* Beauty Salon and the *Praise Jesus* Expert Tailors. Sadly the *Good Health* establishment across the street proved not to be a bar but an aromatherapy salon.

During a brief stop for refreshments and fuel I had to settle for two plastic cartons of *Top Sip* orange juice. I would have bought coke, but one had to consume it on the premises, since the bottles cost more than the liquid inside. In one particularly poor suburb we passed a store whose entire stock consisted of three avocados, proudly displayed behind iron bars. I guess you never know when there'll be a ram-raid by a bunch of crazed vegetarians.

In the smaller villages I marveled at the rustic brick kilns, all themselves made out of bricks. So how do they begin making bricks in the first place? Most impressive of all, however, was the *Bee Collective* (legend: *We serve through sweat*) who were locked in a perennial trading tussle with the peanut butter collective on the opposite corner. Linking all of these was an endless stream of school-girls walking untold miles, immaculate in pink dresses, piles of text-books swaying precariously on their heads, doubtless inspired by their school motto, *Hard Work Pays.* In Africa, I got the feeling there is no other kind of work.

Arriving in Buhoma, the entry point to Lower Bwindi, I was unnerved to find that I was the only guest in an upscale hotel, prices here hideously inflated by the throngs of eco-tourists who come gorilla-trekking. An hour in the presence of a habituated group of gorillas will set you back five hundred US Dollars, so the majority of visitors are sufficiently well-heeled to expect sundowners on the verandah and a choice of steak or tilapia. Since the only budget hostel accommodation in Buhoma was full for the night, I was forced to fake it as a respectable high-income executive, and was put out to discover that I was all alone in the restaurant, having concocted a glamorous if entirely bogus alternative identity for myself.

The staff were never less than polite, though somewhat circumspect around me. I suspected that I only had myself to blame, having probably blotted my copybook on arrival. (Upon learning the cost per night I had informed the manager that I only wanted to rent the room, not buy it outright.) My budget was getting hammered, but any thoughts of ending up in the same state myself were quashed by the need to be bright-eyed and bushy-tailed in the morning. We would have to be at the Lower Bwindi gate before they opened at six a.m. to negotiate the usual bureaucratic paperwork, and it was then an hour's walk uphill before we'd find ourselves in good habitat. Having managed to navigate my way through a fiendishly complicated set of cutlery in approximately the right order, I neatly folded my up-market napkin and turned in early.

Bwindi is a fabulous national park. It has three distinct altitudinal layers, Buhoma being the lowest, 'The Neck' sandwiched in the middle, and Ruhizha astride them both at the upper end. Each has its own set of flora and fauna, and the park is home to the vast majority of the Albertine Rift endemics, the birds I had come to see. It also plays host to an estimated three hundred mountain gorillas, half of the entire global population.

In all there are thirty-six Albertine Rift specialities, all of which live nowhere else, although only twenty-six are found in Uganda, the remainder occurring only over the border in neighbouring DRC. In the end I managed to find seventeen of the twenty-six, including the coveted Neumann's Warbler, which, my trusty if now somewhat battered copy of *Where to Watch Birds in Uganda* assured me, was *diminutive and pitta-like.* And so it was, insofar as it was a bugger to find, crept around furtively on the ground in dense undergrowth, and was poorly endowed in the tail department. With the aid of my guide, 'Sunday' (no prizes for guessing which day of the week he was born on) I also found an Archer's Robin-chat, a pair of Dusky Crimson-wings (cute forest finches) a couple of Grauer's Warblers in trail-side vine tangles, a Handsome Francolin which exploded off the highest point of the trail at Buhoma, and three shy Red-throated Alethes.

On the Mubwindi Swamp Loop we came across fresh evidence of elephants, and proceeded with considerable caution. Happily, although we found further evidence of their destructive power at various points along the route in the form of saplings torn up by their roots, smashed branches and trampled foliage, the herd had moved off deeper into the swamp for the day, presumably in search of water. At one point above Buhoma, we encountered a stern-faced army patrol. Heavily armed, they were evidence that here one is right on the border with the DRC. In 1999, eight foreign gorilla tourists were murdered by a group of Rwandan Hutu rebels, *Interahamwe* based in the neighbouring Congo. After being forced to walk this same remote trail for twenty-four hours, the entire group had been butchered.

Sobering, but hard to square with my own experience. Everyone I met (with the exception of the army patrol who had good reason to concentrate on the matter in hand) was friendly. In Uganda, most people wave as soon as they see a *Mzungu* – the generic word used to indicate a white foreigner – and almost every face is wreathed in smiles as you strike up a conversation. Community projects and collectives seem to have sprung up everywhere, pooling resources for the common good. Folks look out for their neighbours, and good citizenship is expected and respected. I had come with the usual set of narrow, blinkered preconceptions, and was rapidly disabused. It's hard not to like the place.

It's often said that Uganda is a tropical version of my own country, but if that is so, it's an echo of a gentler England, a throwback to a time when Olde Albion was a more forgiving place. It's as if the Ugandans had learned both the language and the niceties of social etiquette from a people that had themselves forgotten the finer points of both in the interim. It's true that my conversations with the youth of Uganda were somewhat sketchy in terms of conventional linear narratives, but we'd get through by mutual determination.

'Hello Sir, how are you?'

'I am well thank-you, and you?'

'You are welcome Sir. Please give me money.'

This would be followed by a brief explanation that I was a penniless bird-watcher fallen on hard times. A handshake would follow, and we would go our separate ways. The truth is, that although my budget was disappearing faster than a Cheetah in

Nikes, I was still considerably better off than almost everyone I met. Rural Uganda is poverty-stricken, and the contrast is all too evident as we western tourists cruise through threadbare towns in our shiny 4x4's wearing designer sunglasses and breathable forest fatigues, checking settings on our precious digital SLR cameras. Most head-balanced provisions I saw were basic foodstuffs, dragged from beneath the cracked surface of subsistence plots. Animals here are gaunt, their life expectancy short.

Nonetheless, there is an aspiration to elegance. Figures along the road were frequently swathed in brightly coloured robes. Each village would reveal a patrician figure wandering down to the speakeasy to sup a Nile beer, sporting a lurid silk shirt and a Panama hat. One generously proportioned lady we passed was swaddled in reams of satin patterned with gold timepieces, her swaying, pendulous breasts contorting the clock-faces into a design worthy of Salvador Dali. The Seventh Day Adventist church was much in evidence, particularly in the poorest towns and villages, suckling on the teat of poverty. The Adventists were not alone; we passed the *Muhinga Deliverance of Christ Church*, the *Kabale God's Way Foundation*, and more controversially, the *Reach One, Touch One Ministries*. If memory serves, it was that kind of thing that got certain parts of the Christian Church into so much trouble in the first place.

Up at Ruhizha I spent a couple of chilly nights in a lodge above the village, where a hot water bottle was thoughtfully provided. There was even a bath, although admittedly only three inches of water could be coaxed from the tap, thus preventing this rarity being used to its full potential. Once again I was the only guest, which meant I had plenty of opportunity to admire the splendour of the canteen décor. To be fair, it was very much a work in progress, as evinced by the plastic windows flapping from nylon cords, each wrapped around a half-completed and insubstantial wooden frame.

The cow of choice in Uganda is the Friesian, and I watched them with profound nostalgia. I could have been back in my childhood home on the Cheshire plains, except that here the Friesian is not pied, but rather is a dust-stained, pink-and-black version of the familiar beast. The cows in turn looked back at me, disapproving and disdainful as I tucked in to one of their former herd-mates. Everything in Uganda is *almost* familiar, separated by just a few degrees from the usual reality. Thus the humble potato here is elevated to the status *of Irish potato*. Logical when you think about it, since it needs to be differentiated from the sympatric sweet potato.

Another day, another drive, this time to Lake Mburo, with most of the trip's entertainment confined to the sizeable town of Kabale. Here one can shop at *The Unique Drug Shop*, or buy *Triple Deccas* at the bed store. Accommodation is available at the supremely Anglophile *White Horse Inn*. This would probably prove to be a better choice than the *Quick Service Motel*, which frankly looked like it offered the kind of services one would prefer performed by ladies who take their time. The road out of town wound between these two establishments and down the escarpment, its crushed quartz surface glittering in the bright sunshine. As we left Kabale, the sign outside Bacchus's Garage wished us a safe trip (although presumably, if my understanding of the capitalist model remains valid, the owners were secretly praying for the odd puncture or two). A petrol tanker delivering fuel was emblazoned with the message *Danger petrol. Better be crazy than lazy.* The marketing team would perhaps benefit from a little international cooperation with the Assam road safety slogan guys.

Mburo was a shot in the arm. After the high altitudes and higher prices of Bwindi I was relieved to have arrived in lowland, low-cost Uganda. Five dollars a night for a hut, and three dollars for a lip-smackingly delicious fish curry overlooking the very lake in which, until recently, the self same fish had swum. With a cold beer close at hand, the hippos aquatic cabaret in full swing, and warthogs dropping by to investigate proceedings, I felt properly integrated into the bush. Admittedly it's not possible to wander freely around the park looking for Fiery-necked Nightjars, but that's only because you'll get eaten in the process.

I had not come to Mburo to see hippos however, fascinating though their antics were. I had come in search of a bird I had tried hard to see in Kenya many years earlier, the African Finfoot. This bird is Donald Duck's dark cousin, the mysterious side of the family that Donald and Daisy dare not mention in polite anatidine society. It is not, strictly speaking a duck at all, but rather is a member of the *Heliornithidae*, a family that has just three members worldwide. Its only close relatives are the Masked Finfoot in Asia and the Sungrebe in South America, so family reunions have been tricky to co-ordinate over the last few millennia.

As a result, the three have diverged significantly in terms of plumage and jizz. The differing first halves of their scientific names (*Podica*, *Heliopais* and *Heliornis* respectively) indicate just how far they have diverged, but they still share an elusive, retiring nature, a striped neck, a brightly coloured bill and a 'duck deluxe' elongated body. They also share a powerful influence over bird-watchers' imaginations, causing us to spend many hours cruising up and down remote river systems in an attempt to track them down. I had glimpsed a Sungrebe on an ox-bow lake in Peru, and had watched open-mouthed as a Masked Finfoot fled across a seldom-visited stretch of the Tembeling River in Malaysia. African Finfoot was the only one needed to complete the set, and was the trickiest of all to find. Except, I had been reliably informed, at Mburo, where finding one was like falling off a log. Mind you, I knew that falling off a log in Lake Mburo was likely to end in tears given the preponderance of crocs and hippos, so I was taking nothing for granted.

I booked the first boat out in the morning, and we puttered our way out across the placid waters, heading for a sheltered bay in the distance. It transpired that seeing the finfoot here was indeed not that tricky. You get in the boat. You put on the lifejacket. You sit still for twenty minutes. Then you raise your binoculars and look at the pretty finfoot. Or in my case, finfeet. Four of them. Swimming in amongst the mangrove roots, diving for invertebrates every now and then, and posing for photos in between.

Skilful manoeuvering by my boatman brought us so close to these incredible birds that I could pick out every last detail; the male silver-spotted black with a coral-red bill, a sleek, handsome devil, the female more soberly dressed in smoky greys and warm buff, dappled and streaked to blend in with the filigree of light seeping through the tangled stems above her. When nervous, they swam with necks pressed flat on the surface of the water, or drifted surreptitiously behind floating logs before peeking out, exposing only a disembodied, piebald tennis-ball of a head with a carrot sticking out in front. Post-finfeet, we cruised the lakeshore for an hour, stealing shrewdly up on Goliath Herons and Swamp Flycatchers, before returning to the jetty and disembarking. A last swing through the driest section of the park produced a Spot-flanked Barbet, Mburo's other speciality, before the long drive back to Entebbe.

I had come to Africa in search of a jewel I thought would require all my skill and resourcefulness to unearth. I left clutching that for which I had come, the country's most precious avian gem having been delivered on a plate. I was also newly enamoured of a country I had not expected to fall for. My opportunity to see a little of Uganda's beautiful countryside had been as delightful as it was impromptu, and I was grateful. The twenty-third pitta was mine, leaving just nine to find. The mission remained on target, with another of its most difficult objectives achieved.

However, I knew that some tough obstacles remained to be conquered. It was time to cast aside the tourist boats and 4x4's, and get intrepid again. Indonesia was calling once more, but this time it was not the wilds of Sumatra that awaited me. I needed to head further east, to more exotic ports of call. The most complex part of the mission needed setting up, and there was much to do. I returned to London and prepared for a logistical nightmare.

Chapter 14

Mad Dogs and Englishman. Halmahera, Sulawesi, Peleng

Nightmare doesn't even begin to cover it. It was early August, and things were going awry. I was tearing my hair out in London trying to finalize an itinerary. Indonesian contacts had gone AWOL. My insurance did not cover me for the destinations I intended to visit. I could not work out visa requirements and restrictions. My printer gave up the ghost. Dates clashed, deadlines passed, paperwork refused to arrive. I noticed that one of the four different travel agents I had been forced to involve had routed me to the wrong airport on Santa Isabel in the Solomon Islands. In Europe or the US, you can just hop on a bus and transit to the right one on arrival. On Isabel the airports are a hundred and fifty kilometres apart and the island has no roads. A black cloud settled over me and refused to budge. It seemed I had exhausted my run of good luck.

In principle, what I wanted to do did not seem impossible; fly from London to Singapore, and onward to Manado in northeast Sulawesi, hopping east to the tiny island of Ternate. A boat would then ferry me to Halmahera, one of the few accessible islands in the world on which Ivory-breasted Pitta is still to be found. Next I'd retrace my steps as far as Manado, before spending a few days at Tangkoko, which clings to the very tip of Sulawesi's most northerly arm. From there a short hop south to Luwuk in central/eastern Sulawesi, the jumping-off point for the island of Peleng, the easiest place to find the little-known Sula Pitta. I'd nip back to Manado before flying south to Denpasar in Bali to look for 'Javan' Banded Pitta. A flight from Bali would take me down to the Lesser Sundas, where I would spend time on Flores and Sumba in the company of an Elegant Pitta or two, before jetting onward to Darwin in northern Australia to find Rainbow Pitta. A skip further east should provide ample opportunity to find a Noisy Pitta near Cairns. Then find a way to get to the remote islands of Manus off the northeast coast of Papua New Guinea and Santa Isabel in The Solomons, for Superb and Black-faced Pitta respectively, before returning to the UK. Simple really.

The Luwuk flight was cancelled. I re-arranged the entire first week of my schedule to tie up with another flight. That got cancelled too. The third configuration stuck, so I booked it in the hope that Merpati might actually keep their word and provide a damn plane. Direct flights down to Bali proved way too expensive, so I settled for backtracking all the way west to Singapore before flying east again to Denpasar. It was not possible to fly directly from Sumba to Flores, so I routed via West Timor. The flight schedules didn't tie up however, so I added a day and a night in Timor to the itinerary. Getting to Manus proved to be a mission in itself. From Darwin I would have to fly to Port Moresby in Papua New Guinea, stay overnight, then continue the next day to Manus. Via Kavieng in New Ireland.

Coming back, it also proved impossible to fly directly to Santa Isabel, or even to Port Moresby. I would have to fly via the dangerous city of Lae on PNG's north coast *en route* to Port Moresby, before then flying on to Santa Isabel in the Solomon Isles. Only it transpired that one can't fly from Port Moresby to Isabel either, unless one stops off in Honiara on the nearby island of Guadalcanal first. Oh, and the flights didn't connect at all well, so I would have to spend a day and a night on Guadalcanal on the way out. And on the way back. The routing had become dauntingly complex, and many of the airlines involved were not exactly famed as the most reliable timekeepers in the world. I booked and hoped for the best. It was all going to be a bit seat-of-the-pants.

There was some good news though. Most if not all visas could be applied for on arrival. I was pleased to discover this, given that I didn't have time to apply for them in advance. Better still, I had at last managed to get some information about Black-faced Pitta (the least known of the family) on Santa Isabel, which appeared to survive on the least developed of the Solomon Islands. Having scrabbled around for months picking up scraps of information, I now had a coherent plan of attack, although my data was sketchy due to the fact that only a handful of people had ever seen the species.

In addition, Andy Mears (my friend from Bath with whom I had seen the Rusty-naped Pitta in Malaysia back in April) called me. He had managed to take a three-month sabbatical off work and would I mind if he came with me for the latter part of the trip? I was secretly delighted, having felt no little trepidation in facing this, the most arduous and unpredictable part of the mission on my own. Since Andy was also a huge pitta fan, a few weeks searching for the most far-flung members of the family together suited us both. We slotted the jigsaw pieces together, and after an inordinate amount of e-mails, phone calls, faxes, carrier pigeons, and semaphore messaging, at last it was done. We had a plan that, on paper at least, would work, and after a final, eleventh hour flurry of flight-booking and wire transfers, everything was set. The last e-tickets came through with less than twenty-four hours to spare, and after a frantic packing session in which the desire to travel light crashed headlong into the need to prepare for every eventuality, I hoisted my back-pack onto my shoulder and high-tailed it to the airport.

Since Andy had already visited some of the Indonesian spots, we had arranged that I would head out on my own, meeting him in Australia five weeks hence. If I was still alive by then, we'd rendezvous in the outback town of Pine Creek in the Northern Territory, sink a few beers and watch a few parrots, before continuing on through Australia together, working our way out to Manus and The Solomons. It sounded like a grand idea.

Twenty-nine hours after leaving London I landed on Ternate, which lies just off the west coast of Halmahera, Indonesia. Halmahera is one of a remote chain of islands known as the North Moluccas, and I was relieved to have made it this far without a hitch. I had enlisted the help of local logistics genius Theo Henoch to sort out my travel arrangements and take care of translation for me, since my grasp of Bahasa Indonesian had scarcely improved since my time in Sumatra. In particular I knew I would need Theo's help when visiting the island of Peleng since nobody there spoke any English, the foreign tourist quotient on the island remaining close to zero.

Although Theo knew little about Peleng, we hatched a plan where I would cover his basic costs while he scouted the territory with a view to building a future bird-tourist business. He in turn would translate, so that I didn't get a haircut when I wanted a beer. Although Theo lives in Manado on Sulawesi, he knew Halmahera well, having already helped a number of bird-watchers get to the few remaining forested sites on the island. What I didn't realize until I arrived was that Theo's very first client, the man who had shown him that the eco-tourist niche existed and could generate an income for him, was in fact the very same Andy Mears with whom I was due to rendezvous in the Australian outback a few weeks hence. Small world.

Theo and I took a taxi down to the quay and were soon speeding across to Halmahera, our attempts at small talk drowned out by the roar of the three Yamaha Enduro outboards positioned in alarming proximity to our heads. The cabin was populated by a few Halmaherans carrying boxes of sago and industrial quantities of insect-proof dinner-plate covers. The cabin reeked of low-grade diesel, so I stuck my head out of the open window and watched the watery world flash by. The short voyage was enlivened by regular sightings of flying fish that changed direction each time they landed, propelling themselves anew. Birds were few and far between, and my vigil produced only a few Red-necked Phalaropes, and a single example of that bird-watcher/comedian's stock-in-trade the Brown Booby. Ten minutes after landing we were delivered to the losmen *Penginapan Handayani Sidangoli* where we were to sleep. It was a Muslim house, clean and tidy, though word of the owners' hospitality had clearly spread to the vast majority of Halmahera's ant population. After a functional dinner I crashed out, exhausted by the long journey, pausing only to flick on the fan in order to keep a couple of co-habiting mosquitoes at bay.

Our horrifically early breakfast was served prior to the chef clocking on for the day, so it consisted of a simple cup of *teh asli*, the local char. This, I am sorry to say, was not as tasty as the cuppas I had enjoyed in Assam in May. It was, however, hot, wet and caffeinated, and in my book, three out of four ain't bad. The reason for my sleep being so violently curtailed was that we needed to be at Anu's place well before first light. I was too excited even to grumble about needing a new hobby with more sociable hours, and we were on the road ahead of schedule.

Anu, I should explain for the uninitiated, was one of the first Halmaherans to entertain visiting bird-watchers, and his house guarded the approach to one of the island's most pristine tracts of forest. This extant forest patch was home to perhaps the most emblematic of all of Halmahera's endemics, the spectacular Wallace's Standardwing. The species was named for Alfred Wallace, identifier of the biogeographic line that divides Indonesia's fauna into Asian species (to the west) and Australasian species (to the east). Wallace was the author of the seminal work, *The Malay Archipelago*, and had himself spent time on Halmahera (which he called *Jilolo*). It's no coincidence that Wallace dedicated the book to Charles Darwin, for both men came up with the idea of natural selection and thus evolution independently at the same time, and Darwin corresponded regularly with Wallace prior to the publication of his *magnum opus, On the Origin of Species.*

The standardwing is a one off. It stands, *sui generis*, in its own genus, *Semioptera*. However, in the larger scheme of things, it is also a member of the fabled birds-of-paradise group of which it is one of the most westerly examples, the majority being essentially Papuan. In common with a number of its congeners, it has evolved extended display plumes and an ornate breastplate, which it puts to good use in its ostentatious display. It was this same display that had brought me to Anu's place. An hour's walk into the forest behind his house was an active lek, where male standardwings had for years congregated to compete against one another for the favours of the comparatively dowdy females. Having met up with Anu we stumbled down the rough trail, flashlights to the fore, eventually arriving at a river crossing where we waited until just before dawn. I amused myself taking photographs of frogs, until Anu signalled that we should approach the lek. After a slippery ascent up one last mud-bank, we were in position with fifteen minutes to spare.

As the sky began to brighten above us, a series of harsh, caterwauling screeches signalled the arrival of the first standardwings. I could make out silhouetted flurries of activity, plumes tossed in every direction as the birds vaulted into the void, leaping five metres above their perches as they cartwheeled and spiralled, ecstatic and unheeding in Eros's grip. Each bird's metallic green breast-shield was extended so that it jutted out at the sides of the breast, lushly iridescent, like Salvador Dali's moustache drenched in absinthe. The snow-white, elongated shoulder plumes, spindly at the base but luxuriously spatulate at the tip, splayed outward in four directions, held aloft but slightly drooping, like helicopter blades at rest. The bird's feet appeared to be clad in luminous orange bootees. The narrow head by contrast was curiously plain, close-cropped, dark brown, with a yellowish fibrous tuft above the small, black bill.

Each individual was truly, weirdly alien, yet also ridiculously flamboyant, the lovechild of ET and Liberace. The standardwing's stage gear is a yardstick. I've seen a few outfits in my time; Bjork, Bolan, Bowie... Bloody sartorial amateurs, the lot of them. Put a standardwing on a stage and *that*, my friend, is show business.

'Always leave them wanting more' was the advice given when I started out as a young musician. It is a lesson that the standardwings have taken to heart. After half an hour of strutting, pirouetting and posturing, they took their leave and exited stage right, leaving us applauding and whistling for an encore. Well before the sun was up it was all over, the performance done for another day. I glanced at my watch; twenty past five. Thrilling though the standardwings' display had been, they were not the reason I had come to Halmahera. I needed to find an Ivory-breasted Pitta. The species lives only on Halmahera, and on the outlying islands of Morotai to the north, and Kasiruta and Bacan to the southwest. It is what is known in the trade as a *restricted range species*. Which basically means your chances of seeing it anywhere else are restricted to zero. Hence my trip to Halmahera.

The bird is something of a bruiser. For a start it measures twenty-five centimetres from the tip of its bill to the end of its tail (which is going it some in pitta terms) and is large-headed and barrel-chested. Whilst it has the usual complement of two legs, one either side, they are even more robust than normal. The bill is broad-based and sturdy. This is a creature that could, should it so wish, open a can of tuna without a tool. In short, we are talking one burly, beefy bird.

The jet-black upperparts and pure white breast do lend it an undeniable air of distinction however. There is something of the orchestral conductor about it, a dapper upright figure, commanding and in control. Since it's a pitta, there has to be the odd flash of colour of course, and the conductor's tails are fitted with an appropriately dazzling lining; a set of glittering azure blue and teal wing-coverts. The *de rigueur* crimson belly completes the sartorial elegance. Some pittas are, dare I say it, a little over the top in the colour department, but the Ivory-breasted has it just right; more Brian Ferry than David Bowie. The call is similarly understated, a little *sotto voce* for a pitta; a rounded, slightly throaty, almost apologetic 'who-wooooh', the cadence lilting, the delivery descending and fading latterly. It's an almost owl-like sound, the cry of a disorientated night-bird lost in the harsh glare of the daylight hours.

All of this I had gleaned from studying pictures and vocalizations during the long winter nights in England. Since arriving in Halmahera however, I had not seen or even heard a pitta. There was work to be done. I wandered through Anu's forest for a few hours, scanning likely looking shadowy corners and listening intently. Not a sausage. I tried sallying off-trail, waiting motionless in cover, and covering more ground, all without success. And then, as is so often the way, after I had all but given up for the day and had returned to the main trail intent on heading out and resting up for a while, I heard the call, soft-edged and unmistakable.

When a pitta calls at close range, there is always a moment of panic. What strategy should one pursue? It's a critical decision that requires the judgement of Solomon. Is the best plan to freeze in order to avoid alerting the bird to your presence? To creep forward to the nearest patch of cover and wait? Or to move to a strategic spot that affords the best view of more open habitat into which the bird could be tempted by playing its call? I usually err on the side of caution, and assume it's best not to move at all until you have a clear fix on exactly which direction the bird is calling from. Then move slow and low, preferably coinciding with a moment during which the bird is vocalizing.

The problem with most pittas is that their vocalizations tend to be decidedly short-lived. In the case of Ivory-breasted Pitta you have two seconds to complete your move before the last vestige of the melancholy call dies away. Nevertheless, those two seconds can be put to good use, allowing you the luxury of sitting on the ground, or clinging to the nearest sizeable tree. Anything that will break up your outline or screen you from the bird will help. Even if the pitta knows you are there, if it cannot see you clearly there's a chance it will move to a spot where it will have an unobstructed view of this potential new threat. At which point of course, you are likely to have an equally unobstructed view of your target.

If the theory is simple, in practice it is often more complex. Taking the queen in chess would, after all, be pretty straightforward if it weren't for the minor inconvenience of your opponent's counter-moves. I decided to follow my instincts in pursuit of my endgame, and when the bird called again, I slunk towards the nearest available cover and sat down on the trail. One and a half seconds, *white pawn to e4*. I cued up the pitta's call, *queen to h5*, and held my breath as the audio lure rang out through the forest. The response was instantaneous; an improbably large black and white shape flung itself through the trees and landed in cover on the ground. It called again, and I could see the quiver of a short black tail as it did so.

I allowed my iPod to run, and as the second call echoed towards the bird, it bounced along the valley, relatively easy to follow given its large size and pied appearance. It hopped up onto a low branch and called again, then moved, quick as thought, parallel to the trail and down into denser vegetation. I slithered along the trail on my belly and hid behind a large fallen log before playing one last pitta call. *Bishop to c4*. The pitta circled, bounded across the trail, and stopped beneath a low, leafy arch, fully in view as it twisted to find me. My camera was already pressed to my eye, and I fired off two shots. *Queen to f7*. Check-mate in four moves, and pitta number twenty-four squared away. It had all been too easy in the end I thought to myself, like taking money from an Old Etonian. This bird was an amateur player, taken in by my ultra-basic *Scholar's Mate* manoeuvre. The sound of my shutter caused the pitta to head for cover, and I watched as it bounded up the slope, disappearing over a ridge and burying itself in the leaf-litter beyond. It called defiantly for the next thirty minutes, but I never saw it again. My victory was rather more than pyrrhic, but equally didn't qualify as an unquestionable surrender. I glanced down at the viewfinder to check my spoils. The image was fairly sharp, and the bird was almost a hundred percent visible, with only a wayward evergreen shoot straying in front of the bird's flank. It would do for now. There would be other photographic opportunities later, I felt sure. This bird was a pushover.

It had grown hot, and activity in the forest was already dying off for the day. Our happy company strolled back to Anu's place and sat on his hilltop, sipping water and admiring the view. I took a snap inventory of his worldly possessions; one sleeping shack, one al fresco kitchen/dining area with ragged palm thatch. A plethora of pineapple plants, most of which appeared to have been pressed into *ad hoc* laundry-drying duties. Three adult chickens, much in evidence, endlessly fussing over ten tiny chicks that were forever getting into mischief, mostly involving my shoelaces. One transistor radio, one oil lamp, one table, two benches, the latter fashioned from a single piece of wood. Just enough to provide the basic home comforts without exactly inspiring envy.

I thought of my chattel-cluttered London life and felt a twinge of shame. We in the western world are so smug in our certainty at having done the right thing in trading close contact with nature for our fine agglomeration of leaf-blowers and electric carving knives. I could probably go my whole life without requiring a ceramic bagel plug or an avocado slicer, but that's unlikely to save me from buying one on impulse, sticking it in a drawer for a decade and then giving it to the charity shop. Meanwhile the plundering of the world's irreplaceable natural resources goes on unabated. Spend a day in a rainforest and you begin to see that the only remaining link between these two disparate worlds is one of supply and demand. We are all complicit, and only now that the causal link between destruction of forest and massive climate change is starting to be understood, have we finally twigged that our species' voraciously acquisitive behaviour might bring about our own downfall. Something is going to give.

After the excesses of rampant western consumerism, my least favourite thing is looking for raptors. I know I've gone on record as saying that I have given up birds of prey, but when the tropical noon heat takes over, there is little else to do but look for the few birds that remain active. Our lunchtime vigil produced a trio of Gurney's Eagles, a New Guinean/Moluccan regional endemic, but little else. Birds of prey are up and about during the heat of the day, because they require warm air thermals to soar above the forest without consuming large amounts of energy. I knew just how they felt. The intense humidity was already sapping my strength, and I lay down on the hard earth, flicking away inquisitive ants and resting my head on my rucksack. I would just close my eyes for a moment...

A couple of hours later I awoke with a start. Rubbing my eyes I became aware that Anu and his family were all giggling at the crumpled, prostrate figure lying in their front yard. I sat up and winked at them, provoking more hilarity. One of the joys of not having access to a mirror for weeks on end is that you lose the self-consciousness that plagues so many social interactions in the developed world. I had on occasion lain down on the pavements of Manchester in my formative years (usually, if I am brutally honest, less affected by extreme Mancunian humidity than by an extreme intake of Boddington's). Such antics had often not ended well. Here in Halmahera, nobody cared. It was freedom of a sort, and I was enjoying the loosening-up process, the shedding of a few layers of Englishness. The problem, I discovered, was learning how to re-adapt to English life when you eventually return to the motherland. I was however, assisted in this process by my other half; any transgression of the unwritten laws of English social etiquette would be met with a stern *you're not in the jungle now you know.*

If only it could be dawn all day. That thought had run through my mind so many times in the rainforest, and here on Halmahera it hit me again. There was a quickening of the forest's pulse in the late afternoon, but it was always subtle compared to the frenzy of activity at first light. We walked the trails again before dark, finding a rare Sombre Kingfisher and the scarce (despite its name) Common Paradise Kingfisher. Papuan Hornbills flap-flap-glided their way across clearings, Black Sunbirds squeaked and tittered their high-frequency gossip, while a Goliath Coucal's deep, liquid boom occupied the other end of the frequency spectrum. The latter does a fine impression of that Latin music staple, the *moose call* (created by sliding a finger across the taut skin of a bongo). It seemed apposite enough, a little Latin heat in the sticky Moluccan dusk; let the Taiwanese tree frogs take care of the jazz. At five o'clock precisely the pittas joined the orchestra, their lugubrious calls ringing out through the distant forest until the lengthening shadows joined forces to drive the daylight underground.

Meanwhile, back in Sidangoli our hosts had prepared dinner, the inescapable *nasi goreng*, crispy *ikan*, sambal and the world's slipperiest noodles. In deference to Muslim sensitivities I had bought cans of coke from the chaotic store next door, before discreetly adding a splash of duty-free rum to the can in the privacy of my room. I offered Theo and Wale our driver a 'special' coke, the latter accepting with an enthusiasm I felt sure would jeopardize the roadside pedestrians on his erratic course home later in the evening. Theo spluttered slightly over his initial sip, which made me worry that I should have outlined the extra ingredient I had added to the Coca-Cola Company's secret recipe more specifically. In any event, our meal went with a swing and the conversation was lively. A power cut rendered my noodle reclamation project all but impossible (not only could I not pick them up, I now couldn't even find them) but candles were swiftly provided to illuminate proceedings. By eight thirty p.m. I was sprawled out on my preternaturally hot bed (the fan being out of action) stippled with sweat but weary enough to drift off to sleep. At least the loss of power had also killed the mind-numbing TV game shows that constituted our hosts' primary entertainment.

The pattern of activities over the next couple of days followed a well-worn routine. Get up painfully early, drive out to remnant patches of forest, look for pittas. One patch (dubbed in a fit of descriptive genius, *The Short Logging Trail*) held the richest rewards. Though partially logged, it still held Dusky Megapodes, a pair of the increasingly scarce Chattering Lory (an endemic North Moluccan parrot) and best of all, three Scarlet-breasted Fruit-doves – amongst the world's tiniest, most beautiful frugivores. I had a further series of run-ins with Ivory-breasted Pittas, but all had reverted to the sneaky behaviour expected of the genus, and despite multiple sorties I was unable to secure any more photographs. I even managed to stumble upon a pair of Nicobar Pigeons, a bird I had not expected to see here, and which I had waited many years to find.

Now I know that pigeons are not everyone's favourite. The familiar 'sky-rat' of urban centres, they are more often regarded as a menace and a health hazard than as one of nature's marvels. Your Nicobar, however, is not your average pigeon. For a start off they are huge, measuring 40cm from one end to the other. Secondly, they are largely emerald green, with a tracery of gold leaf picked out along the back. Their broad tail, startlingly evident in flight, contrasts sharply, being pure white. Most glamorously of all, they have a cloak of long, filamentous shoulder plumes cascading down from their smooth grey heads. The overall impression is of an ageing rebel rocker. (A dead spit for Richard O'Brien as Riff-Raff in *The Rocky*

Horror Picture Show. Not convinced? Well think on; have you ever seen Richard O'Brien and a Nicobar Pigeon in the same room at the same time? I rest my case.) They have a certain louche grandeur as they strut about the forest floor. Suffice to say, if a Nicobar's life story is ever immortalized on the silver screen (which I admit seems unlikely, but then again Hollywood is forever throwing money at turkeys) Bill Nighy would be the natural choice for the lead role.

My last day on Halmahera was spent further east, around Tomares and Tabanalo. I continued to hoover up new birds, including Long-billed Crows, a Blue-capped Fruit-dove and a Spotted Kestrel. All were welcome, but with time running out I was keen to try to find one of Halmahera's Red-bellied Pittas. Although I had already seen the species way back in March (just prior to visiting the emergency room in Mindanao) I wanted to try to photograph the local Halmaheran race, *rufiventris.* Theo had recently located a promising patch of forest, although it required a long climb up through agricultural land in order to reach the remaining habitat. It took us a couple of hours to get up into the good stuff, despite keeping the pace up and only allowing ourselves to be briefly waylaid by a roosting Barking Owl, a rare bird on Halmahera.

By the time we arrived the weather had taken a turn for the worse. After a long hand-to-hand duel with another Ivory-breasted Pitta, which once again steadfastly refused to pose for my lens, I walked further up the trail into wetter forest, and was quickly rewarded with a Red-bellied Pitta calling from extremely dense, mossy vegetation a few metres in from the trail. After a titanic struggle (in every sense of the word; by the end of the contest I was mostly under water like the ship of the same name) I finally obtained a gripping, frame-filling shot of the bird having staked out a tiny gap in the low cover. We yomped back down the now-flooded trail in a downpour, giggling like muddied, truant schoolboys after an afternoon kick-about. (Although my Mum was at least five thousand kilometres away so I'd have to wash my own kit.)

****

It was time to catch the boat back to Ternate before the short flight across the water to Manado. Safely back on Sulawesi, a minivan whisked me up to Tangkoko on Sulawesi's northeastern tip, and I arrived after dark at the famous *Mama Roos*, the accommodation of choice for generations of birders. (Tangkoko's full name by the way is *Tangkoko Batuangus Dua Saudara Nature Reserve.* Righto. *Tangkoko* it is then.) I had included the reserve in my itinerary because Sulawesi, being one of the larger Indonesian islands, is home to a significant number of endemics, and thus promised a fine haul of new birds for my all-important world list. Hence I figured that since I would be in the neighbourhood anyway, it would be foolish, rude even, not to drop in on my way past. I'd convinced myself that it was also justifiable in mission terms, since yet another race of Red-bellied Pitta, *celebensis* (an echo of Sulawesi's original name *Celebes*) lived here. There are at least twenty and perhaps as many as twenty-four races of Red-bellied Pitta all told, depending on which eminent ornithological authority one chooses to follow, and I figured it couldn't hurt to see as many races as possible during the year. Hence a further encounter with a pitta seemed on the cards.

It wasn't the one I expected though. Pittas are, as you are no doubt becoming aware, contrary buggers. When you think you'll see them you don't. When you've searched and searched and completely given up, one invariably offers a glimpse when you least expect it. When it's a nailed-on certainty that they will be vocal they are mute, and when you have become so completely familiar with their behaviour that you can predict in exactly which gap they will next appear, they vanish before popping up right behind you. So I really shouldn't have been surprised when the first bird I clapped eyes on at Tangkoko was an Elegant Pitta.

I had carefully planned my itinerary to include Sumba and Flores, both islands in Nusa Tenggara (aka the Lesser Sundas) well to the south. My thinking was that this would allow me to try for two races of Elegant Pitta, *Pitta elegans maria* and *Pitta elegans concinna*. Since the two races sounded different from one another, it would be useful to see both, just in case they should be split and treated as separate species at some point in the future. It didn't seem likely, given there is quite a bit of variation within each race and that some races of Elegant Pitta are known to migrate reasonable distances (meaning ample opportunity for gene flow between the races) but a sensible mission precaution nonetheless. This very same migratory habit meant that here at Tangkoko, where there shouldn't be any Elegant Pittas at all, I bumped into a bird of the nominate race

P. e. elegans. It had only been recorded three or four times before on the island, and was thus a vagrant. For which in birder-speak read, *intrinsically even more sexy, rare, and exciting.* It was also the first Elegant Pitta I had ever seen, and was hopping about in dry, open forest. As bonuses go, it was enormous. I felt like a city banker who has just hit year-end pay dirt.

The second bird I saw was a Red-backed Thrush, my other main target at Tangkoko. It's in the genus *Zoothera*, which means it's supposed to be almost as difficult to find as a pitta. This one hopped about in full view like a Blackbird on an English garden lawn. A few minutes later I connected with one of Sulawesi's many endemic kingfishers, a Green-backed. Next came a pair of the scarce White-faced Cuckoo-dove, all sooty black except for a white face, the grimy street urchin of the woods. Easy, this tropical bird-watching lark. The rest of my time at Tangkoko passed in a blur of activity, and as I relentlessly whittled down my list of missing species, I strayed further and further off-trail, tracking the most difficult species and hoping for a glimpse of the most furtive residents. It was almost my undoing.

Together with my mandatory forest guide, I had gone off-piste in search of the *celebensis* Red-bellied Pitta, subtly different from the race I had seen on Halmahera. I picked my way through the forest, scanning the floor as I went for any sign of movement, my guide following behind. For some reason, perhaps a subliminal glimpse of an unusual shape or colour, I suddenly felt the urge to look immediately in front of me. What I saw made me recoil in horror, emitting an unmanly series of squawks. Three feet in front of me, coiled and with its head up, was a Wagler's Pit Viper.

The snake was as beautiful as it was deadly, bright lime-green with striking pairs of silver and black bands. The head was diagnostically triangular, with another black and silver line running backwards from the cold, yellow eyes. The creature lay in a small evergreen sapling, directly in my path at waist height. Another two steps and I would literally have walked into it, with consequences I preferred not to think about. My guide looked quizzically at me. I took a slow step backwards before carefully indicating the source of my discomfort. He followed my extended finger and saw the snake.

'Ooooh!' He inched his way closer to me, and in faltering English added, 'I know this snake. One of my guests bite by him.'

I kept one eye on the snake while cueing up my camera and listened to the story. It seemed that my guide's unfortunate guest had walked very close to the pit viper, which as usual had remained motionless until threatened by this large animal's presence. At which point it had struck, biting the intruder on the calf. My guide became animated, as he described how he had treated the wound.

'I kill snake, cut out stomach, chop into small pieces and rub on bite.'

Without taking my eyes of the snake, I whisperingly enquired what had happened next. 'Then we take him to hospital in Manado. They give him anti-venom. He live. Very happy I save his life. He pay me fifty dollars!'

So two happy endings then. I was relieved not to have pushed for three in a row. I circled with infinite care until I was behind the snake to take advantage of the light. The snake-head tracked me every inch of the way, smooth, silent, patient. After a brief check of the back-lit shots in the viewfinder I nodded to my co-conspirator. 'Let's get out of here.'

That night, my last at Tangkoko, I bumped into a group of Dutch birders at dinner. The group included Jan Vermeulen, a big world-lister whose trip reports I had used years earlier in South America, back in the pre-Internet days when information was still a scarce commodity. I showed my pictures to Jan and his crew. Eyebrows were raised, teeth sucked. Someone whistled. Now that I had time to reflect, I realized just how lucky I had been. When you venture into tropical forest, you always know that there are dangers, but for the most part it's a distant, almost comforting concern. It confirms one's derring-do, whilst remaining firmly in the theoretical domain, something that happens to others. This time it very nearly happened to me, and I was shaken. If I had taken just two steps more…I ordered another beer and drank it so fast the bubbles went up my nose. So much for the dignified hauteur of the jungle-wallah.

****

It had been a struggle to get onto the Luwuk flight at all, as it had twice been cancelled when arranging my itinerary. On arrival at the airport Theo and I checked the departures board. Plenty of departures – to Jakarta, Denpasar, Ternate – but our flight was not listed. Upon enquiring, we were directed to desk number eight, along with a number of other wannabe-passengers. Soon our little leaving party was thronged, though sadly we were not joined by our guests of honour, the check-in staff. Eventually an official was procured who hand-wrote boarding cards for anyone who asked for one. We dodged the stampeding hordes and headed for the security check. I glanced back at desk eight, which proudly announced that they were checking-in a Lion Air flight. Desk seven boasted the same logo, also Lion Air. We had apparently checked in at desk seven and a half; beat that Harry Potter. There was still no departure time (indeed still apparently no flight) but having successfully checked-in at a desk that did not exist we were determined to persevere.

We wandered around the terminal looking for clues, spurning the opportunity to buy a cup of coffee in the *Coelacanth* lounge. We bumped into a random stranger from Peleng, who said he had heard a rumour that we were to depart at six thirty. Nine minutes before the departure time, the gate appeared on the screens. We existed! We ran to gate four, where staff denied any knowledge of our flight. Bedlam ensued, until a man in a braided hat said that he didn't think anyone was using gate five. We seized the chance with both hands, and were relieved and amazed to find a security team who confirmed that yes, this was the right gate for Luwuk. The head honcho took my boarding pass, scrutinized it, and gave it back. To another passenger. I managed to retrieve it and headed for the bus. Our crowded, creaking charabanc chugged towards the aircraft with all the doors open to ameliorate the lack of air conditioning. Two people clung to the outside. We boarded Flight 212.

Outside the airport when we had first arrived, amidst the crowds of embarking Sulawesians I had spotted a middle-aged man sporting a baseball cap bearing the logo *Boing 737*. Now, as I boarded the Merpati 16-seater prop. plane it occurred to me that it might come in useful if this airliner also proved able to bounce. The plane had seen better days. The *no smoking/fasten seat belts* signs were hand-painted. The faded décor was, to be fair, enlivened by a hand-painted mural on the inside of the fuselage, a charming work depicting distinctly lunar volcanoes in a range of lurid colours; only the Clangers were missing. I checked the available literature, noting with some alarm the promise of a *live vest* under my seat. The in-flight safety instructions included suggested 'prayers and invocations' for persons of every conceivable religion. They all ran along the lines of, *Dear Lord, in thy mercy, please let this decrepit rust-bucket make it to our destination, and deliver us from falling into the sea.* The view from my seat through the plane's windscreen was also impressive, the cockpit being unencumbered by anything so superfluous as a door. Best of all – and I swear this is absolutely true – when the cockpit window steamed up halfway through the flight the pilot actually wiped it clean with an oily rag. Suddenly I was seventeen again, struggling up the M6 motorway in a windscreen wiper-less Ford Escort that had been a stranger to the MOT process for many years. Only this time I was at twenty-eight thousand feet. I gripped the tattered, threadbare seat and reached for the prayer sheet.

I had prepared for our ultimate destination, the island of Peleng, by learning a few new phrases in Bahasa Indonesian. In my formative years I had been similarly diligent while working in Europe, and had learned how to say *'I like to watch birds'* in German. One night during a trade show when asked whether I could speak German, I proved my polyglot credentials by proudly trotting out the phrase. The impact was more profound than I had expected and the crowd of Germans in the bar fell about laughing. One of them breathlessly explained that owing to a minor mispronunciation I had actually said *'I like to watch people f*cking.'* Since then, it seemed, I had learned little, and I had stubbornly committed to memory *'Saya cari burung burung khusus'; 'I am looking for special birds.'* At least I hoped that's what I was saying.

Having arrived in Luwuk, we hot-footed it to the quay and Theo busied himself with searching for the boat to Peleng. (At face value it should have been a simple enough task. Given our experience at the airport, presumably all we had to do was find quay seven and a half.) We asked a number of locals, but all looked bemused and shook their heads. The same random stranger we had bumped into at Manado airport reappeared and whispered that we were pronouncing the island's name incorrectly. It had recently been amended by government decree to *Peling.* Theo asked for *Peling,* and we were immediately shown to the correct quay. Once *The Aldus* had sailed, Theo snoozed on bales of vegetables whilst I claimed a spot on the prow and scanned the waves for the duration of the four-hour crossing, determined to discover which seabirds inhabit the Molucca Sea in the summer months. I like to think that in my own quiet way I have contributed to the knowledgebase quite significantly. There aren't any seabirds there. (Actually Theo interrupted his siesta for five minutes and pointed out two Common Terns, but I am ruthlessly suppressing this record on the grounds that since I failed to find a single bird during the entire crossing I will look supremely incompetent if it ever comes to light.)

As we steamed into Sabang on Peleng's north coast I did finally spot something; ducks. Three Sunda Teal flew out from a hidden marsh and headed out to sea at speed. I decided that this augured well for our stay, and we set about the task of hiring two *ojeks* (motorbike taxis) to cross the western half of the island to the village of Tataba. I had failed to find much information about Peleng and its birds despite many hours of e-mails and web surfing before travelling. Here's what I had managed to establish:

i) *Only a handful of European bird-watchers appeared to have visited Peleng in modern times. One was Filip Verbelen, a Belgian gentleman with whom I had corresponded extensively throughout the year. As far as I know Filip is the only other man who has seen all the world's pittas during his lifetime. The other was a German academic, Frank Rheindt, who had also chipped in with helpful information. The two of them had passed on the name of a village where we could stay with a local family.*

ii) *Sula Pitta did indeed live on Peleng, though the exact local limits of its presence and absence remained a mystery.*

iii) *There was little infrastructure on the island in terms of transport, accommodation, communication networks etc.*

iv) *The island was not on the tourist circuit. It even appeared to have escaped the attentions of the intrepid backpacker brigade. Proper virgin territory. For the first time since Sumatra, I felt that I was really at the cutting edge of things. Discoveries awaited us, and I resolved to take copious notes.*

v) *Somewhere in the western half of the island lived a recently rediscovered species called the Banggai Crow. No-one seemed to know anything about it, other than it was black, lived in rainforest and was extremely endangered.*

However, Theo and I had, through a chance encounter with a mysterious man on a motorbike at Tangkoko, managed to obtain a few further, precious nuggets of news. We had the name of a useful contact, *Labi,* and the name of the village in which he lived, plus vague directions indicating how to reach the extant montane forest above the village. Armed with these shreds of information, we mounted our chosen motorbikes, balanced our rucksacks precariously across our laps, and headed west. After an hour and a half's ride during which we saw our lives flash before our watering eyes on numerous occasions, we drew up outside a tiny village shop in Tataba in a cloud of dust.

The owners came out to investigate, and advised that yes, Labi lived next door, but that he was away in the hills. They added that we were welcome to lodge with them, and that they were confident Labi would turn up the following day. It being a Sunday, he would surely walk down to the coast to attend church. After a restorative cup of tea and some challenging scones, we dressed for adversity and went to explore the nearby fragments of lowland forest. Four hours later we were soaked in sweat and had seen very little. I had played the call of Sula Pitta at selected points along the trails, but we heard nothing. The forest here was in poor condition having been heavily logged. Agricultural plots had torn great chunks out of what must once have been fabulous pitta habitat. Things were not looking promising. However, to my great relief Labi appeared in the early evening with his colleague Maleso. He confirmed that he would accompany us up to the higher forest in the morning, and that we could stay with his family in the village of Kokolomboi, some three hours climb above Tataba. Having completed the only remaining formality, registering with the local police to obtain the requisite *surat jalan* paperwork, we stripped down our packs to the bare essentials and turned in for the night.

The following morning we were ready before dawn, and clung on to the *ojeks* that would transport us up to Maleso's house at the trailhead. Our gracious host welcomed us and served up an impromptu Indonesian breakfast; *Terang Bulan* (literally *bright moon,* a delicious green sponge containing palm sugar and grated coconut) served with fried sliced cassava. After loading ourselves up packhorse-style with provisions, water and a few other essentials, we began to work our way up through the maze of trails. Maleso and

I set the pace, with Labi shepherding Theo some way behind us, and the two stragglers were soon lost to view on the lower slopes.

Half an hour before reaching Kokolomboi, Maleso explained something in Bahasa. Although I could only follow one word in ten, I was fairly sure he was indicating that he had seen the Sula Pitta here on a previous occasion. I looked at the poor excuse for a thicket in front of me. It was heavily degraded, inundated with bamboo, and a disgrace to thicket-kind. Maleso persisted, and I figured what the hell; at least I would be able to rest my aching limbs for a few minutes.

I sat on the edge of the tiny valley and stared at the paltry amount of cover. There was no birdsong and little insect noise. It was, without doubt, one of the most unprepossessing shreds of forest I had ever had the misfortune to survey. It was obvious that no self-respecting Sula Pitta would tolerate this tawdry habitat, when luxuriant vegetation existed just a few hundred metres above us. I strongly doubted whether any birds at all would be caught dead in such a feebly vegetated spot.

A bird bounced out of the thicket and stood at the base of a clump of bamboo. I knew what it was before I even raised my binoculars, being intimately acquainted with the family's jizz. It was a Sula Pitta.

Here, bold as brass, was this rarest of gems, a bird that so few people had ever seen, hopping about in front of me at close range. I was singularly unprepared, sat in the open, my possessions casually scattered around me. My audio gear was not cued up, and more importantly, my camera was a couple of yards up the slope behind me. This would not look good on my résumé.

The bird had, for sure, already clocked me. I would have to insinuate myself seamlessly into the pitta's world before moving a muscle. I watched the bird, which showed no sign of being in a hurry to leave, nor in fact, of doing anything in particular. Having registered my presence, it was intent only on remaining as perfectly still as I was. It was, to invent a brand new form of contest, a statue-off. I glanced at my watch and noted the period of time that elapsed before the bird moved. It remained rooted to the spot, entirely immobile, for in excess of seven minutes. Eventually it took a couple of exploratory hops within the bamboo. I waited for it to grow accustomed to my presence. The second time it turned its back on me in pursuit of some wriggling prey item, I risked a movement towards my camera. No reaction. The next time it paused to preen its wing-feathers I made up a little more ground. At last my camera strap was within range, and inch by painstaking inch I dragged the camera towards me. Another agonizing minute and I had the camera switched on and at my shoulder. Thirty seconds later I had focused and squeezed the trigger, my first shot secured. The bird fed on unconcernedly, keeping a wary eye on me but quite content. And so our amazing interaction continued for forty-five glorious minutes, until the bird eventually moved on to more fertile pastures. During the whole encounter, the bird never called, never flew. It just loitered in the same small area of cover, eyeing me while gradually revealing every detail of its plumage.

Debate still rages as to whether Sula Pitta is a species in its own right, though it seems likely that it is merely a race of Red-bellied Pitta. Certainly this bird's plumage was strikingly similar to the Red-bellieds I had seen during the last few days on Halmahera and Sulawesi. It was mostly eyeball-searing red, with a crimson crown, lower breast and belly. The upperparts were an oceanic mix of blues and greens, but with a curiously strong metallic sheen. The dark centres to many of the feathers (some of which had dipped-in-ice blue tips) gave it a subtly mottled appearance. The most noticeable difference between this and other pitta species however, was the broad black band that ran across the throat and wrapped round the nape, like an over-enthusiastic muffler. It was a spectacularly shiny creature, and like a multi-faceted gem, the colours seemed to change as the light played upon its various surfaces; a jewel-thrush indeed.

I was delighted. Only my second day on Peleng and the twenty-sixth pitta species could be added to the list. I had some lovely photographs, and had been able to document every last detail of the plumage. I could worry later about whether the bird constituted a good species or was merely a race; for now it was simply a beautiful animal. One of the least accessible pittas* had proved easy to find, and I was hugely relieved.

We continued up-slope and soon reached a huddle of wooden houses with a rank grass main drag; Kokolomboi. Chickens stared out from bamboo coops, mutely appealing for our help to end their

---

* *Sula Pitta lives only on the Banggai Islands (of which Peleng is one) and the Sula Islands (Mangole, Taliabu and Seho) just to the east.*

incarceration. A mother wandered by, her head engulfed by an immense plastic washbowl. Polynesian-style ukulele music drifted through the sticky air, wafting between the immaculately swept, unpainted but not unloved houses. A surreal scene perhaps, but a peaceful one (unless you're a chicken). Labi and Theo joined us, and we sat drinking piping hot, sweet tea on Labi's comparatively splendid balcony. I commented in passing that his house was bigger than that of the *kepala desa*, the village chief. A wry smile followed, with a tacit acknowledgement that yes, a modicum of jealousy existed in the village.

Labi was the town's young thrusting entrepreneur, the man who owned five cows, who had bought his neighbours' land with money made growing vegetables, who slogged back and forth to Luwuk to secure the best prices for his produce.

'Some people on Peleng do not want to work that hard,' he said by way of explanation, 'but I do.'

We were in the presence of Peleng's first, multi-discipline eco-tourist business tycoon, and I felt reassured that the forest's future was in safe hands. With Theo translating, I bombarded Labi and Maleso with questions about the local birds, and listened intently as they educated me about recent developments on Peleng. Labi knew the whereabouts of the 'Peleng Scops-owl', a bird likely to be promoted to full species status in the near future, and confirmed that we could look for it as soon as it got dark. He even claimed to have found a new species of flowerpecker, a tiny wren-like bird that lived in the canopy of the highest forest, and which no western ornithologist had yet managed to see. I was impatient to get into the higher forest, but there was little point in stomping up the trail in the heat of the day, so our newly-bonded crew took a siesta for a couple of hours.

With base camp established, we set about conquering the upper reaches of Kokolomboi's mountain. An hour's steep climb brought us onto an open plateau, fringed with gorgeous forest stretching out along the ridge as far as the eye could see. I asked Labi how far he had penetrated into the forest, and he replied that he'd walked eight kilometres with no sign of the forest thinning out. He also said however, that it could not extend all the way to the coast, since a hilltop market convened twice a month, twenty kilometres to the south. I was puzzled as to why people would climb the mountain to buy and sell produce, given that all the local enterprise seemed to be concentrated along the coastline.

'Well the people on the western side of the hill have only fish,' Labi said, 'and the locals on the eastern side only vegetables. So they meet in the middle and barter.'

We worked the forest until it got dark, and although we heard the strange, urgent squealing calls of the Banggai Crow, we could not catch sight of the bird lurking high above our heads in the canopy. Birds here seemed generally shy, doubtless grown wary after years of hunting, and we saw little in the forest's cool interior. We did hear another pitta however, and I recorded its secondary vocalization, a mournful descending whistle like a forest kingfisher, very different from the typical primary call of the Red-bellied Pittas I'd previously encountered. The bird came fairly close to us, but the tangled understorey vegetation was unremittingly thick, and we were unable to persuade the bird to cross the trail.

This was the kind of behaviour I had been warned to expect from Sula Pitta, and although it was frustrating, I was also reassured that the pittas had reverted to form. No hunter likes a fawn to run up to his feet and nuzzle the gun-barrel. It seemed I had been extremely lucky to see one so easily earlier in the day. Once it got dark we set about tracking down the new scops-owl, and soon succeeded in pinning down an angry ball of tiny claws and tawny feathers in our spotlight beam. Bizarrely the bird called as it flew, highly unusual behaviour for an owl. I was already getting the distinct feeling that normal rules did not apply on Peleng.

Before it got light, Labi took us out to find Peleng Tarsier, an astonishing miniature primate. These adorable fur-bundles live in bamboo, where they cling to the host plant's vertical struts and feast on insects. When you shine a spotlight on them they ricochet from stem to stem at incredible speed, the organic equivalent of multi-play mode on a pinball table. The Peleng variety is blessed with ludicrously large, liquid eyes the colour of antique rosewood, and elongated ears that project, bat-like, upward and outward. Their old men's fingers and toes are extraordinarily long, each equipped with a black nail embedded within a round sucker, like a shard of jellied eel. It's said that Spielberg based the appearance of ET on a Tarsier. If true, it's a poor likeness in my opinion. ET looks way too normal.

By first light we were back on top of the world, and things were astir in the forest. At least two pittas were calling, but again, despite a patient, careful approach, they refused to budge, finding a concealed perch inside the forest and calling endlessly without moving. Unless we resorted to wielding a machete to forge a new trail, it was clear we would continue to have our work cut out, such was the density of the birds' chosen habitat. Other birds were more accommodating. I took notes on a pair of *Phylloscopus* warblers, knowing that no such birds were known on Peleng. I recorded an unfamiliar stilted yet tuneful whistle, and found it to be a markedly unique version of the Rusty-bellied Fantail's song. In time-honoured fantail tradition, this svelte, balletic songster behaved as if pinned to its perch, twitching hyperactively from side to side and defiantly flashing its broad rufous tail in a display of diminutive aggression.

I even managed to connect with a Banggai Crow as it glided from one treetop to the next. I wondered how many western people had ever seen this bird? Ten? Twenty? Although newly enrolled as a member of a club with a tiny membership, I couldn't help thinking that as mythic birds go, the crow was awesomely uninspiring. It's a crow, it's black, and it's very very rare. End of story. I know exclusivity is a wonderful thing, and I may well be laying myself open to accusations of being woefully shallow here, but if I spend a fortune on a limited edition pair of trainers I do also want them to look good when I wear them down the pub.

Another mystery song perplexed me as we retraced our steps back to the clearing. After a staccato, triple-tongue-click intro, it tripped into a short, desultory warble. It sounded vaguely familiar, yet I was sure I hadn't heard it before. After a few near misses, I finally managed to record the song, and upon playback, a bird shot towards me and perched a few inches above the ground. It was a Henna-tailed Jungle-flycatcher, another rare and little known species, and now I realized why the song had seemed so familiar. It was a re-mix of the more widespread Grey-chested Jungle-flycatcher's tune, updated for a modern audience, embellished with a few introductory percussive samples to hook the listener into the first verse. *Come to Peleng...* I imagined the tourist advertising slogans would one day run, *where nothing is quite what it seems.*

We returned to Kokolomboi, packed up and said our goodbyes to our host's wife, kids and excitable dog. Labi escorted us back down the mountain, and we stopped off at the scene of our earlier pitta success. As we rounded the corner, the pitta was hopping about *on the trail.* Clearly a mentalist. I took a few more photographs and thanked the bird for its unprecedented co-operation before we slid back down the hill and collapsed into Tataba's waiting arms.

Our next problem was how to get to the village of Kawalu on the island's northeast coast. Our best bet was to hitch a ride on a truck, but asking around we discovered that they only passed through Tataba every few days. Since we were able to stand unmolested in the middle of the main road drinking our tea, today, it seemed, was not destined to be one of those days. We settled for *ojeks,* and by early evening two shining steeds had drawn up outside Maleso's house. It was agreed that Theo would go with Labi, whilst I would ride pillion behind the other driver, a young stranger who had been summoned to assist. I silently prayed he would turn out to be mature beyond his years, not gung-ho and hot-headed. My prayers went unheeded.

Four hours later I dismounted from the back of the bike and had to lie down for a bit. My pilot lit a cigarette and sat at the edge of the road smoking. If he was a picture of serene calm, I was a gibbering wreck. I had never in my life been so terrified for such a sustained period of time. At least when you meet a deadly snake it's all over quickly; either it bites you or you escape. The ride had felt interminable; I no longer had any sensation in my legs, and I had a number of disfiguring welts on my left calf where I had burned it on the exhaust pipe while gripping the bike's chassis ever more tightly with my knees. My driver stubbed out his cigarette, waved a cheery farewell, and roared off into the darkness.

The house at which we were to stay was in darkness, as indeed was the entire village. Nobody was home. I lay down on a bench on the front porch and closed my eyes. An hour later, Theo and Labi had still not arrived, and I was starting to fear the worst. Eventually, more than five hours after we had left Tataba, I heard the sound of a two-stroke engine in the distance, and a minute or two later the *ojek* spluttered into view. I was hugely pleased to see them. It transpired that our intended hosts were away, but we prevailed upon their neighbours who squeezed us into their modest home.

I weighed up our position. We had long since run out of both rum and beer. Less crucially, we were also very low on water. We had a half-packet of battered crackers. We were liberally caked in grime, but the house we were to stay in boasted neither a bathroom nor running water. I was to sleep on the dining room table. We were however still alive, a fact that I regarded as miraculous given the journey we had just endured. I slept remarkably well.

I wanted to visit eastern Peleng for a number of reasons. First, to establish whether Sula Pitta survived in the coastal forest on this side of the island, given that it had clearly been extirpated from most if not all the lowland forest in the west. Second, to try to photograph a rotund partridge-like creature, the Sula Scrubfowl, whose image as far as I could ascertain had never been captured. Third, to log as many species as I could for Peleng as a whole. Since so few ornithologists had ever visited, there were plenty of potential discoveries to be made. And lastly, I thought we might lie on a deserted sandy beach, drinking rum cocktails while reading a trashy novel, before taking our pick of the myriad restaurants that lined the golden shore. (OK, I made the beach option up.)

Before turning in the previous night I had managed to establish, courtesy of Theo's selfless devotion to his translation duties, that the brother of our host Yason knew where the scrubfowl was to be found. Unfortunately he was sick, so we planned instead to spend a day in the nearest block of forest. We would then (speedy recovery permitting) try for the scrubfowl the following day. The nearby forest turned out to be only a couple of kilometres up the road, and we spent a fulfilling day proving the continuing existence of the pitta in lowland forest. After a long search, a second bird hopped nervously along the trail ahead of us just before dusk. In addition we came across a pair of Helmeted Mynas, a bird that sports an immense quiff that is surely the envy of every rockabilly from Brighton to Bombay.

In the evening, Yason's brother the scrubfowl expert appeared, having risen from the dead. (I think his name was *Lowris* but I suppose it could have been *Lazarus.)* A long discussion ensued regarding how best to find our quarry. We discovered that the scrubfowl was usually found nestling between a knife and fork and in the company of a selection of vegetables. They had been hunted out wherever their territories lay in close proximity to human populations, but if we were prepared to take a short *ojek* ride further east…I groaned.

Innumerable other requirements were discussed, until finally Theo turned to me and said, 'One last thing. Yason wants to know whether he should bring the dogs.' Initially I was stumped. This being Peleng, I suppose I should have expected some non-standard procedures. Then I remembered that the one other bird-watcher I knew who had seen the scrubfowl had visited the same spot.

'When Mr Filip was here, did the dogs come with you?' After a brief conference I was advised that yes, the dogs had accompanied Mr Filip.

'Then we take the dogs,' I announced grandly, and the scene was set.

Bright and early, we once again clambered onto misfiring motorbikes and headed east. The dogs had their own pillion *ojek* seat, and seemed to enjoy the ride rather more than I did. Mind you, they had the ears for it. The forest was not as far away as I had feared, and we were soon working the edge of a wooded area, looking for anything that moved. A pitta called, deep in the forest. Ruddy Kingfishers bickered in the canopy, their rolling machine-gun rattle spitting out of the trees at regular intervals. Every few minutes, the dogs would reappear from the depths of the forest, panting and snuffling and generally having a wild time of it, but still noticeably unencumbered by scrubfowls. I was beginning to experience misgivings about having brought them.

After a couple of hours, we had got nowhere, and Theo and I were waiting to see if anything would drop into a fruiting tree we had located. The day was already warming up, and our chances of finding the scrubfowl were evaporating in the heat. At that moment a volley of barks shattered the peace and quiet. Theo and I looked at each other, before running down the trail towards the commotion. We found both dogs sitting quietly at the foot of a tree staring intently upwards, while Yason and his brother barked furiously at whatever was hiding above them to ensure the bird stayed put. We crept up to them, and there, only two metres above the party, sat a single Sula Scrubfowl. It did not look pleased to see us.

I fired off a few pictures, and we all gazed up at this prehistoric-looking creature. It was roughly partridge-shaped, but with a crew cut and a curiously bare, puckered ear punched into the side of its small, foetal head. This last feature was so unashamedly naked that I imagined if you got close enough you'd be able to peer inside and examine the walnut-sized brain. The russet body was the size and shape of a rugby ball, and at the rear a pair of bright red legs and feet jutted out, terminating in a set of fearsome black claws. It was a hefty bird, and though I wasn't sure what constituted a scrubfowl's staple diet, judging by this individual's bulk it seemed possible that herein lay the answer to the timeless question as to who ate all the pies.

After a short period of paralyzing indecision, the scrubfowl finally decided that it would trust its feeble powers of flight to propel itself far enough to reach a safe haven. With a flight action midway between a wobble and a flutter, it baled out, and we left the bird in peace. It was pleasing to think that our guides would already have figured out that future eco-tourists would pay them more to see these birds alive than they would receive if they sold them for the dinner plate. The dogs appeared less than pleased that we had let the quarry escape after all their hard work, but then they weren't paying to be there. Yason was top dog, and he said it was time to go home.

We packed up and made the four o'clock boat with time to spare, a fact which gave us ample opportunity to study the minutiae of city life unfolding around Salakan's quay. The stevedores unloading a truck full of corn clacked their grappling hooks together in time with the cheery Indo-reggae blaring unstoppably across the harbour. Wooden hand-carts in various stages of disrepair were wheeled up, disgorging their loads into the ferry's fish-reek hold. I cast a critical eye over the *Lady Fortuna*, the craft that was to transport us back to Luwuk if our luck held. The entire boat (quite possibly including the engine) had been constructed from local wood, and was decorated from prow to stern in a fetching moss green and puce livery. Theo and I splashed out to celebrate our success and our continuing survival, and secured the last available cabin, equipped with all mod cons. Well, equipped with all mod cons that fall into the category of bunk beds, broken mirrors or ceiling fans anyway. We were living the high life now and no mistake.

As we steamed out from the dock, the golden minarets of Salakan's mosques peeked out amongst the tree-lined avenues, their opulence clashing uncomfortably with the surrounding poverty. Through my binoculars I could make out cows at the far end of the beach, tearing long strips off the sugar cane. Tethered goats wandered amongst them, clambering over the outriggers to seek out the juiciest morsels.

As I watched the shoreline recede, I felt we had seen the real Peleng, understood what it must be like to function in a community where the majority of trade does not involve the passing of money from one hand to another. It is an island where the man in the street exudes hospitality in a way richer nations have forgotten is possible. I was glad to have had the chance to experience the island's off-kilter magic. Not as glad as I was to have seen Sula Pitta though. If I'd missed it I would have had to return, and I couldn't face another week without a bathroom.

Chapter 15

The Mysterious Mr. Klau. Bali, Sumba, West Timor, Flores

Bali-hai! I was headed straight for the famous holiday island. Actually 'straight' is not strictly speaking accurate. I was headed crookedly for Bali, south via Ujung Pandang in southern Sulawesi, back up north to Manado, and, for reasons best known to the airline route planners whom I personally suspect have all been drunk as skunks for at least the last decade, far too far west to Singapore. I was grumpy about the routing, and for once I couldn't even blame British Airways.

Bali was my gateway to *Nusa Tenggara* (literally *The Southeast Islands*) and was included on my itinerary in its own right because it was rumoured to be the easiest place on earth to see 'Javan' Banded Pitta. You may remember that I had already seen Banded Pitta early in the mission at Khao Nor Chuchi. However, in the upper echelons of pitta taxonomy, something was afoot. I had it on good authority that the Thai and Bornean birds would soon be split off from the Bali birds (which are of the nominate race, *Pitta guajana guajana*) which meant I now had to see it again. It wouldn't count on my year's total (because the various races hadn't yet been split as separate species) but if the Banded Pitta complex *was* split just after I had completed my mission and I'd dropped by to pay my respects on my travels, I would be insured. I know it's ludicrous, but this is how bird-watchers work. Lists are important, and the lists are, for better or worse, somewhat fluid at present. The devil is in the detail, and I was detailed to report to Bali Barat National Park at 0500 hours the following morning.

I landed at Denpasar at eleven p.m. and found a local prepared to drive me to the most westerly point of the island. This, I discovered, is a long way from the airport, and is equally far from the beautiful southern beaches where you can barely make out the sand for the voluptuous women in skimpy bikinis. I found a hotel at two a.m. and was in bed by two-thirty a.m. At four-thirty a.m. my alarm went off. Not happy.

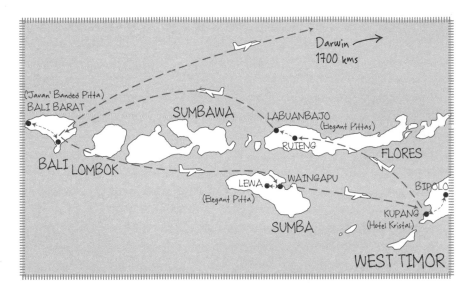

Bali Barat is famous for very nearly having become the last outpost of the *jalak bali*, the Bali Starling. Coveted by cage-bird enthusiasts, the species has been brought low by unscrupulous bird-traders, who have continued to take birds illegally from the tiny remaining wild population, despite knowing that they are critically endangered. The reason this piracy continues unabated is not hard to fathom: a single *jalak bali* may well change hands for upwards of three thousand US dollars. By 2001, only six wild birds were thought to remain alive. Happily, birds have now been reintroduced to Nusa Penida, an island off Bali's south coast, and are rearing families. The species, it seems, may yet be saved. I had decided that, since I would be visiting Bali anyway in search of the pitta, a side-trip to look for the starling was necessary.

I hooked up with Wahyudi my guide, who completed the necessary paperwork to allow our entry to the sanctuary, and after a short, starlit boat ride, we vaulted overboard and waded ashore. A pair of Beach Thick-knees, large waders with inverted banana bills and legs as long as a bloodhoud's face, sprinted away down the beach, squeaking their protest at being disturbed at such an ungodly hour. The beach was bathed in a soft half-light, the kind of dim glow in which one cannot tell where the sea ends and the sky begins. As we teetered between night and day, the thick-knees settled at the far end of the beach, nervously bobbing their heads in the shadows, their outline inchoate.

We climbed up to a vantage point and surveyed the arid scrubland that covered the hillsides. A pair of Black-winged Starlings, almost as rare as the Bali Starling itself these days, shot past at long range but there was no sign of the snow-white, blue-faced Bali birds. Adjourning to the guard hut we chatted to the starlings' protectors, who sat lolling in the shade, cradling their rifles. As we learned more about their work, out of the corner of my eye I noticed a movement, an alabaster arrow hurtling in towards the only bare tree in the compound. Bali Starling, incoming! Clearly this was the way to see them; hang out with the guys with the guns who keep the pirates at bay. I checked the bird's legs, and was gratified to find a complete absence of colour rings, proving that this bird had been born in the wild, rather than being aviary-bred and released. My conscience clear, I could add it to my world list. A second bird arrived, and there was a brief contretemps, during which the first bird raised its crown feathers, creating an effect somewhere between Jack Frost and a King's Road 1980s punk. The birds stared at us out of button-black, blue-rimmed eyes, until with a flick of their jet-black, point-tipped wings, they were gone. Gone, but not, I hoped, forever.

It was still early, so we re-boarded the boat and headed for shore, anxious to keep our appointment with the pittas. Wahyudi led the way to a dust-dry river bed which twisted through the brittle thorn-bush. Within an hour I heard the first pitta call, a hurried, breathy 'wheow', shorter than the calls I had heard many times in Thai forests. The bird played hide and seek with us and won. However, I could hear a second bird responding in the distance, and after a few minutes work I had succeeded in obtaining fleeting views. I spent the next four hours watching the birds, but they were loath to call and never perched up in one spot, remaining resolutely on the ground and forever on the move. I failed in my quest for a photograph, despite finding two different pairs, but at least I had seen them. My insurance policy in place, I spent the rest of the day watching petite Rufous-backed and Small Blue Kingfishers dispatching even tinier arthropods, dropping onto their prey from a succession of exposed perches. In the evening, I admired gangs of stately Green Junglefowls, beetle-glossed chicken-cousins wandering aimlessly through the scrub. As the sun disappeared below the horizon, I relaxed with a beer in a canopy restaurant. The Bali wind that brings the surf-boys ripped through the gaunt trees, threatening to uproot weaker specimens and deposit them in the ocean. I browsed the menu, but the prices were steeper than the Peleng trails, so I decamped to a local roadside restaurant. It was a decision I would later regret.

The drive back across the island was pleasant enough. Every village it seemed featured sculptures of the Hindu God Ganesh. Half man, half elephant and the remover of obstacles. Well I suppose he would be, equipped with both a trunk *and* opposable thumbs. The local temples boasted multi-level thatched towers, each wedding-cake tier topped with a Marx Brothers' wig, the neatly trimmed undersides resembling giant filamentous mushrooms. The tuneless, metallic tittle-tattle of gamelan bells blared out of every shop doorway, matched in its unpleasantness only by the growling noises that had begun emanating from my stomach. Approaching Denpasar, the districts grew wealthier, a fact borne out by the petrol sold at roadside shacks now being displayed in old *Absolut* vodka bottles.

Once within striking range of the airport I found a hotel, and reclined on a sun-lounger, sucking on a beer and trying to blend in with the regular tourists. Since I had taken the precaution of removing my leech socks before arriving I thought I stood a fair chance. However, as I drained the last of my beer, it became alarmingly obvious that all was not well with my innards. I ran to the toilet and was spectacularly ill. Still, I calculated, after so many days in obscure villages with questionable food hygiene, it was a miracle I had not picked up a bug earlier in the trip. It would pass. Sod's law; I finally get to stay in a plush, comfortable hotel, and I spend most of the night in the bathroom.

I was at the airport far too early as usual, a trait I've inherited from my father. When I was a boy, he would invariably have our entire family in position on the quay waiting for the Isle of Wight ferry five hours before it was due to depart. I amused myself by studying the public service notices dotted around the foyer. One warned against the dangers of rabies, listing both animals and countries deemed safe. There is no problem, I can confirm, if one wishes to travel to Bali from Norway carrying a monkey. I filed this nugget away for future use. At the security check I was thoroughly searched, presumably because, surrounded by a sea of surfers, I was the only freak suspiciously devoid of tattoos.

****

The short flight to Waingapu on the island of Sumba passed without incident, other than the unavoidable ones involving my frequent trips to the plane's smallest room. (Actually I imagine the cockpit is the smallest room on a plane, but for reasons of security and politeness I decided not to display evidence of my new ailment there.) By the time we landed I was feeling distinctly peculiar, but in time-honoured British tradition I shook hands with Bona my guide and soldiered on with a stiff upper lip. After a brief delay while the luggage cart was pulled by hand to the arrivals area, I hauled my aching limbs into the indicated vehicle. My driver Mr Ferry (no relation to the famous Brian and no threat to him in the fashion stakes either) whisked me west to the village of Lewa.

We passed through blasted landscapes, the few remaining stunted trees twisting out of the stony soil, emaciated and skeletal, too exhausted to hold on to their leaves. Whole hillsides were in the process of being burned, crackling like snapped wicker canes, emitting coils of thick smoke that curled up into the blackening sky. The only signs of life were in the traditional communal settlements, the tin-roofed, multi-tiered buildings spiking the air like cubist witches' hats. Everything within had a place in the rigid hierarchy; cattle subterranean, people at ground level, corn drying above, with a space for God to inhabit up top. On arrival in Lewa I was introduced to the owner of our homestay, Papa Bill. After the obligatory cup of tea and a slice of bread covered with rainbow sprinkles, I pleaded exhaustion and escaped to my darkened room. (Via the bathroom; a basic, rustic model with a dark squat toilet and a stone tank of cold water.)

The afternoon was a struggle. I was getting weaker, and my bird list reflected the fact: Short-tailed Starling, Asian Dollarbird, Emerald Dove; the common stuff you see on the way to the shops on Sumba. Our evening's owling was cut short by torrential rain, and for once I was grateful.

The next day dawned damp and dreary. I dragged myself back to the same area of forest, and between enforced retreats into secluded bowers, managed to find a few of Sumba's special birds: Apricot-breasted Sunbirds, neatly painted by over-enthusiastic children, shot-through-the-heart Blood-breasted Flowerpeckers, and sprightly Arafura Fantails. My best find was a furtive, silent Sumba Flycatcher keeping a low profile in the shadows, the private detective of the bird world, tan trench coat pulled tightly round the shoulders, a hint of crisp white shirt underneath. Elegant Pittas were audible but not initially visible. Their call here was a whippy, urgent *'whit-ip-wheow'*, very different from the two-note recordings I had of the birds on Flores. They kept themselves to themselves however, flicking through the depths of the forest without leaving a trace, and in my enfeebled state I was not sharp enough to outwit them.

I decided on a change of tack, and fashioned a trail where the forest looked a little more accessible. I sat down amongst the crackling leaves and waited. A pitta called on the opposite side of the road. I cursed my luck and waited on. A second bird called, closer, maybe fifty metres away, but soon lost interest and fell silent. After an hour I had still seen nothing, but at least I was comfortable and could rest. I tried to remain as still as possible, remembering Yothin's wise words from my very first day of the year at Khao Nor Chuchi. *I have a friend who is a very still person. He sees far more than I do. I think that is the secret. Remain unseen.* I concentrated on immobility, restricting my movement to wiping the sweat from my fevered brow.

An hour and a half into my silent vigil, I heard a sound I could not identify. It was sharp, almost mechanical, and seemed curiously out of place in the forest.

'Tak.....tak.'

I puzzled over the possible source, deciding that the sound was not human, but also not vocally animal. It came again, irregular, percussive, misplaced. *'Tak...tak.......tak.'* I swivelled in the direction of the noise, scanning with my optics. On the third sweep I met an out-of-place colour to match the sound, and behind a vertical strut caught sight of a localized but recurring movement. I leaned as far to the left as I could without toppling over, and was rewarded with a partial view of a scene I had never witnessed before.

The colour I had locked onto was a blaze of blue, and it belonged to an Elegant Pitta's wing. The movement I had noticed was the bird's head, jerking downwards as it repeatedly smashed a snail onto a chunk of limestone, a blacksmith at his anvil. *'Tak...tak;'* the smart rap of shell on stone. As I watched, a second pitta bounced into view, and the first bird broke off from his work to call. The interloper responded, both birds drawing themselves up to their full height, erect and alert, bristling with aggression. They faced each other at close range, chest to chest, then bowed, like a pair of Japanese salarymen introduced to each other after a long separation.

The new arrival capitulated and departed. The blacksmith resumed his work, eventually forging a hole large enough to drag the reluctant snail from his home, and swallowing it whole. After a brief check to make sure no morsel remained, the pitta turned and moved off through the forest. I crept forward and found the battered remnants of earlier sessions, which I laid out on the road and photographed, aware of the potential to identify for the first time an element of the Elegant Pitta's diet. Both pitta monographs, I knew, reported a complete lack of dietary information relating to the species. Months later with specialist help, I was able to identify two of the snails as an *Amphidromus* sp. and an *Asperitas bimaensis*, probably of the subspecies *cochlostyloides*. My self-indulgent year had finally produced something of scientific significance, a miniscule mystery solved.

I walked further down the road before stopping to rest on the barriers designed to save errant motorists from plunging to a fiery death on the slopes below. A further lavatorial emergency overtook me, and I dropped my trousers and groaned as another wave of grey-green poison was ejected from my body. Though on a quiet road, a car chose this precise moment to pass by, the occupants staring in unison at the sight of a strange foreigner, trousers at half-mast, smiling weakly back at them. I was past caring, indeed in truth I was starting to care little whether I lived or died. I was sick, really sick, and this, I had started to realize, was more than just your regular, dodgy-curry food poisoning.

I cleaned up as best I could, retrieved my mobile phone and called my friend Kit in England. He worked for a drug company, and I envisaged him surrounded by kindly pharmacists, dispensing life-saving drugs and medical advice in equal measure. Kit answered, listened to my symptoms, and promised to seek the expert opinion of the men in white coats. A few minutes later he called back.

'Could be dysentery,' he said cheerfully, 'I had it once, caught it in Bali. Cost me a heap of new birds. You taking *Doxycycline* as malaria prophylaxis?'

I confirmed that I was, and Kit advised me to check the prescription and take the maximum dose allowed until I started to improve.

'Doxycycline's a broadband antibiotic, it should kill whatever's got into you. Stop birding now. Rest. Drink as much clean water as you can get your hands on. Dysentery isn't trivial.'

I thanked him profusely and hung up. And then continued birding. My recalcitrance paid off, and in the last of the daylight I found my target, a Red-naped Fruit-dove, warming itself in the last rays of sunlight. I felt mildly vindicated that my stubborn stupidity had paid off, but mostly I just felt appallingly ill.

Back in the village we dined at the only available local restaurant. I selected the piece of meat with the least flies and feigned interest in consuming it, though I declined to press the steam-driven ice-shaving machine that helped assemble condensed milk slush puppies into service. We returned once more to the homestay and to the terrors of the bathroom, with which I had now become intimately acquainted. As I hovered above the foetid hole in the ground, wondering how to get cleaned up without simultaneously destroying the bathroom, the power went off. I was plunged into total darkness, and as I squatted in the blackness, unable to see my hand in front of my face, I reflected that this was without doubt, the nadir of my year to date. I felt like death. I was on my own, a long way from a hospital, and stupidly I had left my torch in my room. I was liberally covered in foul-smelling green slime, and could not move in case I tripped and fell into the latrine. I wondered if I died whether they would erect a plaque in my honour, perhaps installing it just above the rusting soap dish. I really did not know what to do, and wished I had never embarked on this pointless pitta misadventure. I yearned to lie on clean white sheets, to drink lemon barley water and sleep for a long time. Most of all I missed my girlfriend and my family. I wanted to go home.

At length, I heard sounds of mechanical activity, and shortly afterwards, the generator started up. The light bulb above me flickered, and after a few false starts, burned anew. I sluiced myself down and crawled back to my room, smiling wanly at my hosts. So very British; don't cause a scene and soldier on. It was a difficult night.

My last full day on the island. If I followed the sound advice I had been given I would miss the remaining Sumba endemics. I fell into my clothes and after a struggle, managed to tie my bootlaces. My driver ferried me out to Watumbela Forest, and I staggered up the trail, which was rocky but mercifully not too steep. I was sweating profusely, and was forced to make frequent unscheduled forays into the forest. Thank God I was birding alone.

After what seemed like an eternity, I made it to the top of the trail, and sat enjoying the gentle breeze that drifted across the hillside beyond. A pair of Sumba Green-pigeons, one of my main targets, crossed from one forest fragment to another. I scrawled their name into my notebook, followed by that of a Sumba Hornbill, which I watched labour across the horizon. A couple of Marigold Lorikeets screamed by, argumentative and lawless. A male Sumba Cicadabird perched up on a lofty snag, and was soon joined by a female. Enough. It was a good haul and I knew it. Time to lie down for a while.

On the way back, my guides announced that we would drop into a local wedding for a few minutes. It was on the way, and they had promised. I was too weak to protest, so we headed to the ceremony. We drove for an hour along Sumba's worst dirt road, pausing frequently to ask for directions, and periodically having to get out of the vehicle to coax it over the rockiest stretches of road. The violent bouncing of the truck did little to ameliorate my condition, and even less to improve my mood. My hosts continually assured me that we were almost there, and just when I was about to finally lose my English reserve, we turned a corner and arrived at the scene of the impending nuptials.

I was introduced to the father of the bride. As the only foreigner present, I was aware that I might well be regarded as the guest of honour, and made a Herculean effort to avoid causing offence by passing out. In order to blend in with the other party-goers, I accepted with good grace the proffered gift of a handful of betel nuts as we took our seats. A series of interminable speeches followed, of which I understood barely a single word. The P.A. system was so bad I doubted whether anyone else caught much of it either.

The betrothed sat on a makeshift stage at the front, sweating regally in the tropical heat. The bride was dressed from head to foot in pale pink, and was visibly wilting. The groom fiddled with his white gloves, and stared fixedly at the hand-drawn decorations around the stage, comprised mostly of fish and boats. I wondered how long they had been sat there prior to our arrival. The maid of honour appeared to have fallen asleep. The young bridesmaid was alternating between fanning herself and cleaning her nails. I really did not want to spoil the intendeds' day, but after joining the reception line, my very presence enough to astonish the happy couple, I took Bona aside and hissed into his ear. 'Listen. I am sick. Really sick. If you don't get me out of here there is going to be a very unpleasant incident involving your head and the rear end of that cow over there. I pointed to the tethered wedding gift at the edge of the crowd. 'We are leaving. Now.'

My urgency prevailed. We would leave imminently. Right after lunch in fact. I managed to lose most of the food piled onto my plate into the waiting mouths of the unruly dogs that prowled the tent. Word spread fast along the canine grapevine, and I was soon surrounded by a suspiciously large group of extremely attentive animals, sat in a neat circle around my chair.

'I love dogs. Always have,' I managed to splutter. 'And they love me.' I giggled hysterically.

This was duly translated by my driver, and everyone laughed. At that moment the family's crazy uncle staggered into the fray, and I seized my chance. I issued profuse thanks to anyone in earshot and fled to the sanctity of the truck, shaking hands with any random strangers who crossed my path. ('Lovely party! And such super dogs! See you soon.') We made good our escape. By the time we reached the outskirts of Lewa my shirt was black with sweat and I was reduced to leaning out of the window. My tongue lolled out of the side of my mouth, my slavering muzzle doubtless resembling that of my new found wedding feast friends.

I arrived back at the homestay just in time to witness an enormous pig being loaded on to a truck bound for the abattoir, a job that took the combined might of the entire family and their sheepdog, 'Blackie' to complete. The pig's terrified, piercing squeals penetrated my chest cavity and rattled around my ribs. I washed, ate more drugs, drank a litre of water and crashed out. Blackie looked in on me, his pig-loading duties now completed, but he did not linger; I suspected I was too much for his sensitive nose to bear.

****

I struggle to remember my last hours on Sumba. I know I managed to get off the island somehow, but the details are a little hazy. I also have a vague recollection of collapsing in the heat on the plains near the airport after totally failing to find one last endemic, the tiny, scuttling Sumba Buttonquail. The rest has been airbrushed out of existence in the interest of self-preservation. Mercifully, despite making me continuously nauseous, after six hellish days the antibiotics were finally working their magic, and by the time I reached West Timor I had started to feel almost human again. On arrival at the Hotel Kristal in Kupang I found myself in paradise. The room featured undreamt-of facilities.

A list of amazing features in the Hotel Kristal bedroom

* *Hot water (for the first time in three weeks)*

* *Enough light by which to read A Guide to the Birds of Wallacea*

* *An actual, sit-down, porcelain toilet*

* *A real bed with clean sheets.*

* *A big fluffy towel. And one of those hanky-sized ones you never know what to do with (I decided it was probably meant for boot-cleaning)*

* *Individual soap in an unopened packet*

* *A mysterious sachet containing something called conditioner*

* *Cold beer in the mini-bar, which could only have been improved had it been served by Kylie Minogue dressed as a squirrel*

* *A restaurant menu that was a.) in English and b.) which included some items entirely devoid of rice and the more obscure innards of animals*

* *A TV with an English language channel*

* *Wireless Internet*

* *Air conditioning*

I slept for fourteen hours and woke a new man. When my young, enthusiastic guides turned up early the next morning, they asked me nervously whether the hotel had been acceptable, noting that it was not the most luxurious in town. I assured them that it was absolutely the best hotel I had ever stayed in.

'What a stud.' A male Golden Bowerbird,
Kahlpahlim Rock Trail, Davies Creek, Queensland, Australia.

Pimp my nest. A Golden Bowerbird's bower.
Note the fresh lichen at the front proving this is an active bower.

The lonely Central Arnhem road at rush-hour, Northern Territory, Australia.

A male Hooded bloody Parrot, Fergusson River, Northern Territory.

Red-necked Crake coming to cheese,
Cassowary House, Cairns, Australia.

Did you spill my pint? Male Southern Cassowary, Cassowary House, Cairns.

Andy Mears, Aaron Joseph and family, Rossun Village, Manus.

Manus Hawk-owl, Rossun, Manus.

Sunset on Manus.

Male Yellow-bibbed Fruit-dove at Jack Daniels' place, Kandriu, Manus.

Santa Isabel from the air.
Note the abundance of Black-faced Pitta hiding places.

Tirotonga village plateau and church, Santa Isabel, Solomons.

The view of the atoll from Tirotonga, Isabel.

Mark Manehage on the pelagic off Isabel.

'Tastes a bit like chicken.' The Prehensile-tailed Skink, Isabel.

Mt Austen, Guadalcanal, Solomons.
Not the worst place to find yourself in transit.

William Manehage, Santa Isabel.

The Manehage clan, Tirotonga, Santa Isabel.
(Veronica and naughty Marister stand on the lower stairs)

'The rarest bird of all', Unawatuna, Sri Lanka.

Detail from a Buddhist temple near Unawatuna, S. Sri Lanka.

An idyllic Sri Lankan beach scene.
Note the reef in the distance which may host seabirds.

Early morning in the hills near Nuwara Eliya, S. Sri Lanka.

Home of the African Pitta: one of the dreaded river beds near Siavonga,
Lower Zambezi valley, Zambia.

The end of the road, Mbendele bridge, Lower Zambezi valley, Zambia,
December 10th. Fantastically under-specified Ford Ka just visible.

We drove north to Bipolo. Alighting from the vehicle my senses were bombarded by flaps and flutters, cheeps and twitters; there were birds everywhere. In three hours I logged one of those glamorous *Zootheras* (on this occasion a gorgeous Orange-banded Thrush) gangs of Yellow-eared Honeyeaters, a fly-by Olive-headed Lorikeet and a courting pair of Red-chested Flowerpeckers. Timor Blue-flycatchers seemed to perch on every snag. Timor Figbirds quarreled noisily in the treetops. Fawn-breasted Whistlers endlessly repeated their workmanlike *'chop-chop-chop-chop-chop-wheat'* from the undergrowth. I tracked down a Timor Stubtail, a tiny, tail-less mouse of a bird, which scurried through the understorey ahead of me, chastising me when I lost the scent with a piercing, scolding *'teenk.'* And just when I thought the stifling heat's monstrous weight had smothered the day's activity, I stumbled upon a resting Tricoloured Parrotfinch, a scarce, multi-hued beauty with a diamond-tipped tail. Quite a morning. Our afternoon session at Camplong did not quite live up to the high standard set by Bipolo, but we still managed to find another stubtail and, right at the death, a pair of Buff-banded Grassbirds skulking in the mother of all thorn bushes.

Back at the hotel, I celebrated with a $4 US steak and chips at the only restaurant in the place. I had lost eight kilos during the last three weeks, and needed to get my strength up. I sipped a beer and scribbled notes on the birds I had seen during the day. I called home and assured all and sundry that rumours of my death had been greatly exaggerated. As I walked back to my room, I noticed the hotel boasted a sports café in the basement. The sign welcoming patrons also depicted items banned from the establishment: shorts, baseball caps, flip-flops. Oh, and guns and knives. Nice to see standards being maintained.

My single day on Timor was over, and I was sorry to be leaving. I had failed to find Elegant Pitta, but since the subspecies here was the same nominate race I had accidentally collided with on Sulawesi, it didn't much matter. After the trials I had endured on Sumba, Timor had been a breath of fresh air, and I was fired up and ready for action again. I felt a frisson of excitement flicker through me at the thought of my impending arrival in Flores, where I had arranged to meet with a mysterious figure named Mr. Klau.

****

If I am honest, Martinus Klau looked less like a Bond villain than I had hoped. His beaming smile, gleaming white teeth and lounge lizard sunglasses did not help create an air of imminent violence. He sported a mop of luxuriant, unruly black hair, not a scalp-baring razor crew cut. His upper body, whilst well proportioned, did not appear to ripple with sinew and muscle beneath his tight-fitting tunic. Nimus, his colleague and our driver for the next few days, was equally unintimidating, owing largely to an impressive Burt Reynolds moustache *circa* 1975, and a similarly welcoming smile. I swallowed my disappointment, and reflected that since we only had five days to find both the local *concinna* race of Elegant Pitta *and* all of Flores's endemic birds, it was perhaps fortuitous that espionage activities would be taking a back seat.

Leaving Ruteng's Catholic bells to fight it out with the muezzin calling the Muslim faithful to prayer, and with a menagerie of cockerels and dogs competing for the heathen vote, we wound our way up into the hills. We almost ran over a Chestnut-backed Thrush on the way, a species I had been too sick to look for on Sumba. It had rained in the early morning, and the dripping forest at Danau Ranamese on the western side of the island was alive with birds. The habitat was in great condition; lush, fecund, and pregnant with possibilities. Cheeky Mountain White-eyes, and perky Flores Minivets flicked about the moss-wrapped branches as we walked slowly down towards the lake, whose mirrored waters lapped gently on the shores of a volcanic crater. Yellow and olive Flores Leaf-warblers gleaned hyperactively in the canopy, and a pair of dowdy Flores Jungle-flycatchers sulked morosely in the gloom of the understorey. A startlingly loud Nightingale-like song led us to Flores's star songster, the bizarre Bare-throated Whistler, whose lovelorn melodies obscenely distended the bare pink skin of its neck. Red-cheeked Parrots streaked past us overhead, tiny jets headed for some distant airfield. Although we did not even hear any pittas, the day had got off to a great start, and I was already warming to Flores.

We could not linger long however, since we had a date with the brothers at the Catholic seminary in Kisol. The monastery provides the only accommodation for miles, and is suitably austere and immaculately maintained. The convivial welcome we received was in stark contrast to the formidably ecclesiastical surroundings; everywhere I looked I was confronted by statuary and iconography, tapestries of the last supper jostling with tessellated cardinals, clamouring for my attention. After noodles and rice, we climbed up into the Ponco Deki hills above town to do battle with the pitta. It wasn't long before I heard its distinctive two-note whistle, and after an hour's work I had teased the bird out of the forest and into view.

I carefully noted the details differentiating this race from the Sumba birds: a broader, brighter golden stripe above and in front of the eye, latterly becoming white, and tinged deep blue near the end. An entirely black throat, extending onto the upper breast as a point, echoed below by an expanded black belly patch. A two-tone tail, whose distal half was grass-green. A textbook bird, and my third Elegant Pitta race of the year. Whilst I felt there were few if any empirically sustainable grounds for splitting the species complex into separate taxa, nonetheless one could not be too careful. My safety net in place, I could cut loose and enjoy myself.

Enjoyment started with dinner. Watched over by Jesus and his disciples, we wolfed down chicken, *ikan goreng*, tortilla-style omelettes and fresh-cut watermelon. I was delighted to discover that the monastery shop sold beer, and we toasted the pitta before getting an early night. The next day we returned to Ponco Deki, and cleaned up on the remaining sub-montane species. A flock of Flores Green-pigeons graced us with their presence at dawn, a Russet-capped Tesia finally allowed good views after I spent an hour digging it out of the undergrowth, and a White-rumped Kingfisher stared imperiously down at us from an elevated perch. Our vigil staring out over the blue hills to the east was rewarded with distant views of the rare Flores Hawk-eagle, and in the evening the unique whooshing wing-beats of a Flores Crow presaged a satisfactory conclusion to a great day.

We drove slowly back to Ruteng, checking-in to a second seminary run by a pair of Italian sisters, wimpled and warmly welcoming. The glacial pace of the service at the Lestari restaurant in town gave us plenty of time to admire the portraits hung around us, evidence of the owner's divided loyalties: Sioux chiefs, Ché Guevara, Yamaha motorbikes and Eminem. The following days were packed with memorable experiences; the chaotic orchestration of hundreds of Bare-throated Whistlers amid the mountain scenery of Golo Lusang, each imitating the sounds around them, the result a Las Vegas symphony of gaming machines all bleeping, ringing and chiming at the same time. A quartet of exquisite Chestnut-capped Thrushes at Puarlolo, feasting on pea-sized, orange *Dysoxylum* fruits. Gorging on local seafood in Labuanbajo with the island of Komodo, home to the famous dragons, as a backdrop. Dodging trucks full of goats on the Potawangka road while looking for Flores Hanging-parrots. Walking the Putri Sari beach at dawn and studying the clockwork antics of Javan Plovers, here further east than their name suggests they should be. And around every corner, another breathtaking, cloud-strewn vista greeted us on this, the most mountainous of the Lesser Sundas.

On the last morning there was just time to buy some natural, saltwater pearls before running to the airport. I hadn't seen a new species of pitta for almost two weeks, and I'd been sicker than I had ever been in my entire life, but this region of Indonesia had been an enriching experience despite the challenges the fates had tossed my way. Now though, it was time to press on with the next phase of the adventure. An irresistible force was pulling me further east, to the last, great, sprawling continent I would visit during the year. I was Australia-bound.

Chapter 16

Billabongs and Bowers. Northern Australia

Australia's not really all that big. In fact it's the smallest continent, a mere eight and a half million square kilometres give or take. You could cycle round its thirty-six thousand kilometres of coastline in less than two years with the wind behind you, punctures and Saltwater Crocodiles permitting. I'd visited the continent a number of times in the past, and had found both Australian pitta species without too much difficulty. Nonetheless, since I had vowed to find all of the world's pittas in a calendar year, I would have to return. Tough gig but someone had to do it.

The plan was relatively simple in outline. Head to Darwin, pop in to Howard Springs southeast of town and catch up with its Rainbow Pittas, before hooking up with fellow Brit, Andy Mears. We'd then hop over to Cairns on the east coast and whistle up a Noisy Pitta. After that, our time was our own. We could, if we wished, fritter money away in the Gold Coast's casinos. Or we could head further south to take in Sydney's vibrant nightlife and world famous cordon bleu cuisine. Wonderful destinations both, that would doubtless feature on any normal tourist's itinerary, but we were birders, and birders don't do normal. If we were successful with the pittas, we'd be fully occupied trawling the sites of abandoned uranium mines, or taking our life in our hands by walking the margins of the northeast's estuaries, home to the most fearsome predators on the planet, the aforementioned coastal cyclist's nemesis, the salties. Not for us the jet-set trappings, the luxury hotels with their pesky chauffered limousines and their obesity-inducing buffet tables. We would dodge the tiresome chore of mingling with super-models and media moguls in Sydney's buzzing bars. Instead we'd get intrepid, heading to far more exciting destinations. One such locale lay deep in the outback, where the whiff of bygone gold-rush fever could still be discerned amongst the eucalypts and the gum trees, where the roads ran railroad straight through the bush to the far horizon, and where kangaroos bounced freely beneath a starlit sky. We would pay a visit to the heaving metropolis that is Pine Creek.

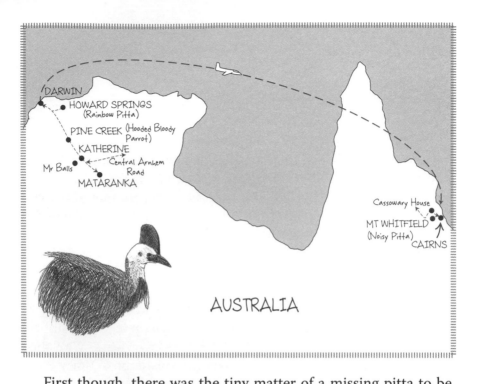

AUSTRALIA

First though, there was the tiny matter of a missing pitta to be dealt with. Although I'd landed at Darwin in the middle of the night, it didn't require a crack orienteering team to point the way to my destination. Which was lucky, since the closest I came to acquiring such a team was bumping into a gaggle of French tourists who were struggling to find their way out of the car park. I stopped to help (and to return their map, which had fallen into the gutter off the bonnet where they had left it). Once on the main Stuart Highway I headed south, turned left in Zuccoli onto Howard Springs road, and parked at the far end. It was not yet four a.m. and the park gates were closed. I was owed a few days' sleep, and gratefully accepted the chance to rest my eyes for a few minutes.

I woke with a start at six forty-five a.m. It was already light, and someone had opened the gates and departed again without me stirring. I was furious with myself. I had only allowed a single day to find the pitta, and I had just blown the precious hour immediately after dawn. Cursing my stupidity I gunned the engine, desperate not to waste any more time.

Deep down though, I suspected my slumbering oversight was unlikely to prove critical; Rainbow Pitta is atypically easy to track down, and is without doubt the most flirtatious of an unremittingly conservative family. Of all the pitta sisters, she's the one most likely to put out on a first date. Daddy Giant Pitta may keep his counsel and stare sternly on from the sidelines, but all the while his wayward daughter will be flashing her rainbow knickers to anyone who glances in her direction. Whilst this might be morally distasteful, she's such a looker that one is obliged to forgive the lack of decorum.

I checked the directions I'd been given and walked towards the trailhead. Ten metres before I reached it, a pitta called. I stopped in my tracks and tried to pinpoint the source. Another call rang out, up high somewhere. I crept towards the trail, moving as furtively as I could, much to the surprise of the forest warden who was tidying the picnic area. 'Looking for pittas?' he yelled, several hundred decibels louder than I would have liked.

I nodded in confirmation, and he waved his arm wildly in the direction of the gum forest. Another high volume salvo assailed me.

'Over there I reckon mate, shouldn't be a drama.'

I smiled politely and nodded again, whilst inwardly cursing my new friend and several bellowing generations of his family before him.

I need not have worried. Frankly, I could have started along the trail with a brass band in full swing behind me and the pittas would still have hopped out to say hello. Within two minutes I had located the calling bird above me, and species number twenty-seven was safely racked up. I grinned smugly, though the ease of the kill limited my sense of satisfaction. I completed the two-kilometre trail at a leisurely pace, and saw six more pittas. Two of them even squared up to one another, standing upright in the open on the trail, settling a boundary dispute. One bird backed off, leaving the victorious male crowing his victory. Their outrageously tarty behaviour notwithstanding, they are a beautiful bird; velvety black head and underparts, lime-green back, red belly patch, accessorized with a jaunty chestnut skull-cap and an ocean-blue wing patch. Simple blocks of colour combined to stunning effect. I tipped my hat to the birds and drove south.

A shotgun pellet-peppered sign welcomed me to town: *Pine Creek. Population 390.* A wrecked pickup rusted slowly in the heat, coalescing inexorably with the thick, red dust that lined the highway. It was early afternoon, and the town was tucked up indoors, sheltering from the murderous sun. I pulled over and stretched my legs, relieved to have escaped the confines of my tin-can rental car. Within minutes I could feel the sun's rays ripping through the thinned ozone, nipping at my reddening neck. I lay down in the shade of a gum tree on the north side of Parson's Terrace and settled in for a snooze while I waited for Andy.

The toot of a horn woke me, and a burry West Country accent rippled through the still air.

'Chris, how are you mate?'

It was Andy, and after five exhausting weeks traipsing across Indonesia I was delighted to see his familiar face beaming down at me from the window of his suitably mud-caked camper van. We adjourned for a beer, and traded stories. Andy had just made it around the Kakadu, the Northern Territory's most famous wilderness. I gave him the once over. No sign of a wooden leg nor a prosthetic limb of any kind; clearly he had managed to stay one step ahead of the salties. I filled him in on my progress, and confirmed to his evident relief that I had caught up with the pitta without any unforeseen problems.

As I glanced around the bar, I noticed an Australian gent sat next to us. He was in his early sixties, face puckered and creased by the sun, and was decked out in a wide-brimmed Akubra hat, beige short-sleeved shirt, khaki shorts and pressed white ankle socks. His stringy physique somehow managed to sustain the weight of an immense beer belly that bore all the signs of a lifelong work in progress. As if to prove the theory, his left hand was wrapped proprietorially around a schooner of Toohey's. A true blue, fair dinkum bloke and no mistake.

I must confess I hadn't selected Pine Creek as our rendezvous point based on the breadth of its cultural events, nor for its wealth of nightlife. This was my second visit to the miniature outback town, and I wanted to return to catch up with a bird I had missed last time round, a bird routinely referred to in our household as 'Hooded bloody Parrot.' I had brought my other half out to Australia three years earlier, and we had stayed at Pine Creek's salubrious caravan park, an establishment that rejoiced in the name of *Digger's Rest*. Relying on out-of-date information I had played a disastrous hand and had completely missed the parrots, which are relatively common around town so long as you coincide with their schedule.

They feed on the flowering trees that line the town's avenues in the early morning, before spending the day in the wilds of the outback, returning to roost just before dark.

Andy and I whiled away the afternoon with parrot-checking duties, but after five hours I was starting to get a distinct sense of *déjà vu*. I should have kept faith though; with barely thirty minutes of daylight remaining, we picked up a pair of small psittacines way in the distance, and our attention was immediately drawn to their curiously weak flight profile as they laboured their way erratically towards us. They landed in a tree just yards from where we stood, and there at last was the bird I'd dipped on my last visit. The male in particular was stunning, pastel blue below with a neat black cap and a broad patch of bright gold in the wing.

I abandoned the usual birding protocol and whooped my approval, causing the owner of the yard in which we were standing to emerge from his property to investigate what was clearly the biggest party Pine Creek had ever witnessed. I set up my telescope and invited him to feast his eyes on this rare bird. He sucked his teeth.

'Oh, yeah, hoodies. We get 'em in the garden most evenings.'

My parade was not to be rained on however, and we retired to the pub for a man-sized steak and a great bottle of local wine. Alfresco dining in an outback town under the stars, and all for the price of a kebab and a pint in London. Definitely as stated in the brochure.

With the parrot under the belt, we headed south at an ungodly hour the next day bound for the town of Katherine and the lonely Central Arnhem road beyond. Here it's just you and the outback, with the occasional wallaby for company. Tinder-dry bush stretches as far as the eye can see, with only an occasional billabong to sustain man and birds alike. In a hundred and fifty kilometres we passed a single apparently deserted settlement, the Aboriginal owners hiding from the glare of the sun within their pointillist-style, traditionally-decorated houses.

The heat is so intense in Australia's desert interior that the middle of the day is a write-off. Nothing can be done beyond skulking in the shade, waiting for the temperature to drop. Hence in order to actually see any birds you need to be out in the field at first light, taking advantage of the optimal conditions until around eleven a.m., then find somewhere cool to enjoy a long, slow lunch, before striking out again at three p.m. Adhering to this regime, we searched for mile after dusty mile until we found our target birds, a pair of bizarre Northern Shrike-tits, their striped, big-bird heads stuck improbably onto little-bird bodies. Along the way we found other birds of the dry interior: diminutive Diamond Doves, solitary Little Woodswallows, and a gang of twelve (naturally) Apostlebirds.

Our long, slow lunch was enlivened by a visit to the nest-site of one of Australia's rarest birds of prey, where we duly chalked up our first ever Red Goshawk, sun-soaked and soporific in the heat of the day. That night we slept near Katherine, at a bucolic establishment named 'Springfield Homestead.' Our gracious hosts provided processed white bread to feed the tame wallaby that arrived to watch us eat.

'His name's Mr. Balls,' the lady proprietress informed us in a voice roughened by a hundred thousand Winfield cigarettes.

'Why's he called Mr. Balls?' Andy asked, a tad unwisely I thought.

A cackle before the bawdy reply; 'get close enough, you'll see why.'

Mr. Balls was soon joined by a white fowl with a red bill, warty facial skin and a mean scowl; an evil antipodean gangster-duck we presumed, demanding bread with menaces. Post-Tooheys we adjourned to our boxy room, disturbing a lime-green tree frog from his bathroom domain in the process. He squeezed down the back of the cistern, and we carefully lifted the lid to find the frog glaring balefully up at us, resentful at the invasion of his watery den.

Our last morning found us in position at the Fergusson River before first light. We spent a productive few hours watching birds coming in to drink at the watering holes: delicately painted Gouldian Finches, more Hooded Parrots, Striated Pardalotes and White-gaped Honeyeaters. So long as we kept still and silent in the shade of the wattle trees on the bank of the watercourse, the birds would come close; a magical experience. How far had these birds flown to find water? Did the same birds visit every morning? Were the birds in each successive knot of Double-barred and Masked Finches members of the same family or unrelated to one another, brought together only by their common need for hydration? We pondered such unknowables as we hoovered up the distance back to the coast, giving a wide berth to the enormous multi-trailer road trains that thundered down the route from Darwin to Alice Springs. In town we whiled away our final hours twitching and missing, failing to find either the famous Rufous Owls in the Botanical Gardens, or any Oriental Plovers at Nightcliff. We settled for studying a procession of canoodling couples, determined dog-walkers and reckless roller-bladers, before continuing our trek eastward.

We crossed the state boundary at thirty thousand feet, cruising smoothly out of the Northern Territory and into Queensland. On arrival we picked up a rental car and switchbacked our way into the hills north of town. Our destination was the legendary Cassowary House, home to a cast that included the owners Phil and Sue Gregory, two bandana'd black Labradors, a family of Southern Cassowaries, and a famous, cheese-loving Red-necked Crake. Sue met us at the door and showed us to our charmingly rickety cabin in the woods, fussing over us to make sure we knew where everything required for the tea-making process was stowed. The cabin wrapped itself around us, comforting and familiar as an old jacket, and we sat on the balcony, feet up with a brew in hand, surveying the tranquil scene before us. For the first time in weeks I could relax.

Not for long though. I had only allowed a few days in which to get to grips with Noisy Pitta, assuming they would be one of the easiest species to find. After chatting to Sue about the best place to eat in the evening, the conversation inevitably turned to birds. 'I'm afraid,' Sue began, with a frown, 'that our pittas have not turned up yet, and since I knew you were coming I called a few folks on the Tablelands, but they all say their pittas have disappeared. It's the drought, birds just aren't on their usual territories.' Contrary as ever; what should have been a cast-iron, dead-cert. pitta had decided to toy with my emotions once again. Not good news. Not good news at all.

On the way into Kuranda to find dinner, we bumped into author Mark Cocker and photographer David Tipling, here gathering material for a new book on which they were collaborating. We introduced ourselves, and as we were shaking hands I noticed Dave was looking in the opposite direction. He caught my quizzical glance and extended his finger in the direction of the elephant in the room. Not literally an elephant in the strictest sense, but a bird on a similar scale. Standing only a couple of metres from us was a male Southern Cassowary with a striped chick in tow.

Typically when pursuing birds, one doesn't have to worry about the hunter getting captured by the game. In the case of the cassowary, it's worth bearing in mind as a possibility. This prehistoric creature is the second heaviest bird in the world. It stands an inch or two below six feet high, and has the not inconsiderable bulk of an Ostrich. In addition, the head is adorned with a fifteen-centimetre triangular bony plate, and the three-toed feet are armed with a lethal inner claw that can disembowel a man in seconds. There are even records in Papua New Guinea of cassowaries doing just that, after which they reportedly watch over their victim's prone body for signs of life. I was even told by a Papuan guide that cassowaries check whether their prey is dead by putting their bill into the injured party's ear. If the casualty reacts, they attack again, gouging the body with that dagger-like claw. In short, if you spill a cassowary's pint, it's best to apologize and buy it a replacement pronto.

The bird had been so close that we had failed to register its presence, subliminally assuming it was a tree, or perhaps a small tower block. The bird started to move, and it moved in our direction. Social niceties were abandoned, and all parties scattered as the bird wandered over to take possession of the patio. Nobody argued.

The next morning as I stood with cup of tea in hand, I could just make out the hulking outline of the cassowary waiting in the dark forest below our balcony. I tossed it a banana skin, which it devoured in an instant. Big mistake. By the time we were ready to leave, our way was barred by the bird-mountain, which was now pressed up against the front door and stood blocking our escape, peering into the cabin with the beady eye of a born killer. There was nothing for it but to wait until our persecutor grew bored and went off in search of other prey to gouge and maim.

Post-liberation, we headed west, tracing the northern boundary of the Atherton Tablelands. Our plan was to climb the Kahlpahlim Rock Trail along Davies Creek. The rock is the highest point of the Lamb Range, and it took us several hours to scramble up into the montane forest that cloaks the mountain's western slope. Despite starting in the dark, we were hot, sweaty and exhausted by the time we reached our chosen habitat. The forest looked uncomfortably dry for pittas, and so it proved; we did not hear a single one during the ascent. However, we knew that with luck, a bonus would await us on the higher slopes.

Andy saw it first; a delicate structure composed of hundreds of interwoven twigs, like a fiendishly complicated child's construction kit. The back wall of the edifice formed a semi-circle, joining the twin peaks that sprouted from either side. It was hollow, with a curved lip to the fore, which was festooned with pastel green lichens. A space in front had been cleared of leaf-litter. It was a thing of beauty, and I knew it had not been put together by the hand of man. Rather, it was the work of an extraordinary avian architect, the Golden Bowerbird.

Male bowerbirds are so in thrall to their mates that they construct their own display grounds, building their bowers and decorating them to attract the females. When a female arrives, the male dances to lure her in, before claiming his conquest and having his wicked way. It's a long and complicated process, and only the male with the best bower will successfully woo his beloved. Just imagine if human relationships worked this way. Your eyes meet across a crowded bar, you buy her a Campari and soda, but deep down in order to win her heart you know you'll have to build the object of your affections her very own private disco before she'll accept you as a worthy suitor. Rather more daunting than the usual, stuttering *'come here often then?'* We were suitably impressed. If the presenters of *Pimp my Nest* ever showed up, they'd just bow their heads in defeat and sidle off.

We hid in cover above the bower and waited. Before long we heard a strange staccato knocking, a rhythmic tattoo that faded in and out. I recorded the sound and played it back. The knocking grew louder, and seconds later, a splendid male Golden Bowerbird landed on a branch above us. He was such a looker that I found it difficult to believe he'd need any engineering qualifications to win the ladies over. In the sunlight the golden-yellow plumage lit up, turning him into an incandescent beacon of love that threatened to set fire to the forest. Filamentous silver feathers gleamed when he turned his head, adding an extra sheen to his lustrous, shining mane. What a stud.

It had been worth the climb, but we needed to crack on and find the pitta. Nearby Emerald Falls held only a flock of Squatter Pigeons pacing the paddock, while a White-browed Robin briefly entertained us as it flitted ahead, following the riverbank. Thinking that a change of altitude might yield results, we headed further inland and spent a few hours trawling the slopes of Mount Lewis, but without success.

As the day wound down we drew up at Kingfisher Park, Julatten, a famous birding site that I knew regularly played host to Noisy Pittas. The owners were friendly and welcoming, but told us they had not seen their regular birds for some time. I cursed the drought as I stomped sulkily about the grounds. What in my mind had been a foregone conclusion was turning into a real struggle, and we were using up pitta options at a rate of knots. At dusk we sat on Julatten's stream bank, and in the last of the light, picked up a silvery torpedo streaking downstream. It might not have been a pitta (it would have to have worn a mask and fins, which would have been a turn up for the books) but it was in any event a creature I was very pleased to encounter: Australia's most singular and charismatic animal, the enigmatic Duck-billed Platypus. An egg-laying, furry, aquatic mammal equipped with a duck's beak up front and the tail of a beaver. Proof positive to my mind that even the good Lord is not averse to the odd session with recreational drugs.

That night we dined with Roger and Mark in the local inn in Kuranda. The bar boasted Guinness on tap, hearty pub food, and an accommodating landlord sporting a handlebar moustache that put Merv Hughes in the shade. Stir in convivial conversation, and a pair of Bush Thick-knees peering in though the doorway to check for stray chips, and you have all the ingredients of a wonderful evening. Only the pitta was missing.

We had a little time before our flight to Manus the next day, and I had a cunning plan up my sleeve. I had seen Noisy Pitta once before up on Mount Whitfield, which pokes above Cairns' surprisingly wild suburbs. It meant another steep ascent, but by now we were inured to such hardships, having developed climbers' calves and thighs of steel. We started early, and by the time the sun was up, so were we. From the ridge at the top we could see planes landing at the airport below. A shimmering haze blurred the city suburbs, stretched out supine to the south. As soon as we entered the quiet, dim forest interior, I cued up audio and played snippets of the Noisy Pitta's refrain, a clipped, three-note whistle.

'Walk to work...walk to work...'

Silence. We ploughed ahead and tried another spot. Another no-show. Could the pittas also have abandoned coastal sites like this? I could understand them upping sticks and deserting the arid interior, but surely they would not have moved far? If they were not here on the coast where at least a modicum of rain had fallen, I was out of ideas. And then came the sound I had been hoping to hear ever since we set foot in Queensland. At first only a short alarm call,

'*kiaaw*', but then, at last, the rollicking song. '*Rrrrork-ke-wreak...*
rrrrork-ke-wreak.' The Noisy Pitta was in the building and preparing
to take to the stage.

Not quite as shameless as the Rainbow Pitta but not a million
miles off, Noisies are larger than life characters, and aggressively
territorial. This bird was no exception, and within seconds of the
first call it came screaming towards us like a heat-seeking missile.
It landed behind a fallen log, and peeped out from one end.

'*WALK TO WORK.*'

The call was preternaturally loud at such close range. The bird
bounced left and came closer still, pausing now and then to shriek at
us again. It crossed the trail and perched up, half-hidden in a clump
of rattan. More calls, more bounces followed, as the pitta described
a wide arc behind us, an irrepressible ball of energy. A chestnut-
capped, lime-backed, black-masked, fiery-bellied bundle of joy, and
most definitely a welcome sight.

Twenty-eight down, just four left to fall. The mission lurched back
into the groove. Despite Noisy Pitta putting up more resistance than
I had expected, I knew more strenuous challenges lay ahead, with
three of the four remaining pittas amongst the most intransigent
of the bunch. The logistics for the next stage of the adventure were
hazy. From here on in I would be taking the path less travelled.
Could I venture off the map and stay on target? It was time to take
the first tentative steps into the unknown, and I steeled myself in
readiness for uncharted waters and strange lands.

Chapter 17

Strange Days. Manus

If you don't know where New Ireland and Manus are, there's no shame in it. Nobody knows where they are except the people who live there. And most of them don't know where anywhere else is. For the record, start with Cape York, the pointy bit at the top of Australia. The big island immediately to the north is Papua New Guinea. Up and right a bit are a pair of islands resembling a boomerang; New Ireland and New Britain. And three hundred kilometres left of the top of New Ireland is another remote blob of land. That's Manus. On most maps it's the one with *Here Be Dragons* striped across it.

We arrived via Kavieng, New Ireland, a little delayed following a lengthy debate about whether we would be stopping there at all, due to a complete lack of fuel on both islands. The pilots decided there would not be enough fuel to complete the round trip back to Port Moresby, PNG, so all Kavieng passengers were shipped back to the terminal. Then detailed weight calculations revealed that yes, there probably would be enough fuel, so they were promptly shipped back again. Despite the preamble, Andy and I arrived at Manus's Momote airport without further incident. Sadly my luggage did not. I was advised to find Mary whose office was in the shed at the end of the runway, just beyond a battered sign that read *guns and ammunition this way.* Mary, I was advised, had gone home, so after registering my missing bags we caught the bus into the town of Lorengau, our base for the next five nights.

The list of things that might cause one to visit Manus is a short one. True, there are Second World War relics that might interest those fascinated by the minutiae of Pacific military history. (I'm still confused though, as to how one can have a major conflict in a region known as *The Pacific*. Is there a race of peace-loving people inhabiting islands in *The Warlike?*) Then there are a few gold deposits, so the odd geologist drops by from time to time. Manus is also a key location for monitoring climate change, so we met a crew of engineers and researchers, flown in to maintain the sensitive equipment that predicts precisely when the seas will roll over our heads. Andy and I

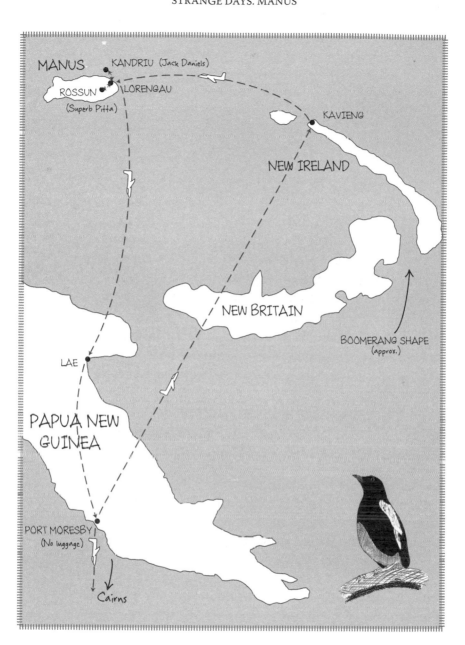

though had come for a different reason. Manus has its own species of pitta. It occurs nowhere else in the world, and thus a visit to the island was necessary in order to track down the little-known Superb Pitta.

We had struggled to find information on the species, since so few people had ever seen it. After a lot of trawling, we came across a data-snippet that suggested we should track down a guy called Aaron, and

305

that we could find him via the good people of the Harbourside Hotel in Lorengau. Armed with this battery of information, we headed out into the unknown. Finding the hotel proved straightforward, and the staff were accommodating, although uniformly unsmiling and keen to avoid eye contact. This is readily explained by the fact that showing one's teeth or gazing directly into a person's face on Manus is a prelude to war. As a result, everyone looks very grumpy and/or shifty at all times.

The establishment had seen better days, its mildewed fascia contrasting starkly with the smart yellow helicopter parked in front. (The latter, we later learned, was the property of the gold-prospecting geologists.) Friday being market day, the town was a hive of activity. The pavements were pockmarked with spattered, brick red betel-spittle, skilfully ejected from generations of mouths. On the street-corner opposite the hotel, a callow youth was doing a brisk if clandestine trade in what we assumed to be some kind of narcotic, but which turned out to be powdered coral. The alkaline in the coral creates the chemical reaction with the dry betel nuts, which in turn gives the drug its kick. I dodged the salesman and raced round to the Air Niugini office next to the hotel to see what could be done about my missing baggage before they closed up for the day. Then I plodded straight back again, having discovered they had closed early. And would remain so until Monday.

Since we had an hour or two to kill, and since I now owned only one battered pair of binoculars and the clothes I stood up in, we went shopping at Lorengau's biggest supermarket. It wasn't particularly super but it was a market, and I suppose one out of two is a fair hit rate. We browsed the aisles, spurning what might well have constituted our only opportunity to buy *Cock* mosquito coils and *Nancy* soap. I enquired about deodorant, but was told there was no call for it. The stale air on our bus journey into town began to make sense. I tried every one of the small shack-shops around the main square, but met with no greater success. This lack of supply, I reflected, did exhibit a peculiar kind of logic. Nobody here smelled bad, because everybody did. I settled for a two dollar, forest-camouflage-friendly, moss green polo shirt, a pair of fake, knee-length Manchester United shorts (oh the shame) and two pairs of *Superdog Executive Business Socks*.

We carried my booty back to our basic room, and set about examining the dubious snacks we had also purchased. All appeared to involve a chemical that reminded one faintly of a cheese left out to die. This noxious and doubtless completely illegal substance had been fired at a succession of misshapen replicas of spaceships, pointy hats and cartwheels, until the marketing department was happy that aperitif-accompanying nibble nirvana had been achieved. We flicked through the four available TV channels, eventually settling on the Australian Rugby League semi-finals, a spectacle that appeared to be gripping the whole island. I poured rum and cokes purchased from Port Moresby's finest duty free emporium, and we sat on the balding lawn to watch the sunset, deciding that the spaceship snacks looked the least revolting option, but realizing within seconds it was a bad call. Having sampled the other two bags it appeared to be a dead heat however, and they all ended up in the bin. The hotel band were tuning up, and their rehearsals in the bar directly opposite revealed that we were soon to be treated to mangled renditions of 'Black Magic Woman', 'Honky Tonk Woman', and a version of 'Run to You' that would have had Bryan Adams reaching for his revolver. It looked like it might be a long night.

The next morning we met Aaron before dawn. We had been advised that he was a potentially edgy character, but he seemed civil enough, though grumpy and shifty as tradition required. Martin the bus driver from the airport also turned out to be our driver for the morning. He looked tired, perhaps worn out by his stint as the waiter in the hotel's restaurant. Either that or his onerous duties as barman had taken their toll. I was pretty sure he had also been the lead guitar player the night before. Happily the band had run out of material by eleven p.m., which meant that we were able to enjoy the full force of the dance music that thumped out of the club located behind our room without further interruption.

Martin ground through the gears, and we bounced up the hill south of town towards the village of Rossun, home, it was rumoured, to both Aaron and the pitta. By evening, we had confirmed that both these things were true, having met most of Aaron's extended family, and heard the pitta call from deep in the forest opposite the village. We had not, however, managed to see the bird, which had resolutely refused to come in either to Aaron's whooped impression of the bird's call, or to our recording of the species. We hung out in the village in the evening, posing for photos, allowing the kids to pull our strange, fine English hair, and watching the antics of a pair of

Manus Hawk-owls, large and curiously romantic owls, who shuffled up close to one another while duetting from a shared branch.

Another night of wince-inducing cover versions followed, but as a soundtrack to Rugby League it worked in an offbeat kind of way. We sorted out arrangements for the following day. Since a tsunami warning had been issued we also tried to figure out how to get up the hill behind the town without skirting the harbour. After lengthy discussion we concluded it was impossible, and settled for a Plan B that mostly involved sitting on the hotel roof and hoping for the best.

The next morning we were in position once again to do battle with the pitta, this time in a different patch of forest. No matter how we varied our tactics, the outcome was always the same; we could hear the bird but we could not see it. We returned to the scene of yesterday's struggle, and squatted in the mud on the only trail that led into the forest interior. This time, however, the pitta's feistiness overcame his fear, and after an hour-long wait, a male flew in high above our heads and called from a hidden spot in the canopy. We held our breath, impatient but immobile, hoping for a break-through. One came. The bird moved position to secure a better viewpoint, and suddenly we had our prize.

Big, black and beautiful, Superb Pitta is an imposing creature. The colour scheme is simple for a pitta, blocks of red, azure blue and dark green rendered impossibly bright when set against the black background of the head, breast, back and tail. The call is a repetitive, urgent, *'wooah, wooah,'* the timbre that of a neurotic dog warning of intruders. With each call, the bird flicked its wings a little, flashing the iridescent blue covert panels to ward off potential rivals. I vowed that the moment I was back in London I would beat a path to Savile Row, there to invest in a silk waistcoat that I could flick to similarly dramatic effect. The pitta towered above us, constantly on the move, unpredictable and slippery, consistently defeating my best efforts to record it on camera. Another twenty-four hours would pass before I had my precious shot, when we persuaded a single male finally to grant us a better view amongst the canopy foliage.

Through a shadowy intermediary, I had arranged for us to visit the offshore islet of Kandriu to search for a few small island specialists (species that shun larger land masses and breed exclusively on the smaller offshore islands). Confusion ensued, largely because the island was also known as *Hawaii*, a name bestowed upon the tiny lump of rock by World War Two US troops, who having clapped eyes on the island's palm trees, had invented this tenuously connected alternative name in a fit of homesickness. Despite bearing little resemblance to its namesake, the name had stuck. Having confirmed that Hawaii and Kandriu were indeed one and the same, a deal was struck, and we agreed to meet at the jetty at five a.m. the next day.

'What's the boatman called?' I enquired.

'Jack...Jack Daniels,' came the reply.

I raised an eyebrow.

'Like the whiskey,' came the confirmatory riposte.

'And he knows the island?' I persisted, keen to confirm that the credentials of a man to whom we were about to entrust our maritime safety were in order.

The answer was reassuring. 'I should think so, he's the owner.'

Our pilot was early, a fact confirmed both by a swinging lantern just offshore, and a lusty if meandering singing voice. Jack Daniels had arrived. We cast off and sped across a mirrored, moonlit sea towards Kandriu.

On arrival, it quickly became clear that life here was simple and unspoilt. The island did not boast a wealth of resources, although its residents would certainly not want for fish, crabs or coconuts. I was slightly concerned that we didn't know the exact location of one of our key targets, the Yellow-bibbed Fruit-dove. As we hauled the boat up the silver sand of a perfect beach, I realized it was unlikely to be an issue. I reckoned it would take about half an hour to walk the entire perimeter, even if we stopped to check every group of trees.

The King of Kandriu dispatched one of his offspring to escort us and we set off, joined by an ever-growing cavalcade of island children who whispered reverentially behind us, helpfully pointing out any birds they saw. We told them the English name of each in turn, and they responded with the local names. We had no problem finding Ebony Myzomelas, tiny dark sunbirds whose song rang from every palm. Halfway round the island we surprised a Melanesian Megapode that scuttered away, its sturdy heels kicking up a spray of sand as it made off. On the northern shore we watched a Beach Kingfisher tearing the legs off a crab it had caught. Only the Yellow-bibbed Fruit-dove eluded us. Until that is, we sat at Jack's table enjoying Mrs. Daniels' excellent carrot cake washed down by the best cup of tea I had tasted in weeks, when a resplendent male dropped in. A more soberly dressed female soon arrived, and our haul of small island specialists was complete.

We spent a happy hour drifting on our backs in gin-clear waters, followed by a spot of itinerant beachcombing looking for conch shells, squeezing sand between our toes, intoxicated by the ozone. We strolled to the end of the sandspit, admiring the Second World War machine-guns still trained menacingly on the island, thrusting out from the rusting hull of a reef-wrecked gunboat. Time slowed.

At length, our idyllic hiatus over, Jack asked whether we would mind the island ladies joining us on our trip back to Manus; since we were paying for the fuel they wanted to take advantage of this rare opportunity to sell their smoked eels and fresh-caught tuna, and to go shopping on the mainland. I toyed with the idea of warning them that if they were planning to stock up on deodorant their luck was out, but thought better of it. We indicated our assent, and our party prepared for the off. The afternoon wind had freshened, whipping up a few white caps, but our progress was steady enough until without warning the engine started to splutter. The boat tugged backwards with every cough, until after one last paroxysm, the outboard died altogether.

'Ah,' said Jack, in an understated, nonchalant tone, 'problem.'

The ladies sighed. We turned in unison, to see his singular figure crouched in the stern, holding aloft the fuel pipe. A solitary drip of petrol clung to the tip, before splashing dolefully onto the deck.

I have managed sales teams for a number of years. When interviewing prospective candidates, I always look for what I term 'Labrador tendencies.' Labradors (gods in canine form) are endlessly enthusiastic. At the end of a Labrador's life, one gently strokes that faithful brow, quietly explaining that a trip to the vet is unavoidable, and that the dog's existence will sadly be brought to an end. The dog will greet this news with a vigorous wag of the tail that will set the whole body in motion, and a boisterous grin that seems to say, 'fabulous news! How will I be killed? Can we go right away? This is great! I'll fetch the leash, you put the back seat of the car down and we'll be there in a jiffy!' Labrador tendencies; unlimited enthusiasm in the darkest hour.

In my finest moments I have occasionally exhibited such traits, and if ever there was a moment for some energetic, despair-crushing *joie de vivre*, this was it. I glanced round the boat and noticed a loose gangplank. I tested it with the heel of my trainer, and it gave slightly. I beamed what I hoped was a winning smile in the direction of our unflappable captain.

'Jack, can I tear off a bit of your boat?' Jack broke off from attempting to wring the last few drops of fuel from the canister.

'Sure,' he said with a grin, displaying an entire graveyard of tombstone teeth.

Andy and I tugged at the timber, and appropriated a slat each. We angled them over the side and began to paddle.

The planks were rather narrow, and the boat rather heavy, but we were gratified to sense an almost imperceptible forward movement. A few strokes more and we were definitely making headway. Our luck was in, the tide was out, and our labours were thus assisted by a gentle push from the sea itself, washing us shorewards. The sun burned pitilessly down on our heads and our progress was painfully slow, but after an hour or so of thirsty work we could make out the jetty ahead. I tested the depth of the water below and found that we were above a long, broad submarine shelf jutting out from the beach. I motioned to Jack that I would jump out and tow us in.

'No!' he shouted, a note of alarm in his voice, 'sting-fish!'

I clambered back down from the gunwale and allowed myself to be educated about the poisonous flatfish which lurked in these waters, and which would surely pierce my bare soles with their barbed, toxic spines.

We paddled on. Suddenly we were in the surf, and it took all of our combined strength to keep the prow pointed towards the beach to avoid being rolled over, but at last our trusty craft nudged against terra firma. Andy jumped ashore and tied us firmly to the jetty. We had made it. Celebrations all round, and a bout of giggling and chatter from the ladies in the stern. Jack continued to smile, insouciance personified, as though our plight had been an everyday occurrence. Given that this was Manus, I suppose that may well have been the case. We said our farewells, and moments later I collapsed onto my bed in our room. We channel-hopped in search of Rugby League. The Grand Final loomed, a head-to-head between the slippery Parramatta Eels and the turbulent Melbourne Storm at the ANZ Stadium. We were going to need a few beers.

To slake the thirst we had worked up on the ocean, we wandered over to the hotel bar and were promptly invited to join the only other resident, a gentleman named Gerhard, originally from Hamburg. By way of polite conversation he announced in an accent that appeared largely unscathed by his forty years on Manus that fifty percent of German schoolchildren believed Hitler was right, but had executed his plans poorly. I smiled weakly and changed the subject.

'You live here alone?'

'No, I have three wives and six children.'

Andy tried again, hunting for safe ground. 'So what do you do for a living on Manus?'

Gerhard trained his piercing blue eyes upon us. 'I run a logging concession.'

We drained our beers and excused ourselves, sidling off to complete the urgent chores I'd just remembered we'd left unfinished.

We absconded to a beach shack selling beer, where we bumped into a slightly dishevelled Aaron. He had clearly already spent quite a few of our pitta-tourist dollars during the afternoon. We sat swigging South Pacific beers (theme song presumably: *there is nothing like an ale...nothing in the world...*) nodding sagely as Aaron pointed out, two or three times, that by drinking here we were saving two *kina* per can compared to the hotel prices. When we made to leave, Aaron insisted on arranging for the local police to drive us the hundred metres to the hotel. We climbed aboard the pick-up, shook hands, and were just about to ask about the crime figures when we arrived at our destination. We strolled back to our room, cracked open a couple of beers and settled in to watch the game.

'And so ends another run-of-the-mill day on Manus,' Andy sighed with a conspiratorial wink.

Our strange days on the island were drawing to a close. The mission clock was ticking, and ideally I needed to stop time in its tracks. Crossing the International Date Line seemed like it might help, but it lay too far east to be of any use in pitta terms. Our only option was to find a place where time might stand still. The Solomon Islands looked like they might just fit the bill.

Chapter 18

Adrift in Time. The Solomon Islands

We flew towards the last recorded home of the Black-faced Pitta, Santa Isabel, the least developed of the Solomon Islands. Our flights puddle-jumped from Manus to Lae, Lae to Port Moresby, Port Moresby to Honiara, and finally Honiara to Santa Isabel. It seemed a long way round when a day's sea crossing, had such a service existed, would have done the job, but such is the way with airlines. We spent a few happy hours in Guadalcanal. The dusty interior of the domestic terminal was enhanced by the many examples of sharp-edged, Day-Glo, graffiti-influenced local art that adorned the walls. Most involved lizards, fish and flowers arranged in a series of geometrical patterns. Amongst them was a more subdued poster announcing the upcoming national population census. The campaign slogan, written in local pidgin, was *Kaont im Everiwan*. We shared the flight to Honiara with a large group of Samoans, whose relatives' nose-rubbing and tears prior to departure were on an epic scale. The Governor General of New Zealand was also aboard, bound for Guadalcanal on a diplomatic mission. He was surrounded by stern lady policewomen, identifiable by their braid epaulettes and severe, scraped-back hairdo's. We reached our mutual destination in the middle of a rainstorm, and watched from the airplane steps as log-drummers and grass-skirted, dancing warriors welcomed the dignitaries, who cowered under enormous rainbow umbrellas.

Leaving Honiara, we had been warned that the previous day's flight had been cancelled due to a waterlogged airfield. A hurried discussion with our fellow passengers, a group of Catholic missionaries on their annual visit to help develop clean water and sanitation systems, confirmed that today's flight would indeed go. The weather was visibly improving as we flew high over The Solomon archipelago, and as we approached Santa Isabel, sunlight flooded through the rain clouds, marbling the surface of the sea like a blanket of pearls. Santa Isabel's airport lay just offshore, squeezed onto a tiny, forested islet named Fera. We swung in to land over a beautiful horseshoe of coral, one wing tip skimming the surface of the ocean. Ahead I could discern the grass airstrip, a narrow

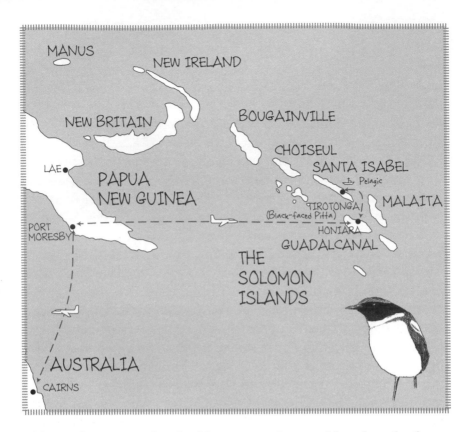

ribbon of green sandwiched between a deserted beach and a forest of waving palms. We bumped to a halt, and the door clanked open. Islanders were scattered across the airfield, and from amidst the throng a stout, genial figure emerged. It was our contact, William Manehage, who had come to escort us across the Maringe Lagoon to Buala, the capital of Isabel Province, and up to the mountain village of Tirotonga.

After a brief stop to purchase provisions, we fought our way up the steep, muddy trails to the village, William, belying his seniority, skipping ahead of us without even breaking sweat, pausing now and then to ensure that his guests were still struggling along in the vanguard. At length we caught sight of the gable end of the village church, perched delicately on the seaward edge of the Tirotonga escarpment. Ethereal, angelic voices drifted towards us through the mist, a perfect blend of Polynesian and Anglican influences, evocative simultaneously of the sang-froid of the English Home Counties and the lush tropicality of the Pacific Islands. The effect was mesmeric, and we stopped to catch our breath and enjoy the music, surveying the environs of the tranquil village. The Solomons' slogan, *Adrift in Time* seemed delightfully apposite.

Tirotonga, home to a hundred or so souls, has been constructed on a tiny plateau, wedged into the mountain like a dinner-plate thrust into an anthill. The school, church and houses have all been constructed using materials carried by hand up from the coast, a feat that in our exhausted state we were barely able to comprehend. It is a true community, populated by the kind of close-knit families where grandparents look after their daughters' babies while the younger women go out to work, often commuting down to Buala on a daily basis. Life in the village is relaxed and relatively serene, pervaded by an almost universal harmony. Although lacking many basic commodities, it was clear that the Isabellians were a friendly and happy people, and we were welcomed by all.

William showed us to our rooms and introduced us to the rest of the family: son Mark who would guide us through the maze of forest trails; Veronica, William's wife who would endeavour to feed us until we burst; her daughter Mavis; and her naughty but captivating little girl Marister, who giggled ceaselessly through the gap where her front teeth should have been. After dinner we sat on the balcony and talked, William and Veronica peppering us with a string of questions. Did I live near the Queen of England? Had I been to her house? How many Red Indians were there in England? None? How many Eskimos then? We drank copious amounts of tea and endeavoured to explain countries of the world to a family who did not possess an atlas, a process during which I discovered just how difficult it is to describe a concept like 'America' from first principles.

In return, we were educated regarding Isabel's matriarchal system, in which land is owned by the women in the family and passed down to female relatives through the generations. We discovered that no-one in the village locked their doors, because there was no crime to speak of. William talked us through the logic of planting the fragrant, waxy-leaved trees that wafted waves of lemon verbena past our noses. Not only did they smell good, he noted earnestly, but they also kept the devil away. We familiarized ourselves with the three Isabellian measures of distance: *not far* means a ten to twenty minute walk, *quite far* means an hour or two, and *far* means you'll be sleeping in the forest. By eight-thirty we were in our bunks, and inspired by the statuary I had seen in Honiara, I dreamed of eagle-beaked Spirit Gods with human torsos and backward-facing feet.

Before dawn, Mark returned as arranged to escort us up into the hill forest. Thanks to regular torrential downpours the trails were treacherous. Progress was slow, not least because, since my baggage was still unaccounted for, I was climbing in a pair of training shoes whose soles were so smooth they would not have marked a squash court. I slipped and slithered my way upwards, liberally coating my only pair of trousers in liquid mud.

It had been exceedingly difficult to obtain information on the last known whereabouts of the Black-faced Pitta. I had managed to discover that it had formerly lived on Choiseul, an island in the northern Solomons, and on the neighbouring Papuan island of Bougainville. However, Bougainville had been unsafe and closed to outsiders for years, and there were no recent records of the pitta there, although it had clearly once been common on the island; at least forty specimens had been collected there prior to the late 1930s. Expeditions looking for the birds on both Choiseul and Bougainville during the 1990s had come up empty-handed, and the bird had not been seen at all between 1938 and 1994 when it was rediscovered on Santa Isabel. The species is undoubtedly rare, and BirdLife International estimates the number of remaining pairs at less than one thousand; a tiny relict population. Following e-mails from two eminent bird-tour leaders, Guy Dutson and Mark van Beirs, I knew that the bird had definitely been seen on Isabel as recently as 2006, though the following year a visiting group had only heard the pittas, which had stubbornly remained invisible in the dense forests above Tirotonga.

Our plan was to work the habitat above the village, focussing on primary forest and secondary re-growth within the patchwork of 'gardens', (mostly failed agricultural plots). We would concentrate our search efforts between four hundred and six hundred metres above sea level, since this was the known altitudinal range of the species. Guy had warned us in advance that Black-faced Pitta was devilishly hard to see, perhaps more so than any other member of a genus which was already hardly renowned for its accommodating nature, and we entered the cool of the forest knowing that we were up against it.

In all, we spent some ten hours in the field that first day. At dawn a little way above the village, we heard the pitta call briefly, a harsh, scratchy, tuneless pair of rising whistles. We sat on the trail in silence, waiting for a glimpse, but the bird soon stopped calling and would not come within range. We hacked a rudimentary trail a few yards into the chaotic vegetation and sat in cover, but the massed tangle of thickets was so solid that the bird would have had to perch on our knees in order for us to see it. We tried more distant patches of forest, and again heard calling birds, but by the end of a frustrating morning session we had succeeded only in logging three separate territories, each of which supported an occasionally vocal but singularly unhelpful pitta. The afternoon unfolded along similar lines. We hauled ourselves up impossible slopes, slid down worryingly steep mud banks, but as dusk fell, had little to show for our efforts.

The next day produced more of the same. We'd find suitable habitat, but where a pitta proved to be present, it always managed to stay hidden. We employed our finest fieldcraft, ran through the full repertoire of our 'men of the forest' moves, but the birds effortlessly outwitted us. We were getting nowhere.

By day three we were fatigued and somewhat dispirited. I had managed to sneak only a momentary 'untickable' glimpse of a bird, and Andy had yet to set eyes on so much as a tail-feather. This exact doomsday scenario had played itself out in my head countless times over the previous months, and I was running out of new ideas we could employ to try to out-think this craftiest of pittas. We had tried all of the spots in which Willam's son Mark had previously heard pitta calls. We had enlisted the help of Samson, the village hunter, but although he was a true 'man of the woods' he too had proved unable to help us conquer our goal. On the morning of the fourth day I asked him in my best pidgin whether the birds had become scarce because the locals ate them.

'Nobody eat im,' came the reply, and then with a grin, the reason; 'nobody find im.' Stupid bloody question really.

Along the trail, we met a distant relative of the Manehages, and in the ensuing conversation it became clear that he had recently heard a pitta in an area of the forest we had not yet tried. I played the pitta's call on my iPod, and he nodded vigorously. Had we perhaps been thrown a lifeline? It was worth a look, and Mark confirmed the details of the location. We wearily clambered up yet another near-vertical incline, our muscles screaming in protest. We crested the narrow saddle at the top and looked down into a new valley, cloaked in forest. It looked perfect.

After a perilous descent, we found a slightly more open area of forest to our right. Better still, the trail on which we sat skirted the edge of the valley, meaning that we were relatively high up, always an advantage in a skirmish. By now there was no doubt in my mind that this was a war, and I was determined that we would have our kill. I cued up the pitta call and fired.

'Hweup-hhweeur.'

The tremulous clarion call rang out across the valley, and echoed back off the cliff opposite us before dwindling into silence. We waited, but there was no answer. I tried another single phrase, and this time as we held our breath, crossed our fingers and sent up a silent prayer, there was a response. Eyebrows were raised. Mark grinned. Samson's rapier-like gaze seared a trail into the gloom. Andy nudged my elbow, and I followed his line of sight to the forest floor. Something was moving. I raised my binoculars and scanned. There was no mistake. Something was perched on a twig ten metres in front of us, wholly obscured within the thicket. We could not see the source of the movement, but the twitching of the sprig continued with agonizing regularity. Suddenly there was a blur of colour as a bird shot across the valley and disappeared into the darkest possible recess on the far side. We exchanged glances; everyone knew what it was but no-one dared to say it.

Ten minutes elapsed, but the bird did not reappear. I decided to go for broke and risk one more burst of audio. Instantly there was a response, and we caught a movement for a fraction of a second as the bird abandoned the lower reaches of the forest and shot into the mid-canopy, still heavily obscured. It called again, and following a brief but frantic triangulation, we figured out where it must be. We scanned again, our searchlight sweeping left and right for the missing prisoner. And then at last, an alien colour scheme, an out of place shape, something feathered not leafy, and I was staring into the eye of a Black-faced Pitta. The bird called, shivering slightly with the effort. I eased my camera into position and pressed the shutter. It clicked reassuringly. Again and again I fired, taking shot after shot in the hope that even at this range, one would be pin-sharp and sufficiently illuminated, that I would find an angle from which the bird's whole head could be seen. Even now, the evanescent creature remained barely visible, motionless, wary, fragile. I held my breath as I took another picture, worried that the camera would move, and that if I exhaled in the bird's direction it might evaporate before my very eyes, blown apart like a child dispersing seeds from a dandelion head.

I pieced together the image, burning it into my memory. I knew that the birds here should be of the nominate race, and sure enough this individual showed the requisite rich chestnut crown and deep ochre breast and belly. The throat was white, with a narrow, pale band radiating out around the back of the neck. The back, dark olive-green, blended perfectly with the surrounding leaves, adding to the bird's shimmering, chimerical mystique. The wing coverts added the only splash of vivid colour, a patch of the palest shining blue, chromatic purity defined, a severed butterfly wing of concentrated light. The panel shone with the lustre of abalone, glowed with the intensity of a Peacock's ocelli. At that moment, it was without doubt, the most beautiful thing I had ever seen. A God made flesh and feathers had revealed himself, and life would never be the same again.

With a dismissive flick of a wing the bird was gone, back to its twilight netherworld of subterfuge and shadow play. We waited for a few more minutes, but it was clear the bird would not return. All hell broke loose on the trail. Andy's grin threatened to split his head in two. I attempted the usual miniature jig and promptly fell over. Mark and Samson laughed like drains, infected by our joy. We crowded around my camera's viewfinder, excited as schoolboys jostling for prime position over a National Geographic piece on African natives promising that first heady whiff of nudity. To my relief, the bird was visible and sharp, the colours readily discernable. At medium range and with such an uncooperative subject it was not going to win a Pulitzer Prize any time soon, but nonetheless it was a coup; the first picture of a Black-faced Pitta ever captured in the field.

We waltzed back to Tirotonga, floating on air, our strained sinews and mauled muscles suddenly forgotten. Half of the village pitched up to look at the photos of a bird they had heard so often but had never seen. It had been a great day, and only the total lack of intoxicants with which to toast our success dampened the party mood.

At around eight o'clock, we saw a lone figure struggling across the plateau. It was William, newly returned from an education conference on Fera. He was laden down with bags, and our field-honed auditory senses indicated that one of the bags was clinking gently with every step. He had stopped off in Buala to buy beer, chocolate biscuits AND cheesy puffs. What a man. I think he was rather shocked by our collective embraces. The time-honoured stereotype of the British as a cold, reserved race bit the dust.

Our key goal achieved, Andy and I now set about documenting Santa Isabel's bird life as fully as the remaining time allowed. We ventured out at night with Mark and Samson and spotlighted Solomons Hawk-Owls. We found the newly described Solomon Islands Frogmouth too, a beast of a night bird with a mouth so wide, no insect within a mile of Tirotonga would be safe. We tramped around the trails, mapping the calling pittas in an attempt to log real data that might help establish a more accurate estimation of the total population size. Along the way we slowly picked off the less common birds: beetle-black Steel-blue Flycatchers, anxious Chestnut-bellied Monarchs, charcoal-grey Melanesian and Solomons Cuckooshrikes, and after hours of neck-breaking scanning of the tree-tops, good views of the impossibly tiny Finsch's Pygmy-parrot. During the heat of the day we sat in a vegetable patch overlooking a clearing above the village, and were rewarded with stunning views of the colossal Sanford's Sea-eagle. An hour later we were privileged to witness two passes by a single, tatty Imitator Sparrowhawk, a globally endangered species about which little is known.

On our last full day we trekked up to higher forest, finding a White-throated Pigeon and gorgeous Superb Fruit-doves, but the star of the show was discovered lurking in the very highest branches of an enormous broad-leafed tree. Smooth of skin and sluggish of movement, this was clearly no bird; we guessed it had to be some kind of reptile. Mark and Samson became visibly excited, and a whispered conference in indecipherable pidgin followed. I knew what was to come, protein being in short supply on Isabel. We reluctantly agreed that they could catch the animal. The question was, how? Samson grinned, exposing a mouthful of betel-stained teeth, and leapt onto the lowest branch. Within minutes he was up in the crown, and before we knew it was standing beside us once more, maintaining a firm grip just behind the animal's formidable jaw.

The creature was a Prehensile-tailed Skink, a half-metre long relative of the lizards, striped cream and brown and with a powerful, box-square jaw. I asked Samson whether the beast bit, and he gestured that it was quite capable of snipping off a human thumb. I wanted to know how he'd reached the ground with all digits intact. He demonstrated how to hold the head while tucking the tail in a loop around the hand, like the strap of a handbag. But how, thus handicapped by his prize, had he climbed back down? He looked puzzled and gestured to his other hand. Well how stupid of me. Clearly one free hand was all that was needed to clamber back down through thirty metres of swaying forest carrying a reptile perfectly capable of cutting short a promising career as an instrumentalist.

Mark dispatched the creature quickly and humanely, and we baked it in a banana leaf. Andy and I were offered a taste of the meat, and we felt honour-bound to accept. As tradition dictates, it tasted like chicken. In a bout of supreme selflessness, we insisted that Samson as the victorious captor keep the intestines all for himself.

'You know,' Mark said as we wheedled tiny shards of dark, stringy meat from between the carcass's miniscule ribs, 'you are probably the first white men ever to eat this animal.' *And we'll probably be the last,* I thought to myself. Dessert was more palatable; a pineapple cut from the side of the trail, washed in the river and quartered with a machete.

Our last day on Isabel dawned, and the view from the plateau over the coral atoll far below us was simply stunning. The Catholic missionaries with whom we had shared the flight out reappeared, and I stood in as official photographer. We were finally able to listen to the finished version of the hymns we had heard being practiced daily, now accompanied by peals of thunder overhead. (I visualized an MC introducing the members of the band. *Ladeez and gennelmen, please welcome tonight's special guest...on timpani: God!*) After a prolonged set of farewells, we set off back down to Buala, where Andy had arranged one last raid on Isabel's biodiversity. We were going on a pelagic.

A pelagic, as the name suggests, involves taking a boat out to sea. Once you get out to a likely looking spot (preferably strategically located over an upwelling current) you simply drop anchor, throw bits of seabird-friendly food over the side, and wait for things to start hopping. We'd explained to William that we needed to get a couple of miles offshore, and despite retaining a healthy skepticism, he had found us a boat and done his level best to obtain the bucket of fish guts we had requested. Sadly for us, Isabellian fishermen gut their fish while sailing back to port, so no offal was to be had in the whole of Christendom. We settled for a kilo of whole fish, all we could afford, and loaded it into the boat, planning to use it to make a DIY version of that most vital ingredient of any successful pelagic trip, chum.

We outlined the plan to William and Mark. First, we would mash the fish up. Then, add a bottle of cooking oil. Lastly, we'd mix in a few pieces of popcorn to aid flotation. Popcorn, it transpired, had not yet made it to Isabel, so we improvised with a few bags of cheesy puffs. The resulting mixture looked and smelled revolting. Perfect. We found a school of tuna out beyond the bay, thrashing about in an attempt to avoid an attacking shark just below them. The frenzy had already attracted a number of seabirds, including Black Noddies, Lesser Frigatebirds and Bridled Terns. However, we had set our hearts on finding the true deep-water pelagic specialists: shearwaters, storm-petrels, perhaps an albatross or two. Andy scooped handfuls of the chum over the stern (watched with some concern by William, who now appeared fully convinced of our insanity) and we waited. Then we waited some more. We explained that certain seabird species could smell the active ingredient in fish blood many miles away, but that it might take a little time for them to arrive. William nodded wearily.

Our seabirds never arrived. At one point a Wedge-tailed Shearwater did fly straight towards the boat, and we cheered at the sight, insubstantial but empirical proof of our wisdom. The shearwater however maintained its bearing and disappeared over the far horizon, completely ignoring our mouth-watering dead-fish-and-cheesy-puff buffet. In the end we admitted defeat, and adjourned to Fera airport's departure lounge. Actually 'departure beach' would be a more accurate description. Where else would one wait, sipping beers bought from Brian's Bottleshop (a shack at the far end of the strip) while keeping an eye out for *the SolAir guy?*

Our check-in monitor duly arrived, borne by a barely-seaworthy outrigger, and we ambled over to the check-in shack, carefully skirting the portions of the corrugated iron roof that hung creaking mournfully in the afternoon breeze. After passengers and belongings had been weighed, we strolled up the airstrip and, waved off by a hundred cheery islanders, boarded the plane.

As Solomon Airlines H4-SID took off, scattering Whimbrels and Pacific Golden Plovers in its wake, I realized I would miss Isabel, with its laid-back attitude to life, its suspicion of technology, its happy sense of community. *Adrift in time* maybe, but when no-one owns a watch, 'Solomons Time' is accurate enough.

We were forced to transit once again through Honiara, this time bumping into the Papuan Prime Minister, immaculate in a suit, tie and sarong. The police band played, stamping up and down the airfield in the blistering heat. The impact of their precise manoeuvres was somewhat blunted however, by the necessity to compete against a local warrior group in full war paint tooting on pan pipes and banging wood blocks. Imagine the Fun Boy Three staging an impromptu jam with The Household Cavalry Marching Band, collectively winging it through *El Condor Pasa,* and you have the effect. The tribute over, the local bigwigs escorted the PM to the terminal building, only to find it firmly locked. A minion was despatched to find the key. A few moments later he returned. With the wrong key. Two more underlings sprinted off to find the head janitor, who eventually appeared brandishing the correct key just in time to meet a junior member of the ground staff unlocking the door from the inside. The PM swept into the lounge, where he encountered a large group of Australian tourists waiting for their flight home. Mistaking them for a part of the extended reception committee, he enthusiastically pumped the baffled holidaymakers' hands, exchanging pleasantries as he went. The local VIPs hovered nervously behind him, too horror-struck to intervene.

On the long flight back to London, I had to pinch myself to check that the thirtieth pitta really was firmly chalked up on the board. Not only had I succeeded in getting to the big 'three-oh', but one of the world's most difficult pitta species had safely been put to bed. Even more critically, it was one of the most geographically remote species, rendering a return trip (expensive in terms of both time and money) unnecessary. Since by this stage of the race I didn't have a lot of either, I was mightily relieved to have added Black-faced Pitta to the list. Having successfully tracked down the pitta, we had joined an exclusive club whose members probably numbered no more than forty, a fitting end for a journey along the path less travelled. Now, home beckoned. After two gruelling months, countless flights, a bout of dysentery and a slew of long days in the field, I needed to recharge my batteries. After three weeks without luggage I was also in dire need of clean socks. I would have a few days to sleep, feed up, and remind her indoors what I looked like. Refreshed and renewed, it would then be time to hit the road again. I prepared myself for a second passage to India.

Chapter 19

A Rare Bird Indeed. Sri Lanka

It promised to be a rather different kind of trip. My long-suffering girlfriend had deigned to join me, and we planned ten days of sightseeing and as much birding as I could sneak into the itinerary. We would stay in comfortable hotels, eat proper food at sensible hours in clean establishments. There would be time enough to take in a few Hindu temples, even, shockingly, to relax on the beach. I consoled myself with the thought that the latter might at least produce the odd seabird sighting.

The main reason for coming to Sri Lanka was, inevitably, pitta-related. Indian Pitta breeds in forests across northern central India, but it is a migrant. As the northern days start to shorten, birds head south to winter in the continent's lower half. I knew that for a pitta they were relatively confiding, and that they vocalized year-round. Their habit of calling morning and evening on the wintering grounds has earned them a Tamil name that translates as *Six O'Clock Bird.* They should be easy enough to find.

Our first stop was Kandy's famous Temple of the Tooth, the focal point of Buddhism on the island. We were shown around by a guide who was strikingly deficient himself in the dental department. We stood beneath the stuffed body of the temple's famous tusker, a ceremonial beast of truly elephantine proportions, which until its death in 1988 had featured in every procession since being captured as a youngster in 1925. His replacement, our guide advised, was 'a rather naughty elephant.' When I enquired how this naughtiness manifested itself, the response was short and to the point.

'He's killed three monks already.'

We strolled through gold and alabaster halls, admiring the collection of Buddhas donated by monasteries around the world. The scent of sandalwood drifted through the shrine as we bought purple and yellow water lilies to present as an offering to the gods, placing them amongst mounds of creamy Frangipani and scarlet Hibiscus. Disappointingly, there was no sign of The Tooth itself, now shown only once in every three years at special events.

SRI LANKA

KANDY

NUWARA ELIYA
(Indian Pitta)

KITHULGALA
(Serendib Scops-owl)

COLOMBO

SINHARAJA

UNAWATUNA
(Sandcastle incident)

Once satiated with culture, our driver Sunil piloted us up through the plantations towards the hill town of Nuwara Eliya, stopping off *en route* at the Blue Field Tea Factory. On the way we passed hundreds of 'Plantation Tamil' tea pickers, each figure bent double, tossing showers of tiny leaves over their heads into collecting baskets. Nuwara Eliya was suffocated in low grey cloud, the cold air clammy, the atmosphere curiously Caledonian. I half expected to hear the skirl of bagpipes. We swished past the near-derelict racecourse, the state of the track making me doubt whether any nag had ever got all the way round without breaking a leg. A group of Shetland ponies waited in vain for foreign-devil hill-trekkers, shivering beneath the pine trees, the rain dripping from their lank, sodden manes. The local market was filled with stringy-legged soft toys and cheap, damp woollens, the street hawkers waving inflatable pink rabbits to attract the punters.

Trekking and shopping were not on our itinerary however. We had come to Sri Lanka's highest town to look for Indian Pitta, whose reputation for being as much of a tart as its Australian Rainbow cousin preceded it. I covered my face as we risked our lives crossing the bus station tarmac that lay between us and a favoured haunt. Engines were revved pointlessly, the air thick with sticky, black diesel fumes. It was a relief to escape into the relatively civilised confines of Victoria Park, a reliable stakeout for our bird. I found a shady spot with sufficient vegetation, played two seconds of tape, and an Indian Pitta flew in above my head. Although aesthetically the pitta was pleasing enough, with its seductive black eye make-up, delicate peach breast and aquamarine rump, the thrill of the chase was conspicuously absent. It was all a little too easy. Game over, I fired off a couple of photos, before we squelched back to the hotel for afternoon tea. Thirty-one down, one to go.

The Grand Hotel lived up to its name, though the grandeur was a little antiquated; cherry wood panels buffed by a thousand dusters to a dull glow, cut-glass chandeliers tinkling gently above our head, a monstrous mahogany piano squatting in one corner of the faded drawing room. Faint strains of *Feelings* and *If You Were the Only Girl in the World* drifted through the hallowed halls. Food dominated proceedings; afternoon tea was followed inexorably by dinner, an immense buffet featuring a hundred varieties of curry followed by a classy chocolate swan swimming in a pool of mint cream. Our dining experience was enlivened by a group of Japanese tourists murdering Olivia Newton-John's *Tak me Home, Kanty Lowds*, their impromptu karaoke foray startling the solo instrumentalist who seemed ill-prepared for a mass stage invasion.

We drove west to Kithulgala, famed as the construction site of the bridge that formed *The Bridge over the River Kwai's* celluloid centrepiece. (In fact the bridge spanned the Kelani River, but marketing men must have their way.) We spent two days in the forest beyond the bridge, finally connecting with the more difficult endemics: a decorous Sri Lanka Magpie, an elusive though vocal Chestnut-backed Owlet, and a clod-hopping Green-billed Coucal. Best of all though was a Serendib Scops-owl, a maddened midget that scowled at our intrusion into its daytime roost beneath a banana leaf. It's an owl that is as beautiful as it is diminutive, with its orange-washed head and peach-suffused breast. The tiny predator perched motionless, as if carved from the very tree on which it stood, the arrowheads on the underparts contributing to a highly effective camouflage.

While sleuthing out Kithulgala's special birds, we happened across another forest resident. I must admit I am not an ardent fan of squirrels, even one as imposing as the Sri Lankan Giant Squirrel. Essentially arboreal rodents, yellow of tooth and sharp of claw, they squeak and chitter from hidden perches in a confusingly avian manner, thus wasting hours of birders' time. (Not to mention the omni-present danger that they'll pinch your nuts.) Black and cream with a pink, bulbous drinker's nose, this particularly impressive specimen of squirelhood sprawled languorously in the treetops, waiting for the pubs to open.

After a brief visit to the local police station, curiously uninhabited by the constabulary but satisfyingly occupied instead by a small group of Pompadour Green-pigeons, it was time to continue our migration south, this time to Sinharaja, Sri Lanka's premier national park. The last of the island's endemic birds trickled in, the highlights a snoozing Sri Lanka Frogmouth, and a Sri Lanka Scaly Thrush lurking furtively in a dank bower. On the final morning a clamber up the hill beside the reserve's approach road yielded the most difficult bird of all, a Sri Lanka Spurfowl that behaved in a highly anti-social fashion, creeping through the bamboo and doing its level best to avoid detection. A very satisfying conclusion.

Now all that remained was to hit the coast and sprawl like giant squirrels on the beach, until the agonizing daily dilemmas of where to have lunch and whether it could decently be considered beer o'clock taxed our sun-addled minds. Sri Lanka's south coast was badly hit by the 2005 tsunami, yet already the reconstruction had restored many of the coastal villages to something approaching their original condition. As we drove through one of the south coast's larger towns, Galle, an immense banner swung into view. Painted in the colours of the Sri Lankan national flag, it bore but a single word, writ large: *REBORN*. Driving east, we passed shacks nailed together with driftwood, single-storey homes with skeletons of future upper rooms creaking gently in the breeze. Palm trees twisted in the wind, bent over at crazy angles yet defiantly surviving. We passed a museum built by tsunami survivors. Someone had painted a message on the front of the building. 'We love the beautiful sea. It's a wonderful gift of nature.' A humbling experience.

There would, it had been agreed with my partner, be no bird-watching at all during our seaside sojourn. Our days would be filled with temple visits, colonial Dutch fort admiration and indolent hours whiled away on the sand. In the evenings we would forgo the usual night-birding, instead sipping cocktails under the stars.

After a few instructive lounging lessons I began to get the hang of it, only weakening on the odd occasion when distant seabirds drifted by offshore. One of two possible noddy species lingered over a distant outcrop, and I wondered if tomorrow I could get away with sneaking my 'scope down to the beach in my rucksack. For the first time in the whole mission, I began to unwind. I slept way past dawn, pottered down to breakfast and took my own sweet time chewing toast and drinking tea. I expressed wonder at items of local jewellery when instructed so to do, and selected the prettier sarong when asked to decide between two potential purchases. I participated in choosing the most agreeable reggae-soaked bar, and helped pick out the richest butterfish curry, the juiciest king prawns, the most fragrant coconut sambal. I ventured into spice markets, emerging triumphant with wraps of cloves, cardamoms, cinnamon and saffron. I hailed tuk-tuks, photographed stilt fishermen, and pretended to understand the finer points of the local religion. Even though I have never really got to grips with the rules of cricket.

In more contemplative moments however, I continued to mull over my imminent future for two different reasons. Firstly, there was still one pitta left to secure, and I knew that success was far from guaranteed. Secondly, I had brought my other half to Sri Lanka with a specific aim in mind.

We'd returned to the shore for a late swim and to catch the last of the sun's rays before beachcombing our way to our favourite restaurant. Unable to lie comatose on the beach having exhausted my supply of trashy novels, I was building an architecturally ambitious sand-castle, ignoring the heckling from my girlfriend who despaired of my inability to keep still for more than a couple of minutes at a stretch. After half an hour's industry, my masterpiece was complete, and I summoned her to admire my handiwork.

'Must I?' she called peevishly from her sun-lounger.

'I think you should', I said, 'I'm rather proud of my efforts.'

With a heavy sigh my mate interrupted her repose, wandered over, and stood next to the cunningly fashioned southwestern turret. She stared open-mouthed at my creation. I couldn't blame her. I was rather proud of the decorative work myself, particularly the message I had spelled out in seaweed in the central courtyard. It consisted of just two words, neatly formed, simple and to the point. *Marry Me.*

It seemed the noble course of action. I had been supported to the hilt in my lunatic endeavour, with barely an objection raised over my determination to sever the ties that bound me to my career. The fact that I appeared intent on setting fire to a CV that had taken twenty years to build passed without comment. Encouraged to indulge my most heart-felt passion, and despite the many months of enforced separation that realizing my dream had entailed, I had scarcely encountered a word of protest. It was time to cement our relationship in a more timeless fashion. The question was, would my proposal be accepted?

The initial response was not quite what I had hoped for.

'Do you mean it?'

After fifteen years together, it was, on reflection, a fair enquiry. I nodded in confirmation, dropping to one knee and whipping out a sneakily purchased pink sapphire as proof of my intent. Still the answer did not come, and I grew worried that the tide would roll in and demonstrate all too graphically the impermanence of things. After what seemed like an eternity, the waves lapping at the ramparts were mingled with tears of assent, and as we kissed I knew I had succeeded in capturing the rarest and most beautiful creature of them all.

Chapter 20

And the First Shall Be Last. Zambia

All's fair, they say, in love and war. Having secured the affections of my true love, only one battle now remained; to find the thirty-second and last pitta.

I had planned to make Zambia my very first port of call back in February, but seasonal considerations and airline intransigence had conspired against me. And so it had come to pass that the first should be last, and only African Pitta now stood between me and pitta immortality.

Back in England, the days had grown short, and the nights were drawing in as the year shuffled to a close; time to head south. I crossed the concourse to board the train heading for London's Heathrow Airport one last time. It was mid-December, and by four-thirty in the afternoon it was already dark. A chill sleet angled down, cast into silver by the streetlights, arrowing into the pavements and sending commuters scurrying for cover. I weaved my way through the mass of bodies hurrying across Paddington Station. A thousand journeys were getting under way, but none, I thought to myself, were quite like mine. As the train lurched forward I felt a wave of *déjà vu* and a tingle of excitement. There was more than a hint of melancholy too, as I realized my grand adventure might be over in a matter of days. Just two more sardine sessions in a pressurized tin tube at thirty thousand feet, before I could burst out into the African sunshine, picking my way through the Miombo woodland to hopefully claim my prize. I was Lusaka-bound, shaking off the gloom of the English winter like a Labrador drying itself after retrieving a stick from a muddy river.

I'd been in touch with a fellow UK birder, Billy Rodger, and though we had not managed to synchronize our travel (Billy had left Zambia the day I arrived) he had promised to leave me notes detailing his exploits. After a long, dusty drive in a fantastically under-specified 2WD Ford Ka through Zambia's southern borderlands, I drew up at the Eagles Nest resort in Siavonga. Here one is as close as it's possible to get to Zimbabwe without actually being physically pressed up against Robert Mugabe or one of his henchmen. The Zambezi river

valley separates the two countries, and I was praying for success here on the northern side, since my only alternative was to venture over the border and plunge into Zim's troubled waters. As I dug out my stash of Zambian Kwacha to pay for my room and gratefully accepted a key, the lady at reception handed me an envelope.

'We have a message for you. From the other Englishman. He left this morning.'

Billy had been as good as his word. I frantically tore open the envelope and scanned the information within.

The first sentence read as follows: *Not good news I'm afraid. No sight nor sound of any pittas despite three dawn 'til dusk days of searching.* My heart sank. As I read through the rest of Billy's missive it became abundantly clear that the rains were late in coming this year. Since the pittas are wet season breeders, they had not yet

331

started to call. The simple fact was that if they were not calling, it was going to be a hell of a job to find them in the impenetrable thickets along Siavonga's river valleys. I had allowed nine days to find the birds, and feared that even this might not be enough if they remained silent. Having travelled for thirty-two hours to get here, it was a bitter pill to swallow.

I mooched around my lakeside chalet, immune to the seductive charms of the view. A weird, half-spider, half-scorpion beast scuttled across the wall until I knocked it down with a well-aimed shoe. I drank more rum-and-cokes than was wise, schemed, cursed and sulked. By seven in the evening I had decided this was simply a test of my resolve, and convinced myself that everything would work out if I remained confident and worked the territory carefully enough. I set the alarm for three a.m., crawled inside my mosquito net, and grabbed a few hours sleep.

I woke at two and assembled my armoury, mentally running through the kit-list as I did so. Binoculars and audio gear, check. Boots and sweat towel, check. Mosquito repellent, torch, maps, water, crackers, check. All present and correct. I drove back up the escarpment, heading east towards Lusaka, and was in position at the Mutulanganga river valley by three fifteen a.m.

I had recce'd the previous day, making sure I could find the path down to the river bed. However, what had seemed so easy the day before was a different proposition now in total darkness. The feeble light cast by my torch illuminated only a few scant metres in front of me, the bushes on either side remaining black as a raven's belly. An animal grunted somewhere up-river, and I stepped backwards and promptly fell over a tree root. I picked myself up and ventured along the river bed, steeling myself to push forward. I had walked perhaps thirty yards when I disturbed a roosting Trumpeter Hornbill, which exploded from its perch a metre or so above my head with a deafening clatter of wings and a screech like torn metal. I sat down in the sand, panting with fear, willing my racing heartbeat to slow. After a few minutes gathering my wits, I pushed on.

I slowly worked my way up-river, the soft, deep sand sapping my strength at every step. I passed smashed tree-trunks and trampled vegetation, and came upon a line of deep, round depressions in the sand, linking one side of the river to the other. *Elephants!* An enormous pile of dung confirmed my suspicions, but close examination revealed that it was far from fresh. Reassured, I pressed on. I stopped at intervals, willing the pitta to call. My advance research had taught me that African Pitta displays before dawn, vocalizing from high in the canopy. As it calls, it jumps vertically in the air, a movement remarkably similar to its Ugandan twin, the Green-breasted Pitta. If one called, it should be easy to locate. Pinpoint the sound, wait for the first glimmer of light, spot the movement, and *bingo*.

It was all so easy in theory. Here on the ground however, things were playing out rather differently. The birds were silent. I was alone in the darkness, staggering about in the African bush, my imagination running riot. Every rustle in the undergrowth was, I felt sure, a ravenous Leopard with a taste for ornithologist meat, licking his lips at the prospect of a feast. Every grunt from the thickets seemed to herald the imminent arrival of a rampaging herd of elephants, which would crush me beneath their mighty feet before picking me up and effortlessly smashing my skull against the nearest sturdy baobab. I rounded a corner, and jumped as a Chacma Baboon skittered noisily through the leaf-litter before loping across the ribbon of coarse-grained sand that stretched ahead of me. Frankly I was petrified, and although I knew every second closer to dawn meant my chances of locating a calling pitta had decreased, nevertheless daylight could not come soon enough.

Soon enough it did, and I breathed easier. Despite my qualms I had covered some distance, sadly without a squeak from a pitta. I walked another couple of kilometres, stopping now and then to bury myself in particularly enticing patches of riverine thicket in the hope of randomly bumping into a pitta going about its clandestine business. Nothing doing. By ten a.m. the African sun was burning the back of my neck. A heat haze obscured anything more than twenty metres away. I slogged my way along the river bed, ineffectually swatting at the crowd of flies that attended my every move and cursing the soft, shifting sand that sucked at my feet and slowed my progress.

By early afternoon I was ready to quit, and I sat down on a fallen tree to rest for a while. Squinting against the sun, I noticed an unfamiliar set of tracks ahead of me. I wandered over to investigate. There in the sand was the unmistakable print of a large cat. I spanned my hand across the paw-print. My outstretched thumb and little finger barely stretched from one side to the other.

Leopard.

I felt a few extra beads of sweat break out on my forehead. *An old print*, I told myself, *probably an animal crossing the bed months ago on the way to some distant hunting ground.* I checked the print again; well defined and apparently made in the recent past by a large, heavy carnivore. I followed the trail. More prints, lots of them, and not linear as I had hoped, but scattered all over the river bed for some considerable distance. The animal had been hunting here recently.

I took stock of my situation: I was alone. I stood perhaps four kilometres from the nearest road, and considerably further from the nearest human assistance. I liked to think I was in pretty good shape after a year of hill climbing, river-crossing and trail-walking, but running at any kind of speed along the sandy river bed was impossible. I was armed with a swingable pair of binoculars and a number of puny potential projectiles, all of which seemed likely to bounce off the muzzle of an advancing feline predator without causing appreciable damage. I weighed the evidence and reached what I felt was a logical conclusion. Leg it.

I covered the return distance to the road in rather less time than the outward journey had taken, despite regularly being thrown off balance by the need to cast nervous glances over my shoulder. I reached the sanctity of the road breathing heavily, plagued by the hornets and hoverflies that buzzed infuriatingly around my ears and flew into my mouth and up my nose. My shirt clung stickily to my chest, streams of sweat cascading down my flanks. I smelled of sour vinegar.

I guzzled water, and reflected that things could be worse. True, I had not had a sniff of the pitta. On the other hand, I was still alive, and had not had to say '*hello kitty*' to any unwelcome visitors. I resolved not to return to the killing ground. My searches henceforth would be in the opposite direction south of the road, and along the Mbendele river beds further to the east. I dozed for an hour in the car, before venturing nervously along the next river bed. I walked until after dark, but again, heard nothing resembling a displaying pitta. One day gone, and no sign of my quarry. Things did not look promising.

The next morning I again drove out of Siavonga in the wee hours, swerving to avoid Square-tailed and Pennant-winged Nightjars roosting on the warm tarmac. A Spotted Eagle-owl swooped in front of the car and perched up at the side of the road, fixing me with its custard-yellow eyes. By three thirty a.m. I had parked off the road at the second bridge, and was stumbling blindly up another river valley, my senses honed by the imminent demise my imagination insisted would befall me at any moment. By noon I was exhausted, and was no nearer achieving my goal. The afternoon was no better, events following the same depressingly familiar pattern. Days three and four unfolded in identical fashion, and by the end of the fourth day I was forced to consider my options.

The problem was, there weren't any terribly appealing ones. I was running out of ideas. I could continue stubbornly on the same course and hope for my luck to change. Or I could attempt once more to reach my only Zimbabwean contact and try to find the birds on the Zim. side of the border. This plan, however, was fraught with difficulties. Even if I could reach my contact who knew where to search on the southern side, I would almost certainly not be able to drive my rental car out of Zambia. I didn't have a Zimbabwean visa, and had no idea if I could obtain one at the border. Even if it were possible, would I be able to get back into Zambia afterwards? How would I get from the border post to the pitta site on the other side? How many days would I need once across? Could I get my hands on any Zimbabwe dollars? (And come to that, given Zim's hyperinflation, the wheelbarrow necessary to trundle them around in?) Given the numerous imponderables, I decided to spend one more full day in Zambia. If I failed to find any evidence of African Pitta by nightfall tomorrow, I would make further enquiries. I drove wearily back to Siavonga and sat nursing a beer at the lakeside, lost in moody contemplation.

I can't honestly say that my fear of wandering through the bush alone in the dark was abating. Only the thought of failure drove me onward, the horror of falling at the very last hurdle pricking me awake in advance of my early morning call. I threw my kit together and reminded myself that today might be my last chance at the site. Zapping my trusty Ford Ka's alarm, I swung myself into the driver's seat and gunned the engine. Familiar by now with the route, I was back in the Zambezi Valley in record time. Today, I assured myself, things would be different. The pittas would sing beneath the stars, vaulting for joy into the Zambian night, and I would be there to watch them.

Nothing had changed. No pittas sang. Dawn came and went, with only African Emerald Cuckoos and African Broadbills to serenade me. By seven a.m. I had already spent three hours hunting, and had nothing to show for it. More out of hope than belief, once it got light I persevered with a scientific approach I'd pursued the previous day. Play a snatch of African Pitta call. Wait motionless for fifteen minutes, listening for a response. Move on, counting off two hundred and fifty paces. Repeat the process. Cover the ground, working one potentially occupied territory after another. Stimulate a pitta to call, despite the late arrival of the rains for which the birds were so clearly waiting.

The parched landscape told the story however; the pittas remained taciturn, if they were here at all. I stomped around one more bend in the river, surprising only a pair of Crested Guineafowl, who spluttered indignantly and ran for cover.

'*Whueep!*' The pitta's emphatic, cartoon-water-drop call rang out endlessly from my iPod, echoing around the forest but finding no response. I waited and waited, praying for a delayed reaction, but instead encountered only silence. I was becoming despondent, my resolve failing, but I forced myself onward. Just a few more metres of sand-shuffle suffering, one last thicket…

I reached a narrow section of the river bed with dense cover on either side. Secreting myself below the bank, I squatted on my haunches and played the call again. And then I heard the sound. Not the call I had longed for, but a curious, mechanical, non-avian double thump. I had heard that sound before, but where? My mind raced, desperate to pinpoint the occasion. Two seconds later it hit me. I had been standing in the Ugandan forest, watching Green-breasted Pittas jumping in the canopy. Now, here in Zambia, the same sound reverberated again. A regular, well-spaced, resonant thump.

'*Bu-doomp!....Bu-doomp!*'

After so many fruitless hours, the wing-beat display of an African Pitta was booming out of the undergrowth. And it was close.

I thought for a few seconds, fighting the urge to run headlong into the thicket. The birds were clearly not vocalizing, that much I knew. This individual had failed to call, stimulated just enough to declare his territory with a wing-beat display. It was highly likely that this would be my sole opportunity. In addition, I probably only had a very short time to locate the bird before it once again fell silent. My mind made up, I crept up the bank, intending to scan the forest floor. I dragged myself up onto a gnarled tree root and stuck my head above the parapet. To my horror, a shape flicked away through the foliage, landing out of sight some ten metres in. I knew it was the pitta. That classic plump, broad-winged, tail-less silhouette of a bird gliding low over the ground was a give-away, but my view had been momentary, fleeting, devoid of colour. I had barely been able to discern any detail, only an outline, a sense of avian character, no more. It was not enough.

I inched my way forward. The bone-dry, brittle leaves conspired against me, went off like firecrackers at every step, each pace an explosion to my heightened senses. Having reached a spot with a relatively clear view, I knelt down on the forest floor, a supplicant at prayer. For ten unbearable minutes I waited, but the bird did not return. Eventually I could stand it no longer, and I cued up the iPod once more. *'Whueep!'*

My senses honed by a year of tuning in to forest nuances, through the tangle of branches I subliminally registered a movement and homed in on the activity. I slowly raised my Leicas and scanned a foot either side, risking a tiny lateral head movement in case the bird was obscured behind some forest detritus. I self-consciously registered the colour map in front of me; brown…green…green…brown….*blue.* Iridescent blue. Coruscating, oceanic, summer sky blue! The bird was so heavily obscured I could scarcely make out any detail, but I knew what that blue meant. It meant the spots on the wing-coverts of an African Pitta. It meant the last of the tribe, the end of a long journey, a lifetime's ambition achieved. It meant the chance to sleep late if I chose, celebratory beers and phone calls home. It meant the world.

As if the bird had read my thoughts, it obligingly flipped across to a looping liana and perched in the open, calm and still in the eye of my personal storm. Snapping its head round in my direction, it weighed me up. I gazed at it for a full ten seconds, collating the details: a broad, bold, off-white supercilium, describing the distance from bill to nape, isolating the crown like a royal diadem. Black face, white throat, green back, yellow breast, scarlet belly. And covert spots, sparkling jewels draped over the wing, purple now at this new angle, matched in their intensity by a shining shoulder patch, etching themselves indelibly into my memory.

Silence; the bird watching me watching him. I inched the barrel of my camera up to the horizontal, focused and fired. The reassuring shutter-click failed to sound. I fired again, with the same result. I looked down at the LCD. An error message flashed up at me. 'BUSY.' *Busy?* I thought to myself, *we're all a little busy my friend.* I slipped the battery pack from its compartment, eased it back in, rebooted and glanced at the display. Systems normal. I raised the camera again and through the viewfinder stared at the branch upon which my target had so recently stood. It was completely and undeniably unoccupied. The bird had flown.

I lay in the thicket for an hour, but the bird did not return. I played the pitta's call one last time, but the gauntlet remained where I had thrown it. I crawled through the undergrowth on my hands and knees, pushing aside the thought of Black Mambas, willing the rendezvous to resume. But the pitta had seen enough, had vanished back into the maze, guardian once more of its own mythic status.

I dragged my heel through the deep sand, marking the spot for future reference and trudged back to the road, emerging, blinking into the morning light. I dumped my gear at the roadside and punched the air. My signature jig followed, miniature and ridiculous. I laughed at my own stupidity, lay down, and pressed my face against the tarmac. I let my gaze travel up the achingly long, straight road, until I reached the spot where it pierced the horizon and disappeared. Silence, except for the boisterous insects. Not a soul was around, no-one to stare at a grinning Englishman a long way from home, celebrating an arcane, thrillingly pointless victory most of the world would struggle to understand. I liked to think the African Pitta would be celebrating too, would know the crucial part he had played in completing the puzzle. Doubtless at this very moment he would be feeding, building his strength for the fevered days ahead. The rains would come, and his song would echo round the dark forests again, a multitude of emotions compressed into a single, liquid monosyllable.

Whether it was the catharsis of finally crossing the finish line, or simply the attritional grind of endless months under difficult conditions, I was suddenly dog tired. My bones ached, and when I tried to stand I found my legs unwilling accomplices. This was not how I had envisaged the ultimate moment of triumph. Surely there was supposed to be a party, with good friends, too much claret, and sausages on sticks. I had imagined balloons, convivial chat, decorative bunting. (Or rather, given the birding context, an extra-limital vagrant Asian bunting.) The reality was starkly different, but as I stood on this lonely Zambian road, a tiny figure lost in the immensity of Africa, it was every bit as satisfying. I leaned against the bridge wall, aware of the sun's warmth on my skin, feeling the blood course though my veins. Victory was mine, the collection complete. Mission accomplished.

December the eighteenth. The Duty Free shop at Lusaka Airport had been dressed to look ever so slightly festive. I was surprised to find a Christmas tree propped in one corner, and as a fellow passenger whisked by, light glinted off the tinsel wrapped around the handle of his suitcase. Of course! Christmas was but a week away, and I was woefully ill prepared. Now only a brief stop at Lilongwe, Mozambique, a seven-hour layover in Nairobi, and two last flights stood between me and my loved ones. We would gather round a fire in Norfolk, my favourite place in the world, now all the more so for having been separated from it for the best part of a year. After months of stifling heat, I longed for a salty slap in the face from a wintry east wind. I shivered in anticipation of the coal shovel scrape, the crunch of frozen flints underfoot as I walked back to the cottage. I would shake the frost from the miniature Japanese Acer in the garden, and plan to buy another Buddleia to replace my latest withered victim. And then we'd curl up indoors, pull crackers and open presents, and wonder once again why we'd cooked sprouts when nobody liked them.

In eleven months I had covered more than two hundred thousand kilometres by aeroplane, truck, motorboat, canoe, motorbike taxi and on foot. I had spent almost thirty thousand pounds, and had lost thirteen kilos in weight. I had seen more than nineteen hundred and seventy species of bird, almost one fifth of the world's total. And I had achieved my mission goal of seeing all thirty-two species of pitta in a calendar year. Every last jewel had been hunted down and captured. I had lived the dream, and lived to tell the tale.

Now it was time to realize another dream. I picked up my bag and walked to the gate.

Homeward bound.

Acknowledgements

I could not have completed my year successfully without the help and advice of countless friends, acquaintances and strangers. I had for years talked about the 'bird-watching community' without truly comprehending the meaning of the phrase. Now I absolutely understand, and I can honestly say that not one person refused to part with often hard-won information when they heard what I was trying to achieve. I am immensely grateful to many people for selflessly offering assistance in many different ways.

Special thanks to Rob Hutchinson and James Eaton/www.birdtourasia.com for initial encouragement, for help in putting together the global jigsaw, and for numerous miscellaneous pieces of advice. Thanks also to Rob for his skill and companionship in the field in Sabah. I extend my gratitude to Frank Lambert and Martin Woodcock for writing their incomparable Pitta monograph, *'Pittas, Broadbills and Asities'* (Pica Press 1996) which remains the seminal work on the family, and which I have used as my speciation authority (although by the time you read this, pitta taxonomy will have changed with regard to two species, Banded Pitta and Sula Pitta). Cheers to Kit Britten, Mike Catsis, Phil Hansbro, Bob Harris, Graham Hogan, Wayne Hsu, Wu Jian-Long, Andy Mears, Hans Meijer, Keir Randall, Mario Rondon, Troy Shortell, and Brendan Sloan for their companionship in the field (and for their collective bravery in testing experimental local liquor rum and cokes).

Thanks go to the following for sharing information on various pitta species: Andy Adcock, Des Allen, Ashley Banwell, Mikael Bauer, Tom Bex, Nick Brickle, Tomas Carlberg, Mark Easterbrook, Mike Edgecombe, Peter Ericsson, Mick Fiszer, Henk Hendriks, Dion Hobcraft, Remco Hofland, Paul Holt, Jon Hornbuckle, Aidan Kelly, Neville Kemp, Gareth Knass, Sander Lagerveld, Kim Chuah Lim, Albert Low, Rob Lucking, Alan McBride, Susan Myers, Wendy Newnham, János Oláh, Tony Palliser, Billy Rodger, Phil Round, Gloria Seow, Brian and Margaret Sykes at OBC, Satish Santanam, Tom Tarrant, Richard Thewlis, Mark van Beirs, Dennis Walls, Sam Woods, Yong Ding Li, and Tamas Zalai.

Thanks to the following for assistance around the world:

India: Peter Lobo for arranging everything at short notice, and Hoon, Basu and Rafiq for actually making it happen.

Indonesia:
- *Bali:* Kuat Wahyudi.

- *Halmahera and Sulawesi:* Theo Henoch for running everything so smoothly (and for trail-blazing with me to Peleng) drivers Roy and Wale, Anu, and Samuel for help in getting from A to B.

- *Nusa Tenggara, Flores:* Martinus Klau for being an organisational powerhouse, and Nimus for services to driving and ostentatious moustaches.

- *Nusa Tenggara, Sumba:* Bona and Mr. Ferry for driving, and Jaap Vermeulen, Colin Trainor, Richard Willan and Vince Kessner for their services to snail identification.

- *Nusa Tenggara, West Timor:* Fridus, Goris and Kanis.

- *Peleng:* Labi, Maleso and the west Peleng team, Yason and all at Kawalu, Simson, Filip Verbelen and Frank Rheindt for setting us off in the right direction.

Malaysia: Mr. Vela for his magic taxi, Kuala Lumpur, and Mr. May for expert river navigation at Taman Negara.

Manus: Aaron Joseph for Superb Pitta access, Jack Daniels for sharing his island with us, and for captaining us back to shore without any fuel.

Papua New Guinea: Daniel Wakra for his help at Varirata.

Philippines, Luzon: Aquilino Escobar for Hamut heroics beyond the call of duty (and Quenilyn Escobar for helping me to track Aquilino down in the first place). Tim Fisher for help with tents and other last minute logistics. *Philippines, Mindanao:* Zardo Goring for saving my life with a banana skin and a length of creeper at PICOP, the staff at Bislig Hospital Emergency Room for stitching me back together.

Sabah: Robert Chong and his staff at Kinabatangan.

The Solomons/Australia: Phil and Sue Gregory at Cassowary House, Guy Dutson for Black-faced Pitta information, Hagen Korinihona at PNG holidays for logistics, William and Veronica Manehage, Mark and Samson for their wonderful hospitality on Santa Isabel, Wilson Maelaua, Kris and Samson 2 on Guadalcanal, Air Niugini for teaching me the art of self-sufficiency. (By the way guys, any sign of my luggage yet?)

Sri Lanka: Sunil de Alwis and Perry Viswalingam at Baurs and Co.

Sumatra: The Way Titias/Danau Ranau crew: Gamal, Toni, Habzi, Bambang and Uyung, Politarius at Ecoventure.

Taiwan: Ruey-Shing (Scott) Lin at Huben, and Simon Liao for help with pheasants, bush-robins etc. at Anmashan.

Thailand: Yothin Meekao at Khao Nor Chuchi, Andy Pierce at Khao Yai, Malee at Doi Chiang Dao.

Uganda: Kalema Livingstone, Robert Bahindi, Gerald T. of the UWA.

Vietnam: Richard Craik at Vietnam Birding and Khahn.

Zambia: Emma, Ian and Mel Bruce-Miller for taking in a waif at short notice, David Hoddinott and Adam Riley at Rockjumper, Callan Cohen at Birding Africa and Jonathan Rossouw for African Pitta gen.

UK: Rob Still and Andy Swash at WILD*Guides* for all things publishing and distribution. Douglas Russell, Robert Prys-Jones and Nigel Cleere for help at the Natural History Museum in Tring. Sarah Whittley at The Pinkfoot Gallery in Cley for inspiration, guidance and whisky-tasting notes. My mother, Sheila Gooddie for help with proof-reading, for encouraging my interest in birds in my youth, and for buying me the pitta monograph twelve years ago. Bernardine Freud for general editing and adverb destruction, Pam and John at Boss Travel for regularly kicking the airlines into some semblance of order. Richard and Sarah Thomas for logistical advice, species data and 'voice of experience' publishing guidance. Brian Unwin, Adrian Pitches at British Birds Magazine, David Callahan at Birdwatch

Magazine, and Steve Gantlett at Birding World Magazine for helping to get the word out. Rob Hutchinson for allowing inclusion of his Wallace's Statndarwing photo. Special thanks to Riaz Cader who went out and obtained the superb forest floor images for the front cover and page 340 almost instantly following a frantic request despatched via Gehan de Silva Wijeyeratne. And last but not least, Killian Mullarney and Mark Constantine at The Sound Approach, the latter for uttering the immortal words, 'you never regret action, only inaction.' Most of all, thanks to my wife Maxine, for having the patience to put up with a perennial absentee who is always away waiting for pittas to show up.

In addition there are many others who helped with odd pieces of information here and there; thanks one and all. If I have forgotten anyone, please forgive the oversight.

For further information regarding pittas, please visit www.pittasworld.com.

Enquiries for the author should be sent to info@pittasworld.com

A percentage of the profits from the sale of this book go to BirdLife International. Bird names used throughout this book follow BirdLife nomenclature wherever possible. For further details on BirdLife International's important work, please see: www.birdlife.org.

The Treasure Chest

A list of pitta species seen during 2009.

Records of additional races of species shown in parentheses.

Taxonomy follows Lambert and Woodock, 1996.

Pittas are listed in the order in which they were seen.
All photos were taken by the author and were the best
I could obtain under trying conditions.

1 GURNEY'S PITTA *Pitta gurneyi*
Male [above] and female at Khao Nor Chuchi, southern Thailand, February 3rd.

2 **MALAYAN BANDED PITTA** *Pitta (guajana) irena* [left]
Male at The Pole Bridge, Khao Nor Chuchi, southern Thailand, February 3rd.
(This species has now been split from the nominate *Pitta guajana guajana*.)

('Bornean Banded Pitta') *Pitta (guajana) schwaneri* [right]
Male at Borneo Rainforest Lodge, Danum Valley, Sabah, Borneo, July 1st.
(This species has now been split from the nominate *Pitta guajana guajana*.)

('Javan Banded Pitta') *Pitta guajana guajana* [not photographed]
Bali Barat, Bali, Indonesia, September 6th.

3 **BLUE-WINGED PITTA** *Pitta moluccensis* [not photographed]
Opposite the Morakot Resort, Khao Nor Chuchi, southern Thailand, February 5th.

4 **MANGROVE PITTA** *Pitta megarhyncha*
Phang Nga, southern Thailand, February 8th.

5 **EARED PITTA** *Pitta phayrei*
Female at Khao Yai, central Thailand, February 9th.

6 **BLUE PITTA** *Pitta cyanea cyanea/aurantiaca* [not photographed]
Khao Yai, central Thailand, February 11th.

7 **WHISKERED PITTA** *Pitta kochi* [not photographed]
Above Camp 1, Mt. Hamut, Luzon, northern Philippines, February 22nd.

8 **AZURE-BREASTED PITTA** *Pitta steerii steerii*
PICOP, Mindanao, southern Philippines, February 27th.

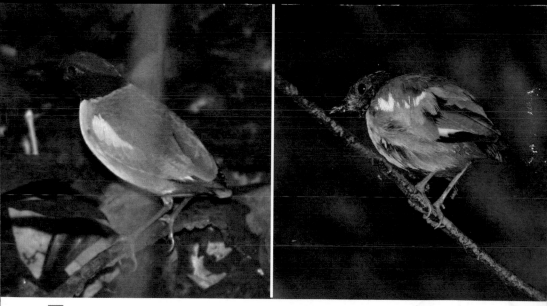

9 **HOODED PITTA** *Pitta sordida sordida* [not photographed]
The Quarry, PICOP, Mindanao, southern Philippines, February 28th.

(**HOODED PITTA** *Pitta sordida cucullata*) [left]
Taman Negara, Peninsular Malaysia, April 12th.

(**HOODED PITTA** *Pitta sordida mulleri*) [right]
Kinabatangan River, Sabah, Borneo, June 28th.

10 **RED-BELLIED PITTA** *Pitta erythrogaster erythrogaster* [not photographed]
The Quarry, PICOP, Mindanao, southern Philippines, March 1st.

(**RED-BELLIED PITTA** *Pitta erythrogaster rufiventris*) [left]
Tabanalo Logging Track, Halmahera, Indonesia, August 25th.

(**RED-BELLIED PITTA** *Pitta erythrogaster celebensis*) [right]
Tangkoko, Sulawesi, Indonesia, August 27th.

11 **BAR-BELLIED PITTA** *Pitta elliotii*
Male, Largerstroemia Trail, Cat Tien NP, southern Vietnam, March 5th.

12 **BLUE-RUMPED PITTA** *Pitta soror soror* [not photographed]
The Swimming Pool Trail, Cat Tien NP, southern Vietnam, March 7th.

13 **BLUE-NAPED PITTA** *Pitta nipalensis nipalensis*
Two shots of the same bird, a male, Kaziranga Tea Gardens, Assam, northeast India, March 30th.

14 **GARNET PITTA** *Pitta granatina coccinea*
Gua Telinga, Taman Negara, Peninsular Malaysia, April 7th.

15 **RUSTY-NAPED PITTA** *Pitta oatesi deborah* [not photographed]
Bishop's Trail, Fraser's Hill, Peninsular Malaysia, April 14th.

16 **GRACEFUL PITTA** *Pitta venusta*
Way Titias, Bukit Barisan Selatan, southwest Sumatra, Indonesia, April 21st.

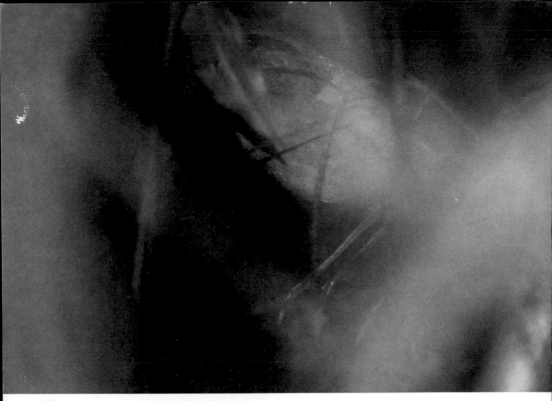

17 **SCHNEIDER'S PITTA** *Pitta schneideri*
Male, Danau Ranau, Bukit Barisan Selatan, southwest Sumatra, Indonesia, April 25th.

18 **FAIRY PITTA** *Pitta nympha*
Female, Huben Village, west Taiwan, May 3rd.

19 **GIANT PITTA** *Pitta caerulea hosei*
Male, Kinabatangan River, Sabah, Borneo, June 28th.

20 **BLUE-HEADED PITTA** *Pitta baudii*
Male, Kinabatangan River, Sabah, Borneo, June 29th.

21 **BLACK-HEADED PITTA** *Pitta ussheri*
Borneo Rainforest Lodge, Danum Valley, Sabah, Borneo, July 1st.

22 **BLUE-BANDED PITTA** *Pitta arquata*
Borneo Rainforest Lodge, Danum Valley, Sabah, Borneo, July 2nd.

23 GREEN-BREASTED PITTA *Pitta reichenowi*
Kibale Forest, southwest Uganda, July 25th.

24 **IVORY-BREASTED PITTA** *Pitta maxima maxima*
Kali Batu Putih, Halmahera, Indonesia, August 23rd.

25 **ELEGANT PITTA** *Pitta elegans elegans* [left]
Tangkoko, northeast Sulawesi, Indonesia, August 27th.

(**Elegant Pitta** *Pitta elegans maria*) [not photographed]
west of Lewa, Sumba, Nusa Tenggara, Indonesia, September 9th.

(**Elegant Pitta** *Pitta elegans concinna*) [right]
Ponco Deki, Kisol, Flores, Nusa Tenggara, Indonesia, September 14th.

26 SULA PITTA *Pitta (erythrogaster) dohertyi*
Western Peleng, Indonesia, August 30th. (This species has now been re-lumped as
part of Red-bellied Pitta, *Pitta erythrogaster*.)

27 **RAINBOW PITTA** *Pitta iris*
Howard Springs, Darwin, Australia, September 19th.

28 **NOISY PITTA** *Pitta versicolor intermedia*
Mount Whitfield, Cairns, Australia, September 22nd.

31 **INDIAN PITTA** *Pitta brachyura*
Nuwara Eliya, Kandy, Sri Lanka, November 16th.

32 **AFRICAN PITTA** *Pitta angolensis longipennis* [not photographed]
River beds near Siavonga, Lower Zambezi Valley, Zambia, December 10th.

29 **SUPERB PITTA** *Pitta superba*
Rossun, Manus, Admiralty Islands, Papua New Guinea, September 26th.

30 **BLACK-FACED PITTA** *Pitta anerythra anerythra*
Tirotonga, Santa Isabel, Solomon Islands, October 5th.